# India, Pakistan, and Democr

The question of why some countries have democratic regimes and others do not is a significant issue in comparative politics. This book looks at India and Pakistan, two countries with clearly contrasting political regime histories, and presents an argument on why India is a democracy and Pakistan is not. Focusing on the specificities and the nuances of each state system, the author examines in detail the balance of authority and power between popular or elected politicians and the state apparatus through substantial historical analysis.

India and Pakistan are both large, multi-religious and multi-lingual countries sharing a geographic and historical space that in 1947, when they became independent from British rule, gave them a virtually indistinguishable level of both extreme poverty and inequality. All of those factors militate against democracy, according to most theories, and in Pakistan democracy did indeed fail very quickly after independence. It has only been restored as a façade for military–bureaucratic rule for brief periods since then. In comparison, after almost thirty years of democracy, India had a brush with authoritarian rule, in the 1975–6 Emergency, and some analysts were perversely reassured that the India exception had been erased. But instead, after a momentous election in 1977, democracy has become stronger over the last thirty years.

Providing a comparative analysis of the political systems of India and Pakistan as well as a historical overview of the two countries, this book constitutes essential reading for students of South Asian History and Politics. It is a useful and balanced introduction to the politics of India and Pakistan.

**Philip Oldenburg** is a Research Scholar at the South Asia Institute of Columbia University where he has taught political science since 1977. He has done field research in India on local self-government, and on national elections, and has been editor or co-editor of ten books in the India Briefing series.

# India, Pakistan, and Democracy

## Solving the puzzle of divergent paths

**Philip Oldenburg**

Routledge
Taylor & Francis Group

LONDON AND NEW YORK

First published 2010
by Routledge
2 Park Square, Milton Park, Abingdon, Oxon OX14 4RN

Simultaneously published in the USA and Canada
by Routledge
270 Madison Ave, New York, NY 10016

*Routledge is an imprint of the Taylor & Francis Group,
an informa business*

© 2010 Philip Oldenburg

Typeset in 10/12pt Times NR MT by
Graphicraft Limited, Hong Kong
Printed and bound in Great Britain by
TJ International Ltd, Padstow, Cornwall

*British Library Cataloguing in Publication Data*
A catalogue record for this book is available
from the British Library

*Library of Congress Cataloging in Publication Data*
Oldenburg, Philip.
  India, Pakistan, and democracy : solving the puzzle of
divergent paths / Philip Oldenburg.
    p. cm.
  Includes bibliographical references and index.
  1. Democracy—India.  2. Democracy—Pakistan.
3. Democratization—India.  4. Democratization—Pakistan.
5. India—Politics and government—1947–
6. Pakistan—Politics and government.
7. India—Colonial influence.
8. Pakistan—Colonial influence.  I. Title.

  JQ281.O43 2010
  320.954—dc22

                                               2010002537

ISBN: 978-0-415-78018-6 (hbk)
ISBN: 978-0-415-78019-3 (pbk)
ISBN: 978-0-203-84715-2 (ebk)

# Contents

# Tables

# Figures

# Acknowledgments

I have for many years taught my introductory course on "South Asian Government and Politics" by starting with Pakistan's political history, followed by India's (in turn followed, in shamefully brief accounts, by the remaining South Asian countries). I used the contrast of their regime types as a way of introducing the dynamics of the politics of each, in a way that I hoped was stimulating for students who knew little about South Asia.

There were a series of opportunities I chanced upon that ultimately initiated this project. First, I was asked to serve as an academic advisor on the South Asia countries for Freedom House's *Freedom in the World* series, starting with the 2004 volume, which forced me to concentrate as never before on the measurement of factors contributing to democracy. I am very grateful to Freedom House for giving me the opportunity to be a small part of a very impressive team effort. Then, in the summer and fall of 2005, I was fortunate to be included in weekly discussions at the Centre for the Study of Developing Societies (CSDS) on the emerging draft of the *State of Democracy in South Asia* report, which greatly enriched my understanding of what democracy means in India and Pakistan. In September 2005, I attended the launch of Meghnad Desai's and Aitzaz Ahsan's book on the issue of why India is a democracy and Pakistan is not, *Divided by Democracy*.

The combination of their presentations and the CSDS discussions moved me to put my long-gestating thoughts on that topic into a lengthy email message to Meghnad Desai. That email text in turn provided an outline for a seminar course I have taught four times in the past two years, to advanced undergraduates in Political Science at Baruch College of CUNY and Columbia University; and to graduate students at the School of Advanced International Studies (of the Johns Hopkins University). The lively intellectual engagement many of those students gave me has shaped the content and presentation of this study. The core outline of this book began as my lecture notes for those courses.

In writing out what were lectures I have preserved to some extent the lack of strict chronological sequence and thematic overlap that the lectures had, and I have felt free to keep my speculative opinions explicitly in place. Although there is a broad chronological organization to the book, there are certain parts of the puzzle – the importance of external aid, for example – that have been discussed separately.

Although others have provided solutions to this puzzle – Christophe Jaffrelot's (2002) essay is the most systematic and insightful, and my arguments overlap and intertwine with his to a great extent – I believe that the argument I have made, and the evidence I have added, is more comprehensive than any of those accounts. I have also drawn on discussions I have had with colleagues, but I am no longer able to remember who provided me with precisely which insight; I hope they will forgive me if they find their ideas in this book. Discussions with Hasan-Askari Rizvi over years in New York and Washington have added immeasurably to my understanding of political change in Pakistan, and those with Yogendra Yadav and others at CSDS have done the same for India.

I am grateful to those who have critiqued a draft, at various stages: Alyssa Ayres, Gurcharan Das, Ajit Kumar, Paula Newberg, Veena Talwar Oldenburg, Saeed Shafqat, Aqil Shah, Farzana Shaikh, and particularly my publisher's two anonymous readers. Christophe Jaffrelot gave the manuscript a meticulous reading; I hope I have dealt to his satisfaction with his critique, which was elaborated also in illuminating discussions with him. I am of course solely responsible for the errors that remain.

The financial support of the Jawaharlal Nehru Institute of Advanced Study, which made me a fellow and provided a wonderful place to work on this project in the summer of 2008, launched what had been a (too) lengthy article into a full-fledged book. My special thanks go to its director, Aditya Mukherjee. While there I benefited enormously from questions and comments received at presentations of this work at the Jawaharlal Nehru Museum and Library, the Centre for Political Studies at Jawaharlal Nehru University, the Political Science department at the University of Delhi, and at Jamia Millia in Delhi.

It has been forty-five years since I first went to India, and twenty-two since I first visited Pakistan. In my years of residence on the subcontinent, I have been privileged and lucky to have friends and colleagues willing to teach me, listen to me, and "discuss." Many of them were tapped for this work, but they are far too numerous to mention. I owe a special debt to Veena, for tolerating a political scientist, albeit one with historical tendencies, and keeping me constantly on my (intellectual) toes.

# 1    Introduction

## Why India is a democracy and Pakistan is not (yet?) a democracy

It is rare for two countries as similar as India and Pakistan to have such clearly contrasting political regime histories. These are large, multi-religious and multi-lingual countries that share a geographic and historical space that gave them in 1947, when they became independent from British rule, a virtually indistinguishable level of extreme poverty and extreme inequality. All of those factors militate against democracy, according to most theories, but democratic systems were the next step from the gradually liberalizing institutions of the state that the British had grudgingly accepted, in response to nationalist-movement demands. In Pakistan, democracy did indeed fail very quickly after independence. It has only been restored as a façade for military–bureaucratic rule for brief periods since then, including the present. After almost thirty years of democracy, India had a brush with authoritarian rule, in the 1975–7 Emergency; but, after a momentous election in 1977, democracy has become stronger over the last thirty years.

Why is it that after sixty years of independence Pakistan is now, and has mainly been, an autocracy, while India is now, and has mainly been, a democracy?[1] In 1947 these two countries were fraternal twins, sharing a deep history of "Indian" civilization, with a largely overlapping genetic and linguistic heritage, and a history of struggle to be free from British rule. They also inherited much of the colonial state, including its legal system, its bureaucratic system, and its constitutional structure. Both countries smoothly started functioning as democracies, with elected provincial assemblies (albeit by the 15 percent or so of adults who were enfranchised) and an indirectly elected constituent assembly, which was divided, with the two parts serving also as a parliament for the successor country.

Many scholars and other experts believed that neither country would develop a stable democracy. Both countries were so desperately poor, so grossly inegalitarian in practice *and* belief, and so prodigiously multi-lingual if not multi-national that sustaining a democracy would be very difficult if not impossible. Pakistan's history indeed conforms to the expected normal pattern of "political development" (see Riggs 1981 for a wonderful dissection of that term's meaning), in which an initial gift of a democratic system from the colonial power breaks down fairly quickly, with either the military or a single party headed typically by a charismatic leader putting an auto-cracy in place.

India is thus the deviant case. As Michelutti (2008: 3) has summarized it: "'Indian Democracy' carries on working despite the poverty, illiteracy, corruption, religious nationalism, casteism, political violence, and disregard of law and order." Rajni Kothari (1988: 155) argues that "India is a deviant case in a much more fundamental sense, in that most if not all the threats to democracy in India come from the modern sector, and from the pursuit of State power by this sector for steamrolling tradition and pluralities in an effort to make the country a modern, united, prosperous and powerful polity." But democracy is now more than just a system for organizing the government; according to Yogendra Yadav (1999b: 30):

> India has, to use Shiv Vishwanathan's memorable phrase, "by-hearted" democracy; this characteristically Indian English expression captures well how Indians have creolized the idea of democracy. They have accepted the Western idea of democracy as their own and then proceeded to take liberties with it as one does with one's own possessions. As a result, the idea of democracy has been localized and routinized.

Indeed, democracy in India has been "accepted and legitimated in the popular consciousness" (Michelutti 2008: 4).

Some resolve the question of India's deviance by claiming that India is not "really" a democracy, or not really a "substantive" democracy. Others are still waiting for the anomaly to be resolved by India falling apart, or succumbing to a (fascist) Hindu nationalism or a (left) revolutionary takeover.

Conventional accounts, however, accept that there is a genuine and persist-ing regime difference between the two countries. Consider the graph we can generate from the Polity IV data for the first three decades of independence, and then the graphs of Freedom House data (Figures 1.1–3).

Freedom House labels India "free" from 1972 to 1974, from 1977 to 1989, and from 1998 to 2007 (and "partly free" in 1975–6, and from 1990 to 1997). Pakistan is judged to be "partly free" from 1972 to 1978 and from 1984 to 1998, and "not free" from 1979 to 1983 and from 1999 to 2007. Pakistan returned to "partly free" status in 2008 (see Figure 1.2). Alternately, the Freedom House data can be graphed to show the average "political rights"/"civil liberties" score, where "1" represents the highest degree of freedom, and "7" the lowest (see Figure 1.3).[2]

The Freedom House sorting depends on scores on "political rights" and "civil liberties" that require democracy to be practiced in the country as a whole. In India, the demotion to "partly free" in the 1990–7 period was due to "methodological modifications," but it is possible that the scores were reduced because of state repression of the Kashmir insurgency.[3] In Pakistan's case, the "partly free" designation in the 1984–98 period, during which elections were held, and freedom of press and assembly were quite

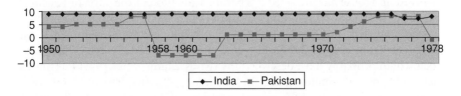

*Figure 1.1* Chart of Polity IV scores for India and Pakistan, 1950–78
Full democracy – 8 and above; Autocracy – 0 and below
*Source*: Country reports at: http://www.cidcm.umd.edu/polity/country_reports/key.asp

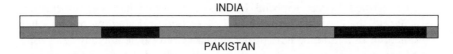

*Figure 1.2* Freedom in India and Pakistan in the Freedom House Assessment,
1972–2008
Key: white = "free"; gray = "partly free"; black = "not free"
*Source*: *Freedom in the World* online at: http://www.freedomhouse.org/uploads/FIWAllScores.xls

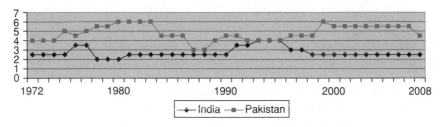

*Figure 1.3* Freedom in India and Pakistan in the Freedom House Assessment,
1972–2008: Average of "political rights" and "civil liberties" Scores
*Source*: *Freedom in the World* online at: http://www.freedomhouse.org/uploads/FIWAllScores.xls

strong, was due to the power of the military to make and break elected
governments, including those with a majority in parliament.[4]

Putting these countries – and the others Freedom House evaluates – into
these categories is largely a matter of careful assessments of the intensity
and spread of certain practices such as arbitrary police action. Changing
a designation from "free" to "partly free" and to "not free" is done only
with a great deal of deliberation by the Freedom House experts.[5] For some
purposes – sorting out the causal links between "democracy" and "development" for example (see Hadenius 1992) – it makes sense to develop an index
of democratization, so that countries are scored as more or less democratic
than others. More recent work, however, has tended to use dichotomized or
trichotomized data (see, among others, Przeworski and Limongi 1997; Boix
and Stokes 2003; D. L. Epstein et al. 2006; Hadenius and Teorell 2005).

Freedom House has provided a separate evaluation of the parts of Kashmir ruled by India (since 1998) and Pakistan (since 2002). Kashmir-in-Pakistan has been labeled "not free" for all the years through 2008; Kashmir-in-India "not free" from 1998 to 2001 and "partly free" from 2002 to 2008. That contrast would probably have described the two Kashmirs after 1947: Pakistan's part "not free" throughout, and India's mainly "partly free" or "not free" (and just possibly judged "free" in the period 1977 to 1983). Like Kashmir, much of India's northeast has suffered almost since independence from a systematic denial of civil liberties in those states where the army has been a constant presence. As Vajpeyi (2009: 36) persuasively argues:

> The [Armed Forces (Special Powers) Act, 1958] [creates] an entirely separate space within India, a sort of second and shadow nation, that functions as a military state rather than an electoral democracy . . . a zone of exception [Jammu and Kashmir and eight states of the northeast] governed by unelected and unrepresentative armed forces (that moreover enjoy complete impunity) should not be thought of as a mere zone of exception, but as a contradiction so extreme that it undoes the totality in which it is embedded, and breaks it down into distinct and mutually opposed regimes: a democracy and a non-democracy; two nations: India and not-India.

As she notes, "the rest of the country carries on as though it is possible to gloss over the reality of military rule as a temporary aberration and a mere enclave in what purports to be the world's largest democracy" (Vajpeyi 2009: 38; see Human Rights Watch 2006 for details on Kashmir). Around 5 percent of India's population lives in that enclave, no small number of people, who need to be kept in mind in the analysis that follows.

## Defining democracy and autocracy

I have chosen here to draw some sort of a line between an autocracy and a democracy, on the basis of where sovereignty ultimately rests: with the people, or with self-appointed rulers. The definition of democracy that essentially requires that elections be free and fair and that no other power (such as the military) can veto decisions made by elected rulers suggests an either/or situation (see Schmitter and Karl 1991; for a succinct essay on conceptualization and measurement of "democracy," see Berg-Schlosser 2007). Some situations would not be clear, in a country in which local political systems are undemocratic in some way (see Gibson 2005), or in which day-to-day politics consists of rulers who are not held accountable or who even flout the law. In my view, those countries are democracies if in a crisis it is the citizenry that remains sovereign. On the other hand, if a strong majority of the citizenry – leaving aside the question of precisely what proportion of the citizenry we are talking about, and how strong the feeling is – concedes the right to rule to a person or institution other than "the people," we would have a "legitimate" autocracy.

Some help in evaluating where India and Pakistan fit using these criteria is to be found in the *State of Democracy in South Asia* report (see also a summary article, deSouza et al. 2008). This report is based mainly on a very careful and convincing opinion survey, conducted in the five major countries of South Asia in 2004. The graph that depicts the "funnel of support for democracy in South Asia" (*SDSA* 2008: 13) shows a "stage one" bar indicating the percentage of respondents who support government by elected leaders. For India the figure is 95, and for Pakistan 83 (Figure 1.4). The "funnel" – perhaps "inverted pyramid" would be a better description – is then drawn by cutting away the base of that possibly superficial support for democracy, by showing five more bars underneath, each of which represents the bar above minus the respondents who have answered questions in a way that negates their support of democracy.

When those who "prefer dictatorship sometimes" or are indifferent between democracy and dictatorship are excluded, India's bar shrinks to 73 percent, while Pakistan's shrinks even more dramatically, to 45 percent. Excluding those who want army rule produces a 59 percent bar for India and a 19 percent bar for Pakistan. Excluding those who want rule by a king has less effect, understandably: 55 percent remain in the Indian inverted pyramid, 13 percent in Pakistan's. Excluding those who want a strong leader without any democratic restraint gives India a bar representing 40 percent, and Pakistan

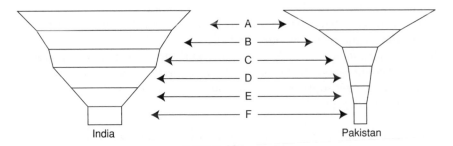

*Figure 1.4* Support for democracy in India and Pakistan, from the *State of Democracy in South Asia: A Report*

Key:
A = Percentage of those who support government by elected leaders (India: 95%; Pakistan: 83%)
B = Excludes those who prefer dictatorship sometimes or are indifferent between democracy and dictatorship (India: 73%; Pakistan: 45%)
C = In addition, excludes those who want army rule (India: 59%; Pakistan: 19%)
D = In addition, excludes those who want rule by a king (India: 56%; Pakistan: 13%)
E = In addition, excludes those who want a strong leader without any democratic restraints (India: 40%; Pakistan: 10%)
F = In addition, excludes those who want rule by experts rather than politicians (India: 19%; Pakistan: 7%)
Adapted from: SDSA (2008: 13).

one representing 10 percent. The final cut excludes those who want the rule of experts rather than of politicians; here India's bar is cut in half, to 19 percent, while Pakistan's (with not much left to it) is reduced to 7 percent. (This can also be expressed as: Only 20 percent of Indians and 7 percent of Pakistanis support government by elected leaders AND do *not* prefer dictatorship sometimes (or are indifferent between democracy and dictatorship) AND do *not* want army rule AND do *not* want a monarchy AND do *not* want a strong leader without democratic restraint AND do *not* want the rule of experts rather than of politicians.)

More directly, "the idea that the country should be governed by the army was endorsed by six out of every ten responses in Pakistan . . . [which is] one of the highest levels of support for army rule recorded in any part of the world" (*SDSA* 2008: 13). In India, the figure is 23 percent. Pakistan's autocratic leaders, however, have claimed to be either presiding over a democracy, or serving as caretakers until a democratic system could be restarted. They have made no explicit claim for the legitimacy of the system of military–bureaucratic rule that has persisted, with only brief breaks, since Pakistan's independence.

Ayesha Jalal argues that, in effect, the two countries are both on the "autocracy" side of the dividing line, labeling India's polity as "democratic authoritarianism" (or, "formally democratic yet covertly authoritarian") and Pakistan's as "military–bureaucratic authoritarianism" (Jalal 1995: 249, 254, 249). The empirical foundation of this categorization is in part summed up by this statement: "Once the analytical spotlight is turned on the dialectic between state structures and political processes, post-colonial India and Pakistan appear to exhibit alternate forms of authoritarianism" (Jalal 1995: 249). To some extent, the reasons to reject this conclusion emerge in our discussion of the belief systems, and the social and economic factors that help us understand the different regime outcomes. (A completely argued empirical counter-argument to Jalal's, however, deserves more time and effort than would be appropriate here.)[6] Underlying the empirical claim is Jalal's conceptualization of "democracy":

> A compound of its formal and substantive meanings, democracy here refers to more than the exercise of citizens' voting rights in elections or even the right to free speech. Though an important feature of democratic processes, elections are only the political manifestation of democratization in the wider social sphere. Democratization's normative or substantive appeal derives from the empowerment of the people, not as abstract legal citizens but as concrete and active agents capable of pursuing their interests with a measure of autonomy from entrenched structures of dominance and privilege. Insofar as dominance underpins any social formation, democratization entails the capacity to resist and renegotiate relations of power and privilege.
>
> (Jalal 1995: 3)

We should recall here Dahl's attempt to replace our use of "democracy" with a newly coined term, "polyarchy." Dahl says he would like "to reserve the term 'democracy' for a political system one of the characteristics of which is the quality of being completely or almost completely responsive to all its citizens" (Dahl 1971: 2). Having outlined his schema of democratization, he says "since (in my view) no large system in the real world is fully democratized, I prefer to call real world systems [high on the scales of liberalization (public contestation) and inclusiveness (participation)] polyarchies" (Dahl 1971: 8). Some years later he notes that "so far no country has transcended polyarchy to a 'higher' stage of democracy" (Dahl 1989: 223).

Dahl's neologism has not been adopted. In the words of one of the most influential articles aimed at defining "democracy":

> For some time, the word democracy has been circulating as a debased currency in the political marketplace. . . . [Dahl tried] to introduce a new term, "polyarchy," in its stead in the (vain) hope of gaining a greater measure of conceptual precision. But for better or worse, we are "stuck" with democracy as the catchword of contemporary political discourse.
>
> (Schmitter and Karl 1991: 75)

Certainly, for the major dataset used by those doing quantitative analysis, Polity IV, the term "democracy" is used. Even those who distinguish between "formal" democracy and "substantive" democracy underline the former's importance *as* "democracy":

> Formal democracies fall far short of the ideals associated with this conception of social democracy. But to dismiss them as merely formal would be problematic and even politically and intellectually irresponsible. Certainly, protection of human rights . . . is immensely important to all citizens in their daily lives. Even the formal share in political decision making represented by voting in regular intervals has often brought real advantages to the many. And governmental accountability to elected representatives restrains abuses of power that are clearly detrimental to the interests of citizens at large. Above all, however, formal democracy opens the possibility of, and is a requisite for, advances toward participatory and social democracy.
>
> (Huber et al. 1997: 324)[7]

Jalal (1995: 3), however, argues:

> Far from representing a neat and sharp dichotomy, democracy and authoritarianism are reflective of ongoing struggles between dominance and resistance. Without blurring the distinction between them it is important to acknowledge that they may frequently overlap irrespective of the formal designation of polities and states as democratic or authoritarian. It seems

more apt to view democracy and authoritarianism as both antithetical and interdependent historical processes, co-existing in a tension while at the same time each informing and transforming the other.[8]

If this is accepted, our general question becomes "Why is India less authoritarian than Pakistan?" But it seems less confusing to follow the consensus formulation that the difference between the two countries, and a durable one, is a difference between "democracy" and "autocracy."

Returning to the issue itself: What explains the difference – however conceptualized – between the two countries? In this book I explore arguments that rest on social–cultural factors, particularly religion; those that see differing socio-economic factors, especially gross social and economic inequalities, and local-arena structures of power; and those that highlight international relations explanations. These arguments are considered at various points within a narrative that proceeds in a loosely chronological fashion. I do that because in the end I am convinced that a path-dependence explanation is the most convincing.[9]

Oversimplifying: India is a democracy now because it was one last year and the year before and the decade before that. With the exception of the period of the Emergency (June 1975 to March 1977), it has been a democracy every year since independence; and each year of democratic experience has, I would argue, enhanced the chances of it continuing as a democracy. Pakistan, in contrast, has had an almost continuous experience of bureaucratic–military rule since at least 1958, and arguably even from Jinnah's "viceregal system" (Sayeed 1968). The periods of procedural democracy have been deeply flawed by the lack of electoral mandates and a constitutional framework in the first period (1947–58), the misuse of executive power in the second (1972–7), and the military's behind-the-scenes authority in the third (1988–99). That said, the free and fair election of 1970 might have at least provided one chance for government by the people in Pakistan, but it was lost in the violent crushing of the electoral verdict, followed by civil war and the emergence of Bangladesh.

In the first months of 1977, the paths of the two countries had converged, and it is not impossible to imagine that after their respective March elections of that year Pakistan could have consolidated democratic rule and India could have become a familiar Third World autocracy. But, in the event, India's free and fair election gave new life and power to its democracy, while Pakistan's rigged election provided the opening for a reassertion of the claim to ultimate authority by the military, and thus a gradual entrenching of the military as rulers.

## The balance of authority between bureaucratic and political wings of the state

The explanatory factor for these "different trajectories" (Jaffrelot 2002) or the "uneven democratic career" (Adeney and Wyatt 2001) that this book relies on more heavily than others is indicated by Jalal (1995: 250) when she notes that "[T]he supremacy of the elected over the non-elected arms of the [Indian] state in itself offered no assurance for the democratic empowerment of the people. . . . India's tryst with destiny brought an indigenous ruling configuration to the centre stage of state power, but not a commensurate democratization of politics at the social base." I believe this misses the point. While perhaps not "commensurate" with "supremacy of the elected," there has been significant democratization of politics along a number of dimensions in India, including in the belief in democracy and in the practice of voting, in which members of the "social base" participate in greater numbers than those on the "centre stage." The Pakistan of today, on the other hand, has *never* experienced the "supremacy of the elected" over its state apparatus.

Fred Riggs, writing about the developing world more generally, argues that "premature or too rapid expansion of the bureaucracy when the political system lags behind tends to inhibit the development of effective politics. A corollary thesis holds that separate political institutions have a better chance to grow if bureaucratic institutions are relatively weak" (Riggs 1963: 126). He goes on to put forward one part of his "paradoxical" view:

> It has become axiomatic in modern public administration that bureaucrats *ought* to be selected on the basis of universalistic, achievement criteria, best expressed in an examination system; and that employment should be for a career. . . . Yet the merit system cuts at the root of one of the strongest props of a nascent political party system, namely spoils. . . . No doubt a career bureaucracy of specialists is administratively more capable than a transitory bureaucracy of spoilsmen. But, by the same token, the career bureaucracy can project greater political power on its own, resist more successfully the politician's attempts to assert effective control. What is lost in administrative efficiency through spoils may be gained in political development.
>
> (Riggs 1963: 127–9; emphasis in the original)

In his later work Riggs presents the hypothesis that

> the most likely causes [of the disruption of Third World representative governments] arise from an imbalance between the effective power potential of constitutive systems and the state bureaucracies under their authority. Angered and frustrated officials, anxious to protect their income, perquisites and status will, under the leadership of a military cabal and with popular support, seize power and attempt to restore order and security while promoting developmental ambitions.
>
> (Riggs 1993: 226)[10]

We can add another element of the bureaucratic mindset if we follow Przeworski (1986: 58–61) when he argues that establishing democracy means "institutionalizing uncertainty" and writes: "For authoritarian bureaucrats, the introduction of democracy constitutes an ideological defeat, a collapse of their very vision of a world that can be rationally commanded to one's will. Uncertainty is what they abhor ideologically, psychologically, and politically" (Przeworski 1986: 59).

Most Third World countries are governed by a combination of military and civil bureaucrats, and "constitutive" authorities such as democratically elected officials, revolutionary parties, a regnant clergy, or a charismatic leader heading a "guided democracy."[11] There are continuing struggles for domination between the two "wings" of the state. Thus another way of framing our empirical question would be: *What allowed Indian elected politicians to assert and maintain their dominance of the bureaucratic and military branches of the state, while that has proved to be impossible in Pakistan?*

My argument focuses on examining the balance of power between elected politicians and the state apparatus when political choices are made, either focused on a particular event, or over a period of time. In the first part, I examine the colonial period, and in particular the years around the moment of independence on 14–15 August 1947, and the three decades afterwards.

In the colonial period, the balance is affected by the stronger and more autocratic bureaucratic tradition in what is now Pakistan. Bureaucrats became partners in the effort to create Pakistan, and so took power almost on an equal footing with the Pakistan-movement leaders. Bureaucrats in India, in contrast, had to demonstrate their loyalty to new political masters, particularly after independence.

It is, however, more important that the Indian nationalist movement was far older, broader, and more deeply rooted than the Pakistan movement. The authority of the Congress political leadership had been well institutionalized by 1947, and a thick layer of local and regional leaders had been brought into a very large and disciplined organization. Likely post-independence issues had been thought out, in part during solidarity-producing spells in British jails. The Congress had both mass and momentum as it took power.

Jinnah had been the sole towering leader of the Pakistan movement. He did not mobilize supporters and develop leaders in the Muslim-majority provinces that were to become Pakistan until very late, during the 1945–6 provincial assembly election campaigns. Congress had achieved a comparable position of mass support twenty-five years before, and had organized two India-wide mass civil disobedience campaigns since.

At independence, the superiority in power of the politicians vis-à-vis the bureaucrats was much greater for the Indian elected leaders than it was for Jinnah and his cohort. That contrast was reinforced when Jinnah chose to become governor-general rather than prime minister, and set in place a "viceregal system" of rule. Nehru became prime minister in India with a real commitment to democratic practices, which he demonstrated to his party leaders and members of parliament.

Indian politicians managed to write a constitution within two years; held adult-suffrage and free and fair elections in 1951–2; and dealt with the linguistic-states issue soon after. It took eight years for Pakistani politicians to resolve issues of the national language, the federal structure, and the place of religion in the state – by which time there had been a quasi-coup by Governor-General Ghulam Muhammad; rigged elections in the states of West Pakistan; and an emphatic defeat of the Muslim League in the Bengal elections. The Congress politicians enhanced their legitimacy by winning elections in every state as well as in Delhi. They could keep their bureaucrats in line; while the bureaucrats had seized the initiative in Pakistan by 1954.

Crucially, mid-level Pakistani politicians of the Muslim League, which was strongest in the Muslim-minority provinces that remained in India, discovered that as Urdu-speaking refugees they had great difficulty forging new political support networks in places where there were existing opposition-party groups, with citizens speaking a different language. They joined the bureaucracy to get a share in power.

At the same time, Pakistan's military was called on – to a much greater extent than India's – to secure the new country and help deal with the bloody exchange of population. It was also weaker than the Indian military, having had to build new units in the army, and develop logistical systems and training institutions almost from scratch. Even so, it succeeded in fighting India to a stalemate in Kashmir, which gave it legitimacy as an effective guardian institution – one that was disciplined and honest, unlike many politicians – when it chose to intervene in 1958, and renew its lease on rule in 1969. India's military, by the time it was given massive infusions of resources after the shock defeat in the India–China border war of 1962, and full-scale, if short, wars in 1965 and 1971, had been kept under tight control by the politicians and the civilian bureaucracy.

Pakistan's political leaders were unable to resolve the language issue and the question of just how Islam would feature in the constitutional order, and lost both legitimacy and power as a result. First the upper-level state officials and then the military asserted their authority and ultimately explicit control over the system. While the initial result seemed to be a disciplined state that brought about significant economic development, ultimately the shutting down of the democratic process led inexorably to the break-up of the country in 1971. Although the new government of Zulfiqar Ali Bhutto was able to establish relatively quickly a new constitutional order and political authority over the state apparatus, the autocratic elements of his rule, and the weakness of other parties and leaders, allowed the military to step in again, and retain direct or indirect control of the state up until the present.

In India, the Congress won both at the Center and in every state in the first elections. Nehru's leadership and the legacy of the Congress movement ensured that the elected representatives were unquestionably in control, and capable of resolving major questions about the secular state, linguistic states and the national language, and ultimately the defeat and split of the

Congress Party itself. At the same time, the Supreme Court was able to increase its autonomy and power, even as in Pakistan the courts were constrained to ratify the seizure of power by the bureaucrats and the army. The breakdown of democracy of Mrs Gandhi's emergency rule ended not in a regime change but in the re-equilibration of the system.

Although the social and economic structures of power in both countries were essentially autocratic, there is little evidence of that seriously determining what the state did, although there is a great deal of evidence that the interests of local power-wielders were well served by the actions of the state. In both countries, there were comparatively open societies, with freedom of speech and of association preserved, though perhaps marginally less so in Pakistan. There has been a much stronger development of civil society in India, again built on the legacy of the Congress movement, but strengthened by regular elections and the development of local self-government institutions.

The second part, focused roughly on the second thirty years, begins with a detailed examination of the implications and aftermath of the two elections held in March 1977. Arguably, Pakistan was more democratic than India in the two years before that election; afterwards, India took a giant step towards a re-energized and broader-based democratic system, while Pakistan wound up with a military regime that based its legitimacy on a program of Islamization, and began the process of deeply entrenching the military in a position of ultimate power in the system. In India, new popular forces were unleashed, reflecting to some extent a change from a "command economy" relying on planning and state enterprises to a "demand economy" relying more on the market – ultimately accelerating with the crisis-induced economic reforms of 1991. Hindu nationalism also emerged, even as groups like *dalits* (ex-untouchables), "other backward classes," and women were increasingly involved in democratic politics. The question of how significant the religious difference between the two countries might be is examined in this context. We also consider the influence of external links; it is clear that Pakistan's military alliances with the United States in particular have had a significant effect in strengthening that side of the political balance of power. India had no comparable set of relationships with countries or movements abroad.

The decades after 1977 have seen the entrenching of the Pakistan military not only in government, as it played king-maker when not directly in power, in the dozen years when there were elected governments, but also in the economy (setting up and running an array of business enterprises) and in society. No one and no party has been able to develop deep political roots to challenge that military leadership, nor have sparks of civil-society activism ignited sustained political action. In India, in stark contrast, there has been a deepening of democracy.

The evidence for this argument comes largely from a broad range of secondary sources. Fortunately, there have been many fine scholars, historians, political scientists, and anthropologists who have made similar arguments drawing on their own and others' research, and on a wealth of empirical studies in both countries. Since I am not always able to check their data and inferences with my own direct knowledge, I have often presented their own words rather than summarize what they have to say. In the conclusion I locate the solution of this particular empirical puzzle, as I see it, in the more general literature on what determines whether a country will become, or remain, democratic or autocratic. In particular, the theoretical frameworks – and large-N studies – that search for answers in the record of economic development need to be examined. I also try to suggest some lessons for understanding the political trajectories of the South Asia neighbors of India and Pakistan.

Both India and Pakistan have undergone rapid and profound political change since independence. Since 1977, India has not had a system-threatening crisis; and its politics, while continuing to develop along many dimensions, has done so at a pace much slower than before. Pakistan, on the other hand, has been more volatile, with regime changes in 1988 and 1999 and again in 2008. More significant changes are quite likely to occur at any moment, and it is tempting to wait for them; but that is obviously no way to complete a study. The argument I make thus takes into account events – and analyses of those events – up to the end of 2009, an arbitrary but convenient finish line.

I have spent many decades engaged in research and teaching on South Asia, and more than a decade of residence in India, so the establishment and future of democracy in India and Pakistan is not just a matter for disinterested political analysis, but something I care about personally, thinking of myself as a quasi-citizen of both countries. It is perhaps that perspective that explains my belief in the great value of examining these two cases: these are special countries, grounded in multiple great civilizations, whose future history, I hope and trust, will be positively path-breaking.

## Notes

1 At the time of writing – January 2010 – Pakistan has an elected government, but it probably should not be called a democracy, since the military retains control over things like nuclear policy and has not given up its (unspoken) claim to veto political decisions not in the national interest.
2 Until 2003, countries whose combined average ratings for political rights and for civil liberties fell between 1.0 and 2.5 were designated "Free;" between 3.0 and 5.5 "Partly Free", and between 5.5 and 7.0 "Not Free." Beginning with the ratings for 2003, countries whose combined average ratings fall between 3.0 and 5.0 are "Partly Free," and those between 5.5 and 7.0 are "Not Free."
3 "Methodological modifications" also explained its return to "Free" status in 1998, which is also when Kashmir began to be evaluated separately (*Freedom in the World 1993–94*: 303; *Freedom in the World 1998–99*: 223).
4 The shift from "Not Free" to "Partly Free" occurred because the 1985 elections meant the "initiation of a democratic process that may be hard to halt" (*Freedom in the World 1985–86*: 49–50).
5 This comment is based on my service as an academic advisor for Freedom House in recent years. The methodology, including the very detailed checklist for each of the subcategories, is available in each recent volume of *Freedom in the World.*

6 Jaffrelot (2002: 251) remarks:

> For Jalal, India suffers from such centralization of power that its democracy is largely "formal", while Pakistan is gradually emerging from its authoritarian tradition. Jalal formulated this interpretation at a moment when Pakistan was indeed engaged in a phase of democratization, while India, caught up in ethnic tension, was showing an increasing tendency towards authoritarianism. However, when placed in the context of the last fifty years, this reading no longer stands up to scrutiny.

See also Hasan (2001: 330–1):

> [Her] attempt to obfuscate the dichotomy between democracy in India and military governments in Pakistan and Bangladesh does not carry conviction. . . . [Her] attempt to discover the common strand of authoritarianism in the political experiences of India and Pakistan reveals her insensitivity to the important achievements of Indian democracy.

See also Adeney and Wyatt (2001: 114).
7 Collier and Levitsky (1997) explore this question with respect to procedural democracy. See O'Donnell and Schmitter (1986: 13–14):

> Political democracy per se is a goal worthy of attainment, even at the expense of forgoing alternate paths that would seem to promise more immediate returns in terms of socialization [a combination of "social democracy" (see Huber et al. 1997: 324) and "economic democracy"]. Not only is the probability of their success much lower and the likelihood of their promoting an authoritarian regression much higher, but the taking of such paths seems to require, at least in the interim, the installation of a popular authoritarian regime which is unlikely to respect either the guarantees of liberalization or the procedures of political democracy. . . . [I]t is by no means clear whether such a *via revolucionaria* will in the long run be more successful than incrementally and consensually processed change in making socialization compatible with the values embodied in liberalization and political democracy.

See also Welzel and Inglehart (2008).
8 The choice of language here – "reflective of," "apt," "processes" of democracy and authoritarianism – makes it hard to know precisely what is meant.
9 In general, I adopt the framework Dankwart Rustow uses, as John Waterbury describes it (1997: 383):

> Rustow staked out a well-defined position in what might be called the contingency school in explaining the initiation and institutionalization of democracy. The opposing, structuralist school emphasizes socioeconomic and occasionally cultural preconditions for democracy. These schools are not warring camps, nor are their positions mutually exclusive.

10 Thirty years later, Riggs is seeking to explain the "basic fragility of all third world regimes," and argues that "we need to recognize so-called 'military authoritarian' rule, as more meaningfully, bureaucratic polities" (Riggs 1993: 200). "A bureaucratic polity is . . . a political system . . . governed by the logic of power, ambition and greed, as exercised by bureaucratic rulers whose use of power cannot be restrained by any other institution, whether it be a traditional monarchy or a modern constitutive system" (Riggs 1993: 206).
11 According to Waterbury (1997: 385), a term coined by Ayub Khan.

# Part I

# The first thirty years of independence

As India and Pakistan began their independent existence, their leaders had to make important choices about the shape of their political regimes. Both countries had to come to terms with their inheritance of British Raj institutions, which included not only the military and civilian bureaucracies but also the very structure of the political system, as enshrined in the Government of India Act of 1935. Within this period of twenty-five to thirty years, Pakistan struggled to produce a constitution, while building a new country almost from scratch. It then came under military rule for thirteen years, ending with another partition, when its eastern wing fought for independence and became Bangladesh, with India's help. India, far more successful in writing a constitution and putting it into action with free and fair elections, none the less was challenged when many states rejected Congress rule in 1967, and when the 1971 Pakistan crisis forced it to go to war again. At the end of this period, India slipped into quasi-authoritarian rule, when Prime Minister Indira Gandhi declared a state of emergency in June 1975.

There are six major areas we need to explore here. The first is the inheritance of colonial rule, out of which the balance of power between politicians and the civil and military apparatus of the state is constructed. For Pakistan, that inheritance was of a comparatively strong bureaucracy and a comparatively weak political establishment, so that the two wings were very nearly balanced in terms of power. For India, in sharp contrast, the result was a power balance that strongly favored the political, both because of the far greater strength of the political side, and because of the comparative weakness of the bureaucrats. Having described that balance, we take an initial look at the role of the military, and discover that it begins to assert itself in Pakistan only after a few years of independence, and in India hardly at all in the initial phase. We then look at the character of the nationalism(s) which the rulers in each country held and promoted; then the choices made in the first critical months by the two unquestioned leaders, Nehru and Jinnah, and the political practices legitimated in the first decade or so of independence. The counterfactual questions have always been intriguing. Had Nehru died and Patel lived, what would India's regime trajectory have been? Had Liaquat been given the chance to govern for as long as Nehru, what would

Pakistan's trajectory have been? What if Nehru had succumbed to the temptations of charismatic leadership that he so famously set out in his anonymous article of 1937? What if the principles outlined in Jinnah's equally famous speech to the inaugural session of the Constituent Assembly on 11 August 1947 had been followed, and the battles over the "Islamic" nature of Pakistan avoided, at least for a time? Both countries tried to work out the place of religion in politics and government. In India, the issue had to do with preserving secularism, while Pakistan attempted to decide just what role Islam would play in the new state. Finally, we consider the struggle to institutionalize democracy, focusing on representation in the two countries, federalist arrangements, electoral history, freedom of association, press freedom, and the rule of law.

# 2　Inheritances of colonial rule

Newly independent India and Pakistan inherited a colonial state apparatus and a set of constitutional institutions produced by decades of the reform of colonial rule, culminating in the Government of India Act of 1935. Both had nationalist movements aimed at replacing colonial rule. But India's inheritance differed significantly from Pakistan's. At independence, the state apparatus in what was to become Pakistan was stronger than it was in the areas that were to become India, while those who held popularly ratified political power in India were much stronger than their Pakistan counterparts.

Consider the "balance" of political authority derived from popular support – what Iftikar Malik (2001: 363) calls the "political sector within the state structure" – versus the authority of the state apparatus. In India, the balance favored the political authority, as is suggested by the efforts Sardar Vallabhbhai Patel had to make to defend and retain the Indian Civil Service (ICS) and other senior services. In Pakistan the balance favored the state apparatus. As Aitzaz Ahsan (2005: 98) remarks:

> The question often asked is: how did the civil and military bureaucracy wrest power from the politicians at the very outset of Pakistan's creation? The answer has to be that it never relinquished it. Jinnah was the only politician who could have subordinated the bureaucracy and the army to supreme democratic will. . . . But Jinnah died merely a year after Partition.

And, in fact, Jinnah never did subordinate the bureaucracy. Ahsan (2005: 99) describes how, under Jinnah, Chaudhri Muhammad Ali set up a "Planning Committee of the Cabinet" which "became the alternate, indeed the real 'cabinet.' . . . Thus bypassed by the bureaucracy and divested of decision-making powers, politicians began to look feeble." Nothing remotely like this happened in India.

My argument here is that the balance of power at the moment of independence clearly favored political leaders in India, while it was closer to having political leaders and state apparatus more or less equally powerful in Pakistan. This was so mainly because India's political leadership had greater absolute strength than Pakistan's. But, also, Pakistan's state apparatus had a level of power more like that of its immediate British colonial parent, while India's had had its power weakened. The historical sketch that follows high-lights the factors that contribute to the development of these contrasting pictures (see also R. Kumar 1989; Sarkar 2001).

## The strength of the state apparatus

Jaffrelot (2002: 253–5) outlines the case for the importance of the differing inheritance of the state apparatus. Having described the gradual process of British colonial governmental reform, with the "gradual devolution of power to Indians at the local, and then regional, level," he argues that

> The whole territory of the Raj did not benefit in the same way from the colonial apprenticeship of democracy. The provinces that would later become the principal components of Pakistan [Punjab, North-West Frontier Province (NWFP), and Balochistan] were among the least solidly anchored in this tradition. [Owing to its position on the frontier, the Punjab was] more militarized than others, and became a real laboratory for the bureaucracy and in particular for the Indian Civil Service. . . . District Magistrates literally reigned over their territories. . . . The Lawrence brothers, who administered Punjab after its annexation [in 1849], embodied better than anyone this mixture of paternalism and autocraticism.[1]

Possibly significant even for post-independence Pakistan, "[John] Lawrence was delighted that the separation of the judiciary and executive, which he believed was ruining the North-Western Provinces [i.e., the area around Agra and Allahabad], was not to be reproduced in the Punjab" (Stokes 1959: 244). Although Dalhousie adopted this system for administration in the Central Provinces and Awadh (Oudh) – major parts of what was to become India – he did so for different reasons (Stokes 1959: 248); and, in any case, the administrative traditions of the other presidencies and provinces, the so-called "Regulation Provinces," especially Bengal, were autocratic in a different way.

Sayeed (1968: 281), discussing the situation after provincial governments were elected in 1937, notes that the powers of the deputy commissioner, particularly in the "Non-Regulation Provinces" of the NWFP and Punjab, were such that in a broad range of activities "the people in the countryside depended almost entirely upon the goodwill and leadership of the Deputy Commissioner. This seriously undermined the role of the politician for he could neither put forward vigorously the interests of his constituents, nor was much patronage available to him at the district level." In contrast, "the administrative system of the Regulation Provinces with its careful definition of the rights of the citizenry and the restrictions it placed on the authority of the district officer enabled the growth of political consciousness in these

Provinces" (Sayeed 1968: 281–2). There were few Regulation Provinces-tradition bureaucrats in post-independence Pakistan, as is clear from the under-representation of Bengalis in the Central Secretariat (Jahan 1972: 26). Had there been more, the autocratic–paternalistic Punjab tradition might have been diluted.

As Jaffrelot points out (2002: 254), "The weight of militarism in Punjab and the NWFP is not explained solely by the deployment of troops for security reasons, but also by the fact that these two regions soon became sources of recruitment for the army." This would presumably mean the socialization of men into a decidedly non-democratic modern organization, but also would reinforce existing attitudes, as Dewey (1991: 262) suggests: "all the locally dominant castes in the great Punjabi recruiting grounds have value systems . . . which hold the warrior up to admiration as the finest sort of man." That would also tend to reinforce respect for officials who acted decisively, army fashion, rather than by temporizing with the excuse of considering all opinions.

The civilian bureaucracy was also shaped into an autocratic mode by the requirements of an agricultural economy that was dependent on a massive canal irrigation system in the Punjab. As Imran Ali (2004: 135) argues: "The cultivator became much more dependent on the government than under rain-fed agriculture. The centralized irrigation management thus furthered the submission of the citizen to the state." The process of trans-ferring the land, managed by the lower bureaucracy, was very corrupt, and "the British did little to curb these malpractices, not wishing to alienate valu-able support groups. As a result, both rent seeking behaviour and access to arbitrary authority were already embedded during colonial rule. They were to reemerge with even greater alacrity [sic] after 1947" (Imran Ali 2004: 135). It is also true that senior civil servants – Chaudhri Muhammad Ali most notably – worked in partnership with political leaders to make Pakistan a reality in the 1940s.

As the British gradually introduced democracy, the Punjab's rural areas were given an overwhelming segment of the representation. The landed elite, many of whom had military ties, were particularly prominent.[2] After the 1919 reforms, the military vote in Punjab was estimated at 32 percent of the electorate (Yong 1995: 187). In the immediate aftermath of independence, the alliance of politicians with the civil and military bureaucracy became crucial. Tan Tai Yong (1995: 192; see also Yong 2005: 308–9) concludes that the association of Punjab with the army meant "the militarization of the administration of the Punjab" and the "conjunction of the military, civil and political authorities into a unique civil–military regime . . . not replicated anywhere else in British India, nor indeed the empire." After independence, "it was this powerful and well-entrenched civil–military alliance that took over the state apparatus and ensured the survival of the 'moth-eaten' and fragile state of Pakistan." Anthony Low (2002: 266) con-curs and adds:

[I]t is not too difficult to see why independent Pakistan should . . . have become a deeply entrenched military–fiscal state. For it stands in a direct line of succession from the Clive–Hastings model of a British military fiscal state in the eighteenth century, through Washbrook's 'very military state' in the first half of the nineteenth century . . . before being ultimately forged into its present form in the further extraordinary circumstances of the traumatic Partition in 1947, the unending conflict with India over Kashmir, and the desperate need at independence somehow to hold a ramshackle new state together. For all sorts of reasons habits persistently reinforced over two centuries and more are not to be easily sloughed off.

Thus the state apparatus that Pakistan inherited came out of a tradition of good government that was both more militaristic and, on the civil side, more autocratic-paternalist than the state apparatus the Indian politicians faced (see Imran Ali 2004). Even so, in both countries "the period of legislative development from 1909 to 1947 was also . . . the period of centralization of the supreme executive power in the hands of the higher bureaucracy. By the time the British left, they had amassed all real power in the hands of top civil servants" (Waseem 1989: 60). Yet the Pakistan bureaucracy became more politics-minded than India's, because in the years immediately after independence it was captured by members of the elite classes who had fled from India; who, faced with the difficulty of gaining power through democratic means, chose instead to rule in government as civil servants (Waseem 1989: 112–13).

India also inherited part of the "Punjab school" state apparatus, and a substantial number of Punjabi Sikhs in the military. But while the Punjab was the governmental heartland of Pakistan, even before 1971, the part of Punjab that remained in India was on India's periphery. The civil-service tradition that was preponderant in India came from the Regulation Provinces, so was not as autocratic. As important, perhaps, was the effect on the civil service of Gandhi's 1920 call to government servants to quit their jobs, even though few actually did. From then on, at least in terms of rhetoric, it was almost traitorous to serve the British openly, in the army and in the civil service. In practice, those Indians who joined the civil service often were sympathetic to nationalist goals but probably not to Congress methods. The near-hatred of the Congress and "politicians" more generally comes through strongly in memoirs of British ICS officers of this time (e.g., those in Hunt and Harrison 1980). The extent to which Indian members of the civil services shared those views would be hard to determine.

Indians in the army were loyal to the British, at least up to World War II and its immediate aftermath, even taking into account those who served in the Indian National Army, who were recruited after being captured by the Japanese. According to Kundu (1998: 6; see also pp. 33–49): "the almost total exclusion of the military in the nationalist struggle meant there was no mystification of the soldier as hero. When independence came, no military man would be in a position to challenge the right-to-rule of those nationalist leaders who became India's democratically elected representatives." These words could almost certainly describe the civil servants as well. They had clearly chosen to serve the British loyally, undoubtedly relishing the high pay and high status, while their countrymen in the nationalist movement were making sacrifices of jobs and comfort. Although many would have been sympathetic to the nationalist movement, they were far from "heroes" at independence. The power and authority of the state apparatus they constituted would have been undermined and weakened when it came to dealing with their new political masters after 1947. And no civil servants of the stature of Chaudhri Muhammad Ali, Ghulam Muhammad, and Iskandar Mirza in Pakistan received formal positions of political power.

## The strength of the nationalist movements

While the comparative power of Pakistan's and India's state apparatus as of 1947 is significant, the comparative power of those in political authority was far more important. Some nationalist leaders had won elections in the years before independence, but that was not the major source of their power. India's leaders were in a comparatively far more powerful position than their Pakistani counterparts mainly because of the differing character of the two nationalist movements. That in turn explains much of the contrast in the balance of power and legitimacy vis-à-vis the state apparatus in the initial years of freedom. To oversimplify the argument that follows: India's nationalist movement was much older than the Pakistan movement; reached a mass public much earlier; was directed democratically (by and large); and valorized non-violence and a respect for the rule of law. The Pakistan movement was a generation younger than the Congress; became a mass movement twenty-five years after the Congress did; was directed in a less democratic fashion; and at a critical point in 1946 resorted to mob violence to make its political point.

Let us first consider the factor of the two movements' duration. Founded in 1885, the Congress was the oldest nationalist movement to win independence in the wave of decolonization after World War II.[3] Its sheer age is less significant perhaps than one consequence of that age – the need to have a succession of generations of leadership (see Rudolph and Rudolph 1964: 6; Kothari 1988: 161–3). Oversimplifying, there were three generations, with Pherozeshah Mehta, Dadabhai Naraoji, Surendranath Banerjee, Madhav Rao Gokhale, and Bal Gangadar Tilak, among many others, in the first; Mohandas Gandhi, Motilal Nehru, C. Rajagopalachari, and Maulana Azad in the second; and then the post-Gandhi generation of Jawaharlal Nehru and Subhas Chandra Bose. To some extent, these men were chosen, or at least blessed, by one or the other stalwart of the preceding generation – Gokhale anoints Gandhi who anoints Jawaharlal. Many if not most of these "tall leaders" had significant followings, and represented – and felt they represented – particular geographical or other interests.

The Muslim League, in contrast, was essentially a single-generation organization, even though Jinnah did not fully emerge as "the" leader until ten years after its founding in 1906. No one of a second generation challenged, let alone supplanted, Jinnah. Compared to the Congress, there were not many leaders of any kind, much less those with popular support.

Had Gandhi not taken over the reins of the Congress after World War I, it might have remained an organization working the system through petitions and representations, and contesting elections to fill posts that the British had released to "non-officials," with an occasional agitation of the swadeshi variety. Given what was to happen in Ceylon – though that clearly did not happen in isolation from the situation in India – a smooth transfer of power was indeed possible by taking that path.[4] The path of revolutionary or terrorist violence that some had already chosen, especially in Bengal in the decades before Gandhi returned to India, would certainly have put pressure on the British to leave, but would have produced a decidedly non-democracy-minded leadership.

The Gandhi-directed nationalist movement's contribution to the emergence of India's democracy obviously cannot be easily summarized. It did indeed, in stages, become significantly a mass movement – though not one that was built from the bottom up. There were literally millions of ordinary Indians who became caught up in nationalist fervor, beginning twenty-five years before independence (for vivid accounts, see Shahid Amin's "Gandhi as Mahatma" and Raja Rao's novel *Kanthapura.*) The equivalent fervor emerges among most Pakistanis-to-be only two years before independence. The Congress organization – crucially, rearranged by Gandhi on linguistic-province lines – becomes a formidable instrument with a thick layer of local and regional leadership, and literally decades in which to become institutionalized, in terms of committee structure, leadership elections, lines of communication, etc. While obviously not successful in drawing in everyone, the Congress was something of a "rainbow coalition." As an unintended consequence of the interaction of Gandhian protest technique and British notions of rules of special treatment for political prisoners, men and women of a wide variety of views and backgrounds met together in jail with plenty of spare time to develop bonds of common purpose that went beyond the rhetoric of the annual meetings. The leadership of the Muslim League never sought that advantage.

The Congress from the outset placed itself in opposition to the British, claiming to exclude no Indian from its cause. Arguably, Indian nationhood was generated by that opposition, since it was hard to see what made "Indians" a "nation," as many pointed out.[5] But Indians did share a common denominator: their economic and political position vis-à-vis the Raj. As Meghnad Desai (1993: 227–8) notes, "the argument for Indian nationalism was at its outset [in the late nineteenth century] framed in terms of economics. . . . The language of Indian nationalism in those days was almost exclusively economic tariffs, the Sterling/Rupee exchange rate, the immiserising effects of the British rule, etc." Or, as Deshpande (1993: 13) puts it: "During the colonial period the major impetus behind the nationalist struggle – getting it an all-India character – is the notion of an enslaved economy." In later phases the movement against British rule changed from polite argument to street demonstrations and direct action: first "swadeshi" (see Deshpande 1993: 16–21), then the revival of self-reliance symbolized by *khadi*, and finally the focus on the salt tax in the 1930 movement. The economic dimension of imperial rule remained prominent.

Without a common religious, linguistic, ethnic, territorial, or historical identity, what developed was something of an economic and therefore a political identity: Indians were "Indian" because they were *collectively* exploited economically and suppressed politically by the British. One's "home place" on the subcontinent was quite circumscribed in terms of language and culture and socio-religious institutions. A particular caste (*jati*) was local, and not India-wide. But there was an overarching common market that included princely India, and people would move or be moved and resettle as plantation and industrial labor, as workers on the railways, and so on. Being an "Indian" made sense as someone who was part of the economy, even if there was cultural and social fragmentation. It was clear, of course, that the cause of that economic harm, and the suppression of India's ability to make economic progress, lay in the *political* injustice of colonial rule.

The Congress strove to bring in all elements that opposed the British, promising, in effect, that once colonial rule was ended the other problems of India's cultural and other diversity would be solved by the economic and political energy unleashed by freedom. Gandhi was, to be sure, bitterly disappointed that the transformations he had sought to bring about during the movement itself did not happen. Indians did not adopt non-violence as a principle rather than a tactic; or accept a complicated notion of an Indian people-hood grounded in tolerance and respect; or agree to the transformation of the idea of property into something called "trusteeship." Yet Gandhi was to accept, reluctantly and sometimes in despair, that the goal of freedom from colonial rule was paramount.

The Muslim League, while committed to Indian (and then Pakistan's) independence, was as committed to the safeguarding of the Muslims as some sort of a collectivity – only in the last stages of the movement, as a nation – in an independent India. From time to time, collaboration with the British was justifiable in order to achieve that end. Certainly, there was no impulse to quit serving the British. In the process of gaining independence for Pakistan, Muslims working with the British government were part of the patriotic effort to preserve fellow Muslims, of whatever linguistic and ethnic type, from what they saw as the threatened onset of Hindu majority rule.

It was clear to the Muslim League leaders that the adoption of democracy in an independent India would mean permanent minority status for Muslims, who were a quarter of the population. Farzana Shaikh (1989: 233) argues persuasively that it was not simply the number of voters that would matter:

> [E]lements that sustained the politics of Muslim representation were also grounded deep in a tradition the sources of which were believed to lie in divine revelation. . . . While the thrust of Muslim opposition was more ostensibly concerned with the political disadvantages that such [liberal-theory] representation would bring to bear upon Muslims in India, it rested upon a more profound critique of the ends of Western representation. This questioned the theory of individual representation and denied that men's political commitments were independent of their religious faith. It rejected the justice of arithmetical democracy and called for the restoration of moral superiority as a condition of men's claim to power.

The Muslim League had been founded as an organization of the elite in 1906.[6] It was not until the mid-1930s that it even began to work as a political party building support among voters – at a time when there was a very limited franchise – and it never became a mass movement with national reach, on the model of what the Congress had become.

The fateful paradox of the League's efforts even then was that the core of its initial support came from the provinces – especially from Uttar Pradesh (UP) – in which Muslims were a minority, while in the Muslim-majority provinces that were to become Pakistan its political fortunes lagged (see F. Robinson 1992 for a detailed and convincing discussion). But in 1945–6 the League won 75 percent of the Muslim vote for the provincial assemblies (Jalal 1985a: 172).

In the 1937 elections, the Muslim League did very poorly in Punjab, NWFP, and Sindh, and not that well in Bengal, where it won thirty-nine of the Muslim seats, while independents won forty-three. The Krishak Praja Party (KPP) of Fazlul Huq came in third with thirty-six seats. The KPP, however, received 31.5 percent of the Muslim votes to 27.1 percent for the Muslim League. The KPP victories were all rural seats, mainly in East Bengal. The Muslim League won only one of the Muslim seats in Punjab, and none in Sindh and the North-West Frontier Province (Sen 1976: 88–9).

When Britain declared India to be at war in 1939 without consulting "any Indian elected body" (Low 1997: 298), the Congress representatives in the central and provincial assemblies resigned en masse. Three years later Gandhi began the "Quit India" movement, and the entire Congress leadership was put in jail for several years. The Muslim League, however, cooperated in the war effort, in which the Indian state was fully mobilized. Bengal had a Muslim League ministry, but by the end of the war "Jinnah's main lieutenants in Bengal had lost all credibility, and he had no ties with the new crop of leaders in the Bengal League" (Jalal 1985a: 108). The Unionist Party continued in office in Punjab, despite its internal problems. The Muslim League "failed to win Punjabis at the top" (Jalal 1985a: 98) and in the countryside: according to the March 1945 report of the Punjab chief secretary (quoted by Jalal 1985a: 98; see Baxter 1977), "during the last year the Islamic appeal behind the League has failed to galvanize the rural Muslim population."

Percival Spear (1961: 402) claims that "the Congress Ministers [who had to resign in 1939] in general departed from the seats of British power amid mutual expressions of regret. They had won the respect of the British and in their turn had come to know them better." Not that this was an easy process. As Woodruff (1964b [1954]: 244), writing of the 1919–37 period, notes:

> India . . . was proceeding to popular government . . . by the English method of prolonged argument and crisis upon minor crisis. It is not easy for a Guardian [ICS officer] who has been trained in knowledge of the good to make over his charge to someone who manifestly has not; on a different level, it is hard to serve where you have ruled.

But, for the next six years, Congress politicians and British administrative officers were clearly on opposite sides. The Indian officials were presumably torn, if ICS officer Ashok Mitra's remark (Mitra 1991: 81) is representative: "I never thought then [1942] that the British would be diabolical enough to be working for splitting India asunder. Was that because I was in the steel frame myself and inwardly shirked facing the moment of truth?" British officialdom probably preferred the "natural" leaders to be found in the countryside to the urbanized (lawyer) leadership of the Muslim League and the Congress, with whom Indian civil servants shared at least a class identity.

Less than a decade after the 1937 election, there was a huge shift in votes. The results of the 1945–6 provincial assembly elections, which were in effect a referendum on whether Muslims wanted an independent Pakistan, "proved that in Bengal the Pakistan movement was mass-based and democratic" (Sen 1976: 197). The Muslim League won an astounding 83.7 percent of the Muslim vote (Sen 1976: 198).

In Punjab, the elections were fought "on the old lines with personal, tribal and factional rivalries, not party creeds, dominating the choice of voters" (Jalal 1985a: 22). Even as the 1946 election campaign began, "most League branches in districts, rural and urban alike, were still on the drawing boards" (Jalal 1985a: 146 n), and "its coffers were empty. Yet it had the smell of a party about to have victory thrust upon it" (Jalal 1985a: 146). According to F. Robinson (1992: 52), "Not surprisingly, the political decisions of landholders rather than the popular will of Punjabi Muslims decided that the League should rise and the Unionists decline." Ian Talbot (1980: 89–90) makes the same point but adds an important element:

> The Muslim League succeeded in the 1946 Punjab Elections because it used religious appeals and traditional channels of political mobilization

more effectively than the Unionist Party. This was possible because it had captured the support of many of the landlords and *pirs* [religious leaders] who had previously provided the backbone of the Unionist Party's strength in the countryside. During the elections *pirs* issued *fatwas* to their *murids* to support the League; landlords used their economic influence and their leading positions within the *biraderi* networks. . . . Most importantly, [the League] presented Pakistan not only as a religious imperative but as a cure for all their problems. The League's ability to provide answers to the economic dislocation of the countryside caused by the War was the key to its success in winning over the Punjabi villagers. Votes were traded off for immediate material benefits and for the promise that Pakistan's creation would solve their social and economic difficulties.

In a province with a 57 percent majority Muslim population, the League won seventy-five of 175 seats, with 32.8 percent of the vote (compared to 23.1 percent for the Congress and 20.2 percent for the Unionists) (Jalal 1985a: 150).

In the North-West Frontier Province, however, the Muslim League "had no real machinery with which to conduct its campaign. Its provincial organization was a façade, incapable of functioning, let alone competing with the Frontier Congress' strong party apparatus" (Rittenberg 1988: 194). The Frontier Congress narrowly won the election, gaining 51.9 percent of the vote in the Pakhtun constituencies, compared to the Muslim League's 39.4 percent (Rittenberg 1988: 201). In the province as a whole, the Muslim League received 38.8 percent of the votes cast (the turnout was 62.2 percent of an electorate of 604,563), while the Congress and its ally the Jamiat-ul-Ulama-i-Hind received 42.6 percent (Rittenberg 1988: 246). In Sindh the Muslim League won twenty-eight out of thirty-four seats, where it formed the government (Sayeed 1968: 135). But these results did not directly bring Pakistan into being, as Anthony Low (2002: 271) points out:

Unlike India . . . Pakistan did not achieve independence as a result of a resounding electoral victory, but as a consequence of the fateful decision to partition the sub-continent. The difference here was seminal. It meant on the Indian side that the immense importance of Congress' electoral success in securing independence gave electoral procedures there an unchallenged legitimacy which persists to this day.

The Muslim League leaders from the places where voter support was comparatively deep and strong (though only ten years old) either chose or were forced to move to Pakistan, leaving most of their supporters behind. They had to find new roots in Pakistan. In the areas that became Pakistan, the Muslim League roots were even shallower, dating from two years or less before independence. There was no comparison to the nationalism-derived momentum and strength that the Congress movement-turned-party was able to display in India.

In the endgame of the Raj (1945–7), during the interim government, politician–administrator relationships became quite significant, at least in Delhi. It is important to note that this was a very limited set of people – an intimate elite. Consider V. P. Menon working with Sardar Patel, and Chaudhri Muhammad Ali with Liaquat Ali Khan. It is likely that the process of establishing trust and respect between civil servants and the Indian politicians was significantly more difficult than it was when it came to Muslim League politicians and (Muslim) civil servants.

The Indian higher services had more to prove, in terms of showing that they could work loyally and keeping their own biases and judgments under wraps, because they were still in the camp of the enemy. Kundu (1998: 46–7) claims that "both jawans and commissioned Indian officers had to defend themselves against the charge of doing nothing to hasten *swaraj* in contrast to the personal participation of millions of common people active in the nationalist movement." When the article that in effect guaranteed the privileges of the ICS came up in India's Constituent Assembly, one member said: "This guarantee means that they were the rulers under the old regime and that they will continue to be so in this regime. This guarantee asks us to forget that these persons who are still in service – 400 of them – committed excesses thinking that this was not their country". (as quoted in Shiva Rao et al. 1968: 721). The Muslim civil servants, on the other hand, could be seen as allies in the cause by Muslim League and other non-Congress Muslim leaders (see Potter 1986: 130–1).

Mushirul Hasan argues that it was Gandhi who made the difference in setting India's course, and he contrasts his beliefs and actions with those of Jinnah, who "stayed clear of the dusty roads, the villages inhabited by millions of hungry, oppressed and physically emaciated peasants, and the British prison where so many of his countrymen were incarcerated for defying the colonial government" (Hasan 2001: 333):

> While Gandhi walked barefoot to break the Salt Law and to galvanize the masses by culturally resonant and action-oriented symbols, a pensive and restless Jinnah waited in London to occupy the commanding heights of political leadership in Delhi. While Gandhi treaded [sic] the path fouled by Hindu and Muslim zealots in the riot-stricken areas of Bihar and Bengal, Jinnah was being crowned as the Governor-General of Pakistan.
>
> (Hasan 2001: 334)

The irony is that by the time Jinnah took power Gandhi had lost his position as the unquestioned leader of the Congress.

## Nationalisms

The political foundations of India and Pakistan consisted both of inherited state and regime structures – the bureaucratic organizations, legislatures, local executives, and constitutional framework (the Government of India Act of 1935 in particular) – and differing ideas, in both, of who "the people" were at the core of the nation-in-making of each country. Both had to engage in simultaneous state-building and nation-building. We ask: In what way, and to what extent, did the differing nationalism(s) to which they committed themselves affect the choices in the first decades of independence that stabilized and strengthened a democratic system in India, and undermined it in Pakistan?[7]

There is an important argument that *the* prerequisite for a consolidated democracy – Rustow (1970: 350) calls it a "background condition" – is to have an agreed-upon "national unit," a country whose people constitute a community (see also Schmitter and Santiso 1998: 79). British colonial rule and India's nationalism had generated some sense of what India's territory and citizenry would be well before independence, including who would *not* be included. There was never a demand that Ceylon be included, or Nepal, or Burma, even though Burma was administered by the government of India until 1937, and Ceylon was clearly culturally and historically tied closely to India. The Pakistan resolution of 1940 was itself unclear whether one country or two was being demanded, so it was only in 1947 itself that an approximation of the territory that Pakistan would control was understood, with the partitioning of Punjab and Bengal being major changes from an initial conception. And even then it was an imperfect understanding, since the status of the princely states was left unclear. Although India was changed as well, as Pakistan was subtracted from its territory, its core conception remained.

Thus India and Pakistan were different in this crucial aspect of having a clear national unit. Indians had this prerequisite established to a significant degree before they began the other democratic consolidation processes. Pakistan was missing most of Kashmir – whose initial letter was in the acronym "Pakistan" (while the "B" for Bengal was not) – and had no time before beginning to build its democracy to understand itself as a single country, let alone develop a "feel" for its territory. It is likely that the mass of its citizenry literally had no idea of what the country Pakistan consisted. The many leaders who came from places that remained in India had to develop a new territorial feeling, even when they understood in their head what Pakistan was.[8]

It is useful to think of two strands of nationalism in pre-independence India, both of which survive in post-1947 India. One ultimately becomes "Hindu nationalism" and the other its opponent, variously called "secular" or "inclusive" nationalism. I accept that nations and nationalism are counter-intuitively related; as Hobsbawm (1992: 10) puts it: "Nations do not make states and nationalisms, but the other way round." The nineteenth-century nationalism that has its origins in notions of social and religious transformation need not depend on there being an actual Indian nation.[9] A few members of the elite can claim to be part of an encompassing nation-in-making even if there is no "people" of India who all think of themselves as "Indian." The same is true for those who asserted that an Indian nation was a myth, that the true nations were two (or more): Hindu and Muslim, Aryan and Dravidian, or the very many defined by a mutually comprehensible language.

The Hindu nationalist strand begins – in the standard narrative – with the Brahmo Samaj, and continues with organizations such as the Arya Samaj and the Ramakrishna Mission. This strand claims that Hindus have been weakened by "evils" – customs such as *sati* and child marriage and the caste system – that allowed first the Muslims and then the British to conquer India. Becoming independent again required removing those evils, and that was to be done by founding institutions and by mobilizing public opinion to get the British government to ban the most egregious customs. Reform was not confined to the Hindus at large, but also becomes a goal for groups like the Sikhs and the non-Brahmin castes.

Somewhat later, a nationalism emerges that is focused on Indians' rights as British citizens vis-à-vis the British government, beginning with civic associations looking to gain influence in issues of local government, especially in the Bombay presidency. I have argued earlier that this comes to have as its kernel an economic identity. But it also adds the Hindu nationalist strand, when Tilak, perhaps seeking to evade British sanction by masking political processions as religious ones, transforms the Ganapati festival in the 1890s into a nationalist statement. It is no accident that Hindu–Muslim riots ensue, or that the novel *Andandamath* (and the patriotic song that it contains, *Vande Mataram*) emerge from Bengal as rallying points. It is not surprising that Sir Sayyid Ahmad Khan warns Muslims against joining in the new-formed Congress, and that the Muslim League is formed in 1906 to demand separate electorates.

This Hindu nationalist strand was significantly modified in its use by Gandhi, when he added a *bhakti* (devotional) flavor, as it were: an emphasis on prayers and congregational song – albeit including those of other religions. This made it possible, for a while, for Hindu–Muslim cooperation to occur, from the Lucknow Pact through the Khilafat Movement, featuring things like Swami Shraddhanand speaking from the pulpit of the Jama Masjid in Delhi in 1919. But its collapse was accompanied by the founding of the Rashtriya Swayamsevak Sangh (RSS) in 1925, and the publication of Savarkar's *hindutva* ideas (see Jaffrelot 1994).

Congress-led nationalism, "secular" and featuring "Indian" as an economic identity, certainly generated the most popular support in much of India, especially in the early 1930s. There was an array of groups and parties that kept away. Muslim opposition solidified around the Simon Commission/Nehru Report controversies (1928–9). Some Sikhs, fresh from a triumphant recapture of the gurudwaras in their 1920s movement, stayed separate. The Justice Party gained real strength in Madras; and a separate Bengali nationalism added to the complexity.

One major place in which Congress-led nationalism did not operate directly was princely India. Since there was freedom of movement and communication, nationalism and the freedom movement's ideas were presumably known to many in the princely states. At least until the 1930s and the 1940s, there were not many agitations or demonstrations, because the Congress and other parties were not allowed to organize there. There were popular movements, as in Kashmir, and enlightened rulers who advanced education and infrastructure development that helped support the laying down of human capital in places like Baroda and Travancore.

As the princely states were integrated into India after independence, could it be that their inhabitants were "behind" the rest of India in exposure to the ideas of the nationalist movement, as well as missing the multitiered Congress organization that existed elsewhere? Perhaps, as political mobilization began in a free India, the Hindu nationalists competed on a more level ideological playing field with the Congress, which was still emphasizing the economic common denominator. *The* goal of the country was no longer juridical independence, but the "real" independence that would come from economic transformation, particularly industrialization, necessarily in a single capital and labor market (see Nayar 1974).

For those in the former princely state areas, however, where the state' majority community typically had a marked religious identity, a religious identity might have seemed more valid to more new citizens. Might this help explain why the map of Jana Sangh and then Bharatiya Janata Party (BJP) strength in the 1980s and 1990s in north India seemed to fit well on the map of the former princely states?[10] Yogendra Yadav and Suhas Palshikar (2008: 16), however, assert that "today, it would be hard to detect the boundaries of princely and British India in the map of democratic politics."

Copland (2005: 207–14) argues that the support the right-wing Hindu-oriented parties received in what he calls "Middle India" (mainly in what is now Rajasthan and Madhya Pradesh) was due directly to the support of many of the particular ex-rulers, but also to "the political values imparted to the region by centuries of *darbari* [courtly] rule" (Copland 2005: 209). Most significant, in Copland's view (2005: 213–14), are those that served to protect Muslims under princely rule:

[A] number of ex-princes and princely family members . . . brought to the BJS [Bharatiya Jana Sangh, the predecessor of the BJP] a vision of the state as a powerful, paternalistic institution with the moral and physical capacity to enforce a Hindu majoritarian compact that would, at the same time, minimize social violence by guaranteeing the right of non-Hindus to reside and work and worship in their local communities. That is exactly the vision of the state that the BJP is currently trying to sell the Indian people. . . . It is a vision that, until recently, many, if not most, Indian Muslims have glumly embraced for want of practical alternatives.

It is quite possible that this idea – explaining perhaps the reduction in Muslims' assertion of their rights after the destruction of the Babri Masjid – has affected the rest of India as well.

Undoubtedly it took many decades for Hindu nationalism *qua* electoral force to emerge from under the blanket of Congress nationalism, but the two strands were always present. Whether Hindu nationalism is less compatible with a democratic regime than secular nationalism then becomes the crucial question, which we shall consider below. In the first decades of independence, though, claims for political representation based on religion were delegitimized in India since religious nationalism had torn the country in two, and there was a "never again" idea abroad (see Brass 1994: 172). The horrendous ethnic cleansing of partition had perhaps also caused Indians to step back from pursuing "communal" agendas; deaths in Hindu–Muslim riots are few until 1961 and 1964 (see figure 1.2 in Wilkinson 2004: 12). "Sub-national" identity claims were based on language divisions, which, in the event, could be handled with relatively little disruption.

In Pakistan, the contradiction of multiple nationalisms certainly contributed to the collapse of its initial democratic regime, and ultimately to the break-up of the country (see Oldenburg 1985; Shaikh 2009: 46–80). The claim of the "two nation theory" was that the Muslims of the subcontinent, mainly by virtue of their shared religion, were a separate nation and therefore were entitled to a separate country. In the initial years, this was recognized to imply a right to migrate to Pakistan, though that was certainly never formalized in any way, and would clearly be impossible to implement completely, since one-third of the Muslims of undivided India were left behind in India. In the aftermath of the break-up of the country in 1971, a substantial group of "Biharis" – Urdu-speaking migrants who left India for East Pakistan – were not able to move to Pakistan. Many of them had actively supported Pakistan in the 1971 civil war, and all of them were clearly not welcome to stay on in the new Bangladesh. Their claim that they were Pakistani citizens and therefore should be allowed to go to Pakistan was not granted for many years. Ultimately an agreement was reached to allow a portion to move to Pakistan, but a substantial number remain in Bangladesh, thirty-seven years later, essentially as stateless persons.[11]

On the other hand, non-Muslims were *ipso facto* not denied Pakistani citizenship; and, indeed, many remained in Pakistan, especially in East Pakistan. The separate electorates that had provided seats for Muslims in the 1946 provincial elections gave way to reserved seats in post-independence elections (see Baxter 1977: 181; Park 1954: 71; Shaikh 1986: 82–5). Separate electorates had not found a place in either the constitution of 1956 (under which no elections were held), or the Ayub constitution of 1962, or the Legal Framework Order of Yahya Khan's government, or the 1973 constitution. They were reintroduced by President Zia in 1977 (for non-Muslims) and abolished again for the 2002 election by President Musharraf's regime (Hamid Khan 2001: 898–9; European Union Election Observation Mission 2002: 22). Although non-Muslims seem to have had equal citizenship (with the exception that non-Muslims are barred from a few of the highest offices of state), that the Hindus of East Pakistan provided the numbers to give that wing a majority of Pakistan's population did play a significant role in the crisis of 1971, following the only one-person, one-vote national election ever held in united Pakistan (see Oldenburg 1985). Post-1971, the "equal citizenship" problem has continued, but only 3.7 percent of the population are non-Muslims (including the *Ahmadiyya*).

Along with a common religion, the claim was made that the Muslims of the subcontinent had a common language: Urdu. The crack that opened in 1948 in Pakistan's unity was on the question of the national language (Oldenburg 1985). That crack was never mended, and ultimately was a major contributor to the division of the country. Even now, Urdu remains the mother tongue of only 7.8 percent of the population of Pakistan,[12] although it is the "language of wider communication," as a second language, for advanced literates, who were 23 percent of the population in 1984 and now are a major-ity (see Tariq Rahman 2002: 9).[13] However, its status as a national language does not depend on the number of Pakistanis who know it; rather it is bound up in the history of the Pakistan demand.

The nationalism promoted in post-independence Pakistan was anti-democratic to the extent that it denied the rights of the majority, defined largely by language, but reflecting a "Bengali"–"non-Bengali" divide. That problem ceased with the new Pakistan of the post-1971 era. The other major point of contention in Pakistan's early years – the rightful place of Islam in the political fabric of the country – remains unsettled (see Shaikh 2009). That problem contributed both to the nationalism that drove the Bengalis out of Pakistan, as I have argued (Oldenburg 1985), and to the failure in constitution-making that led to the anti-democratic dismissal of the first Constituent Assembly and ultimately the coup of 1958 (McGrath 1996).

Rather than strengthening the hand of the leaders of Pakistan vis-à-vis the state apparatus in the initial phase of its existence, the nationalism of the Pakistan movement brought to leadership men whose political roots were left behind in India. They had to compete with home-grown leaders for whom nationalism (and devotion to Islam) was secondary to working a democracy in their own economic, social, and cultural interests. In West Pakistan, those men tended to be the powerful men who had long ruled in the countryside. The ruling economic class, and many politically active pro-fessionals in the cities, had been decimated by the departure of Hindus and

Sikhs, especially in the Punjab. Those who came from India to replace them were ardent nationalists, but if they joined government they tended to do so as bureaucrats.

In East Pakistan, Muslim League politicians had to confront the leaders of the small farmers and the intelligentsia, such as the students who had enthusiastically worked for Pakistan in the 1946 election and who became the shock troops of the Bengali-language movement. They were concerned to preserve Bengal's cultural heritage, especially its language. Ultimately this was conceptualized and popularized as the "internal colonialism" argument about the "two economies" of Pakistan and the exploitation of the East Wing by the West Wing (see Jahan 1972). In 1954 the Muslim League was comprehensively turned out of office in East Bengal.

The incumbents of the state apparatus in the Pakistan central government claimed as much legitimate authority as the political leadership once Jinnah and Liaquat had died, and in effect seized power in 1954. It did not help that, once those two leaders were gone, the Muslim League suffered a series of splits (though it controlled the government at the Center and all the provinces up to 1954) and "party careers increasingly depended on bureaucratic patronage rather than organizational promotion" (Waseem 1989: 119–20). It is important to remember, though, that with the acceptance of the 1956 constitution Pakistani politicians had gone a long way towards resolving the issues of the place of Islam in government, the national language, and reasonably just federal arrangements. Pakistani nationalism had certainly not proved fatal to the democratic system. When the military took over, it was on a "patriotic" rather than a "nationalist" basis: to save "the country," not "the nation."

Both India and Pakistan emerged in 1947 at best as "nations-in-making." In India, because there was no obvious binding factor that would make the country a national unit – no common language, religion, or dominant ethnic community – the nationalist movement drew on opposition to British colonial rule, and particularly its exploitative economic system, to unite Indians. The officials who continued to serve the Raj were to some extent seen as the enemies of freedom; and that position, coupled with the particular administrative history of most of India, put the politicians who took power in 1947 in nearly complete control of the state.

It is necessary to insert a cautionary note here on the inevitability of a democratic system for India. Phillips Talbot, in a lengthy appraisal of the future(s) of India called "The Independence of India" and dated 19 March 1947, speculates on what would happen in "Hindustan" (a post-partition India without Pakistan):

> As soon as political stability is achieved, current evidence suggests that economic planning and control will become the main arena of partisan debate. . . . To carry out such ambitious programs – and, indeed, to avert

chaos – realistic Indians expect a strong, tough-minded government to administer [India]. Political democracy is a rudimentary, though growing, political concept in India. Current trends suggest that the most likely initial form of government is an oligarchy based on the consent of middle-class elements and spokesmen of peasant and worker movements. Opponents, it may be expected, would call it a dictatorship; at least the signs point to strongly authoritarian rule.

(P. Talbot 2007: 256)

Since Talbot had by then had many years of contact with the Indian political elite, and practice in analyzing and judging political trends – and doing so with great acuity and accuracy – this prediction has to be taken very seriously. It was not self-evident that even India would be a democracy post-independence.

It is doubtful that anyone would have been more optimistic when Pakistan's chances of continuing democratic rule were to be predicted. Talbot (2007: 347), writing in December 1947 after returning to Pakistan – he does not visit Bengal – for the first time since independence day, sees as one of two positive points "the determination of its Muslim population never again to submit to Hindu-controlled India. . . . The ministers [of government] can be assured of general, even fanatic, support in any conflict with India." The rest of his analysis, and a letter written two years later (P. Talbot 2007: 357–68), deals mainly with the economic situation and the Kashmir conflict, and the strong commitment by leaders and ordinary citizens alike to the country being run on Islamic principles. He reports that the administration has managed to come together, and marks the passing of Jinnah; but while he notes the diversion of budgetary resources to the army – because of the genuine feeling of an existential threat from India – he makes no prediction about whether Pakistan's democracy would survive. What does come through Talbot's account is the extent to which Pakistan had succeeded in dealing with the crisis of its birth through strong administrative government; few political leaders are mentioned. Two elements of Pakistan's nation-building – at least in West Pakistan – that were to prove destructive of its democracy were clear: the value of India-as-enemy to unite Pakistanis, and the commitment to relying on Islam.

### Notes

1  See also Waseem (1989: 53–6, 554–6) and Stokes (1959: 243–8). Philip Woodruff [pseudonym for Philip Mason], in *The Men Who Ruled India*, provides an evocative description of the "Punjab tradition" as opposed to the rest of the colonial service (Woodruff 1964a [1953]: 324–43, 370–8). We find this also in the short stories of Kipling, especially in "The Head of the District" and "William the Conqueror." For an important general discussion of differing administrative traditions, and their relevance to the present-day Pakistan Frontier areas, see White (2008a).

2 It should be noted that the British introduced at least consultation with local notables, later elected from a very limited franchise, in the major cities of the Raj very early in their rule. Madras was given a municipality in 1687, and Calcutta and Bombay in 1726. Karachi had a Board of Conservancy in 1846, and became a municipality in 1852. The bulk of "local self-government" institutions are first established after 1857, including those in the cities of Dacca, Chittagong, and Comilla (1864) in East Bengal, and Lahore, Rawalpindi, and Ferozepore (1867) in what is now Pakistan. See Tinker (1968: 30–1).

3 There is an argument about whether it "won" independence or was "given" it. See S. Epstein (1982); Mahajan (2000); Potter (1973).

4 One is tempted to argue that Sri Lanka's long-standing ethno-political difficulties were in part the result of having it "too easy" in the British period: they were not forced to combine in resistance to colonial rule, to forge a leadership class crossing the Sinhala–Tamil divide, perhaps maturing during a spell in jail together. Democracy was delivered almost before they asked for it.

5 Right at the beginning of John Strachey's canonical book, *India*, we find: "What is India? . . . There is no such country . . . India is a name which we give to a great region including a multitude of different countries." He goes on to list the differences in language, race, religion "as wide in India as in Europe" (Strachey 1894: 1–2). Morris-Jones (1988: 101) remarks: "Strachey had been so reassuring [to the British]: there could be no Indian nationalism because there was no such country as India and no such people as Indians."

6 Waseem (1989: 64), citing S. Shamsul-Hasan (ed.) *Plain Mr Jinnah* (Karachi, 1976), notes that "only 11 out of 35 members of the Simla Deputation were not titled" and that "the original membership qualifications of the Muslim League included the ability of 'reading and writing with facility' and an income of not less than Rs. 500 a year," which I estimate would be the equivalent of 200,000 rupees today. (I base this on my reading of Tirthankar Roy's [2007: 77] graph of the daily agricultural wage, which in 1906 was about a quarter of a rupee, which is 1/2000 of Rs. 500. The equivalent wage rate in 2009 was about Rs. 100 per day.)

7 The question of comparable nationalism(s) has been explicitly explored by Ian Talbot (2000); I have looked at the question in Pakistan (Oldenburg 1985). The literature on nationalism in India is enormous; clearly, no quick summary of that is possible.

8 The classic evocation of this is Sadaat Hasan Manto's story "Toba Tek Singh."

9 See Bayly (1998); Kumar (2002); Nandy et al. (1995: 56–69); Tinker (1967); Srirupa Roy (2007); and many others.

10 Harold A. Gould (1993: 304) takes note of the BJP victories in the 1991 election in the southern border districts of UP which have "long traditions of pre-Independence dominance by princely states whose largely Rajput and other elite caste descendants still use their inherited charisma, networks of personal influence, and what remains of their economic power to try and preserve what remains of their landed wealth and traditional status."

11 The numbers are contested: 173,000 were officially repatriated to Pakistan, and many managed to get there by traveling (illegally) through India, but there were still 300,000 in Bangladesh (McKinsey 2007). In May 2008, the Bangladesh High Court ruled that those who were minors in 1971, or were born after independence – about half the stranded population – would become Bangladeshi citizens. For a detailed scholarly discussion, see P. Ghosh (2007).

12 Census of Pakistan, 1998; available at: http://www.census.gov.pk/Mother Tongue.htm; accessed 23 May 2007.

13 According to the 1998 Census, 51.1 percent of the population is educated at the Middle level and above. See http://www.statpak.gov.pk/depts/pco/statistics/pop_education/pop_education_sex.html; accessed 23 May 2007.

# 3   Politicians and bureaucrats in the first years of independence

Despite the bloodbath that had already occurred, and the clouded horizon that indicated even more killings and the massive movement of peoples across the border, the actual transfer of power took place amidst scenes of great joy, with inspiring speeches by both Muhammad Ali Jinnah, as he convened Pakistan's Constituent Assembly on 11 August 1947, and Jawaharlal Nehru "at the midnight hour" four days later. There was no doubt expressed there about both the challenges to be faced, and the political system under which they would work: both countries would be democracies, and they would be led by those who had won freedom, and could justly claim the people's mandate to rule (see P. Talbot 2007: 313–40). The task of actually governing, however, required a partnership with the bureaucracy, and it quickly became clear that the two countries would be very different in this respect.

It became necessary to deal not only with the transfer of political power and the transfer of physical assets but also with the partition of the government's personnel, the civil bureaucracy and the military. On 1 January 1947 there were 101 Indian Civil Service (ICS)/Indian Political Service (IPS) officers who were Muslim (18.4 percent of the total Indian ICS/IPS); ninety-five of them opted for Pakistan. Only forty-three had ten years or more of experience, and only twenty-one held the rank of joint secretary or higher (Braibanti 1963: 365–6). More than a quarter of the total Pakistan ICS–IPS officers for the first year of Pakistan's independence were British, some of them in senior positions. After that the number of British officers rapidly diminished, to 12 percent in 1954, but there was a significant British presence in the Establishment [Personnel] department and the Civil Service Academy until 1960 (Braibanti 1963: 370–1).

Significantly for Pakistan's political development, there were few Bengalis. According to Jahan (1972: 25), citing a later work by Braibanti, "only one of the 133 Muslim Indian Civil Service/Indian Political Service (ICS/IPS) officers who opted for Pakistan was a Bengali Muslim."[1] In 1955 there were no Bengalis among the nineteen secretary-rank officers, and a total of fifty-one Bengalis in the higher ranks of the Central Secretariat – 7 percent of the total (Jahan 1972: 26). In the same year there were fourteen Bengali army officers, compared to 894 from West Pakistan (Jahan 1972: 25).

In India very few British ICS officers stayed on. The chief secretary of Uttar Pradesh wrote: "Some European officers have expressed their willingness to continue in service. They need not trouble" (Hunt and Harrison 1980: 244). Indian ICS officers were a different matter, of course; as Patel said in the Constituent Assembly, "Many of them [ICS and similar senior civil servants] with whom I have worked, I have no hesitation in saying that they are as patriotic, as loyal and as sincere as myself. . . . These people are the instruments. Remove them and I see nothing but a picture of chaos all over the country" (Misra 1986: 7, taking the quotation from Shiva Rao et al. 1968: 722). Presumably the great majority of the 417 ICS officers who did not opt for Pakistan (calculating from the table printed in Misra 1977: 383) were already in place in India.

Pakistan's newly built bureaucracy must have had more refugees than India's; and, as the administrative apparatus was expanded, even more refugees were recruited. Waseem (1989: 112–13) makes the critically import-ant argument for a link between that recruitment and the problem of finding a support base when one is a refugee politician:

> The large influx of refugees [from India] . . . strengthened [the] bureaucratic hold over the society. . . . These urban refugees emerged as the support base for the refugee leadership of Muslim League, especially in the non-electoral context of Pakistan's politics. . . . [T]he migratory leadership of the Muslim League as a whole represented an in-built pressure group against the holding of general elections. . . . The absence of sufficiently large concentrations of refugees in the countryside would only have indicated bleak chances of the return of refugee candidates from the rural constituencies. The talented individuals from amongst the refugees, instead, showed keen interest in government employment. . . . [B]eing merely 10% of the total population of united Pakistan, the refugees claimed [as of 1951] almost 60% of seats in the recruitment for the highest stratum of the central services in Pakistan.

By the early 1960s, more than a third of public servants had come from what was then India, and 57 percent of the refugee civil servants were from UP, Delhi, and East Punjab (Waseem 1989: 114). Important for Pakistan's path to the 1971 civil war, I would suggest, is Waseem's judgment (1989: 114) that "the refugee bureaucrats lent a pervasive character of socio-cultural superiority to the state apparatus, largely through adherence to the symbols of Moghul India and the rich literary heritage of Urdu." Clearly, this was a major factor in empowering the bureaucracy vis-à-vis the politicians.

The bureaucracy, and particularly the "steel frame" part of the enlarged Indian Civil Service that became the Indian Administrative Service (IAS) and the Civil Service of Pakistan (CSP), had been very powerful when serving the British. It was desperately needed to deal with the enormous logistical challenges of rebuilding a governmental apparatus that had been weakened in several ways. In addition to being under-strength because the recruitment of new members was essentially ended during the war, they were strained by the uncertainties of an unknown political future and by the severe violence, from the "Great Calcutta Killing" of 1946 to the hundreds of thousands killed after independence day. The settled pattern of administrative authority, which was lubricated by networks of classmates and former superiors and juniors, was ripped apart, along with the physical displacement to different locations and the departure of almost all the British officers. This was particularly difficult for Pakistan, and the debt owed to the service of those in the state apparatus was perhaps correspondingly greater in Pakistan. Indeed, the two ships of state stabilized remarkably quickly.

It is possible that administrative officers retained a real aura of authority, particularly in Pakistan. What Justice Munir wrote in the Inquiry Commission Report on the Punjab disturbances of 1953 could be mistaken for something written by Kipling: "[This inquiry] . . . has given us an opportunity to ask our officers, on whom lies the burden of administration, to bear this burden in the traditions of the steel-frame, when we saw the erect figure of a district officer in the middle of an excited procession, a soft smile on a firm mouth, determination written on his face" (as quoted in Goodnow 1964: 70–1). In 1954, Governor-General Ghulam Muhammad "carried out a bureaucratic–military coup" (Jalal 1999 [1990]: 179). He essentially took over the government, and the most important portfolios in his "Cabinet of Talent" were held by military or civil-service members (Goodnow 1964: 72). None of them, it should be noted, was Bengali.

Ghulam Muhammad was succeeded as governor-general by Iskandar Mirza, who had served in the British Indian Army and then, from 1926, in the Indian Political Service. Addressing the Civil Service of Pakistan Association in 1957, Mirza puts the CSP on a high pedestal (from *Dawn*, 19 March 1957, as quoted in Goodnow 1964: 74–5):

> The great Indian Civil Service which, with the passage of time, became surrounded by a fabulous halo of efficiency, resources and heroism was to a large extent staffed by men who faced exile and physical distress in the pursuit of their imperial ideal. Today our ideal is far nobler than that of the pre-independence civil service and we must bring to its pursuit the sacrifice of personal vanities and a noble disdain of petty fears and cheap favours.

Evaluating the CSP in the period up to Ayub's coup, Goodnow (1964: 230) notes its "major accomplishments," including being "successful in bringing a degree of order out of chaos," and collecting revenues. But he immediately points out that "the bad features of British administration . . . were evident in the transplanted institution." He continues (Goodnow 1964: 230–1):

The C.S.P., like the I.C.S., was autonomous. It controlled its own recruitment, training and indoctrination, disciplinary procedures, performance ratings, promotions and transfers, and administrative investigations. In the interests of public tranquility, it sometimes prevented public meetings or silenced the press, and occasionally an uncooperative politician was placed in jail. . . . Pakistan's legislature . . . could not control [the CSP] because the higher services had been given considerable constitutional protection against political influence. To protect competence, responsiveness was sacrificed.

And independence, according to Goodnow (1964: 241), did not change civil servants' attitudes:

Many British administrators in India regarded the native politicians as nuisances who had to be tolerated if the façade of self-government were to be maintained. The higher civil services of Pakistan have retained this attitude. They tend to assume that no politician can be trusted to act in the public interest.

But the problem, in Goodnow's view (1964: 244), was not the individual CSP officers, but "because the civil and military bureaucracies in Pakistan have a monopoly on organized power. There are no countervailing powers . . . [no] strong political party with grass roots support . . . [or] effective and independent local governments." It is important to note that Goodnow, himself "a bureaucrat of sorts" (Goodnow 1964: vii), was working and researching in Pakistan from 1954, and so is analyzing an institution (and its officers) with which he is directly acquainted.

The period 1947 to 1954 in Pakistan, from the standpoint even of the next few years of quasi-democratic rule, seems to be a slightly distorted colonial-rule system. In Daechsel's (1997: 152) words:

When Liaqat Ali Khan was assassinated in 1951 and Governor General Ghulam Muhammad dismissed the constituent assembly . . . the last nails were driven in the coffin of Pakistani democracy. No strong party system had emerged which could force the steel frame under its supremacy. All important policy matters continued to be in the hands of the same agencies that had controlled them prior to independence. The bureaucracy managed the allocation of resources through an administrative process while the army shielded the bureaucracy and gave directives in foreign policy matters.

Or, as Jalal (1999 [1990]: 193) puts it:

The interplay of domestic, regional and international factors had brought about a decisive shift in the institutional balance of power; bureaucrats and generals had triumphed over politicians and the complex dynamics of Pakistan's political process were no longer relevant to the actual building and consolidation of the state.

Steps such as the dismissal of the government of the North-West Frontier Province a week after independence, the rigging of provincial elections in the early 1950s, and the army-initiated negotiations for a US–Pakistan military arrangement indicate that Pakistan was very much a "bureaucratic polity" from the beginning.

In India, the "heaven born" senior civil servants of the erstwhile ICS came under attack by some Congress leaders, though they were staunchly defended by Vallabhbhai Patel (for details, see Potter 1986: 146–9). Bidyut Chakrabarty (2006: 89–90) quotes a speech by a member of the Constituent Assembly, Shibban Lal Saksena: "The Civil Service as the Steel Frame . . . enslaved us [and] they have been guilty of stabbing [the] Nation during our freedom struggle. [W]e should not, therefore, perpetuate what we have criticized so far." Patel guided the process of first ensuring the continuance of an all-India service (see Misra 1977: 299–308), and defended the value of an expert, non-partisan civil service, as well as providing his stunning testimonial in the Constituent Assembly debate (quoted above, p. 37). Nehru, who was concerned particularly about the danger to law and order obvious in the communal situation (Chakrabarty 2006), also came round to giving support to the constitutional guarantee of the continuation and relative autonomy of the all-India services.

None the less, it is worth asking how much effect the ambivalent position of a history of at least superficial loyalty to the British government of ICS and other senior officers had on their relative power vis-à-vis the politicians. The Indian members of the ICS had for some time been caught in the contradiction of favoring eventual Indian independence and taking a job serving the British, but certainly by the 1930s they expected and wished for a quick end to British rule. The Punjab ICS officer Mangat Rai wrote that during his district training in 1939 he was struck by " 'the extent of disloyalty to the British government.' He did not meet a single Indian 'who advocated the continuation of the regime' " (Potter 1986: 126). That did not mean that they favored a new regime governed by leaders like Gandhi: "When Zinkin (ICS, Bombay) arrived in 1938, he found ICS Indians in that province 'nationalist almost to a man, though profoundly ambivalent about the Congress,' because 'they wanted an India which they could run, not a Gandhian India' " (Potter 1986: 127–8). But when independence came, and the Congress took power, ICS and other senior officers were easily absorbed, and felt free to use their power to maintain their privileges and positions (Potter 1986). Chakrabarty (2006: 91), quoting IAS officer B. P. R. Vithal, believes the steel frame was retained because "the Congress leaders who took office . . . shared the social background of the senior civil servants whom they inherited from the colonial state." Chakrabarty (2006: 91) points out that "even Nehru, who was a hard taskmaster, felt comfortable dealing with the post-1947 crop of senior civil servants who, being generally urban-based and English-educated, spoke his cultural language."

This was probably far less true in the states in which Indian Administrative Service officers served. According to Potter (1986: 151), "as democratic politicians swarmed in, many political administrators defined the new situation as political interference." But, although there may have been cases where civil servants outmaneuvered politicians, in most cases the politicians ruled, and they knew it. In one account, a chief minister said to an ICS secretary, "You may think you are doing your duty, but if I think you are going beyond it, remember I am the judge" (Potter 1986: 151–2).

It was immediately apparent that the ICS and other British-era services, focused as they were primarily on buttressing British rule with a lean and mean administration centered on maintaining law and order and collecting revenue, would not be able to provide both the expanded services and the development expertise that a liberated India would require. As Nehru put it:

> We have a democratic system now and necessarily structure of government must fit in with this. Secondly, we are faced with enormous problems of development and reconstruction and they have to be tackled with speed as well as efficiency. The old British system had no such problems to face and therefore was meant to deal with a static and more or less unchanging state of affairs. Today we are faced with a dynamic situation which requires a rapid pace of development and continuous adaptation to changing conditions. We have thus to bring our administrative structure in line with this, or we fail.
>
> (Chakrabarty 2006: 85–6)

There was indeed a special recruitment of senior civil servants into what becomes the Indian Administrative Service, including men from the provincial services. Very soon the services were opened to women, and places were reserved for scheduled castes and scheduled tribes.

For decades more, however, recruits came mainly from the elite classes and castes – that being fluent in English was a requirement of admission helped filter out others – through the pipeline of educational institutions of "public" schools and elite colleges. But the enlarging of the net of recruitment, and the significantly larger numbers of new officers admitted – a pattern that is repeated in the various states – must have modified the English club atmosphere of the ICS/IAS to a significant extent.[2] According to Potter (1986: 144–5), the departure of the British ICS officers opened up many senior positions to Indians, who would have been younger and less experienced than their predecessors, and thus perhaps less sure of themselves in their relationships with politicians.

True, there was a formidable network of power and influence built by men (sic) linking to classmates in school and college, or batch-mates in the services who shared the experience of training in Mussoorie's IAS Academy and elsewhere, and who became the carefully mentored "juniors" of experienced senior officers. Those men knew intimately how the machinery of government worked, and controlled literally the rules and the files and the forms (and forms of behavior, such as the manner of notating files). It is likely that, even decades after independence, a British ICS officer from the early twentieth century, if not earlier, would have found the routine of governing utterly familiar. The lines of command over the intermediate and lower services, down to the office peons, were kept clear of political interference, as far as possible.

When the new politician captain and his senior politician officers took over on the bridge of the ship of state – or rather ships of state, because the pattern repeated itself at the state and district levels – the tussle between them and the bureaucracy was intense (see Taub 1969). As Kothari and Roy (1969: 56) put it, in an influential study that effectively generalizes from a survey of administrators and politicians in Meerut District, "the onslaught [sic] of representative politics, impatient of time-consuming administrative procedure and rigid rules and regulations and bent upon quickening the pace of the distribution of divisible and indivisible benefits, has put the administrative system on the defensive." The consequence was that administrators "do try to seek political leaders' support and establish good relation with them but this does not reflect their responsiveness to representative politics. It is symptomatic of their search for security. In other words, administrators have still to recognize and accept the change in system goals and orient their normative referents and role perceptions accordingly" (Kothari and Roy 1969: 59).

In Jalal's (1995: 249–50) view, the colonialist core of the state was not much disturbed. But, even under the British, the bureaucrats had developed working relationships with politicians, and in post-independence India the bureaucrats did share the nationalist goals of India's rapid economic development, political independence, democracy, and rule of law. The later recruits to the civil services were enveloped in what has been called a "patronage-democracy" (Chandra 2004: 115–42), in which a nexus of mutual (financial) convenience developed between politicians placing their kinsfolk and supporters in jobs, and ultimately the buying and selling of transfers and promotions (see Wade 1982, 1985). It is not at all clear, however, that such a system was widespread in the early decades after 1947, or even the extent to which it exists now.[3]

The Indian politicians who came to power were overwhelmingly members of the Congress, and took strength from their achievement of independence, even with the great costs of partition. The Congress was also strengthened, ironically, by the tragic death of Gandhi, which at one stroke brought all the leaders together in a moment of catharsis – and removed a proponent of a very different future for the Congress and the country, someone who would have been annoyingly very hard to disregard. The Congress's lines of communication were intact, and could easily be extended into the former princely states, as they came into the Union. As long as Nehru was alive, and to a significant extent even after, the central leadership could govern using the two parallel tracks of government and party, and the party lines of authority (and carrots-and-sticks) extended throughout the country. Most important, the Congress was strongly supported in all the areas that became India, and few of its leaders were left behind in Pakistan – the major and significant exception being the Khan brothers of the NWFP – or came as refugees to India. It was not until decades later that Indian refugee politicians came to power, and then mainly at the state level – for example, leaders like L. K. Advani of the BJP; Tara Singh of the Akali Dal; and leaders of the Communist Party of India (Marxist) (CPM) in Bengal.

The contrast with Pakistan is stark. The politicians who had "won" Pakistan – Jinnah and the core of the Muslim League – were enthusiastic-ally supported in the new country, but the most important of them came from the Muslim minority provinces of undivided India (see I. Talbot 1999: 91–3). They were mainly Urdu-speaking, and their supporters who came to Pakistan – settling mainly in Karachi and other cities – were not enough to provide continued electoral support (see the analysis of Waseem 1989: 112–13, quoted above). Some Muslim League leaders were accommodated by being given Constituent Assembly seats that had been won in Bengal. But they literally did not speak the language of those whose electoral support they would need and, as important, they did not have networks of political lieutenants in place to mobilize them. In Punjab they found them-selves in a place where there was a powerful party machine of ex-Unionist Party landlords.

That is, the Pakistani politicians who did have strong roots and an "at home" familiarity with the state and society they occupied after 1947 were generally those who came late to the Muslim League and were never in the ruling circle around Jinnah. The Bengal leaders Fazlul Huq and H. S. Suhrawardy lived in Calcutta. Fazlul Huq in his long political career in Bengal was in and out of the Muslim League. Notably, he became the premier of Bengal, leading a coalition of his party, the Krishak Praja Party (KPP), with the Muslim League from 1937 to 1941, after which he formed a new ministry opposed to the Muslim League and was expelled from the League. Having been "pushed to the extreme point of joining the League within six months of forming the Ministry" (Sen 1976: 250), he was "made to introduce" the Pakistan Resolution at the Muslim League meeting in 1940 (Sen 1976: 251). Suhrawardy – who had also been Muslim League premier of the united Bengal province – did not immediately shift from his Calcutta base to Pakistan and, even then, not to East Pakistan. Indeed, he joined with Gandhi in a successful effort to keep the peace in Bengal (Suhrawardy 1987: 34 [Talukdar introduction]).

In Punjab, the Muslim League mass mobilization and success in the 1946 elections was in part due to the loss of support of the Unionist Party, weakened by the death of its major Muslim leaders – Fazl-i-Husain in 1936 and Sikandar Hayat Khan in 1942. But the Muslim League's efforts, and the emergent Islamist feeling, quickly eroded the base of Unionist Party workers; the League took the opportunity to bring local landlords and *pirs* into the movement (see I. Talbot 1999: 67–71). As Talbot (1999: 73) puts it, the Punjab Muslim League "was in some respects the Unionist Party rein-vented in that it mobilized support in 1946 through the time honored 'tribal' allegiances and appeal to a localized Muslim identity based on the Sufi shrines." The Muslim League leaders who emerged were, however, sorely lacking in the experience of governing.

Pakistan politicians of the ruling Muslim League soon saw the mass support they had mobilized in 1945–6, and brought to a peak with the achievement of independence, melt away. In Bengal, it was the movement for the recognition of Bengali as a national language that was most significant in weakening its base. In Punjab, "politics reverted to the tradi-tional pattern of landlord dominance. The factional rivalries amongst the rural elite which had split asunder the Unionist Party re-emerged in its Muslim League successor shortly after independence" (I. Talbot 1999: 133). The community most dependent on the all-India leadership, that of the Urdu-speaking refugees, was itself struggling to find new roots. The other provinces had not been very significant in the Pakistan movement, except, in the case of the NWFP, as an opposition bastion. The power of the Muslim League politicians in Karachi was thus almost entirely derived from their occupa-tion of positions in the government, and from their alliance with fellow refugees in the bureaucracy.

They would have to rely almost entirely on the state apparatus to implement the League's policies, and its relationship with the bureaucracy was one of trust and alliance. According to Waseem (2007a: 193):

> The executive managed to amass all power in its own hands and relegate the legislature to a secondary position in the business of the state. A cult of unity, couched in the Islamic discourse of nationalism and the charisma of Jinnah, was crystallized in the form of deification of the state. Gradually, a "bureaucratic" center was entrenched against "political" provinces.

The result is neatly summed up by Burki (1969: 243; see Jalal 1999 [1990]: 63):

> The 1948–58 decade saw the disintegration of the Muslim League Party; the seven political parties that were formed out of its fragments produced nine highly unstable governments in as many years. In the provinces the situation was no better; in Dacca and Lahore new coalitions between

political parties were rigged up almost as fast as the old ones broke down. The politicians at the center and in the provinces, while they themselves worked out these political jig-saw puzzles, were quite content to let the day-to-day administration be handled by the CSP. The situation admirably suited the CSP; it flourished and thrived in the near political vacuum in which it had been called upon to perform. Independence had brought little change. Before 1947, the ICS officers had no political bosses who could exercise effective control over them (those in England were too far away to be effective); after 1951 (that is, after the deaths of Jinnah and Liaquat Ali Khan) the Pakistani leadership was not capable of exercising any such control.

Burki adds a footnote: "The situation in India was totally different. The political maturity of the Congress Party and the effective leadership of Nehru rationalized the position of the Indian Administrative Service vis-à-vis the emerging political structure" (Burki 1969: 243 n). In sum, just after independence, the Muslim League was weaker in Pakistan than the Congress was in India, even with Jinnah and Liaquat in power, and the Pakistan bureaucracy was given greater authority than the Indian bureaucracy: the balance of power favored Indian politicians and Pakistani bureaucrats.

## Controlling the military

In these first few years of independence, the civil services played a far more significant role in governing both India and Pakistan than the military services (essentially the army in both countries). The balance of control has two elements: the relationship of civilian bureaucrats to the military, and the relationship of the military and the political rulers (see Kohn 1997). In India, politicians controlled the military using the civilian bureaucracy; in Pakistan, politicians exercised direct but increasingly weaker control over the army, particularly after the death of Liaquat Ali Khan in 1951.

Ayesha Jalal (1995: 250) concludes that "The containment of the military proved to be a critical factor in the institutionalization of India's formal democracy," and adds, "albeit one resting on the well-worn authoritarian stumps of the colonial state [which were the civilian bureaucracy and the police, whose existence] mitigated the need for an overt dependence on the military." She contrasts this with Pakistan, where "the logic of consolidating central authority where none previously existed saw Pakistan's civil bureaucrats and senior military officers stealing the march on parties and politicians" (Jalal 1995: 250–1). Stephen Cohen (1963–4: 427), analyzing India's civil–military relationship, has a different interpretation:

> Just as important as an obedient military is to the maintenance of the liberal democratic model of civil–military relations, is the existence of a competent, respected and democratically committed political elite;

the mere repetition of the slogan "civilian control" is not enough to guarantee its existence: that the civilian leadership must demonstrate its capability to rule is no less important than that it maintain the tradition of apolitical professionalism in the military.

Although both military organizations came out of the British tradition of political neutrality and professional pride, Pakistan's army had arrived at the point of a possible coup in 1954, while India's did not even come close during that initial period of Nehru's rule, or has ever come close since then.

Already in the period of the interim government led by Nehru (1945–7) the control of the military came into sharp focus with the problem of what to do about those who had formed and joined the Indian National Army (INA), and with the naval mutinies of 1946. There was an upwelling of popular support when the British put three INA leaders on trial in 1945 and Nehru put on his lawyer's robes to defend them. "Yet, later on," writes Nirad Chaudhuri (1953: 351), "after coming to power itself, the Congress again grew cool, if not cold, toward the I.N.A., and with reason. Dependent as it was in military matters on the officers and soldiers of the Indian Army who had fought with distinction for the British, it could hardly persist in glorifying men who had gone over to the enemy." A "political army" model would not have been accepted (see Cohen 1990 [1971]: 162–3; see also Nawaz 2008: 18–19). As the Rudolphs (1964: 8) point out: "unlike Indonesia and Burma, India did not start its independent life with a political army that claimed a share in the nationalist movement and the winning of independence." Nor did Pakistan; according to Shuja Nawaz (2008: 19): "overall, the Muslim officers who attained senior ranks in the fledgling army of independent Pakistan, played little or no part in the political thinking of the freedom movement."

Is Cohen correct in seeing India's "competent, respected, and democratically committed political elite" as a crucial factor for explaining why India was able to maintain and even enhance civilian control of the military? Was there no such elite in Pakistan, so that civilian control eroded, to the point that the military was perhaps invited by Governor-General Ghulam Muhammad to take over in 1954? We can consider along the way, as it were, the question of why Pakistan has seemingly conformed to the blueprint of a coup-ridden Third World country, while India has not.

The fundamental cause of the failure to establish civilian control of the military in Pakistan is indeed probably the weakness of the political leadership, once Jinnah had passed from the scene.[4] But other factors were also important. The Pakistan army at the moment of independence was put under far greater pressure than the Indian army. It had to deal with the huge flow of refugees and was soon at war with India over Kashmir, but with fewer resources and many more problems than the Indian army had. As the defense forces were divided, it was the Pakistan army that had to build up even the basic regimental structure out of bits and pieces, as there was not even one all-Muslim regiment in the united Indian army. It had few, if any, facilities such as training academies and ordnance factories. The Pakistani share of the common supplies was held up by India once the two countries were skirmishing in Kashmir. And there were too few Muslim officers to man the new armed forces, forcing Pakistan to use British officers for a considerable length of time after independence. Ayub Khan, the first Pakistani commander-in-chief, took over only in 1951.

The Pakistan army, facing a much larger and better-equipped Indian army, acquitted itself well in Kashmir, even though it was forced to demur when asked to attack by the political leadership, including Liaquat shortly before his assassination (see Schofield 2000). Hasan-Askari Rizvi (2003a: 76–9) describes the support from virtually all Pakistanis for a strong military. That was reflected in parliament, but parliament had very little input into defense policy. In fact, Rizvi (2003a: 77) points out that "defense and security policy making was the exclusive prerogative of the top bureaucrats of the defense ministry and the military top brass. Once the policy outlines were determined, the top brass enjoyed much autonomy in its implementation. The same applied to defense expenditure." This was even true of military aid. According to Cohen (1973: 18), "Ayub Khan . . . engaged in negotiations with the U.S. for arms assistance without formal political approval." As Rizvi (2003a: 77) puts it, "the decision to enter into security arrangements with the U.S. . . . was taken by the political leadership on the initiative of the Army commanders." Saeed Shafqat (1997: 30–1) notes that those discussions occurred perhaps as early as August 1951, but certainly by a year later.

The military undertook traditional "aid to the civil" operations as well. When the anti-Ahmadi agitation threatened to get out of hand in the Punjab in 1953, there was no hesitation in calling the army in, and declaring martial law. As Rizvi (2003a: 78–9) reports, "The army authorities brought the situation back to normal within a few days and then launched the 'Cleaner Lahore Campaign' to improve civic conditions. By the time the city was handed back to the civilian administration [two months later], it was presenting a new and cleaner look." Ayub Khan served as defense minister for almost a year in 1954–5.[5] According to Aitzaz Ahsan (2005: 106), he "felt himself free to trespass on the civilian domain;" he adds: "the tragedy is that no politician or civilian superior challenged, chastised or resisted Ayub. None even tried to read him the law or the rules of government business to remind him of his due station in life. . . . None reprimanded him. . . . None chose to remove him."

An attempted coup in 1951 – tagged with the name of the legal process ("The Rawalpindi Conspiracy Case") – in which plans were made to assassinate the (British) army commander and others was easily discovered and crushed. Perhaps because of the link of politically committed army officers and members of the Communist Party of Pakistan, no "lesson" of the danger of an army takeover seemingly was learned by the political class, and no explicit steps were taken to guard against it.[6] On the eve of the army coup of 1958, according to Rizvi (2003a: 81):

> The military commanders maintained a highly professional profile, emphasizing discipline, efficiency, training and a strong service pride. They were in command of their house, which was orderly and well maintained. This strengthened their position vis-à-vis the political leaders, who were faced with social turbulence and political fragmentation. The civilian leaders were not in a position to assert their leadership over the military. Rather, they attempted to cultivate the military so as to strengthen their position, and, thus, the military was able to play a key role in decision-making not only for the matters that related to its professional interests, but it also influenced priorities in the civilian and political domains.[7]

Once a coup has occurred, to be sure, the explanations for subsequent coups change.[8] The metaphor that comes to mind is getting a disease (malaria?) which goes into remission, sometimes for decades, but which can recur, perhaps triggered by something special. The "cure" for the disease of military intervention is some sort of revolution, typically brought on by the comprehensive defeat in war of the military, or a transition to democracy that is bolstered by a certain level of economic development and income equality.[9] It is of course not impossible to think of a scenario for extracting the military, returning it to its prime purpose of defense of the country, and possibly "coup-proofing" the subsequent democratic regime.[10]

We shall consider the importance of the US–Pakistan alliance in Chapter 8, and in Chapter 9 the extent to which the Pakistani military has entrenched itself not only in politics but also in the economy and society in recent decades, thus giving itself a degree of autarky that its civilian counterparts cannot match. That material base – at least in terms of having a military budget that was more than adequate – began in the immediate post-independence years, and was clearly buttressed by major military aid, from the US in particular. It has contributed a great deal to altering the balance of power in the military's favor.

In India the situation for the military was very different indeed (see Kundu 1998: 2; McMillan 2008: 740). So different that it appears to be a non-issue. The question of how the military is controlled by civilians hardly appears in the standard accounts of India's political history. As Stephen Cohen (1988: 139; his emphasis) sums it up: "from the perspective of sustaining India's democracy, the Indian armed forces have made a major positive contribution as they have carried out their duties with competent professionalism, and they have made a *negative* contribution in that they have not sought power, or even influence." Although India had to rely on its military immediately after independence to defend Kashmir against first the "raiders" invading

Pakistan, and then its army, there was no need to fear that the very existence of the country could be militarily threatened by Pakistan. The Indian military, unlike Pakistan's, had no incentive to search itself for aid and supply arrangements.

The Indian military was no different from the Pakistani in adhering to an ideal of politically neutral professionalism. When the British first recruited Indians as officers immediately after World War I, they selected men who were non-political: "Collectively, they were the most reliable, politically inert, aristocratic, and conservative group the British could select" (Cohen 1990 [1971]: 119). And although "many" of the next generation of recruited officers "came into the army under the influence of national ideas" (Cohen 1990 [1971]: 121) they accepted the transfer of power to Indian and Pakistan governments as fully legitimate. At that time, according to Cohen (1990 [1971]: 169), "the military in fact, was not disposed toward intervention, despite its increased activities in domestic and civilian aid tasks and external defense. . . . The military was content to be left alone and permitted to rebuild its precious organizational integrity."

Lloyd and Susanne Rudolph argue, relying on interviews with Prime Minister Nehru and others, that it is not so much the desire of the military to rule, or the explicit controls placed on the military by civilians that matter. The military steps in to fill a political vacuum:

> Senior Indian officers who attended Sandhurst with their Pakistan counterparts remember a shared military past and see little difference between themselves and Pakistani generals. Prime Minister Nehru and Defense Minister Chavan concur. They agree it was not inordinate ambition or a special taste for politics but the failure of the political classes to govern effectively that persuaded the Pakistani army under Ayub Khan to seize power. It took power, Mr. Nehru believes, "naturally," "automatically," when politics failed. It seems reasonable to senior Indian officers that when politicians "play ducks and drakes," as they did in Pakistan, rather than shoulder their responsibilities, the army should step in to "put things right." But in the absence of a serious failure of politics Indian army men will adhere to a standard learned under the British, to "know their place."
>
> (Rudolph and Rudolph 1964: 5)

It needs to be underlined that the implication here is that the military in India also, if things became bad enough, would have a duty to intervene.[11]

The organization and position of the armed forces was quickly changed, with the effect of fracturing its power in the political system as a whole. The position of commander-in-chief was abolished, and the equalizing of the positions of the three branches had the effect of diminishing at least the symbolic importance of the army.[12] The order of precedence that ranked military officers was changed so that they now were much lower down, compared to a large new group of politicians and even civil service officers. The civil service control of the ministry of defense was strengthened (see Cohen 1990 [1971]: 171–3). And the elitist character of the army began to change: "The army became less attractive to India's upper classes [and] the formal status of the armed forces was sharply reduced. . . . In their place have come the sons of noncommissioned officers (NCOs) and junior commissioned officers (JCOs) . . . one generation removed from the peasantry" (Cohen 1988: 105). The same was not true of the civil services, who were also not as physically isolated as military men living in carefully fenced off army bases (cantonments), so it is likely that the gap in pay and prestige and power between the civil and military wings of the state became much larger in India than it was in Pakistan, making an alliance of respect and shared interests less likely.

It is also worth looking at the crafting of civilian control of the armed forces in India (see Trinkunas 2005: 8–13). When independence came, India did not need to retain proportionally as many British officers as Pakistan did, and replaced them more rapidly. Those new officers had neither the experience nor the stature to challenge the leadership of a very popular freedom movement. Although there were ten times as many Sikh officers in the army as their percentage in the population (see Haq 1993: 209–10), "no single ethnic group dominates the Indian armed forces" (unlike the Pakistan army, where Punjabi interests were safeguarded) (Cohen 1988: 139). No head of any of the armed forces has ever held a formal position in the cabinet, as Ayub did in Pakistan. The defense ministry has always been firmly in the hands of civilians. That tradition has continued: although serving military officers are invited to contribute to discussions of security issues, and obviously have a role in choosing weapons systems, in personnel policies, and the like, the final decisions on those matters have always been firmly in civilian hands.[13]

Was there an explicit effort to "coup-proof" India? Nehru personally was vehement in his denunciation, in principle, of the military (see Cohen 1990 [1971]: 104–6); more generally, "it was a rare Indian intellectual who could find anything to admire in the British Indian Army or its theories of the martial races. . . . For most of them – including Nehru – the military remained barbaric and mercenary" (Cohen 1990 [1971]: 106–7). It would seem that Nehru and the initial governing leadership very consciously sought to preserve the British-derived traditions of the Indian army, including the routines of a firm retirement age, of fairly short, fixed terms in particular positions, with rotation functionally and geographically, once one "graduated" to positions beyond the command of particular units. Whether deliberately done or not, such practices made it difficult for coup-minded officers to get together for coordinated actions.

These policies became firmly established: after India's first unambiguous military victory, in the 1971 war with Pakistan, army chief General Manekshaw, who was a hero of the campaign, demitted office on schedule two years later. The government waited until two weeks before his scheduled retirement to give him the honorary title of field marshal, and he played no political role later. Retired military men have been appointed as ambassadors or governors of states, including, from time to time, states with active security problems, such as Kashmir. They have rarely entered politics; and, when they have, they have not been very successful. In the 1950s, "the efforts of General Cariappa, the first Indian to hold the office of Commander-in-Chief, to lead the forces of order and cultural fundamentalism have made little impression nationally or regionally" (Rudolph and Rudolph 1964: 7).[14] More recently, General Khanduri became chief minister of Uttarakhand, having served as minister of transport in the 1999–2004 National Democratic Alliance (NDA) government; but he was, professionally in the military, an engineer. Jaswant Singh, who held major portfolios in the BJP-led governments of the 1990s, listed his profession as "military service" in his parliamentary biodata. He served as an officer for a while from 1957, and "resigned to join politics."[15] I believe no other military man has held high elected office.

The Rudolphs (1964: 19) remark on the Indian army's tradition of professionalism, but point out that if politicians "yield to the temptation to strengthen themselves by developing friends or allies among military men they will inevitably draw the military into politics." Taya Zinkin (1959: 90) suggests some larger considerations, having to do with class and culture. She claims that, for one thing, "India has a middle class sufficiently large to make a military dictatorship impossible." Moreover, "this ruling middle class is predominantly Hindu. Military dictatorships look as absurd against a Hindu background as they look natural in the Middle East." But Zinkin also believes that "[Indian] politicians may have failed to fulfill all their pledges, but they have at least tried and nobody can accuse them, as in Pakistan, of spending their entire time playing musical chairs for office. . . . All that a military dictatorship would have to offer is civic cleanliness." The Rudolphs (1964: 6–7), however, are not so sure that a ruling middle class prevents military intervention:

> The propensity to popular authoritarian rule is most likely to play into the hands of military leadership. The authoritarian character created by the traditional family, the attraction of cultural fundamentalism to the urbanized lower middle classes, and the appeal of order, discipline and efficiency to the professional classes, now marginal features of Indian political life, are susceptible of mobilization by military leadership under the right circumstances.

When these appeals finally appeared at the center of Indian politics, with "order, discipline, and efficiency" during Mrs Gandhi's Emergency rule, and then the "cultural fundamentalism" of BJP-led Hindu nationalism, the military was not involved, either as mobilizer or as an institution that took advantage of those developments.

While the Indian government maintained a sizeable military force, once the Kashmir ceasefire was implemented (1 January 1949), it was not very active nor was it well supplied or developed. That only changed with the growing crisis that led to the India–China war of 1962. The humiliating defeat that India suffered, although in part due to diplomatic blunders and a purposeful neglect of the military and then political interference by the leadership, symbolized by the defense minister Krishna Menon, served to undermine any claims to political authority the military might have had. It had failed in its first duty of preserving the country's security. That was redeemed to a considerable extent when the military fought Pakistan to a stalemate in the 1965 war, and then wholly in the triumph of the victory in 1971. The comprehensive defeat of the Pakistan military apparently may well have been a lesson that Indian military took to heart: taking power, and becoming entangled in politics, as their Pakistani counterparts had done, was a recipe for weakening the prime goal of protecting the country.

Pakistan had been defeated, but China and the United States had emerged as potential military enemies. In the years following, even as India moved to develop a nuclear weapon and continue its modernization and expansion of its military, there was no temptation to intervene in politics. It is telling that the only hint of such a thing was the rumor that, as it became clear that Mrs Gandhi was heading for defeat in the 1977 election, her son Sanjay asked the military to intervene (see Khushwant Singh 1979: 141, who reports this "slander" and its denial by the defense services chiefs).

Militaries seem to be very tradition-bound, at least in their ceremonial and culture. In both Indian and Pakistani armies there are immediately visible signs of continuity with the British army, from the appearance of the cantonments to the style of moustaches. Since Pakistan's coups have been carried out by the seniormost officers, with the subsequent regime headed by the army chief, there has been no overturning of the duty to obey higher ranks. The internalization of the transfer of the duty to obey "the political masters" probably did not happen in Pakistan, because, almost simultaneously with the replacement of the last British commander-in-chief by Ayub Khan in 1951, Liaquat Ali Khan was assassinated, which "left the field to political leaders who lacked national stature" (Rizvi 2003a: 68). The governor-general himself soon held the door open to active military political involvement. The "tradition" now has become one that legitimizes an army takeover (see Kennedy 2005). In India, on the other hand, the politicians the military was duty-bound to obey had smoothly shifted from heroes of the freedom movement to effective government leaders, and even a globally recognized statesman, Jawaharlal Nehru. By the time the débâcle of the 1962 India–China war occurred, something which could be blamed on the politicians, the habit of obedience to civilian authority had been practiced, at the top, by five Indians who had served as army chief (twenty-three have held the position – as of November 2009 – compared to twelve Pakistani army chiefs). The Indian military tradition is now one of acceptance of civilian and political authority.

## Jinnah and Nehru

There is a justifiable reluctance to claim that these two particular individuals shaped let alone determined their country's political history, given the significance of nationalist movements, colonial state inheritance, and the factors we shall examine later: security-driven and other political choices and constraints, and socio-economic and socio-cultural structures and forces. Yet Jinnah and Nehru did make specific contributions to the way government practices developed in the first year (Jinnah) or decade (Nehru) of independence, and in some accounts those contributions were crucial to the direction the two regimes took.

Both were towering figures: "[T]he role of Jinnah in independent Pakistan was largely shaped by the nature of his induction into the state and the way he mediated between the contending individuals, groups and parties. This in turn had a tremendous influence on the way the authority of the new state was exercised" (Waseem 1989: 93–4). Nehru also towered above his cohort, although that cohort was far larger and more diverse than Jinnah's (for a disinterested evaluation, see Corbridge and Harriss 2000: 24–31).

There are some significant choices that both men made from Day One, as it were, that need to be analyzed for our purposes. It is not that each set out a plan of action which was coherent and could be labeled "democratic" or "autocratic." Jinnah often acted democratically, and Nehru had more than a few autocratic moments,[16] but there was definitely at least a style, a tone, to what they did that quite possibly influenced the differing course each country took. For Nehru, it was something that became reinforced by his long stay in office. For Jinnah, it legitimated the actions of two of his successors as governor-general. There is a slight case to be made for a doctrine of necessity, something like: "Nehru had to deal with a broad range of competing political forces and so had to be inclusive and respectful of the opposition; Jinnah had to deal with a chaotic situation."[17] And of course there were major differences in the institutional back-up each man had, particularly in terms of party organization.

### *Jinnah*

Jinnah clearly did not believe in having anything other than a democratic, parliamentary system in Pakistan (see, for example, Jinnah 2000: 125). A. G. Noorani (2001: pt 1) writes that "his vision of Pakistan was of a democratic secular state based on the rule of law." But it is possible to argue that his acts spoke louder than his words: his beliefs about how to govern and his idea of what Pakistan should be did not seem to take into account the danger of compromising the principles of democracy, even given the crisis situation Pakistan found itself in. As Ardeshir Cowasjee (2008c) writes, in semi-serious vein, "He professed to be a democrat, but in reality was a benign dictator who harmed no one. He merely put his foot down when necessary – and that was most of the time."

Jinnah chose to become the first governor-general of Pakistan, not its first prime minister, while India had Lord Mountbatten as its first governor-general, followed by C. Rajagopalachari. Part of the reason for Jinnah's choice was undoubtedly that the alternative on offer was having Mountbatten as joint governor-general of the two countries, and Jinnah had a well-founded belief that Mountbatten favored India, and was certain to be difficult to deal with, since he was likely to continue to want to wield some power.[18] Sayeed (1968: 228) explores Jinnah's decision in considerable detail, concluding that he did it "in accordance with his own temperament and the tenor of his times." Noting his own view that "Pakistan at that time needed its founder as its Governor-General," Sayeed emphasizes a sentence of a *Dawn* editorial of 13 July 1947: "Whatever the constitutional powers of the Governor-General of a Dominion may nominally be, in Quaid-i-Azam's case no legal or formal limitations can apply" (Sayeed 1968: 231).[19]

Having described Jinnah's exercise of the governor-general's powers, Sayeed concludes: "Thus, here was a Governor-General who was not only more powerful than his other contemporary Governors-General, but also more powerful than his predecessors, the Viceroys of India" (1968: 251). In Qureshi's summation (2008: 83):

> Jinnah chose to become Governor General as well as Speaker of the Constituent Assembly, along with holding the ministerial portfolio of Kashmir Affairs, while also being the president of the All Pakistan Muslim League. . . . [He] concentrated executive, legislative, and political positions all in his own hands. . . . [He] presided over cabinet meetings, reducing the prime minister to the level of just another minister. Not only that, Jinnah would consult bureaucratic heads of departments over the heads of their political masters, that is, the ministers. None of this could in any way be justified by reference to any kind of democracy.

As Jinnah took on all these roles, and confidently exercised ultimate power, he seemed to act on the model of the temporary dictator in the Roman republic, there to get the country through a major crisis; he certainly did not explicitly reject democracy.

But if Jinnah did bequeath to Pakistan what Sayeed calls a "viceregal system", and if his choice of having executive power concentrated to deal with the founding of the new country, and to deal with issues of national identity, became institutionalized, then he contributed directly to putting Pakistan on its path to autocracy.[20] Sayeed (1968: 259–60) argues:

> The [administrative] machinery that was carried over from the British days largely rested on the Governor and the Central civil servants

placed in the Provinces. This machinery was not related so much to the Prime Minister as it was to the *primum mobile* of the Pakistan constitution at that time, the Quaid-i-Azam. . . . There was no doubt that this machinery served a highly useful purpose, considering the nature of the problems and the quality of Pakistan's political leaders. But the unfortunate result was that the administrative machinery was kept in full gear even after the emergency was over on the plea that the Central Government could not afford to dismantle it because of the irresponsibility and immaturity of political leaders. What was never realized was that political leaders could not become mature and responsible as long as this machinery was retained in its full vigour and power.

This is a strikingly prescient description of the justification each time the military, with the bureaucracy's willing help, has intervened in Pakistan's politics, and sought to perpetuate its rule, from Ayub to Musharraf. As Alavi (1983: 78) puts it: "Jinnah's unintentional contribution to the future of Pakistan was a demotion of the political leadership in favour of the bureaucracy."

Subsequent heads of state with a taste for power – Ghulam Muhammad and Iskandar Mirza – made full use of the precedents Jinnah established. The first was Jinnah's dismissal of the Congress government of the NWFP, arguably undermined by the plebiscite that favored the provinces joining Pakistan (boycotted by the Congress, but none the less undoubtedly an expression of the majority's will [see Rittenberg 1988: 244–5]). Sayeed (1968: 272) comments: "The precedent of dismissing a Ministry which had a majority and then commissioning another man to form a Ministry in the hope that the latter would soon be in a position to produce a majority was bound to lead to political instability in the Provinces."

On the other side of the ledger, Jinnah took care to tell the civil service that its role had changed. Speaking to the gazetted officers at Chittagong on 25 March 1948, he said:

> (1) You have to do your duty as servants; you are not concerned with this political or that political party . . . your duty is to serve that Government [that forms] for the time being as servants not as politicians. . . . The Government in power for the time being must also realize and understand their responsibilities that you are not to be used for this party or that. . . . I hope it will not be so but even if some of you have to suffer as a victim – I hope it will not happen – I expect you to do so readily. . . . (2) . . . [W]ipe off that past reputation: you are not rulers. You do not belong to the ruling class; you belong to the servants. Make the people feel that you are their servants and friends.
>
> (Jinnah 2000: 162–3)

Yet, in a similar talk to civil servants in Peshawar in April, it is significant that Jinnah (2000: 192–4) focuses again specifically on the problem of officers being asked to act incorrectly by politicians in power, and talks vaguely of giving the citizenry a "fair deal" with "justice done to everybody." The expectation is clearly that the bureaucrats will behave well when dealing with citizens, and be victimized when dealing with politicians in government. Jinnah promises to work out ways of protecting them.

Jinnah was not willing to yield to politicians or political activists who challenged his views or policies, and that had devastating consequences. In A. G. Noorani's (2008: 82) judgment, and citing McGrath (1996), "Mohammad Ali Jinnah maimed and mutilated democracy in the infant state that he had founded." In particular, he cannot escape personal responsibility for not fully understanding the depth of feeling and the danger to the country (in a charitable interpretation), or acting as an arrogant dictator (as the Bengalis believed), when it came to the question of the language issue (Oldenburg 1985). In his speech at a public meeting in Dhaka on 21 March 1948, and repeated in greater and even more forceful language three days later at the Dhaka University convocation, he declared that Urdu would be the sole state language, adding that "anyone who tries to mislead you is really the enemy of Pakistan" (Jinnah 2000: 150). Not only did that lead inexorably to the political agitation on the issue that ultimately led to the emergence of Bangladesh; it also suggests at best a tin ear when it comes to understanding what democracy means. Even if there was some reason for making Urdu a national language (having to do with its prominence as a mother tongue in the "nation" of Muslims of the subcontinent, including those in India), how could he have denied the language of the majority of the citizenry – Bengali was the mother tongue of 55 percent of the population – the status of an associate national language?

Had Jinnah somehow been able to understand the justice of the demand for Bengali, and start a process of compromise, it is just possible that a constitution could have been completed more or less at the same time as India's, and elections held right away under its provisions. Instead, it took nine years from the date of independence to adopt a constitution that recognized Bengali as a national language and gave "parity" to the East Wing. The prospect of elections to be held under that 1956 constitution helped precipitate the army coup of 1958.

Jinnah's contribution to Pakistan's future political regime was not solely on the side of adding to the power of the state apparatus vis-à-vis the politicians and pouring salt into the wound of the national-language issue. He had built the Muslim League as a movement and won Pakistan's freedom with it. It was perhaps not his responsibility to see – given his age and service, and the great challenges of setting a new country on its feet – that the party would need to be transformed once the goal had been reached, perhaps by developing "an economic and social programme designed to mobilize both the support of the landowners and the peasants" (Sayeed 1968: 298). Here also, however, he was not far-seeing. Having decreed that Urdu would be Pakistan's sole national language, he continued his 21 March 1948 Dhaka speech with:

I tell you once again, do not fall into the trap of those who are enemies of Pakistan. . . . We are not going to tolerate quislings and fifth-columnists in our State. . . . Very often it is said, "Why cannot we have this party or that party"? Now let me tell you . . . that we have as a result of unceasing effort and struggle ultimately achieved Pakistan after ten years. It is the Muslim League which has done it. . . . Now this is a sacred trust in your hands, i.e., the Muslim League. . . . Are mushroom parties led by men of doubtful past to be started to destroy what we have achieved or capture what we have secured? . . . Well, if you are going to serve Pakistan, if you are going to reconstruct Pakistan, then I say that the honest course open to every Musalman is to join the Muslim League Party and serve Pakistan to the best of his ability. Any other mushroom parties that are started at present will be looked upon with suspicion. . . . Honest change is welcome, but the present emergency requires that every Musalman should come under the banner of the Muslim League, which is the true custodian of Pakistan, and build it up and make it a great State before we think of parties amongst ourselves which may be formed later on sound and healthy lines.

(Jinnah 2000: 150–1)

In April, Jinnah repeated the message in the North-West Frontier:

The Qaid-i-Azam warned the people against the grave national emergency existing both internally and externally and stressed that under the circumstances they should have only one political party. He advised the people not to believe in new mushroom-like political parties organized by erstwhile anti-Pakistan elements . . . and said, "You have seen, you have realized, that it is the Muslim League and the Muslim League alone that has saved the Frontier Province from going into the clutches of the Hindu Raj. . . . Do you think that the Muslim League can give you the right lead or those who are against us, those who were in the enemy camp? Are they entitled to look after Pakistan or we?"

(Jinnah 2000: 204–5)

As Binder (1963: 125) puts it: "The assumption on which the partition of India was executed was that the officers of the League represented the will of the Muslims of the subcontinent. Nor was Jinnah or Liaqat slow to equate the membership of the League with the Muslim 'nation' itself." Perhaps the explanation for Jinnah's difficulty in accepting the legitimacy of opposition parties comes from his life-long experience of being in the minority, in formal councils, during negotiations with the British, in discussions with Congress leaders, not to speak of in India's society.[21]

Liaquat apparently followed in Jinnah's footsteps, though it is more likely that these were shared views. According to Allen McGrath (1996: 67):

Liaquat's approach to party politics was direct and forceful. Those who form other parties were traitors, liars, and hypocrites. Words like "dogs of India" were part of his vocabulary when discussing opposition. He equated opposition to the Muslim League with opposition to Pakistan itself, and made it clear publicly that he would not tolerate the existence of an opposition party as long as he lived.

Yet, when it was proposed that Jinnah be exempted from the rule that members of national or provincial cabinets could not hold office in the League, "Jinnah refused the exemption, saying that his constitutional position as governor-general made it his duty to hold the balance 'evenly and fairly amongst such parties as may come into existence or be formed from time to time'" (Binder 1963: 126; citing *Dawn*, 29 February 1948 for Jinnah's words). With the institution of that policy, for reasons Binder (1963: 128–9) explains, "any hope that the government may have had of using the League to further its policy, or explain that policy to the public, was lost."

Jinnah died before he could have had much impact on the conventions and customs of parliament (which is where Nehru made a significant contribution favoring democracy). He attended only a few sessions, as it began to meet in February 1948 (an inference from Riaz Ahmad et al. 1981: 139–41), and it is not clear whether his active participation in legislatures in the 1920s (see Wells 2005: 241–2) was brought to bear in that setting. Qureshi (2008: 81) intriguingly argues that "Jinnah's understanding of how democracy works reflected his apprenticeship in the British Indian Legislative Council and not the Westminster type, which Jinnah neither experienced nor understood."[22]

On the question of where Islam should fit in the constitutional order, Jinnah did provide the charter that many Pakistanis who are committed to democracy treat as a cornerstone of the polity. This was in his 11 August 1947 speech to the Constituent Assembly, which contains the famous line, "you will find that in course of time Hindus would cease to be Hindus and Muslims would cease to be Muslims, not in the religious sense, because that is the personal faith of each individual, but in the political sense as citizens of the State." But Jinnah had died before the Constituent Assembly even began to work on what was to become the Objectives Resolution, where the debate between modernist Muslims, quite secularist in their orientation, and the *ulama* was joined. There is no evidence that Jinnah's views had any weight in that context, let alone served as a trump card against the *ulama*. The compromise the Objectives Resolution represents has survived against the pressures brought by the *ulama* and Islam-minded politicians until the present, but it has also frozen almost all prospects for modernist reform.

Pakistan's formal democracy was deeply flawed in the period from independence to Ayub's coup in 1958. Some very basic issues were not fully and effectively resolved. The mandate to the Muslim League to create Pakistan, delivered in the elections of 1945–6, did not include a mandate for particular policies. That was possibly a conscious choice: since it was necessary to form a united front around the single demand of "Pakistan" – which was at that moment very far from a likely British concession – it might have been necessary to omit discussions of divisive issues, such as language, federal arrangements, and the place of Islam in the new country.[23] Neither Jinnah nor Liaquat was able to act decisively to resolve them, once freedom had been won.

There were other less-than-democratic features of politics in this period. Liaquat, after Jinnah's death, "was all-powerful and wanted to retain this power. Because he did not enjoy the popularity of the Quaid, he used his ascendancy to ensure that the Muslim League alone ruled all the provinces, and further that only those League leaders were made chief ministers who were loyal to his person and owed their advancement to him" (K. K. Aziz 1976: 14). There was no democracy within the Muslim League.[24] As K. K. Aziz (1976: 14) points out, "There was no opposition party in the country. Nor was there any leading public figure who could appeal to the imagination of the people and lead a movement against this 'dictatorship.' "

Provincial governments in the NWFP, Sindh, and Punjab were dismissed by the central government in the first two years of Pakistan's existence, and the subsequent elections in those provinces were flawed (Wilder 1999). Although the Bengal election of 1954 was free and fair, the government was dismissed weeks later and governor's rule imposed, after uncontrolled riots between Bengali and non-Bengali Muslims; the prime minister declared, "one thing is certain – the Centre will never allow this province to again incur the danger of disintegration" (Sayeed 1967: 73).

After 1954, when an unelected governor-general exercised a veto over parliament, opposition parties and leaders did emerge. The Bengali ones had a popular mandate, but they operated under severe constraints imposed by the central government, including the governor-general and then president. K. K. Aziz (1976: 84) remarks: "It is not far from the truth to say that Pakistan was a one-party State from 1947 to 1954, and in some ways up to 1956." Hamza Alavi (1983: 74) forcefully underlines the result: "Pakistan was, from the outset [i.e., 1947], in the hands of a military–bureaucratic oligarchy. In the first decade, the bureaucracy was the dominant element."

It is likely that a younger Jinnah living longer would *not* have built the foundations of a democratic system the way Nehru did in India. At a minimum, Jinnah would have needed the equivalent of the Congress movement-turned-party to set the party system of Pakistan on a truly demo-cratic path. The Muslim League would have needed to have a thick layer of political leaders well connected to their constituents, and Jinnah would have had to be willing to hand power to them, or at least share it substantially. There is little indication even in Jinnah's political life history that suggests he would have been prepared to do that. Only one man was allowed to emerge as a significant force: Jinnah's chosen deputy and successor, Liaquat Ali Khan. Liaquat was a crucial partner in winning Pakistan, and certainly was a highly skilled leader, who handled both economic issues and relations with India very well when he was prime minister. But he was a leader who continued Jinnah's viceregal system with relish, and might well have moved Pakistan towards a one-party system.

### Nehru

If only because he lived sixteen years longer than Jinnah, Nehru's contribution to setting India on its democratic course was far greater than Jinnah's perhaps partial responsibility for the course Pakistan unambiguously took some years later. There is no doubt that Nehru legitimately spoke for India. The dominance of the Congress under his leadership, winning every national election and virtually every state assembly election while he was alive, is eloquent testimony to that. True, there were many major policy issues on which he did not get his way, but he still commanded overlapping majorities of support, and there was no one who rivaled him in stature. And he was eloquent in his articulation of what democracy meant for India, in his writings and speeches, interviews and discussions. We do not know, of course, how much of that was received and adopted by ordinary citizens – probably not that much, given that most of the eloquence was in English. Yogendra Yadav emphasizes the "discursive chasm between elite and masses" (Yadav 1999b: 15). Referring to "Nehru's schoolteacher-like mannerisms," Yadav argues that

> If we focus on the flow of ideas, it was clearly a one-way traffic. Ordinary citizens were autonomous in this realm only to the extent to which they misunderstood, deliberately or otherwise, the ideas they received from above. . . . If you were born in the right kind of family . . . Indian democracy could appear very much like an authentic or at least a "developing" liberal democracy.
>
> (Yadav 1999b: 12)

On the other hand: "The achievements of [the Nehruvian] phase, and of Nehru in giving a long-term institutional base to democracy in a fragile moment, must not be undervalued" (Yadav 1999b: 15). There is a checklist of items here: Nehru's energetic campaigning in the general elections, even though he could have won as easily by a more relaxed, long-distance effort; his hands-on direction of the Congress Party; his punctilious regard for parliamentary conventions, including a formal respect for the tiny numbers of opposition party members who had managed to be elected; his "working" the federal system through party and governmental links to the chief ministers; his accessibility, reaching literally into his home, and willingness to listen to all and sundry (see Desai 2005: 28). He did not react to press criticism by attacking press freedom, and he dealt with court decisions that went against him (e.g. on land reform) by getting the constitution amended, if necessary.

Khilnani (1997: 40) says "parliamentary and party procedures were priggishly followed," but Morris-Jones (1964: 237–8) is more generous: "account must be taken of the profundity of the ideological commitment of many of India's rulers to the Westminster model. Even of Nehru himself, headmaster though he was, it makes sense to say that if opposition had not existed he would have found it necessary to invent it."[25] Gopal (1979: 304) focuses first on cabinet government:

In the framework of democratic institutions that Nehru strove to install in India, the weakest link was Cabinet government. He insisted that all important matters should at some stage be brought up in Cabinet; there were numerous Cabinet committees and consultation was frequent; the deficiency was in spirit and animation. But at least the procedures of collective policymaking were established, for life to be later instilled in them. This was the work of Nehru, achieved against the drive of his own personality and despite the eager subservience of mouldering mediocrities who claimed to be his colleagues.

Nehru's conduct in parliament was similarly inspired:

He took seriously his duties as leader of the Lok Sabha and the Congress Party in Parliament, sat regularly through the question hour and all important debates, treated the presiding officers of the two houses with extreme deference, sustained the excitement of debate with a skilful use of irony and repartee, and built up parliamentary activity as an important sector in the public life of the country.

(Gopal 1979: 304)

Gopal (1979: 304) concludes with a striking argument: "By transferring some of his personal command to the institution of Parliament, he helped the parliamentary system take root. This ensured that no one else would be able to dominate Indian politics as he had done. One of his greatest achievements was the preclusion of a successor in any real sense." (In Pakistan, the leaders of the Muslim League displayed a "cavalier attitude toward Parliament" by presenting legislation for *pro forma* debate after vigorous discussion and decision within the parliamentary party [Callard 1957: 87].)

As Austin (1999: 27, citing Ranga 1986: 283) says, "The strongest curb on the Prime Minister's arbitrary use of power came from Nehru himself. He both fought and yielded to the 'slow elephantine movements . . . of democratic methods', recalled long-time peasant leader and Congressman N. G. Ranga." Nehru also recognized his limitations in the broader areas of policy implementation. With the possible exception of foreign affairs, where he had no clear rivals in any sense, he understood that India had to be governed through institutions such as parliament, party, and the bureaucracy, and that even a leader as all-powerful as he seemed to be had political capital that could not be spent promiscuously. At times, even on matters on which he felt deeply at odds with his political followers, Nehru was forced to give way, as on the question of linguistic states. True, in that case it only happened when there was a law-and-order crisis following the death of the fasting Potti Sriramulu. His fortnightly letters to the chief ministers are justly famous. He sought to persuade and inform and not infrequently twist arms.

Nehru did these things vigorously for fifteen years, which is almost a generation in India. There is no doubt that those of the political class who came under his direct and indirect influence were indeed drilled in that school-masterish way in the practices of democracy. It was a relentless inculcation of democracy-as-routine, marred by undemocratic episodes such as the dismissal of the Kerala government in 1959, and the tolerance of colonial-era measures such as preventive detention. As Meghnad Desai (2005: 29) puts it: "Having had nearly two decades of a democratic leadership at its start, India got addicted to democracy." While Nehru lived, the critical first test of a democratic system – the peaceful handover of power to an alternate party and government – did not happen, and would not happen until 1967 at the state level and after the trauma of Mrs Gandhi's Emergency and the 1977 election that followed at the national level. Nor were the economic and social and military crises that he managed without stepping outside democratic means – a foreign exchange crisis in 1958, conflict over land reform, the battle over the Hindu Code, the defeat in the India–China war of 1962, among others – as deeply disturbing as those that were to come after his death. But there is no doubt that India's democratic foundations were laid down under his rule, while across the border Pakistan suffered through a governor-general's coup, an army coup, and a spell of "guided democracy," with the internal rift between East and West Wings continuing to widen. It is not at all hard to imagine that an India deprived of Nehru's leadership at an early stage would have looked a lot more like Pakistan seventeen years after independence.

## Secular state, Islamic state

In his speech of 11 August 1947, Jinnah succinctly affirmed a "secular" position not at all different from the contemporary one in India. This suggests that, despite the problems generated by his "viceregal system" and his forcing Urdu to be the sole national language, had he lived a few years longer, he might have been able to resolve the critical problem of just how Islam would be incorporated into the new state. There were others in the Constituent Assembly who shared his views, but not his authority. In the event, it took too long for a compromise formulation to find its way into the draft constitution, and the heightened activism of religious movements produced a major crisis with far-reaching consequences: the anti-Ahmadiyya agitation of 1953.

Still, Jinnah's position on Islam reflected a broad view of the relationship religion ought to have in the new state – one that Ayub Khan also accepted, and implemented in one area, in the provisions of the Muslim Family Law Ordinance of 1961. It is not until the 1970s that the "Islam card" is played once again, first cynically by Zulfiqar Ali Bhutto and then in dead earnest by General Zia ul Haq. It is then that those in authority attempt to make Islam a guiding and active principle of state policy, rather than an encompassing and vague umbrella that sheltered, but was separate from state activities. We shall examine below, in Chapter 7, whether the precepts of Islam and of Hinduism, in part as revealed in "Islamization" in Pakistan and in Hindu nationalism in India, contribute substantially to making a country democratic or autocratic.

In India, the Constituent Assembly built on the foundation of the secular position of the nationalist movement under Gandhi's direction, and then under Nehru's command. Nehru himself was a man who believed deeply in the exclusion of religion from public life, even though he was exquisitely sensitive to its central place in Indian civilization.[26] The political leadership deliberated in the shadow of the tragedy of partition, which was blamed on the use of religion as a political tool by the Muslim League under Jinnah. None the less, religion was not a major issue in the Constituent Assembly debates, where the problem of the national language and social justice were center stage (Austin 1966). Although political parties with a Hindu agenda were formed to fight the elections of 1951–2, they did not do well. Yet the effort to legislate a significant reform of Hindu personal law met with spirited resistance, and was only a partial success.

### India as a secular state

India's Constituent Assembly, with the Muslim League members not participating, began to work on a constitution in January 1947, when the British were still far from conceding an independent country of Pakistan, but when the consequences of mobilizing a people on the basis of religion was already starkly evident. Gandhi had long before made clear his deeply felt objection to strengthening the nationalist movement by appealing to an exclusivist Hinduism, although he also insisted on the value of infusing religious values – those of all religions, not just one's own – into politics. That the Pakistan movement had finally succeeded in mobilizing popular support with the cry of "Islam in danger" was for Gandhi and the secularist Congress leadership a tragic outcome, and not an excuse to make India into a Hindu state, whatever that might mean. Nor did the Hindu nationalists of the Hindu Mahasabha and the Rashtriya Swayamsevak Sangh have much overt support. Hindu nationalism (*hindutva*) only becomes a major force in Indian politics in the 1980s.

The Constituent Assembly included the freedom of religion within the fundamental rights without serious objections raised by anyone, but that applied most directly to the individual's right to beliefs and practices, including the right to proselytize (see D. E. Smith 1963: ch. 4, for an extended discussion of these issues). On the other hand, the state was given the right to step in and reform religious practices – hardly surprising given the efforts by Gandhi to ensure the freedom of all Hindus, especially the "untouchables" he renamed "Harijans" (God's people), to enter temples, and to transform the religiously sanctioned institution of caste. His ideas were based on his religious beliefs, but his political opponent, Dr B. R. Ambedkar, a major leader of the "untouchables" and the chairman of the drafting committee, also supported state-directed reform. The socialist Nehru, leading a substantial like-minded group in the Assembly, also supported that position.

Enforcing what was to become a "universal" notion of human rights against particular religious restrictions, symbolized by the "directive principle" included in the constitution to adopt a universal civil code (abolishing the separate codes of personal law), would inevitably mean greater interference in the practices of some religions than in others. A reformed Hindu Code was passed after a great deal of resistance in 1955 and 1956, but there has been no serious progress towards a universal civil code – to match the universal criminal code that the British had instituted a century earlier. Although the word "secular" is not included in the preamble of the constitution until Mrs Gandhi's Emergency, the principle of the secular state was accepted from the beginning. According to D. E. Smith (1963: 155), Nehru, drawing on Western ideas of secularism, "defined the secular state as a state which protects all religions but does not favor one at the expense of others, and does not establish any religion as the official creed. . . . For Nehru, the secular state is the *sine qua non* of modern democratic practice." Gandhi and his followers supported a secular state of this kind, but on the basis of Hindu philosophy (D. E. Smith 1963: 146–52). A state divorced from religious partisanship, however, probably received broad and visceral support mainly from the opposition to the justification of Pakistan, evident in the rejection of the argument that Kashmir "belonged" to Pakistan purely because a majority of its population was Muslim. It was so much a non-issue that Austin (1966), in what is still the definitive study of the making of the Indian constitution, does not mention the issue of secularism.

Once the constitution was ratified, and particularly after the first elections (of 1951–2), most matters of religion were handled through the legislative process. Critical issues included conversions to Christianity and the role of foreign missionaries; Hindu temple administration reforms; religious instruction in schools and regulation of schools run by religious organizations; and the passage of the Hindu Code Bill (these are the major issues discussed in D. E. Smith 1963). In the next decade, the most notable event that was explicitly "Hindu" was the mass demonstration in favor of legislation banning cow slaughter, and featuring a large number of *sadhus*, in front of parliament in November 1966, sponsored by various Hindu organizations which resulted in police opening fire, the resignation of the home minister, and quite possibly some votes for the Jana Sangh Party in the 1967 elections.

Hindu–Muslim riots were few and far between throughout the 1950s, and only gradually increased in salience in the 1960s. There was a major riot in Calcutta in 1964, precipitated by the disturbances in Kashmir because of the theft of the hair of the Prophet, which in turn caused riots in East Pakistan. Major riots occurred in Ranchi in 1967, and in 1969 in Ahmedabad, where a thousand or so died. These and the large number of riots in the early 1970s in Western UP and in Maharashtra did not seem to have general, let alone national, political roots. Nor were there political consequences comparable to the disturbances brought on first by the linguistic states issue, for example, or the Naxalite rebellions of 1967–70. Hindu nationalism does not begin to gain traction until the late 1970s.

It is hard to interpret these things as suggesting either the strength or weakness of Hindu influence on political practice, and Hinduism's favoring or undermining of democracy. Hindu influence is seen in the reality or the hypocrisy of "tolerance," especially in local arenas; the continued tyranny of the ruling upper castes, or the beginnings of serious challenge to their unfettered power. It is also impossible to measure the extent to which caste and gender inequality rooted in Hindu belief was undermined in this period, but it is likely that the implementation of reserved seats for scheduled castes and scheduled tribes, the enforcement of the right of temple entry regardless of caste, the reforms of the Hindu Code Bill that went some way to giving women rights, and other such measures did have some impact. Yet, on the whole, the many contradictions between Hindu and democratic beliefs remained stark. On the other hand, the major episode of authoritarian rule in India in this period – the imposition of Mrs Gandhi's Emergency – has no obvious "Hindu" roots.

### Pakistan as an Islamic state

In Pakistan's Constituent Assembly, in sharp contrast to India's, religion was center stage, although in Pakistan's first year (until Jinnah's death), according to Binder (1963: 117), the "Islamic character of the state" was not "the central issue of Pakistani politics," despite the number of public pronouncements on the question. Our difficulty is in sorting out the real from the symbolic importance of Islam in the constitutional arrangements of the new state. None of the major leaders of the Muslim League had an Islamic agenda for governance; the slogan of "Islam in danger" had come late in the Pakistan movement. Before then, the separation into a sovereign state was for giving Muslims the right to rule over themselves, and the assumption was that such rule would be automatically "Islamic." The groups and leaders that *did* have an Islamic agenda had in some cases – most importantly the Jamaat-i-Islami, led by Maulana Maududi – actively opposed the creation of Pakistan, for sound Islamic reasons: that the "nation" for Muslims was the *umma*, the world-wide community of believers, not a territorially defined "nation" living in the Indian subcontinent.

Jinnah's statement in his inaugural address to the Constituent Assembly on 11 August 1947 that a citizen's religion "has nothing to do with the business of the state" and the assertion that non-Muslims would be equal citizens of Pakistan, free to practice their religion fully, was not acceptable to religious leaders. Yet Jinnah's view was not unrepresentative of either politicians' or citizens' ideas. In Wayne Wilcox's (1966: 347–8) judgment, "very few of Pakistan's leaders saw the state goals as anything other than social, political, and economic. They were not intent upon re-creating seventh century Arabia in Pakistan. . . . [They] proposed to create conditions favorable to the realization of the [religious] ideal, not to legislate the ideal itself." Those leaders, most notably Liaquat Ali Khan, were squeezed between the non-Muslim members of the Assembly who sought to have Jinnah's pledge fulfilled, and the *ulama*, who had only a handful of members, but great strength outside the Assembly. This three-way struggle was first apparent in the debate over the Objectives Resolution, passed in March 1949, and later incorporated into successive Pakistan constitutions as a preamble (for an important, almost contemporary, analysis, see Binder 1963: 142–54; see also McGrath 1996: 68–73).

As with other decisions on constitutional provisions that were to follow (see Callard 1957: 87), this resolution was formulated in secret, within the Muslim League. On 2 March 1949, "to the great satisfaction of religious Muslims . . . and perhaps to the bewilderment of the uninitiated, the newspapers announced . . . in screaming headlines 'Sovereignty over the entire universe belongs to God Almighty alone' " (Binder 1963: 142, citing the quotation from the Resolution printed in *Dawn*). The Resolution goes on to say that God "has delegated [authority] to the State of Pakistan through its people for being exercised within the limits prescribed by Him," which immediately sparked the debate on whether the "limits" could be determined by "its people" and their "chosen representatives," or by those learned in Islamic law, the *ulama*. A further clause stated that in the constitution to be framed "the principles of democracy, freedom, equality, tolerance and social justice, as enunciated by Islam shall be fully observed." Provisions were to be made for freedom of religious practice for Muslims and non-Muslims alike, along with other fundamental rights. Binder (1963: 147) underlines the inconsistencies in the Resolution on just who or what is "sovereign": "if sovereignty belongs to God, that did not prevent Pakistan from being a 'sovereign independent state' in the second paragraph. . . . [S]overeignty resides in the state of Pakistan, and not in the people of Pakistan."

In Binder's (1963: 150–4) account, there was some "furor" over the "enabling clause" of the Resolution, which directed that the constitution be framed "wherein the Muslims be enabled to order their lives . . . in accord with . . . the Holy Quran and the Sunna" (Binder 1963: 143). Considered along with the paragraph granting rights to the minorities as a "step to enshrine the *two nation* theory" (Binder 1963: 150), it was interpreted by the *ulama* as a requirement to establish *sharia* as the law of the land. But, for the non-traditional national leadership of the Muslim League, it meant that the Muslim majority would legislate in democratic institutions according to their understanding of Islam. These and other ambiguities meant that, although the Resolution was passed ten days later (with the vote divided on religious lines, Muslim against Hindu), "the real issue of the nature of an Islamic state was not yet joined, nor was it even clearly defined" (Binder 1963: 154).

Although subcommittees of the Basic Principles Committee were quickly formed to flesh out the Objectives Resolution, not much work was done for the rest of the year on these issues, by which time India's Constituent Assembly had completed its work and seen a new constitution inaugurated on "Republic Day," 26 January 1950. Disagreement over the nature of the Islamic state was not what kept the constitution from being written. Rather, the Muslim League leadership – which continued to monopolize real discussion and decision-making, ignoring ordinary members of the Assembly – had to wrestle simultaneously with foreign and domestic crises. These included Kashmir, refugee resettlement, and the disruption of trade with India caused by the decision not to devalue the rupee in 1949. It was not as if they needed a new constitution since the British Act that established the Constituent Assembly as a legislature provided an adequate legal framework, which also allowed them to hold provincial assembly elections in 1951, 1952, and 1954. The serious stumbling block at this point was the issue of federalism, in which the political goals of Liaquat to maintain his power became entangled with the need to have a constitution that would deal with Bengal's majority status (see Binder 1963: 200–7).

Soon after the passage of the Objectives Resolution, the Ahrar, a militant Muslim offshoot of the Congress that had opposed Pakistan, began an agitation against the *Ahmadiyya*.[27] They demanded that Ahmadis be declared non-Muslim and that their most prominent member, Foreign Minister Sir Zafrullah Khan, be dismissed. The agitation was supported by the establishment *ulama* and the Jamaat-i-Islami, who then began cooperating on broader questions relating to the Islamic state issue. In early 1953, this culminated in serious disturbances in Lahore, which forced the use of the army to restore order. By then, the particular Islamic state question had been entangled in Muslim League politics, as famously summarized in a metaphorical fable in the Munir Report on those disturbances (see Sayeed 1967: 70). In 1974, Zulfiqar Ali Bhutto declared the Ahmadiyya to be non-Muslim, as a way of establishing his Islamic credentials, and they have continued to serve that purpose for other politicians.

The *ulama* had demonstrated their strength, but this crisis did not bring them greater power. A draft constitution was finally framed, one that was acceptable both to religious leaders and to secular politicians. It was a constitution that "reflected a religious orientation," and the Jamaat-i-Islami declared that it was "to a very large extent Islamic in character and urged its adoption" (McGrath 1996: 126–7). But the governor-general, Ghulam

Muhammad, in effect staged a series of coups: having dismissed Prime Minister Nazimuddin the year before, he then dismissed Nazimuddin's successor, Muhammad Ali Bogra, who had managed to get a constitution draft completed, and asked General Ayub to take over the government (Ayub refused). Ghulam Muhammad then dissolved the Constituent Assembly, an act ratified a year later by Justice Munir. Ultimately a new Assembly approved another constitution, one quite like that of 1954, but Pakistan had been set firmly on a path to authoritarian rule, overtly so with General Ayub's coup of 1958.

The de facto rejection of democracy by Ghulam Muhammad and his successors Iskandar Mirza and Ayub Khan had nothing to do with Islam per se. (It is worth noting the remarks of F. Innes, whom McGrath [1996: 111] describes as a British ICS officer who remained in Pakistan, and quotes, writing in 1953: "Islam is perhaps the most democratic of all religions, and it follows that the Pakistanis, as Muslim people, are enthusiastic for democracy.") Binder (1963: 375), writing of the 1956–8 period, notes that "the claims and the ideals of Islam remained largely irrelevant to the difficult problems that dogged Pakistan's progress."

This reduction in the importance of those advocating an effectively Islamic Pakistan was signaled in 1954. Justice Munir, in the hearings on the Punjab disturbances,

> [had] pressed the *ulema* and religious political leaders . . . to define a Muslim. The results . . . stressed the inconsistencies of the answers given, and were used to discredit [them as] participants in constitution-making. . . . The hearings of the Munir commission were symptomatic of a change . . . which took place as a result of the Ahmadi riots. The strongest voices in constitutional debate were now those arguing for a secular constitution.
>
> (McGrath 1996: 102)

When Ghulam Muhammad dissolved the Assembly, Iskandar Mirza, on leave as governor of Bengal and "acting as the chief spokesman" for the government, said that "the electorate was . . . 'illiterate' and needed further training in democratic institutions. Until that was accomplished there would be a need for 'controlled democracy'" (McGrath 1996: 135). In McGrath's (1996: 141) analysis of Ghulam Muhammad's "attack on Pakistan's parliamentary democracy," he notes that "while democracy lacked leadership, the forces opposing it did not."

It is ironic that Pakistan's most liberal Islamic measure, the Family Laws Ordinance (see Fazlur Rahman 1966) was promulgated by Ayub Khan, and then insulated from legal challenge (Abbott 1966: 366). It has remained in place despite the Islamization policies of Zia's regime. Freeland Abbott (1966: 352–3) argues that although "by almost any standards one chooses to adopt, Pakistan is not a secular state [and though Ayub's 1962] Constitution contains . . . obviously religious [i.e. Islamic] articles, it also contains many articles usually associated with a secular state." Abbott (1966: 368) makes an even stronger claim: "while Pakistan may not be a secular state, neither is it a religious state in the sense in which that term is usually understood in the West. . . . Pakistan is in the process of finding out what an Islamic state is." This constitution – once again of the plain "Republic of Pakistan" – still required that the president be a Muslim. When Fatimah Jinnah ran for the office in 1964, she received the support of the Jamaat-i-Islami, despite a *fatwa* issued by some *ulama* declaring that "in Islam a woman could not be head of state" (Hamid Khan 2001: 302).

Islam did not directly affect politics and the character of the state in either the Ayub or Yahya Khan regimes, and hardly made an impact in that of Zulfiqar Ali Bhutto. There were "concessions to Islamic sentiment" in the 1972 interim constitution (Hamid Khan 2001: 479), and the 1973 constitution made Islam the "state religion." Other Islam-related provisions of earlier constitutions were retained, such as "no law shall be enacted which is repugnant to the injunctions of Islam as laid down in the Holy Quran and the *sunnah*" and the establishment of a Council of Islamic Ideology (Hamid Khan 2001: 502). The constitution's second amendment, enacted in September 1974 after some demonstrations in May, declared the Ahmadis a non-Muslim minority (Hamid Khan 2001: 516–17). Islam did not figure significantly in any of Bhutto's domestic political moves – Pakistan's turn towards the Middle East is another matter, to be discussed below.

Although "Islam is our Faith" was an oft-repeated slogan of the Pakistan People's Party (PPP) in the 1970 and 1977 elections, the achievements listed under "Islam" in the 1977 manifesto were mainly superficial (changing the name of the Red Cross to the Red Crescent Society; changing the weekly holiday from Sunday to Friday). The manifesto plans for the next five years listed under the heading of "Islam" were of minor importance. In the thirtieth year of independence, "Islam" remained more slogan than a significant political feature either of collective action or institutional structure or citizens' political ideas or motives. Almost none of Pakistan's heads of government or state had been overtly pious; and the Islamic parties, though deferred to, had mobilized, every now and then, only a small part of Pakistan's population.

Just as "Pakistan" was something of a slogan (although it became much more) in the struggle to secure Muslim rights and a just share in governance in an undivided independent India, in some ways an "Islamic Pakistan" was more a slogan used to mobilize followers than a goal of the Muslim League leadership. But in both cases the slogan took on a life of its own, committing Pakistanis to incorporating Islam into the fabric of the state, whatever their personal inclinations might have been. There is no indication that the beliefs of Islam themselves propelled the bureaucrats and the generals to take over the running of the state, nor were differences in religious belief crucial in weakening the power of the politicians, compared to the mishandling of the language and federalism issues, and the mismatch of refugee politicians and bureaucrats with those they were hoping to lead. It was only with the inauguration of a project of "Islamization," particularly after 1977, that "Islam" played a role beyond restricting moves towards a thoroughly secular state, perhaps on the Turkish model, and became politically significant. Even then, I shall argue in Chapter 7, it is sufficiently complex a religion and set of practices (and groups) that it is not necessary to use it to explain why Pakistan was unable to sustain a democratic system.

## Notes

1 Jalal (1999 [1990]: 32) believes the actual total number of Pakistan-opting officers was around 200.
2 Potter (1979: 28) provides a useful list of ICS memoirs; for one collection of IAS memoir-essays, see Nigam (1985).
3 I believe that Chandra's evidence for the extent and significance of this system is thin, since I have observed in my own field research over the years (Oldenburg 1976, 1987, 2005) that there is a great deal of government activity, including the implementation of particular programs and the recruitment, transfer, and promotion of government employees, from Class IV employees to gazetted officers, in which rules and regulations are followed, albeit with some discretion exercised from time to time. I do not believe my research experience is unrepresentative, although I cannot make that argument in detail here.
4 See Jinnah (2000: 225) for Jinnah's polite but pointed reminder to the officers of the Army Staff College, Quetta, on 14 June 1948, that

> I should like you to . . . understand its true constitutional and legal implications when you say that you will be faithful to the Constitution of the Dominion . . . that the executive authority flows from the Head of the Government of Pakistan, who is the Governor-General and, therefore, any command or orders that may come to you cannot come without the sanction of the Executive Head.

5 He claimed to have been asked by the governor-general, Ghulam Muhammad, to take over the government at that point (see H.-A. Rizvi 2003a: 80; Nawaz 2008: 89).
6 See McGrath (1996: 150–1) for a short discussion of the special procedures and secrecy of the trial that underlines the Liaquat government's view of the "balance between liberty and security." See Jalal (1999 [1990]: 119–24) for a detailed analysis.
7 See Cohen (1990 [1971]: 178–9):

> Pakistan demonstrated that professionalism does not prevent military involvement in politics. . . . In former colonial states the military might be said to be "too professional" because it is technologically and temperamentally more modern and capable than the rest of the political system. Impatient for results, and fearful of a decline in its resource base (or its reputation), the military steps into politics in order save itself by saving the nation.

For a description of the various partnerships of the 1950s, see Siddiqa (2007): 70 ff.
8 The literature on the causes of military coups is enormous. A good recent review and intriguing attempt at measurement of coup risk (paying attention to "coup-proofing") is Belkin and Schofer (2003).
9 There has been a lively recent discussion of the relationship of level of economic development and the consolidation of democracy. See, among others, Przeworski

and Limongi (1997); Boix and Stokes (2003); D. L. Epstein et al. (2006); Houle (2009). We shall return to this issue in the concluding chapter.

10 For "coup-proofing" in the case of certain Middle Eastern countries, see Quinlivan (1999). See also Horowitz (1991: 514–21; 532–59). Stepan (2007) directs us to his earlier work: "On the negative effects on many democracies of such 'prerogatives', which can occasionally last for decades after direct military rule see the chapter 'The Military in Newly Democratic Regimes: The Dimension of Military Prerogatives' [Stepan 1988: 68–92]."

11 As Nehru wrote to Krishna Menon on 27 January 1952, "Few people think of the Army, Navy and Air Force. They take them for granted. Our Defence Services are good and loyal. But if any sudden changes took place in India, nobody can say what the Defence Services might do" (quoted by Gopal 1979: 164).

12 This was done in Pakistan by Bhutto between 1972 and 1976, when the army's power and legitimacy were weakened by the defeat in the 1971 war. See Gowher Rizvi (1985): 218–19 and H.-A. Rizvi (2003a): 144–5.

13 "The Indian armed forces are [in the mid-1980s] under strict constitutional constraints and play a very limited role in the central decision-making process, although they have somewhat more operational authority than many of their foreign counterparts" (Cohen 1988: 138). See also Siddiqa (2007): 253–4 (n. 33), in which one technique – a "double file" system – is outlined.

14 Cariappa became commander-in-chief on 15 January 1949; with the inauguration of the constitution a year later, the president of India became the commander-in-chief.

15 Parliament of India website: http://164.100.24.167:8080/members/biodata. asp?no=77&mpname=Singh+Shri+Jaswant; accessed 12 August 2008.

16 See Nehru's (1941: 433) famous warning about himself, published anonymously in 1937: "Men like Jawaharlal . . . are unsafe in a democracy. . . . [H]e has all the makings of a dictator in him. . . . His overwhelming desire to get things done, to sweep away what he dislikes and build anew, will hardly brook for long the slow processes of democracy. . . ."

17 As Jalal (1999 [1990]: 62) argues, "But in the initial months of independence without strengthening executive authority at the centre it would have been impossible to underwrite the sovereignty bestowed upon the territories constituting Pakistan." See also Jalal (1985b) for a detailed presentation. Waseem (1989: 92) accepts Jalal's view, and expands on it.

18 As he in fact did in India, according to Hodson (1968: 123): "Mountbatten as constitutional governor-general of independent India exercised more direct executive authority in certain spheres than he had enjoyed as autocratic viceroy."

19 Jinnah probably shared that view. As Noorani (2008: 82) reports, Jinnah "told the officers of the Staff College at Quetta on June 14, 1948, that 'the executive authority flows from the Head of Government of Pakistan, who is the Governor-General.'" Noorani calls this "constitutional nonsense."

20 See Jalal's objection (1999 [1990]: 62), which is that no individual's actions could explain the "complex historical processes that have worked to shape the balance between elected and non-elected institutions of Pakistan." On the other hand, see the sources cited by Wilke (2005: 194, n. 15).

21 I owe this point to Christophe Jaffrelot (personal communication).

22 Qureshi (2008: 83–4) notes that "Jinnah's political apprenticeship had been spent in [the British Indian Government, in the] kind of a set-up that gave the impression of providing representation to people, whereas in reality it was tightly controlled by the chief executive;" that he "was handicapped by an absence of higher education" and "did not read much beyond daily newspapers." So "Jinnah could not be expected to institute what he was not aware of." Jinnah served in the Bombay and India Legislative Councils for all but twelve years between 1910 and 1947;

the "elections" to those bodies were more like selections – by a small group of "non-official" leaders – and he was often elected unopposed (see Hayat 2008: 74).

23 See Oldenburg (1985: 731) for speculation on why Pakistan was "a place insufficiently imagined," in Rushdie's memorable phrase from his novel *Shame*.

24 See K. K. Aziz (1976): 84–94. K. K. Aziz (1976: 72 n.) illustrates what he calls "the Muslim League's undemocratic approach to politics." He blames Liaquat for there not being "any attempt to make his party more democratic" (K. K. Aziz 1976: 79).

25 See also Morris-Jones (1957: 329) for a rebuttal of the idea that parliament was "no more than Pandit Nehru's 'durbar'."

26 One of Nehru's most eloquent statements of this is to be found in his will (Nehru 2007: 741–3), in which he explains why, even though he did not want any religious ceremonies after his death, he wanted a handful of his ashes to be immersed in the Ganges – not for religious reasons but as his "last homage to India's cultural inheritance" – and the bulk scattered from an airplane. Indira Gandhi, however, had full religious ceremonies performed and the bulk of the ashes immersed, with only a handful scattered.

27 This community – sometimes referred to as "Ahmadi" or "Qadiani" – was founded in the nineteenth century in Punjab; and, while its members assert their Islamic faith, elements of their belief are rejected by mainstream Muslims.

# 4 Institutionalizing democracy

The constitutional question of how religion would be institutionalized was of comparatively less importance than the question of how the people were to be represented. It was evident that in both countries some sort of federalist arrangement would have to be made. In Pakistan, this issue was tackled in the Constituent Assembly, but proved to be so difficult that it was a major factor in the inordinate delay in drafting the constitution. In India, a critically important part of the solution to the problem – rearranging the states on a linguistic basis – was arrived at after the constitution was implemented. We also examine other crucial pillars of an institutionalized democracy – elections, and the associated freedoms of association and of the press – that are necessary also to ensure that political leaders govern with the consent of the citizenry. That consent is at the core of their ability to command the state apparatus, because they can then claim to act as legitimate representatives of the people. The rule of law requires the judicial system, which had been integrated with the colonial state apparatus, to develop a degree of autonomy sufficient to hold politicians, bureaucrats, and the security forces (military and police) accountable.

## Representation and contested federalism

In Pakistan, the issue first appeared as the question of the national language, which Jinnah had declared to be Urdu alone. The problem for the Bengalis was not simply that the mother tongue of 55 percent of the Pakistan population was Bengali, while Urdu was the mother tongue of only 4 percent. For reasons I analyze in my essay "A Place Insufficiently Imagined" (Oldenburg 1985), the demand that Bengali be made a national language along with Urdu was rejected by Jinnah and the Pakistan central government. Bengal's majority was a problem for those ruling Pakistan – mainly leaders whose origins were in the Muslim minority provinces – because they felt that they were central to winning Pakistan and saw the resistance to their decisions as traitorous. They drew on the argument of "weightage" (see Shaikh 1989: 158–9) that they had made in the Pakistan movement, when the aim was to safeguard Muslims as a minority within undivided India. Under British rule, the argument was used to give them seats in any elected body in Muslim-minority provinces greater than their proportion of the population, on the grounds that as descendants of the Muslim rulers from whom the British had only formally taken over in the mid-nineteenth century they had an ancestral right to rule, or were in some sense the natural rulers of India.

The "two nation" formula then is subtly modified: "two nations" implied "two nations equally entitled to rule," which in turn implied "the (numerically) inferior nation has to be given added weight." With independence, ironically, these founders discovered that they were *still* in a minority, as Urdu speakers and as transplants in places with very different political histories. So they developed formulas that would give "parity" between East and West Wings of the country.[1] One involved noting that the numerical population difference was an artifact of the large Hindu minority in Bengal, so there is a devaluation of their citizenship (at best) or an outright labeling of them as alien (at worst). From this comes the attempt to keep the separate electorate system, and, arguably, the genocide that occurs in 1971 (Oldenburg 1985).

Other constitutional efforts involved keeping the provinces separate, with equal representation for each province. That East Pakistan had one province and West Pakistan four neatly gave West Pakistanis a veto power over the majority. There was a period where West Pakistan became "one unit" – part of a grand compromise with the Bengalis, which also involved the recognition of Bengali as a national language – and in certain circumstances, when the two houses of parliament sat jointly, a majority could rule. But that did not last, and the fact that substantial numbers of West Pakistanis rejected "one unit" and majority rule is telling. Democracy depends on citizens accepting the myth of "one person, one vote." If leaders, from the founding fathers on down, did not accept that, let alone internalize it, then democracy becomes more difficult to legitimize.

The idea of parity survived the army takeover of 1958: the electoral college of "basic democrats" in Ayub's 1962 constitution was split fifty–fifty, East and West Pakistan. But the position of Bengalis continued to erode, as Pakistan's "decade of development" wound up favoring West Pakistan for commercial and industrial development, making East Pakistan in effect a raw-material-exporting quasi-colony. Owing in part to largely Punjabi racist anti-Bengali attitudes, citizens from the East Wing made scant progress in the bureaucracy and the military, and even their advantage in education wasted away. Gowher Rizvi (1985: 212) argues that Ayub's exclusion of politicians from decision-making "was particularly disastrous for the regime in East Pakistan [since] East Pakistan's involvement in the regime was virtually non-existent." Politicians were banned from office until Ayub, without much enthusiasm, became one himself, and allowed the revival of political parties. Ayub relied on both civilian and military bureaucrats to run the country, along with a loyal set of politicians, in particular Z. A. Bhutto. Rizvi (1985: 217) considers "the failure to build institutions based on popular consensus and the determination of the civil–military bureaucracy to monopolize decision making" to be crucial in explaining Pakistan's break-up.

India also had to deal with the question of federalism and the question of a national language. These problems were thought at the time to be system-threatening. Nehru resisted the reorganization of the states on a linguistic basis, even though that had been implemented in the Congress organization since 1920. He was worried that there would be demands for further divisions of India. When he was forced to concede the demand for a separate Andhra state, following the fast-unto-death of Potti Sriramulu, a States Reorganization Commission was formed. Within three years the map of India was redrawn, with the exception of splitting Bombay into Gujarat and Maharashtra (which happened in 1960) and the emergence of Punjab and Haryana in 1966 (see Chandoke 2007: 120–7). There have been disputes about border territories, and demands for regional autonomy within states, and occasional demands for new states. Some of these were granted, but "Brass's rules" – a scholar's summary of the political principles and practices that explain the success or failure of linguistic demands (Brass 1994: 172–4) – remain in force, and have, on balance, helped to keep India unified, and helped bring about a more genuine federalism in the past decades. The national-language dispute, similarly, after major protests in places like Tamil Nadu, was solved through the political process by the mid-1960s. The Nehruvian slogan of "unity in diversity" seems accurately to describe India's condition, particularly after the wars with China (1962) and Pakistan (1965, 1971).

The reign of the Congress gradually eroded, particularly after the death of Nehru. In 1959 he permitted the democratically illegitimate dismissal of the communist-led Kerala government. In the aftermath of the startling Congress defeats in the 1967 elections in many major states, the central government made ample use of "President's Rule" – the central government takeover of states where governments were unstable, usually because of "floor-crossing" by Members of the Legislative Assembly (MLAs). As with the linguistic-states issue and the national-language issue, and indeed with many crisis-inducing issues (e.g. the economic crash associated with the droughts of the mid-1960s), a very messy and barely principled politics, in a very rough-and-tumble way, slowly transformed the political systems at the state level. Party defectors were punished by being defeated, and the politics of shifting coalitions, and central intervention and playing games with local leaders resulted in the Congress Party being changed, under Indira Gandhi's aegis, into a top-down organization, while its erstwhile state-based leaders established themselves as a local opposition.

Mrs Gandhi, taking a cue from various left-leaning colleagues like Mohan Kumaramangalam, gradually extended the "command economy" into more sectors, but that ended with the failure of the attempt to nationalize the wholesale trade in food grains in 1973–4. That marks the beginning of what becomes a liberalization agenda that comes to fruition in 1991. But, for our purposes, a more significant aspect of her radical politics was her attempt to institutionalize a "committed" bureaucracy and a "committed" judiciary. A Congress Party document prepared by Chandra Shekhar, Mohan Dharia and others says: "The present bureaucracy under the ortho-dox and conservative leadership of the ICS with its upper-class prejudices can hardly be expected to meet the requirements of social and economic change along socialist lines. The creation of an administrative cadre *committed* [emphasis in the original] to national objectives and responsive to our social needs is an urgent necessity" (as quoted in Potter 1986: 155–6).[2] Mrs Gandhi aimed to make the civil-state apparatus not only a junior part-ner in rule but also a loyal arm of the political leader. Had she succeeded, India could have become a familiar guided democracy.

The logical outcome of these tendencies was Indira Gandhi's declaration of a state of emergency in June 1975, which ushered in a twenty-month period of mild autocratic rule, to which there was hardly any overt resistance (although more than was reported in the censored press). It appeared that India's democratic system had (finally) failed, and the "India exception" to the typical Third World pattern had been resolved.[3] This was indeed the reaction of Third World countries, as Norman Palmer (1976: 107), quoting an unpublished paper by Leo Rose, summed it up:

> In most other Third World countries the developments in India were greeted without surprise, and with general approbation. As one observer has pointed out, "The Third World interpretation of recent developments in India . . . [is that] the Emergency [is] a movement away from an essentially democratic to a modified command system, as a further proof that democratic development models are inappropriate for the so-called emerging nations."

India experts did not disagree. One of them, Richard Park (1975: 996), an elder statesman of the study of Indian politics, noted: "There are many participants in, and close observers of, the Indian scene who do not accept Mrs Gandhi's assertions, and who believe that she has established autocratic rule in India to protect herself from the Courts and to further tighten her grip on personal political power" – and provides, in an extensive footnote, references to many newspaper and magazine articles. His own evaluation concludes:

> One step towards a closed political society has led to another. The his-tory of such movements warns us that more steps in the same direction are likely to follow, rather than a return to anything close to the status quo ante. . . . In the widest sense, however, the task ahead for India is to construct a political order that is more suited to its own genius. The political crisis of 1975 is only the most severe of many that have arisen

since 1947. The constitutional and party systems established in 1950 have been tried; the experiment, in general, has been the most successful in Asia – perhaps anywhere in the developing world. But it is not adequate for India.

(Park 1975: 1013)

For analysts like Park, it only remained to see just what sort of autocratic regime India would adopt. Army rule was unlikely, at least right away. A "great leader" guided democracy on the Ghanaian or Indonesian model perhaps would work. There might yet be a renewed outburst of communist revolution – the Naxalite revolts had been effectively crushed five years before – with the strains brought on by increasing inequality from the introduction of the green revolution into the countryside. Or some sort of a fascist system, with corporatism and a party with young thugs intimidating opponents, and rigged elections, could be instituted.[4]

Just when Mrs Gandhi seemed to have chosen autocracy, Pakistan was apparently building the foundations of a new democratic regime under Zulfiqar Ali Bhutto's leadership. He was clearly so popular that no one doubted he would win the elections of 1977. Indeed, some have said that one of Mrs Gandhi's motives for calling the election of 1977 in India – which led to her humiliating defeat – was not wishing to be unfavorably compared to Bhutto and Pakistan. We shall return in Chapter 6 to an interpretation of the startling events of 1977, where there were unexpected changes of direction in both countries, setting India on a path to more deeply rooted democracy, and Pakistan on to one of more and more entrenched autocracy. But we need first to analyze the historical roots of both countries' electoral experience.

## Elections

Elections are obviously one of the core elements of "procedural" democracy. Although there were elections in India under colonial rule, the Raj not only limited severely the scope and powers of elected government; it also held in reserve a de facto veto of decisions of whatever elected bodies there were. In this, there was little difference between the areas that were to become India and those that were to become Pakistan. In the period after independence, the paths began to diverge.

We consider first Pakistan's electoral history. Wilder notes (1999: 16, citing Waseem 1994) that, because of the "Punjab tradition" of civil administration, it took longer to introduce elected members in the legislative council of Punjab and the NWFP than elsewhere, and so "at the time of Independence the regions that became part of Pakistan had much less experience with elections than those that became part of India." It should be noted that Bengalis had a tradition closer to that of most of the rest of India.

None the less, Wilder (1999: 16–17) argues that these democratic initiatives were so strong that after independence "even the country's military rulers have felt compelled to hold elections in some shape or form to seek political legitimacy." But he continues: "While the legacy of elections and representative rule was strong, however, the legacy of bureaucratic rule was much stronger." Wilder then sets out the consequences:

> The fundamental electoral dilemma confronting Pakistan's ruling elites since Independence has been how to accommodate the legacy of rule by elected representatives without threatening the legacy of bureaucratic rule. The objective has always been to hold elections that would legitimate but not change the *status quo*. . . . [The strategies] include the following six: (i) rigging elections; (ii) promising but postponing holding elections; (iii) holding local rather than provincial and national elections; (iv) holding indirect rather than direct elections; (v) holding non-party rather than party-based elections and (vi) writing new constitutions or amending old ones in order to strengthen presidential powers and reduce those of elected representatives.
>
> (Wilder 1999: 17; see also Kennedy 2005)[5]

Citing the government of Pakistan's 1959 *Report of the Electoral Reforms Commission*, Wilder (1999: 17–18) proceeds to show how the Punjab elections of 1951, the very first elections held after independence, were rigged (Waseem et al. 2006: 10 say there were "procedural malpractices").[6] The elections in the NWFP in 1951 and in Sindh in 1953 were also rigged.[7] The Bengal elections of 1954, however, were apparently not rigged (Chowdhury 1974: 107). At least, Richard Park, writing within weeks of the election, does not mention anything of the kind (Park 1954). All of these elections were held with full adult franchise.

Pakistan finally was able to institute a constitution in 1956, under which popular governments in Karachi and in the provinces continued to function. A general election was scheduled for February 1959, but was forestalled by the Iskandar Mirza–Ayub Khan coup of October 1958. The causes of that coup, as typically recounted by scholars (see Newman 1959; Sayeed 1959; Wilcox 1965), do not include a particular fear of what the elections would bring in the way of popular support for democracy. At most, President Iskandar Mirza's well-founded fear was that the politicians who were likely to succeed (leaders of the Muslim League in West Pakistan and the Awami League in East Pakistan) were going to replace him as president.

Waseem (1989: 125) sees a broader cause. He claims "the establishment" feared the election because of the "rising potential" for electoral and agitational politics of the "non-statist" Awami League and National Awami Party:

> [With] the "statist" parties [Muslim League, Republican Party] being in an extremely weak position . . . the only way out for the government was to opt out of the parliamentary system altogether. It was feared that even a statist party such as the Muslim League would outgrow the bureaucratic control after getting the public mandate in the ensuing elections.

Pakistan was not to have a fully free and fair election until December 1970 (see Wilder 1999: 20–5). In between, five indirect elections were held under Ayub's guided democracy.

The 1970 election was an aberration: the next election, which Bhutto won in 1977, was rigged, and there have been serious questions about every election since. According to Ian Talbot (1999: 240–1), "the reality seems to be that a certain PPP victory was inflated by malpractices committed by local officials, which may have affected [15–20 percent of the] seats."[8] Weinbaum (1977: 614) concludes that "whatever the extent or origins of the election irregularities, in just a matter of days the legitimacy of the entire electoral exercise had been irretrievably lost." The next election held was that of 1985, as Zia ul Haq gradually relaxed his rule, but political parties were not allowed to contest. There was no need to rig the actual voting. The election of 1988, which brought Benazir Bhutto to power, was reasonably free and fair, but the military had engineered the opposition alliance.[9] The 1990 elections were at best questionable in that regard,[10] but the 1993 elections were seen to be reasonably correct, as were the 1997 elections (conducted with a caretaker government in power), despite the "astounding victory" of Nawaz Sharif (Waseem 1998: 131). Once the military came to power in 1999, things grew worse. The referendum that made General Musharraf president of Pakistan was a blatant fraud, and the 2002 national and provincial assembly elections had their results skewed by a whole array of indirect and direct government interventions.[11] I shall discuss the February 2008 elections, which had significant irregularities but probably produced a fair result, in Chapter 10.

Although all of these post-1971 elections – conducted under the constitution of 1973 – were supervised by a chief election commissioner, there is a pattern of "overzealous local officials," narrowly legalistic judgment of complaints of irregularities, intimidation of women voters, and measures taken against the most recent incumbent party (Wilder 2004). From 1985 onward, it is the military, behind the scenes, which was responsible for the dismissal of both Benazir Bhutto governments and the first Nawaz Sharif government. The low turnout after 1985 probably reflects the voters' judgment of the validity of elections conducted under the military's authority (see Table 4.1; and Islam 2001: 1337).

The figure for 2008, in the face of a call for a boycott by several parties, particularly in Balochistan (where indeed the turnout was only 32.6 percent),

*Table 4.1* Voter turnout in Pakistan elections post-1971

| 1977 | 1985 | 1988 | 1990 | 1993 | 1997 | 2002 | 2008 |
| --- | --- | --- | --- | --- | --- | --- | --- |
| 55.0% | 52.9% | 43.1% | 45.5% | 40.3% | 35.2% | 41.8% | 44.6% |

*Source*: Adapted from *International IDEA Handbook of Electoral System Design* (2005); IDEA website: http://www.idea.int/vt/country_view.cfm?CountryCode=PK; accessed 26 May 2007; 2008 figure from Election Commission of Pakistan, table posted on 20 February 2008 (262 constituencies). The turnout in West Pakistan in 1970 was 54 percent (Waseem 2000: 148).

perhaps indicates a revived belief that elections would matter, since the army had not manipulated the campaign (as General Musharraf had done in 2002) and had been explicitly ordered by the chief of the army staff, General Kayani, not to interfere on polling day.

It is clear that the comparatively rare experience of casting a ballot in Pakistan, for most citizens, has been from the beginning not very meaningful, and is often that of being "taken" in a con game. In Wilder's (2004: 102) words, "the primary purpose of [nearly all of Pakistan's elections] was to legitimize the retention of power by the unelected institutions of the state rather than to transfer power to elected institutions."

India's electoral record is altogether different. Although both countries shared the experience of elections in British India, it is likely that many more (and a greater percentage) of leaders of India-to-be had been elected to urban local bodies, given the more rural complexion of the areas that were to become Pakistan. Jawaharlal Nehru, in the 1920s, served as the elected chairman of the Allahabad municipality, for example.

The pattern of campaigning to reach a mass audience was clearly set in the 1937 provincial elections, at least for the Congress: grueling hours on the trail, with speech after speech to small and huge crowds, and close contact with voters (Nehru 1941: 360–1). As Nehru famously described his own campaign (Nehru 1941: 360):

> In the course of about four months I traveled about fifty thousand miles, using every kind of convenience for this purpose, and often going into remote rural areas where there were no proper means of transport. I traveled by airplane, railway, automobile, motor truck, horse carriages of various kinds, bullock cart, bicycle, elephant, camel, horse, steamer, paddle-boat, canoe, and on foot. I carried about with me microphones and loud-speakers and addressed a dozen meetings a day, apart from impromptu gatherings by the roadside. Some mammoth gatherings approached a hundred thousand; the average audience was usually twenty thousand. . . . For us it was something much more than an election campaign. We were interested not only in the thirty million voters but also in the hundreds of millions of others who had no votes.

Vanderbok and Sisson (1988: 137) look at the electoral data for that election and conclude that it "had a lasting impact on electoral practice in India."

Pre-independence elections were based on a very limited franchise. Meghnad Desai (2005: passim) insists that *the* decision that put India firmly on a democratic path was that of the Constituent Assembly to adopt universal adult franchise. He calls it "revolutionary" because "nothing in Indian history justified it" (Desai 2005: 26). To be sure, Ceylon was given universal franchise in 1931, while still under British rule, and Pakistan managed to hold adult franchise elections in the provinces, starting in 1951, even without a constitution having been framed.[12] Ayub had to overrule the recommendation of the Franchise Commission he had appointed (under pressure from the intelligentsia) for direct universal adult franchise elections, rather than the indirect elections he favored (Hamid Khan 2001: 292–4), in which all citizens would only vote at the local level, for the "basic democrats." It is not likely that the Indian decision was as path-breaking as Desai believes, though the difficulties in conducting a free and fair election for a majority illiterate, unpracticed citizenry were great. Nor does this decision differentiate India from Pakistan.

The electoral system was firmly established even with the first general elections in India in 1951–2, for representatives to both the national parliament and state legislatures. That descriptions of how an election is conducted tend to be repeated, from those first elections up to the present is largely due to the presence of a genuinely autonomous and increasingly powerful Election Commission. Its diligence in registering voters and parties, issuing and enforcing rules of campaign conduct, and organizing the election-day effort to ensure a free and fair vote has contributed mightily to the legitimacy of democracy in India, and to the centrality of elections in that democracy.

True, in each of these areas there are severe problems. The registration of voters produces very defective rolls. Election rules on campaign finance are routinely ignored, and all efforts to purge the candidate roster of people with criminal charges pending – and there are many in that category – have failed (Das 2008; Narayan 2009). While violence has gone down as the security effort has been beefed up (typically by holding the elections in different areas in phases, with four or more dates over a month's period), there are still cases of intimidation and "booth capturing."[13] Vote fraud no doubt persists at a non-trivial level, particularly in certain areas: dead people vote, live voters are denied the vote, etc. (Narayan 2001). On the other hand, Krishna (2007: 143 n) reports that in his large sample "I rarely came upon an instance of someone's name missing from [the electoral roll]."

With the major exception of most elections in Kashmir, elections in India have been judged to be free of rigging and blatant distortion of major proportions. The chief election commissioner, on occasion, has boldly and forcefully confronted the government in power. Most important, there have been *so many* elections, fairly evenly spaced out in time: fifteen elections to parliament, as many (or more) to most state legislatures, and frequent local elections as well. The practices and almost ritualized behavior have remained the same, more or less. Now there are electronic voting machines, where before there were paper ballots. The period of the campaigning is about the same (a month or so before the election date); only the festival atmosphere has dimmed a bit, as the Election Commission has enforced regulations against plastering posters everywhere, and using loudspeakers anywhere and at all times. Parliamentary elections now take place on four or five days, and violence has been reduced as a result. Parties assign agents to observe the casting and counting of ballots, and the official counting is done with the strictest security – but transparently; and so on. Indian voters know the routine as well as the officials who run the elections do.

While Pakistani and Indian elections are similar in their mechanics and supervising institutions and rules, the *experience* of elections has been very different. India has had a history of many, regular, almost entirely free and fair elections for more than fifty years; and Pakistan, sharing with India a pre-independence history of limited-franchise elections, has had only a few elections that were not rigged in some fashion, and – even more important – has had the frequent experience of election results being overturned by military-led fiat. When asked an open-ended question about the meaning of democracy, 22 percent of Indians and *zero* percent of Pakistanis said "elections" (*SDSA* 2008: 242–3).

## Freedom of association

"Free and fair elections" require more than a system that allows all citizens to vote without fear and with an assurance that their vote will be counted. The choices must be meaningful, which means that freedom of association and of speech must exist. In a modern representative democracy freedom of association means that, at a minimum, political parties can organize the selection of candidates and conduct a campaign, develop programs, and attract (and sometimes protect) supporters.

In open societies other associations also feed into the political process: interest associations like labor unions, issue-oriented groups or even movements, like the environmentalists, and social groups interested only in sponsoring sports teams or concerts but which (at least in some theories of democracy) are vital in setting patterns of democratic behavior.

While the British vigorously catalogued and kept themselves informed about the various associations that emerged along with the colonial state, they did not control them. Religious reform movements, associations for the uplift of women, education societies, and of course social and civic associations formed in the early nineteenth century in a significant way. There is now a huge historical literature and argument that touches on this. For our purposes, it is noteworthy that the British before independence cracked down on terrorist groups and the Communist Party (after its formation in the early 1920s), but treated groups such as the Congress with annoyed tolerance. By and large, such associations were free to hold meetings and processions, and present petitions, and even engage in Gandhian *satyagraha*, which involved carefully orchestrated breaking of the law, followed by jail terms that were not unpleasant, though sometimes not short. Issue-based associations, like the Congress Socialist Party, could be accommodated as a semi-autonomous group within the Congress. The Pakistan movement, particularly after 1937, was able to attach other parties and groups.

Parties organized to contest municipal and legislative elections came into existence in the 1920s (see Mehra 2003). By the time of the 1946 provincial assembly elections, there were major parties – to give a few examples – based on economic interests (the Unionist Party in Punjab, the Krishak [Peasants'] Party in Bengal); on ethnic or religious identity (the Akalis in Punjab, the Hindu Mahasabha, the Ahrar), as well as the catch-all Congress and Muslim League.

After independence, the number of parties expanded in both countries. Only a few had a nationwide presence, and a few others were major factors in the politics of particular provinces.[14] Not many of them can be called mass parties, even when they exist only in a particular region. Pakistan has banned communist parties, but India has not (and there are several of them), but otherwise there has been a remarkable range of parties more or less free to operate in both countries – although, obviously, with significant restrictions in Pakistan in non-democratic periods. Other associations are banned from time to time, typically for being "terrorist," and include hard-line religion-based organizations, separatist and revolutionary groups, and the like. Both countries regulate parties and other associations, requiring them to register, and have written and public constitutions. Indian associations, typically NGOs, have to register to obtain permission to accept foreign funds. In both countries, associations and parties that oppose the government may find themselves in trouble with the laws and regulations, but typically this results in restriction of activity rather than outright suppression.

When political party leaders are put in jail, it is usually because criminal charges have been brought against them – corruption and murder cases are not infrequent. There is still a British colonial system of "externing" people from a district or even state, when they are deemed to be trouble-makers or criminals, essentially on the say-so of administrative authorities. In Pakistan this idea has in recent years been extended, as it were: at one point, the leaders of the three major parties – Nawaz Sharif, Benazir Bhutto, and Altaf Hussain – were in effect forced by the military government to live outside the country. India by all accounts has a denser associational landscape than Pakistan, but it is hard to make valid comparisons or even obtain reliable data. The crucial point, for our purposes, is that, while somewhat constricted, freedom of association exists in both countries, though significantly less robustly in Pakistan.

## Press freedom

The freedom of the press – now encompassing other media – is at the same time impressive and problematic in both Pakistan and India, though to different degrees. In India, the print media have operated freely since even before independence, with the crucial exception of the period of the Emergency (June 1975–March 1977). Since that experience they have developed an investigative vigor that is often very impressive. It is only within the last decade, however, that non-governmental television stations have made an impact; and, even today, radio is essentially government-controlled, as far as political society is concerned (see Ram 2000: 241). The government has not been shy about co-opting journalists with everything from copious press releases and other public relations efforts, to special privileges, such as paid junkets and support for cooperative housing societies. Only the largest and most economically successful newspapers and broadcast networks can hold out against those inducements. The government has also rewarded and punished newspapers through the allocation of newsprint and government advertisements.

Most significantly, there is little protection for journalists from harassment in the courts in India. Courts can require the appearance of editors to answer charges of defamation filed by ordinary citizens, or "hurting the sensibilities of a particular community." This is designed to intimidate and punish by forcing the hiring of lawyers, the costs of making an appearance, and adverse publicity. If the government joins in actions of this kind, as in the hounding of Tehelka.com, for example, the damage to press freedom can be severe.

On the whole, however, the press has served as the "fourth estate" in significant measure, serving to hold government to account on occasion, to the extent of forcing major leaders to resign. It has certainly been able to provide the forum for competing parties and candidates to disseminate their views, and has also represented an important platform for organizations and individuals of civil society to present alternative positions and analyses. It is no longer true that only the English-language media – catering to an elite that is very influential without being all-powerful – has a large impact: there has been a flowering of newspapers and magazines and television programs in Hindi and other of the major languages.[15]

In Pakistan in the last decade, the print and television media have probably been the "freest" sector of civil society. In the past, there were periods of severe restrictions on the press, particularly during periods of direct military rule. The title of the best study of the Pakistani press is *The Press in Chains* (Niazi 1986).[16] Its author notes that as early as 1948 "three progressive periodicals . . . were proscribed by the Muslim League government of the Punjab" (Niazi 1986: 50) and "during the first seven years (1947–1953) of Pakistan, in the Punjab alone, 31 newspapers were banned" (Niazi 1986: 62, citing the Munir Commission Report). Niazi's summary of the "democracy period" (1947–58) is that "in spite of a plethora of the Press laws . . . bequeathed by the alien rulers, the Press played its role with a certain tinge of defiance" and quotes from I. H. Qureshi's introduction to a book published in 1982: "The Press was much more independent during the first 11 years of Pakistan than it has been ever since" (Niazi 1986: 75, quoting from Rehman 1982: xi). According to Niazi, General Ayub Khan's seizure of power in 1958 "heralded the beginning to a completely chained Press for all times to come" (Niazi 1986: 79).

It was only with the loosening of General Zia's regime in the mid-1980s that the Pakistani press revived and became more and more professional. Paradoxically, the emergence of a popular and effectively independent set of television stations is roughly dated from the onset of General Musharraf's military regime. As Zaidi (2008a: 116) notes:

> In 2002, when the last elections were held, there was only one private TV channel in the country; today there are perhaps more than thirty private news and information channels, in all major languages. With constant information, analysis, and chatter about even minuscule political tremors and developments, much of Pakistan's society has become involved and informed about what goes on in the country.

But some problems remain. In Freedom House's recent assessment: "journalists continued to encounter official attempts to restrict critical reporting as well as high levels of violence."[17] In May–June 2007, with Musharraf's regime in something of a crisis of democratic legitimacy, it reacted in part by banning the broadcasts of the most important television stations, though it was quickly forced to retract the ban. With President Musharraf's declaration of Emergency on 3 November 2007, independent television stations were yanked from the airwaves. The government of Pakistan went to the extent of using pressure to get broadcast facilities in Dubai suspended. That was followed by the imposition of a highly restrictive "code of conduct" – featuring strictures on criticizing the president – for the elections of 2008.[18] With a new government in power, media freedom has been increased. Reporters were able to reach and report on the family of captured Mumbai attack suspect Ajmal Amir Kasab before the government was able to hide them away.

The difference between English-language and Urdu and other vernacular media in Pakistan is probably greater than the differences in India, with the English media being less subject to government pressure than the Urdu media (Menon 2000) and also – at least in the view of the elite – more "responsible." The pressures on the media not to challenge the government have been constant, even on the English media. Government pressure can be illustrated by considering the experiences of Pakistan's major daily, *Dawn*, more than fifty years apart. Niazi (1986: 63) writes:

> [On 16 November 1953] *Dawn* appeared with the following banner-headline: "GOVERNMENT TAKES ACTION AGAINST *DAWN* AND *EVENING STAR*: Advertisements stopped; Members of staff outlawed." The report said that the Government had decided that all "patronage" extended to *Dawn* would be stopped and that no members of its staff would have access to any Government office or [be] invited to any function. [Niazi's citation is to *Viewpoint*, 8 April 1977.]

In June 2007 readers of *Dawn* found on its online homepage the following announcement:

> Since December 2006, the DAWN Group is facing massive advertising cuts equivalent to two thirds of total government advertising. . . . This period first witnessed the government's exerting of harsh pressures on our daily evening newspaper – The STAR – by attempting to intimidate and harass journalists with false cases and concocted charges, and by a failed attempt to implicate the writer of this letter, as CEO of the Group, in a totally fabricated incident of terrorism and illegal weapons possession.[19]

The intimidation can also be physical. Nicholas Schmidle (2008), who was forced to leave Pakistan probably because of an article on the Taliban in Pakistan published in the *New York Times Magazine*, notes:

> A couple of weeks ago, a spokesman from the Information Ministry said that "the media in Pakistan is the freest ever in the history of the country." In many ways, he was correct; drawing-room columnists can be as critical as they wish to be. But opinion-writing shouldn't be confused with reporting. And every journalist working in Pakistan knows that crossing certain undefined lines can become a risky, often life-threatening endeavor.

Schmidle describes several cases in support of this last statement.

According to the Reporters Without Borders 2007 report on Pakistan, "Harassment and threats remain the preferred methods of the security services. Reporters Without Borders recorded more than 40 such cases in 2006."[20] If this is the case for foreign and nationally published reporters, the situation for local journalists must be even worse. Whether there is true freedom of the press in local arenas, or perhaps even in regions, is an open question. The Reporters Without Borders introductory summary of the year 2007 in the entry on Pakistan in the Annual Report is printed in bold face:

> It was an *annus horribilis* for journalists in Pakistan. Six reporters were killed, nearly 250 arrested and more than 100 incidents were recorded of threats and physical assault. The brutality came from all sides: the army, Islamists, political militants and local organised crime. And Gen. Pervez Musharraf, rocked by a protest movement launched by judges and lawyers, made life impossible for privately-owned television and radio stations.[21]

The election of February 2008 was, however, reasonably well reported, and the new government is unlikely to be as insensitive to press freedom. However, according to Reporters Without Borders, "The press is caught in a vice between the Taliban which has stepped up its attacks and the security forces who continue in their old ways of harassing journalists. [The authorities] deemed it necessary in March 2009 to block television news channels Geo News and Aaj while they were covering demonstrations by lawyers."[22] Pakistan remains a very dangerous place for reporting. Still, the press has certainly not been cowed.

## The rule of law

The legal system is arguably the oldest governmental institution India and Pakistan have – much of both civil and criminal law, and the judicial system, seems to have barely changed from what the British created in the mid-nineteenth century. But a set of laws does not itself make a "rule of law": we need to know the extent to which the rule of men or a rule by autocratic institutions (where laws are modified by fiat and where, crucially, those who make the laws are not bound by them) is trumped by a rule of law at each period in the political histories of the two countries.

In the conclusions of their fine-grained analysis of the rule of law in India and China, Ocko and Gilmartin (2009: 94) point out: "The 'rule of law' is not inherently democratic. The appeal to law, in fact, defined in both imperial China and colonial India ideological foundations for profoundly authoritarian forms of governance." I follow the conceptualization adopted by the World Justice Project for its Rule of Law Index project, as summarized by the report of the Vera Institute of Justice report to the Project: "the definition [of the rule of law] emphasizes equity, accountability, and avoidance of arbitrariness and is rooted in fundamental principles of human rights as well as the more traditional concept of the supremacy of the law."[23]

Procedural democracy does not require the rule of law in its broad sense – just that the rules of choosing representatives and leaders are proper and obeyed. But when we add the requirement that for democracy there may not be any person or any institution other than the people and their elected representatives to choose the government and hold it accountable the rule of law becomes significant. If there is no rule of law to punish and thus prevent coercion and fraud; if the laws that are made by the people are systematically ignored by the rich and powerful – then you have no democracy. Yet if the rule of law is bent but not broken; if on most occasions, or for most decisions, almost all citizens can vote as they please, and those they choose to govern are able, most of the time, to make laws as they themselves see fit, and those laws are mainly obeyed – then democracy, albeit blemished, could still be said to exist (provided we can adequately judge what is meant by "most," "almost all," and "mainly").

We should also like to take into account the significance of the decisions and the laws. If the people can exercise their full power for crucial decisions, as when Indian citizens threw out Mrs Gandhi in 1977, or when periodic elections produce significant changes of government, that should matter more than whether they have much say in arcane matters of day-to-day government, say, on something like taxation policy. For assessing the extent of the rule of law, people getting away with murder on a regular basis is worse than people getting away with driving over the speed limit. Given these problems, it would seem to be impossible to devise an empirical test of when the rule of the powerful – which has always been a part of every existing democracy – eclipses or erases the rule of law and the power of the collective citizenry.

We can talk about the rule of law as a less complex phenomenon, by focusing on the judicial system itself. Here we need to ask whether, by and large, rules of procedure are followed; whether participants in the system have access to competent lawyers; whether judges have autonomy and security. We are hampered by the way the judicial system has tended to be studied: in India and Pakistan, most legal activity takes place at the district level but is the least studied. Constitutional issues decided by the highest courts receive the most attention, even though that happens rarely. Clearly we need to consider both of these arenas in making an assessment of the extent to which a rule of law exists.

In Pakistan, according to Paula Newberg (1995: 248):

> Citizens have believed, often with good reason, that courts are accessible and useful. Belief, however, sometimes overwhelms proof. As arenas for relatively open political debate, the courts are generally viewed as unsullied, apolitical institutions within a compromised, corrupt and highly politicized state. As institutions of judgment, however, they more often support than challenge state power.[24]

Ardeshir Cowasjee (2008b) makes a similar point about the legal system as a whole:

> It seems to some of us laymen, out here in the legal cold, that many of our lawyers are now bent on the destruction of institutions rather than on their preservation or resuscitation. The masses at large are untouched by the judiciary, the lawyers and their courtrooms. They have other matters that preoccupy them – such as staying alive. And besides, to them, historically, the courts and courtrooms have always appeared to be the domain of the rich and powerful, not of the poor and needy.

The judgment of the team leader of the government's own "Access to Justice Project" (originally funded by the Asian Development Bank) is equally damning (M. Sarwar Khan n.d. [ca 2006]). He notes the "appalling situation" of poor-to-nonexistent court infrastructure; calls both citizens and the lower judiciary "victims" of the senior judiciary's neglect; and points to the "falling standards of judicial decision-making."

The 2007 "chief justice" crisis in Pakistan highlighted the precarious position in which even the highest judiciary finds itself. The crisis occurred because Chief Justice Iftikhar Chaudhry refused to resign when asked by the president and chief of the army staff General Musharraf, even when put under the severe pressure of being asked in the presence of the prime minister and the heads of the intelligence agencies. That refusal was unexpected, since there had been a long history of judges knuckling under to the demands of the executive. When General Musharraf, three months after taking power in October 1999, required the senior justices to swear a new oath of allegiance, most of them complied – including Justice Chaudhry – and those who refused left quietly.

Indeed, the pattern of compliance had been set in 1954, when the courts did not provide a remedy to the Constituent Assembly, which believed itself to be sovereign, after the governor-general arbitrarily dismissed it. Chief Justice Munir of the Federal Court gave in to the pressure to ratify his decision (McGrath 1996: 196; see also Amjad Bhatti 2008). Four years later, when President Mirza declared martial law, Justice Munir ruled in *Dosso* v. *Federation of Pakistan*: "A victorious revolution, or a successful *coup d'état* is an internationally recognized legal method of changing a Constitution [and, after that change,] the national legal order must for its validity, depend upon the new law-creating organ" (as quoted in McGrath 1996: 214). The so-called "doctrine of necessity" was applied in several subsequent arbitrary transfers of power. "Just as the Dosso case legalized the 1958 coup," writes Ian Talbot (1999: 257), "so the Supreme court . . . legitimised Zia's extra-constitutional assumption of power, [empowering] the Chief Martial Law Administrator . . . to 'promulgate legislative measures' and to amend the 1973 Constitution" (see also Newberg 1995: 162–7).

The impartiality of the higher judiciary has also been called into question after a new regime has been installed, particularly during periods of military rule. Perhaps the most significant example would be the court decisions that ultimately led to the execution of the deposed prime minister Zulfiqar Ali Bhutto in 1979.[25] As Newberg (1995: 173) puts it: "Bhutto's conviction caused profound public dismay with the civil courts for years after their verdicts. It was assumed that the military government had found a way to eliminate its most profound opposition by influencing the justices and judicial decision."[26] With few exceptions, the higher judiciary has bent to the indirect or direct pressure of the military–bureaucratic executive, even during the "democratic" period of 1988–99. That was perhaps most shamefully apparent in November 1997, when a mob of party supporters of Prime Minister Nawaz Sharif stormed the Supreme Court as the embattled chief justice was hearing a contempt-of-court case against the prime minister. Sharif ultimately forced the chief justice's resignation, after some hard political games played out in literally competing courtrooms. The higher courts have never even begun to carve out a sphere of autonomy comparable to that of the Indian Supreme Court, but the Pakistan Supreme Court's decision to reinstate the chief justice (July 2007), along with a startling mobilization of the legal profession in his favor, may mark a significant turning point.

On 3 November 2007, however, President Musharraf, in all probability anticipating a court ruling that would debar him from running for another term, declared a state of emergency and dismissed the chief justice and several other judges. He also required all the other judges of the Supreme and Superior Provincial Courts, if they wished to continue in their positions, to swear an oath of allegiance to a new "provisional constitutional order." A significant majority refused, and certain of the senior judges that opposed the president were put under house arrest, along with their chief lawyer supporters. The coalition government elected in February 2008 ultimately dissolved because Nawaz Sharif's PML-N demanded that the dismissed judges be restored and the newly appointed judges be removed, while the PPP hoped to come first to a compromise concerning several things: the tenure of the restored judges, particularly former Chief Justice Iftikhar Chaudhry; the fate of the judges appointed after the 3 November 2007 state of emergency; and broader constitutional issues concerning the powers of the president. These issues were resolved on 22 March 2009, when Chief Justice Chaudhry was reinstated, the day after the retirement of the judge who had replaced him.

Pakistan's political path depended heavily on the personal character and thinking of the principal men involved in this crisis, rather than on the institutions they headed. The questions that were raised in the first six months after the February 2008 elections are indicative. Would the former chief justice and his strong supporters in the legal community, who had staked out a significant increase in judicial power, continue where they had left off? Was Nawaz Sharif – who in his previous term as prime minister had been willing severely to curtail judicial autonomy – truly converted to a commitment to an autonomous and powerful judiciary? Was Asif Zardari's seeming objection to the return of the pre-3 November courts simply a matter of his perception of how unjustly he felt he had been treated by them, or did it rest on a different perception of what constitutional status the judiciary should have? It remains to be seen whether the legal community, energized at least at the apex level of Supreme Court and Provincial Court bar associations, has been turned into a powerful force for a rule-of-law system, not just at the superior court level, but extending to the district level as well.

Pratap Mehta (2005: 158–60), terming the Indian judiciary a "deeply paradoxical institution," argues that the courts have accumulated great power, even managing to limit parliament's right to amend the constitution. But they have also become an "institution of governance," in effect making laws in place of parliament, pronouncing on public policy, and have even "directly taken over the supervision of executive agencies." But it also shows signs of weakness: "with the partial exception of the Supreme Court, most of the institutions of the judiciary remain in a permanent state of crisis. The complaints usually leveled against other institutions of the state – inefficiency, poor enforcement, corruption, are increasingly applied to the judiciary as well" (Mehta 2005: 160).

Much the same dual nature applies to the legal system as a whole. At the highest levels, investigative organizations like the Central Bureau of Investigation (CBI) and the senior officers of the Indian Police Service operate a system that quite frequently resists the influence and power of those it deals with who are breaking the law. On the other hand, the autonomy and integrity at the top is being called increasingly into question, and is in any case overshadowed by the pervasive culture of corrupt and ineffective enforcement of the law at state and district levels, which constrains the system as a whole from delivering timely justice with anything like reasonable frequency. One consequence is that there are large numbers of government officials – including elected representatives, some in high positions – who have sometimes dozens of criminal cases pending against them. That is only partly the result of the ease with which one's opponents can get a criminal case filed, and the near-impossibility of getting the clogged and corrupt courts at the lowest levels to process cases efficiently once they are registered. But, even if some cases are spurious, it certainly does not help the legitimacy of a democratic system if those who are making the laws are themselves perceived to be egregious law-breakers.

There is a copious literature discussing the transformation of the Indian judiciary, particularly the increasing autonomy and power of the Supreme Court, in the decades since the constitution was inaugurated in 1950.[27] There have been instances of the higher courts caving in to the government, most notably during Mrs Gandhi's Emergency. That suggests perhaps that the courts' record is not a matter of their internal strength, but rather of not having been confronted by a demand to ratify anti-democratic institutions and practices. Still, the rule of law has, on the whole, been upheld with vigor at the national level.

It is at the district level of the legal system – the state-level high courts are truly betwixt and between that level and that of the almost entirely "clean" and reasonably effective Supreme Court – where the foundations of the rule of law are, and they are at best terribly weak.[28] Perhaps that is because these institutions were among the first established by the British, and they have had a long time to decay, including during colonial rule. Going to court is very much still a way of pursuing or initiating a dispute, not of settling one (see Cohn 1959: 91, as cited in Lindsay and Gordon 1993: 369). Criminal cases are as often as not about the exercise of local power. And the system is scandalously slow and callous, with literally millions of people charged with crimes, or attempting to get justice in a civil court, spending a lifetime trying to get out of the clutches of greedy and incompetent lawyers, corrupt court officials, and indifferent (and often also corrupt) judges. Not to speak of the police.[29]

This is not to say that, from time to time, real criminals are not caught and punished or that real disputes are not brought to a close. Sometimes that even happens at a reasonable speed, and often justice is done. But it is something of a lottery: the odds of winning are low, but the hopes of winning are somehow never dashed.

The situation at the grassroots in Pakistan is not much different. According to one police investigator interviewed by Mohammad and Conway (2005: 634), "law is only for poor people. For those who are rich, have connections and other resources, there is no torture, no law. A poor person, even if he or she is innocent, has to endure the persecution of the system."[30] As Babar Sattar (2007), an elite lawyer who is writing about his own ability to deal with the administration, notes: "The law as a protector of individual rights is an alien concept to the citizenry, especially in the rural areas. They witness and endure a law that is used as a means of oppression and extortion and need their local elites as mediating agents to seek access to the law and law enforcing agencies."[31] Scholars Yasin and Shah (2004: 111–12) sound the same note, concluding that the system of justice is "a simple and workable system, but in actual practice justice continues to evade the common person. Procedural weaknesses and attitudinal trends combine to deny justice.... [T]here is a lack of equality between powerful and wealthy litigants and under-resourced litigants. Therefore the confidence in the courts is low." What seems to be different in India is that confidence in the higher judiciary remains strong. The *State of Democracy in South Asia* report (2008: 251) found that only 9 percent put a "great deal" of trust in the courts in Pakistan, compared to 27 percent in India, with 12 percent having no trust at all in India, compared to 30 percent in Pakistan. The views of "elite" and "mass" respondents differ significantly: for example, 41 percent of Pakistan's elite respondents trusted the courts "somewhat," compared to the mass respondents' 23 percent (in India, the figure was 31 percent for both mass and elite).

The quality of policing in Pakistan does not seem to differ very much from India's, and neither country has modified very much what was essentially a colonial system. The Pakistan system is neatly described in the International Crisis Group's (2008a) report, *Reforming Pakistan's Police.* In sum:

> For all the shortcomings of the Police Act of 1861, the British gave their Pakistani successors a tried and tested system of civil and criminal justice. Although that system was primarily designed to protect colonial interests, it nevertheless ensured, in large measure, law and order and a functioning criminal justice system. Pakistan retained the Police Act, but under power-hungry bureaucrats and inept rulers, both civilian and military, the criminal justice system in general and the judiciary and the police in particular went into decline, serving neither the state nor the citizen.
> (International Crisis Group 2008a: 4)

When Musharraf came to power, he "pledged to transform Pakistan's ill-disciplined, politicised and violence-prone police into an efficient, apolitical and service-oriented force. Six years after the order was passed into law in 2002, the police remain inefficient, corrupt and brutal" (International Crisis Group 2008a: 1). Ayaz Amir (2008), a very influential columnist and Member of the National Assembly (MNA), reported a particularly brazen case of the police killing someone, with a large number of witnesses, in a "[fake] encounter" incident in his constituency. That such an incident happened in a constituency represented by a prominent, upright, and outspoken MNA, who had in fact been actively involved in the selection of the supervising officer of the area, and who was likely not to succumb to pressure to keep the incident under wraps (Amir reports that an attempt was made), constitutes proof that the police are steeped in a culture of the use of unjustified and illegal violence.

Pakistani citizens apparently have a good deal of contact with the court system as such. According to the mammoth 2004 survey (some 54,000 households/respondents) conducted by CIET International (Cockroft et al. 2005: xvi–xvii; see Cockroft et al. 2003: xii), 6 percent of households had contact with the courts "in the past two years," and 56 percent of the households who had contact with the courts were satisfied with the experience. Z. K. Bhatti (2006) critiques this survey and others that disagree with the CIET findings (which also show quite positive evaluations of the police), analyzing the conceptual issues that might explain the divergence. He then adds:

> It must also be noted that even CIET news can only be considered to be good if our expectations . . . are extremely low. . . . Citizens are more likely to contact union council leaders for their legal problems than courts. When they do contact state justice machinery, service is not likely to be satisfactory. 56% of citizens were not happy with their police contact. 44% were not satisfied with their court contact. . . . Most important worry is that all categories of disadvantaged clearly have a raw deal. Citizens, if vulnerable or less educated or female, are less likely to seek police help, are less likely to have faith in courts, are less likely to initiate police contact, and are less likely to be satisfied with police contact.

As part of a larger study on the new local government system, S. R. Khan et al. (2007: 166–249) conducted a "benchmark study on law-and-order and the dispensation of justice" that is impressively comprehensive and careful. They analyze a sampling of criminal and civil cases and interview participants in villages in the four major provinces, discovering significant differences in the kinds of disputes, and some differences in the efficiency of the court system. But the general impression from the masses of descriptive data they provide is one of enormously and unnecessarily drawn out proceedings; cases pursued to establish prestige; with many ending by being abandoned, or in out-of-court and secret compromises after years of court appearances. Only 40 percent of cases "reached some resolution" (S. R. Khan et al. 2007: 235).

It is worth quoting at some length their major findings. They report that "despite the differences across the provinces, there were some common themes":

> Firstly, women across the board were the target of the informal system. . . . This is particularly the case in the practice of *karo-kari* [honor killings, a particular problem in Sindh]. Secondly, across the board, the poor shunned the police and the courts. . . . Thirdly, the rich were more likely to engage the formal system as a mark of their status, and because they could purchase justice.
>
> (S. R. Khan et al. 2007: 232–3)

This meant that:

> For the most part, the poor got rough justice [i.e. very little justice], although there were a few cases in which the poor were given lighter punishments than prescribed by the law, but only after they had been put through the grind in the court. Influentials used the courts to settle scores and the police and the courts obliged, and seemed to collude with them in harassing the poor.
>
> (S. R. Khan et al. 2007: 234)

The researchers learned from semi-structured questionnaires that "more than half [of the respondents said] that it was difficult to register a case with the police and most indicated that this was the case because police wanted a bribe. Only 7 percent thought that the police were fair and most indicated that they only went to the police when there was no alternative" (S. R. Khan et al. 2007: 233–4). The picture at the level of the "common man," then, is hardly one of a rule of law: getting justice would seem to be almost an accidental outcome.

Both India and Pakistan have had to wrestle with the extent to which religious law, particularly personal law, can be accommodated within the broader legal system.[32] In India, as the Rudolphs put it, "the opposition between legal pluralism and legal uniformity is not likely to yield a smooth progressive historical narrative in which society moves inexorably from the first to the second. Whether regarded as benign or malign, identity formation, in the form of religiously based personal law, seems to be alive and well" (Rudolph and Rudolph 2001b: 56). In the first parliament in 1947, Nehru's government introduced the Hindu Code Bill, in which "aspects of Hindu personal law – marriage, divorce, succession, inheritance, property and women's rights – were to be 'secularized'" (Austin 1999: 22), and after a great deal of political opposition it was finally passed in 1956 (see Overstreet 1970). The equivalent bill to "secularize" Muslim personal law has not been proposed, let alone passed, so a universal civil code, called for in the Directive Principles of State Policy of the Constitution, is nowhere in sight.

Indeed, the effort of the Supreme Court in 1985 in the *Shah Bano* case – to apply to Muslims the provisions of the civil code concerning the maintenance of a divorced wife – provoked a major political crisis, one that strengthened Hindu nationalist sentiment (see Jacobsohn 2003: 106–7). That in turn led, with many twists and turns, to the destruction of the Babri Masjid in December 1992, and the riots in which Muslims suffered disproportionately in the following weeks. The call for a universal civil code remains a political football. It is worth emphasizing that a common criminal code, instituted by the British, remains in force, without any politically inspired demands for change to accommodate particular religious laws. Whether the people's sovereignty and the "rule of law" is fatally compromised when certain non-universal "islands" of law are allowed to exist is an important question, debated with passion when it comes to certain issues, particularly women's rights, in present-day India.

According to I. Yilmaz (2005: 125), "modern Pakistani law, despite its constitutional commitment to observe the injunctions of Islam, operates on the basis that the state law is the only legal authority." But the state's power to shape family law is limited: "some segments of society simply refused to adhere to the law as reformed by the state" (I. Yilmaz 2005: 125). However, we need to question the common perception that local Hindu or Muslim religious leaders inevitably harm "modern" principles of individual rights by issuing religious injunctions and enforcing them.[33] Martin Lau (2006: 210) makes a striking argument that "Islam's main contribution to the legal system of Pakistan in the 1990s was its incorporation into public interest litigation and its role in the advancement of fundamental rights." And in addition, according to Lau (2006: 211):

> [The] rise in the importance of Islam [in Pakistan's legal system] is a result of judicial self-assertion rather than of deliberate governmental policies. The appropriation of Islam has amplified the power of the judiciary. Under the mantle of Islam, Pakistan's *shariat* courts have been able to circumvent virtually all constitutional mechanisms which protect legislation against judicial review.

Sounding a less positive note, Lau remarks that the "flexibility of Islamic law in the hands of Pakistan's higher judiciary" produces a problematic "legal uncertainty" that "exposes the judiciary to the risk of political bias" and affects the separation of powers (Lau 2006: 211).

The rule of law in both countries varies not only by the religious community to which it applies but also by geography. In Pakistan, the significant case (others might exist, e.g. in the Northern Areas and in Azad Kashmir) is the Federally Administered Tribal Areas (FATA).[34] There, the Frontier Crimes Regulation "authorizes tribal leaders to administer justice according to Sharia and tribal custom."[35] A recent US State Department report elaborates:

> Tribal leaders are responsible for justice in the FATA. They conduct hearings according to Islamic law and tribal custom. The accused have no right to legal representation, bail, or appeal. The usual penalties consisted of fines. Federal civil servants assigned to tribal agencies oversee proceedings and may impose prison terms of up to 14 years.[36]

There is an additional layer of justice: "Reports of religious extremists and militants forming parallel administrations, including justice administrations, in FATA increased during the year. Public executions were the most visible manifestation of this trend."[37] Informally, in the rest of Pakistan, disputes are settled using "custom" and the good offices of traditional leaders in a very large number of cases, including cases of theft, murder (and especially "honor killings"), and marital disputes (see S. R. Khan et al. 2007).

In India, the rule of law in designated "tribal" areas is also different. There is something like the FATA situation in some states in the Northeast: the sixth schedule of the constitution allows the government to permit the use of certain customary law, both criminal and personal, including constituting traditional court-like bodies. The provisions for appeal of decisions seem to fold into the regular Indian legal system.[38] Large portions of the northeastern states, and significant portions of others where scheduled tribes are concentrated, are designated "tribal areas" or "scheduled areas"[39] within which, most importantly, non-tribals are not allowed to acquire land, either from tribals or from the state, and (at least in the past) the rights of moneylenders were restricted. That provision has been applied more generally in many states, for scheduled tribe people.[40] In addition, there are areas – Kashmir and the northeastern states, most notably – where there have been decades of army quasi-rule (allowed by the Armed Forces (Special Powers) Act, 1958), including effective legal immunity (see Vajpeyi 2009: 36).

We have noted that the distortions in elections – and, it might be added here, in day-to-day government activity – that stem from corruption and from the existence and actions of wielders of social and economic and political power *ought* to be managed through the legal system. Given the capacity and record of that system, however, that is hardly a tenable hope, in either country. But do Pakistan and India differ in this? It is notable that in both countries the military in general tends to be insulated from judicial oversight, particularly in places like Kashmir, India's Northeast, and the borderlands, especially FATA, in Pakistan. Given the far more important role of the military in Pakistan, that diminishes the reach and significance of the legal system much more in Pakistan than in India. It is also true that in Pakistan the government, even in civilian periods, has not been held accountable in the courts to the extent that it has in India, and of course civilian periods are a small part of Pakistan's history. On the other hand, the impact of the 2007 lawyers' movement against the Musharraf regime suggests that the legal system can be tapped in order to change Pakistan's course in a democratic direction. Lau's argument that Islamization has given the courts a means to enhance their autonomy suggests that there is the potential for them to help guarantee a democratic system, once it is in place.

The rule of law, on balance, is significantly sturdier in India than it is in Pakistan at the highest levels of the system, but equally filled with holes at lower levels. There are ongoing attempts at legal reform in both countries, and to the extent that they are successful – and the impact of increasing ties to a globalized political economy that seems to require legal regimes of clarity and integrity might prove decisive – the virtuous-circle relationship between the rule of law and democracy should be established.

Creating and maintaining some fundamental institutions of democracy proved to be more difficult in Pakistan than in India. It was obvious that some sort of federal system would be necessary for both countries. In India, the linguistic-states demand was accepted in principle and enacted for almost the entire country relatively quickly, within a decade of independence. Far from opening the door to fragmentation and weakness, that redrawing of state boundaries has on balance probably strengthened India's unity, and thus the platform for its democracy.

In Pakistan, the federalism issue was complicated by the concurrent one of what the official language should be, and the problem of dealing with the minority Hindu community that remained, almost entirely in East Bengal. A majority of the population of Pakistan had Bengali as a mother tongue, but that majority included the Hindus, who were to be equal citizens – except that they were excluded from the office of head of state, and were kept in a separate electorate, against their wishes. Although Pakistani leaders managed to reach the federalist compromise of "parity" between East and West Wings of Pakistan and gave Bengali its appropriate status as an official language, as well as agreeing on the provisions on Islam, the process had weakened democracy fatally.

The death of Jinnah and the assassination of Liaquat had removed the only politicians capable of wielding authority over the bureaucrats. By 1953 and 1954, after rigged elections in the states of West Pakistan and the massive repudiation of the Muslim League in the Bengal election, the unelected bureaucrats Ghulam Muhammad and Iskandar Mirza, with overt support from the military, could seize power by dismissing the Constituent Assembly, obtaining judicial ratification of that step, manipulating the political leadership of the new Assembly, and finally staging a coup. The only free and fair election of this era in Pakistan, held after twelve years of military rule, resulted in the break-up of the country. That probably reduced the legitimacy of elections for the military in the 1988–99 "democracy" period, but also for Zulfiqar Ali Bhutto, whose party rigged the 1977 election, and some of whose opponents invited the military in to resolve the crisis. The press in Pakistan was not as free as India's in most of this period.

In India, a constitution was written with comparative dispatch, allowing free and fair elections, with adult suffrage (as in Pakistan), to be held on time, five years after the original Constituent Assembly members (who also sat as a parliament) had been indirectly elected. The legitimacy of the political leadership was enhanced not only by the free and fair regular elections that followed but also by the vigor of associational life and an active press. Bureaucrats certainly exercised significant power, but always under political leadership. The Supreme Court and the superior judiciary in India also established early on an autonomy that the Pakistan superior judiciary has not yet reached.

India's was hardly a consolidated democracy, given that the Congress continued to rule in Delhi until 1977, but it had been institutionalized to a significant extent, with freedoms of association, of expression, and of electoral contest put into active practice, along with a judiciary strong enough to protect them. Pakistan's democratic institutions, when they were allowed to exist, were too often window-dressing for the civil and military bureaucracy that wielded real power, unchecked by the courts. In both countries, however, there remains the issue of whether those in the offices of government, whether elected or not, are the ultimate decision-makers in the allocation or regulation of political goods. Is it not possible that those who have social and economic power are the arbiters of politics as well?

## Notes

1  See Shaikh (1989: 195–6) for a statement of how parity reflected ideas of "just" representation in pre-independence India; her argument – including her statement "parity then was not just an issue of immediate political urgency for Indian Muslims in the 1940s, but a restatement of the most authentic values of their political tradition" (Shaikh 1989: 196) – probably applies as well in undivided Pakistan.

2  Note that the judiciary in the British colonial state, and then in India's parliamentary system, is not independent of the fused legislative-executive, except for a significant autonomy slowly carved out by the Supreme Court.

3  See Neville Maxwell's famous judgment when reporting on the 1967 election: "[while Indians would soon vote in] the fourth – and surely last – general election . . . the great experiment of developing India within a democratic framework has failed" (as quoted in Guha 2005).

4  See, e.g., Shourie (1978) and Datta-Chaudhuri (1976). Also: Rudolph and Rudolph (1978), and the chapters in Hart (1975). There has been no definitive scholarly study of the Emergency. Among the more useful book-length contemporary accounts are Henderson (1977); Drieberg and Jagmohan (1975); and S. Sinha (1977). Mayer (1984) has a persuasive interpretive analysis.

5  The validity of this analysis has been strengthened, since General Musharraf, who took power *after* Wilder wrote this, followed this script almost in its entirety. One could add another item to the list: establishing a "King's Party" and rewriting rules to favor it (after which election-rigging is deployed to ensure its victory). See Wilder (2004: 103) for a table of "Electoral Strategies to Preserve the Status Quo" that brilliantly collates strategies from "rigging elections" to "creating a

malleable judiciary" to "promising but postponing and/or canceling elections," with examples from 1951 to the present. See Gilani (2008) for a discussion of the topic.

6  Waseem presents a synopsis of Pakistan's electoral experience (for which see Wilder 1999: 17–33) in the course of a discussion of how scholars differed in their styles of analysis of each set of elections. See also Waseem (2000).

7  "Massively rigged" according to the Human Rights Commission of Pakistan's Elections database, which does not cite a source. See the website: http://www.hrcpelectoralwatch.org/his_persp.cfm; accessed 25 May 2007. Choudhury (1974: 106–7), drawing on "a report" of the Electoral Reform Commission, confirms at least that the allegation of rigging was detailed and widespread. Palmer (1975: 181, 322 n. 5) cites *Gazette of Pakistan (Extraordinary)*, 24 April 1956, p. 922, as the source of the sentence "It was widely and persistently complained that these elections were a farce, a mockery and a fraud upon the electorate." See K. K. Aziz (1976: 71) for the critique in greater detail, but without that sentence.

8  See Mujahid (1980) for some detailed evidence of rigging, and also the *White Paper on the Conduct of the General Elections in March 1977* issued by the Government of Pakistan in 1978.

9  See the report of the National Democratic Institute team, concluding that the elections were conducted in a "relatively fair and orderly manner" (executive summary); available at: http://www.accessdemocracy.org/library/228_pk_foundation_1_1_29.pdf; accessed 26 May 2007.

10  See the report of the NDI on the 1990 election; available at: http://www.accessdemocracy.org/library/227_pk_elections90_9_105_117.pdf; accessed 26 May 2007.

11  See the European Union Observer Mission's report; available at: http://ec.europa.eu/external_relations/human_rights/eu_election_ass_observ/pak/finalreport02.pdf; accessed 26 May 2007. See also: Wilder (2004); International Crisis Group (2007b); Waseem et al. (2006); Waseem (2007b).

12  See Jalal (1999 [1990]: 145). Palmer (1975: 179) notes that the Objectives Resolution, "adopted by the Assembly in March 1949, seemed to indicate [that there would be] representative national and provincial Assemblies elected by the people on the basis of adult suffrage."

13  Where irregularities have been proved, the Election Commission "countermands" the poll, and holds a repoll some weeks later. Those repolls apparently work – though they are almost never reported in the press – and, in any case, the percentage of affected polling stations is very low.

14  There is an enormous literature. For India, the basic works include: Weiner (1957); Manor (1988); Sridharan (2002a and 2002b); Yadav and Palshikar (2003). For Pakistan, see K. K. Aziz (1976); Wilder (1999); International Crisis Group (2005).

15  For general overviews, see Sonwalkar (2001: 747–52); Ram (2000); R. Jeffrey (2000); and Swami (2009). The phenomenal increase in the importance of the Hindi press is wonderfully analyzed by Sevanti Ninan (2007). For an interesting case study, see Ståhlberg (2002). It is something of a mystery that press freedom as a separate topic is not discussed in the general surveys of either Indian or Pakistani politics. For up-to-date assessments, see the Reporters Without Borders website: http://www.rsf.org/article.php3?id_article=20785 and the annual Freedom House publication *Freedom of the Press* (in the 2008 edition, India's press is still labeled "Partly Free" and Pakistan's "Not Free").

16  Niazi has published sequels: *The Press under Siege* (1992); *The Web of Censorship* (1994).

17  Freedom House, *Freedom of the Press* [2009]; available at: http://www.freedomhouse.org/template.cfm?page=251&year=2009; accessed 17 December 2009.

18 Some of the television operations agreed to the code of conduct – e.g., GEO and ARY – and were allowed to return, though with the very significant live news interview programs not allowed.

19 Available at: http://www.dawn.com/events/appendix/index.htm; accessed 26 May 2007.

20 Available at: http://www.rsf.org/article.php3?id_article=20794; accessed 13 September 2009.

21 *Annual Report 2008*; http://www.rsf.org/article.php3?id_article=25678; accessed 7 May 2008.

22 Available at: http://www.rsf.org/en-rapport74-Pakistan.html; accessed 13 September 2009.

23 *Developing Indicators to Measure the Rule of Law: A Global Approach*, p. 3 [p. 44 of the encompassing document: *Rule of Law Index* (Vienna: World Justice Forum, 2–5 July 2008; available at: http://www.lexisnexis.com/documents/pdf/20080828015427_large.pdf ; accessed 12 March 2009).

24 See also International Crisis Group (2004b); Islam (2001): 1340–2.

25 The Supreme Court judgment (650 printed pages) provides the details of the case; see *All Pakistan Legal Decisions* Vol. XXXI (February 1971).

26 For a concise and balanced discussion, see Taseer (1980: 186 ff.), who reports interviews with senior PPP leaders, and says that "doubt was often expressed of the legal cases against [Bhutto] although his involvement in similar activities [i.e., crimes committed by the Federal Security Force] was accepted" (Taseer 1980: 188).

27 *Inter alia* Austin (1999); Dhavan (2000); Rudolph and Rudolph (1987: 103–26); Rudolph and Rudolph (2001a); Z. Hasan et al. (2002); Dhavan (2003); Mehta (2005).

28 There are far too few careful studies of the judicial system at that level. See Moog (1997); Mendelsohn (1981). For a hundred-year-old satirical account of "a law suit" that suggests that not much has changed, see Pritchard (1900?).

29 For an account that presents paradigmatic cases, see Vasudha Dhagamwar (2006: 267–97), a chapter titled " 'Prisoner at the Bar: Are You Rich or Poor?' ". For an overview of the history and current practices (and thoughtful suggestions for remedies), see Human Rights Watch (2009).

30 Although this article is based on extensive interviewing and observation, it may not accurately describe the situation outside the North-West Frontier Province. For other recent essays, also having a fairly narrow focus, see S. S. Ali (1999) and Baxi et al. (2006).

31 See Z. K. Bhatti (2006) for a careful analysis of various surveys on police–citizen interaction and Pakistan's justice system more generally.

32 See *inter alia*: Kennedy (1990); Kozlowski (1995, 1997); Larson (2001); Jacobsohn (2003); I. Yilmaz (2005); Lau (2006).

33 As Kozlowski (1995: 927) notes in his careful study of the decisions of a *mufti* in Hyderabad in India: "Looking at such a situation reveals that shariah has obviously changed, adapted itself to new social, political and economic circumstances while maintaining its independence from the state."

34 See Madsen (1996: ch. IV, "Autonomy, Democracy and the Rule of Law: Human Rights in 'Intergenerational' Conflict in the Tribal Areas of Pakistan"); S. S. Ali (1999); and S. S. Ali and Rehman (2001).

35 Freedom House, *Freedom in the World 2007: Pakistan*; available at: http://www.freedomhouse.org/template.cfm?page=22&year=2007&country=7247; accessed 4 June 2008. This is not confined to FATA, however; according to Freedom House:

> Feudal landlords and tribal elders throughout Pakistan adjudicate some disputes and impose punishments, including the death penalty or the forced exchange of brides between tribes, in unsanctioned parallel courts called

*jirgas*. In April 2004, responding to growing concern over the potential for abuse inherent in this practice, the Sindh High Court issued a ruling that banned all trials conducted under the jirga system in the province. However, such judgments continue to take place.

36 US Department of State, *Country Reports on Human Rights Practices – 2007: Pakistan*; available at: http://www.state.gov/g/drl/rls/hrrpt/2007/100619.htm; accessed 4 June 2008. See also International Crisis Group (2006): 7–9.
37 US Department of State, *Country Reports on Human Rights Practices – 2007: Pakistan*; available at: http://www.state.gov/g/drl/rls/hrrpt/2007/100619.htm; accessed 4 June 2008.
38 I have not been able to find up-to-date sources on just what the practices are; the closest is S. K. Ghosh (1987: 138 ff.)
39 For states in the sixth and fifth schedules of the constitution. See the Ministry of Tribal Affairs website for a link to listings, by state, of the specific areas: http://tribal.nic.in/index1.html.
40 According to the report of the Delhi-based Asian Indigenous and Tribal Peoples Network, *The State of India's Indigenous and Tribal Peoples 2008*. Available online at: http://www.aitpn.org/Reports/Tribal_Report2008.pdf; accessed May 24, 2010, these provisions have been "ineffective" (p. 17). See McMillan (2005: 110–30) for a concise description of colonial and nationalist policies on scheduled tribes.

# 5 Who (really) governs?

The question of "who (really) governs?" implies that the Pakistan and Indian governments are simply façades for a power structure that exists in the economy, in society, or, indeed, outside the country's borders. The centrality of this question comes from the definition of democracy that includes the requirement that there be no significant veto power over the citizen *qua* voter, that the citizens are not puppets, with their decisions countermanded by non-elected wielders of power. A typical expression of this appeared in the weekly column of the respected Pakistani Member of the National Assembly, Ayaz Amir (2009):

> Politicians in Pakistan live under a great illusion. They think they run the country when actually they do nothing of the kind. More than even the red-stripe wearers in General Headquarters, it is the captains of industry, commerce, banking and real estate who run things from behind the scenes and wield real power. Politicians represent the face of things. The string-pullers are different.

This is a matter of degree. To be sure, certain interest groups and local "big men" exercise a disproportionate amount of influence and even power: there is, on the ground, no real "equality" of citizens on election day, except in principle.[1] But does that make democracy into a sham? Again, it depends on one's standards: in a strict interpretation, there are no existing democracies, only polyarchies, and even those are weakly representative and accountable. But we can attempt to compare India and Pakistan on the dimension of the extent to which those extra-state actors and institutions determine what the government does. I shall leave the discussion of whether forces outside the borders – countries, international regimes, etc. – decisively or marginally influence the difference of regime until later, in Chapter 9. It is safe to say, however, that no external power has exercised a veto over the regime-defining choices made in either country.

At the other extreme, the micro-levels of village and neighborhood (and occasionally in slightly larger territories), there are cases of a singular "ruling class" and, in particular, a local "big man" whose word is law, whose interests govern how policy is implemented. From a different angle, one can see sectors of interests and issues in which particular societal institutions not sanctioned by the state – some religious societies, for example – exercise significant political authority, and not just over willing followers.

We are looking here for differences between India and Pakistan in this regard. It is not easy, however, to find the evidence, especially when we realize that a great deal of power in unambiguously democratic systems is wielded by unelected party officials, campaign finance donors, religious leaders, and many others. Perhaps the best way would be to analyze critical political decisions, in order to discover just who influenced them, and how much. Such studies do not exist in either country. We do have some evidence on whether voters cast their ballot according to what others tell them (their husband, for example). The organization of my discussion below points to an additional problem: politics in both countries is meaningful at local, provincial, and national levels, and it is not at all clear just how the various structures of power relate to each other across those levels. The results of our investigation will thus be at best inconclusive, but I hope that the analysis will at least enrich our understanding of the question itself.

## Ruling classes in the country and at the provincial level

The prime candidate for a "real" ruler, a power behind the throne, is a ruling class. It is hardly surprising in countries as large as India and Pakistan that there is no unitary "class structure" in either country, and there is no proof that classes "for themselves" exist. There are certainly economic and social categories that we can call classes, but by and large there is very little class consciousness (see Rudolph and Rudolph 1980: 161). Indeed, the pattern is one of fragmentation and cross-class linkages, with patron–client relationships the most prominent. These make it impossible to argue that at the macro-level of the country as a whole – and probably also at the provincial level, and even generally at the district level – at any given moment, on any particular issue, let alone consistently and continually, "a" class, or its "leadership" has exercised rule.

In considering the balance of power between the state apparatus and the political leadership, we must of course understand the roots of the power bureaucrats have. In a pure Weberian rational-legal state, compliance is the result of a system of rules; and officials, appointed and promoted on the basis of merit and expertise, enforce those rules. Those to whom the rules apply see them as legitimate. And the power of the state apparatus derives only from the political process, ultimately exercised by those in power in a democracy – the representatives of the people. In a neo-patrimonial state, of the sort Christopher Clapham (1986) sees as typical of the Third World, there is a blending of the legal-rational with the patrimonial, and compliance comes from a greater dose of coercive and charismatic power. Again, patron–client relationships assume great importance. Autocratic regimes can encompass both kinds of state, and the state apparatus has alternate sources of power. (We are not considering one-party autocratic regimes, or theocratic regimes, or monarchies, or personal dictatorships, since none of those types fit, or is likely to fit, the India and Pakistan cases.)

For India and Pakistan at the macro-level, we would need to analyze *the extent to which* a number of things are true about the links of non-state groups to those in political leadership, and the civilian and military bureaucracies. I suggest a non-exhaustive list:

- *The extent to which* the military/bureaucracy is a social/economic extension of a particular category of people from which it takes direction or from which it draws support;
- *The extent to which* the bureaucracy and the military constitute something of a "state-apparatus class," significantly autonomous from the political system (and its "state class") to allow it to dominate the political wing;
- *The extent to which* the democratically elected leadership takes direction from, or draws support from, a very narrow base of economic and/or social institutions, to whom it caters;
- *The extent to which* the "classes" (categories) that direct/support the military/bureaucracy overlap with those that direct/support the politicians;
- *The extent to which* the bureaucracy/military take direction, or draw support, vis-à-vis the political wing, from external institutions/countries.

There is, as far as I can tell, no agreement on the deep description of either India's or Pakistan's political economy in general that would allow us to make those fine-grained judgments. Our problem is even more complex: in both countries we really should be talking about "political economies" in the plural – still at the macro-level – typically focusing on regions that may or may not be congruent with juridical (provincial, divisional) boundaries.[2] Within each province-state, we need to consider segments of the state apparatus, particularly the bureaucracy and the range of paramilitary forces, armed constabulary, and ordinary police. At an even "lower" level, we need to pay attention to how politics and economic and social power are connected in the village and other places small enough to allow most participants to know each other as people rather than as unnamed types of people, or as someone in a named role.

### India

There are, to be sure, bold statements that suggest that political systems of both India and Pakistan are simply the window-dressing for a hidden system of social or economic dominance. For example, in Harry Blair's summary (1980: 259) of what happened in the Emergency in India, according to a class analysis: "the pluralistic veneer of parliamentary democracy stripped away, leaving the underlying reality of elite class dominance." Blair presents his model as a rough analytic framework drawing on the work of a number of authors, mainly Marxists, with many problems he himself discusses. Blair's model has "dominant" classes: landlords, the national bourgeoisie (large capitalists), and "professional elites" (civil service, military, and intelligentsia). He also makes note of "intermediate classes" – small farmers, perhaps the industrial proletariat, the petty bourgeoisie, and government and white-collar workers – and "inferior" classes: landless agricultural workers, perhaps the industrial proletariat, and the urban "lumpenproletariat" (see Blair 1980: 246).

Pranab Bardhan (1984), in a widely accepted formulation, speaks of "three dominant proprietary classes": the industrial bourgeoisie, the rich farmers, and "the professionals [in the public sector] (both civilian and military), including white-collar workers" (Bardhan 1984: 51). Bardhan recognizes that these are "classes" in the plural, distinguishing India from "most advanced capitalist countries where the dominant class [note the singular] is somewhat more homogenous" (Bardhan 1984: 60).[3] He discusses the conflicts among them, arising from differing interests (speaking of "the plurality of proprietary classes with multiple veto powers) in the dominant coalition in India" (Bardhan 1984: 73), and argues that "While the autonomous power of the state can clearly increase if none of the classes constraining state action dominates the others, the Indian experience suggests that the very nature of class balance and heterogeneity may also make the proprietary classes more interested in the maintenance of democratic processes" (Bardhan 1984: 75–6). Having outlined the many ways in which those processes have worked, and allowed popular ferment and assertion, he says in his concluding paragraph: "it is possible that the dominant coalition may . . . find it prudent to make substantial sacrifices in striking downward alliances with some of the subordinate classes and restore the ability of the system to compromise and muddle through" (Bardhan 1984: 83). Yet somehow there is something called "the" dominant coalition, acting as a person ("find it prudent") to deal with other person-like entities ("the subordinate classes") which he himself recognizes to be internally highly fractured, and far from even groups with corporate coherence.

Paul Brass (1990: 272–6) provides a succinct critique of Bardhan, looking at each "proprietary" class. He argues that "in other words, businessmen as a class have relatively little influence over the direction of economic policy, but individual businessmen and business houses may nevertheless prosper in India's 'mixed economy' by influencing the implementation of government regulations" (pp. 273–4). Brass claims that it is only the "professional bureaucrats" who wield "effective power" in India (p. 274), and that "the broader professional and urban classes constitute a 'ruling class' in Mosca's sense of the term rather than Marx's, in that they constitute the source for recruitment of the administrative groups" (pp. 274–5). Finally, he says, "Bardhan's analysis of the class hegemony of the rural rich farmers is somewhat oversimplified" (p. 275), in part because "as early as the early 1960s

. . . the class of middle and upper peasantry had become dominant in most state governments" and that "it seems strange . . . to include as members of a dominant ruling coalition in the country as a whole a class that acts primarily as a constraining, restraining and frustrating force against the implementation of Government of India policies at the state level" (p. 276). In sum "rich farmers . . . like big industrialists and businessmen, operate effectively within and gain benefits and privileges from a system they do not like and which does *not* [Brass's emphasis] serve their class interests . . ." (p. 276).[4]

Focusing on the industrial sector, the Rudolphs state flatly that "India . . . has no national classes" (Rudolph and Rudolph 1980: 161), and explain that "the domination of the means and relations of production by state capitalism in the organized sector severely limits the objective conditions for industrial and financial capitalism in India to become a conscious, organized force in politics" (Rudolph and Rudolph 1980: 164). Although Vanaik (1985: 60) writes of "the ruling class bloc" (consisting of "different factions and sections of industrial capital, agrarian and industrial bourgeoisie" with a "petty bourgeois mass base"), in the analysis that follows, these categories do not figure as such in the description of India's mid-1980s political economy. In more recent work, even that which explicitly embraces class analysis (e.g., Corbridge and Harriss 2000), terms like "elites" replace "ruling class." For Leela Fernandes and Patrick Heller the "hegemonic" New Middle Class (NMC) does not seem to act on politics in that sort of way: "we contend that the contours of the NMC can be grasped only as a *class-in-practice*, that is, as a class defined by its politics and the everyday practices through which it reproduces its privileged position" (Fernandes and Heller 2006: 497; their emphasis).

In India taken as a whole it seems clear that socially and economically powerful groups and individuals outside government deal with a powerful state with various strategies, most of them hidden. They develop financial and other links with parties and particular politicians crucial in making policies that affect their interests, and with bureaucrats who implement the programs that emerge. They also form old-fashioned interest associations – such as the Federation of Indian Chambers of Commerce and Industry, and the Confederation of Indian Industry – that put public pressure on the government, and work to shape public opinion through the media. There is no explicit alliance of these people, companies, and groups with powerful interests in the agrarian sector, except perhaps for a handful of firms that operate in the agro-industrial sector, such as sugarmill-owning companies. Indeed, agrarian interests powerful in state and local arenas are almost entirely absent from the national arena, except for the occasional farmers' march on Delhi, so to label them as part of a "ruling coalition" seems problematic.

It is also hard to see even the professional bureaucrats as a "ruling class" (let alone, as Brass suggests, the broader intelligentsia), even though those who serve parliament and the ministries clearly help shape policies. They certainly can use their network of classmates and civil service batchmates and officers they have served, or who have served under them, to supplement their official lines of command, allowing them, sometimes, to get things done with a nation-wide reach. But it is rare that the bureaucrat consistently holds the upper hand in the relationship between the professional bureaucrat and the elected politician. That is as much a partnership or a tussle for control. And the professionals of the other significant segments of a largely autonomous state – the uniformed military and the courts – do not explicitly act in concert with their brethren in the rest of the government. While it is true that it is hard to imagine the Indian state seriously threatening the institution of private property, or even the core interests of the very wealthy, that does not mean that the category of the "propertied" is anything more than a loose collection of individuals and groups with (largely) overlapping interests. It is not a "dominant coalition" of (self-aware) classes that act coherently to preserve and exercise their power, let alone a coalition of three apex "classes."

In between the village level and Delhi, so to speak, there are provinces (states).[5] The level immediately "above" the village and other face-to-face localities (places where everyone knows the name of everyone else) is the arena of the "big men" and other intermediaries between ordinary citizens and the state. The state is continuously present in localities typically only in the person of the schoolteacher and a few other government functionaries, and perhaps in the person of the *pradhan* (headman). Those intermediaries include lawyers, low-level political party workers, NGO activists, and the *naya netas* ("new leaders") Krishna (2002) has identified. Many of these are marked by their ethnic identity, although there are links that are more class-like, such as those with school classmates or with co-workers. Those active at this level are almost always men.

In the more local part of this arena, there is certainly a *category* of influential or powerful men who operate in this intermediate arena, serving as MLAs, as chairs of municipal committees or senior leaders of major city government, as powerful leaders in district and block-level *panchayati raj* institutions, and in the associated party structures. Some are leaders of gangs, if not of "mafias" (a word that has been adopted in the English press, at least). Others have a base in business or other organized interest groups. I suspect that the crucial locales where these leaders most commonly meet are, during the day, in and around the district government offices, especially the courts, and, in the evening, at private functions of fellow notables, such as weddings (see Michelutti 2008). While there are undoubtedly certain markers these notables share – they would tend to come from certain castes, and be linked to the more significant economic enterprises of the area, for example – it is hard to see them as constituting a "class" in any empirically valid sense of the term. We can reject K. Balagopal's label, but accept the validity of his description of this category:

A typical family of this provincial propertied class has a landholding in its native village, cultivated by hired labour, bataidars [sharecroppers], tenants or farm-servants and supervised by the father or one son; business of various descriptions in towns – trade, finance, hotels, cinemas and contracts – managed by other sons; and perhaps a young and bright child who is a doctor or engineer or maybe even a professor at one of the small town universities that have sprouted all over the country during the last two decades.

(Balagopal 1987: 1545)

A crucial point here is the blurring of the "rural–urban" divide, which has only increased in the two decades since Balagopal wrote, as road and rail and telecommunication infrastructure has continued to make physical movement and information-flow easier and easier.[6] Impressionistically, we see institutions of democratic government playing a minor role in providing public services or even holding officials accountable, let alone in shaping private activity. Government bureaucrats are more significant, though the impact of corruption might in fact enhance the reach of the otherwise powerless. It is fair to say, though, that it is only rarely that a named group (let alone "class") "rules" in these places. Politicians, who maybe represent their social and economic group as much as they do their constituents more generally, but are none the less committed to a democratic political society, are very much in evidence as players in the game of power.

At the other end of this space between Delhi and a face-to-face locality lie the institutions of government of the state, typically concentrated in the state capital (see Jenkins 2004; A. Sinha 2005; Yadav and Palshikar 2008). To what extent are the democratically elected representatives, of legislative assembly and state government cabinet, actually making crucial political decisions? Leaving aside the important question of the extent to which they act at the behest of national-level party or other leaders, to what extent are they frontmen for a category of (real) rulers – a coalition of dominant castes, for instance, or what Sanjaya Baru (2000) calls a "regional capitalist class"?

Francine Frankel, in the conclusion of the comprehensive two-volume work she edited with M. S. A. Rao on *Dominance and State Power in India*, argues that

neither [Marxist nor behavioral approaches] can deal with the special complexities created by modern Indian history of the different historical origins, social composition and policy orientations of the public and political institutions [the institutions of the state largely inherited from British rule, and the political institutions of post-1950 parliamentary rule respectively]. It is the complexities specific to the Indian experience which made these institutions competitive with each other, and transformed them into *arenas of conflict* [her emphasis] between upper caste and middle class groups determined to protect their social and economic privileges, and lower castes and poorer classes aspiring to share in or overturn them.

(Frankel and Rao 1989–90: II, 500–1)

None of the chapters on specific states – eleven of the major ones are analyzed – suggests that there is any caste or class group that translates even the limited social and/or economic dominance of a specific region of the state into political power that goes unchallenged or has lasted very long, especially in the recent past. Oliver Mendelsohn (1993: 840 and passim) has indeed argued persuasively that "dominant castes" are "disintegrating" under the impact of a whole set of political, economic, and social changes.

Sanjaya Baru (2000: 223) sees the emergence in many states of a "regional capitalist class," one that has "agrarian origins and agrarian roots." Members of that class have "invested in regional political parties to gain political support at the state level and entered into collaborations with foreign investors to gain market leverage over national big business" (Baru 2000: 223), so "the link between the emergence of regional capitalism and regional parties is too stark to be ignored" (Baru 2000: 226). These classes may well overlap with the "dominant [intermediate] castes" that clearly contribute to the newly powerful state-based parties. In the case of Andhra, Baru speaks of "Kamma capitalists" dominating the Telugu Desam Party (TDP), and suggests that in Tamil Nadu many of the new regional capitalist class "come from intermediate and backward castes" and support the Dravidian parties (Baru 2000: 221–2). But detailed empirical evidence that substantiates the power and reach of such classes is not presented, even for Andhra.

Yogendra Yadav and Suhas Palshikar (2008: 20–1) lay out the case for their seventh (of ten) theses on state politics, and conclude:

if one was looking for evidence for the famous quip that governments are nothing but the executive arms of the capitalist class, many states in contemporary India would fit the bill. . . . As state politics gains greater autonomy vis-à-vis national politics and the central government, its capacity to resist corporate and other organized interests appears severely eroded, often producing regimes that act as the agents of dominant classes.

(Yadav and Palshikar 2008: 21)

Although Yadav and Palshikar name a few states in which this is done "brazenly," there is, again, no reference to detailed empirical work that would establish the validity of this thesis. And "classes," let alone "dominant" ones, do not appear as significant political players in the analyses of important scholars writing in one of the few works in which state politics is systematically compared (Jenkins 2004).

While there is no doubt that newly powerful political groupings can be characterized by economic and social background, there do not seem to be powerful caste leaders who are not themselves politicians holding party or elected office. Regional capitalists, on the other hand, do not often become directly involved in politics, but no individual (or business house) controls even a party, let alone a government.

## Pakistan

Hamza Alavi (1972) has provided a seminal account of the post-colonial state, with Pakistan as the paradigmatic case. Since so many have indeed relied on his analysis, Alavi's argument is best presented in his own words. For Alavi (1972: 61), the "metropolitan bourgeoisie" that imposes colonial rule, in addition to replicating "the superstructure of the state which it had established in the metropolitan country itself,"

> has to create state apparatus through which it can exercise dominion over *all* [emphasis in the original] the indigenous social classes in the colony. [That state apparatus is] "over-developed" in relation to the "structure" in the colony. . . . The colonial state is therefore equipped with a powerful bureaucratic–military apparatus and mechanisms of government which enable it through its routine operations to subordinate the native social classes. The post-colonial society inherits that overdeveloped apparatus of state. . . . At the moment of independence weak indigenous bourgeoisies find themselves enmeshed in bureaucratic controls by which those at the top of the hierarchy of the bureaucratic–military apparatus of the state are able to maintain and even extend their dominant power in society, being freed from direct metropolitan control.

The state apparatus, in Alavi's (1972: 62) definition, "does not . . . consist only of the bureaucratic–military oligarchy. Where democratic forms of government operate, politicians and political parties too form a part of it." Alavi's (1972: 62) "central proposition" is that

> The state . . . is not the instrument of a single class. It is relatively autonomous and it mediates between the competing interests of the three propertied classes, namely the metropolitan bourgeoisies, the indigenous bourgeoisie and the landed classes, while at the same time acting on behalf of them all to preserve the social order in which their interests are embedded, namely the institution of private property and the capitalist mode as the dominant mode of production.

This relative autonomy of the state is under-girded by its economic resource base. Ayesha Jalal (1999 [1990]: 295) argues for the importance of the international connection:

> With decision-making firmly in the hands of a ruling alliance drawn mainly from the top echelons of the bureaucracy and the army, although

loosely tied to dominant classes and interest groups, there was an obvious equation between the actual wielding of state authority and the structures of economic power and social control. Consequently, the relative autonomy of the Pakistani state from the internal class structure came to rest in large part on the closely nurtured connections of its senior state officials – civil and military – with the centres of the international capitalist system.

The assertion that the state's relative autonomy "in large part" rested on international links is not convincingly supported.

The state in Pakistan has, much more than in India, a "rentier" character. The rentier-state perspective and argument says that the more the state can draw on resources other than those extracted from its own people, the more it can provide security and development *without* making itself accountable to taxpayers. This gives autocratic regimes more staying power.[7] Rentier states draw their resources from things like oil exports, or from remittances, or military and other foreign aid if the country is of great strategic importance. Such states float above their own society, as it were, drawing sustenance not from the populace, but from outside the country. If the ordinary citizen is not taxed at all (as in the oil-rich states of the Gulf at some points in time), then demands from below for accountability of the government, let alone representation in it, are likely to be weak. Even in an economy that is not overwhelmingly dependent on rents charged to outsiders, like Pakistan's or India's, indirect taxes that are levied almost invisibly can serve the same purpose.[8] Even if demands from below emerge, they are unlikely to succeed against a strong fortress state controlled by a unified and developed military, as in Pakistan. If the military continues to exercise substantial control over Pakistan, as seems likely, it is improbable that organizations in civil society, or even political parties, will be able to expand their power vis-à-vis the state (see Candland 2007b).

Indeed, the major challenge to the military–bureaucratic rule of Pakistan's first twenty-five years came not from indigenous propertied classes, nor from any popular upsurge based on some sort of "no taxation without representation" demand, but from regionally based political movements. A notable feature of the politics of Pakistan then – and of the provinces before 1971 that became present-day Pakistan – and continuing to the present is that most major political leaders come from the elite classes, especially the rural land-owning elite. When in government they have certainly protected and advanced the interests of their immediate relatives and associates, but there is no evidence that they are dependent on non-politician members of the elite, organized or unorganized. Even when Z. A. Bhutto came to power in the name of the poor, with the slogan "Bread, clothing, shelter," the promise of the eradication of "feudalism" through land reform was not kept, and the nationalization of industries did not survive long.[9] Alavi (1983: 89) argues that Bhutto's ultimate downfall in 1977 came when he made "the fatal mistake [of alienating] also the most powerful class in which he had established a base, the landowners," when he nationalized "the agro-processing industries, namely cotton ginning, flour milling and rice husking." He goes on to describe (unfortunately without providing empirical detail) the power of those hurt by the nationalization:

> Cotton ginning mills, flour mills and rice husking mills are, in the main, owned by [a] section of landowners who, since the exodus of the Hindu trading classes in 1947, have also established themselves as the main traders in agricultural commodities in *mandis*, or local markets at the district and sub-district levels. The *mandi* organization is an extremely powerful and effective network that extends all over the country and its tentacles reach out into every village and town.
>
> (Alavi 1983: 89)

Other sections of the landlord class have also been changing. Ayaz Amir (1996), in an opinion column reprinted approvingly by S. Akbar Zaidi (2005a: 24–5) in his magisterial work on Pakistan's economy, argues that "feudalism" in Pakistan is a "waning force," with only a few areas left where the great landlords survive, so that "feudals" – the inheritors of smaller and smaller tracts of land – depend on political parties to become elected rather than the other way round.

The more likely explanation of the congruence of provincial policies and elite class interests continues to be the class composition of the bureaucracy and the military and, in their brief periods of influence, elected politicians. The "establishment" can tolerate and protect political leaders who join parties, make speeches, and stand for election. And the leaders can count on reasonably decent treatment when the plug is pulled on democracy, although some of those jailed – which does not happen often – have been handled roughly. With the exception of leaders of the Islamic parties, the Muttahida Qaumi Movement (MQM), and the more traditional "tribal" leaders of Balochistan, most of the politically active form an "intimate elite,"[10] which helps explain the movement in and out of the cabinets of military presidents, and relationships that bridge ideological differences. It may be that the emergence of the lawyers as shock troops in the demonstrations against General Musharraf, in the aftermath of his clumsy sacking of the chief justice in March 2007, heralds a new role for an educated middle class that has helped create modern industry along with retaining its role in the state, media, and higher education. But it is still just a small part of the elite, and not very significant in politics.

It is hard to analyze patterns of power at the provincial level in Pakistan. A striking feature about the Pakistani press coverage of politics is how rarely provincial politics features. That is, there are plenty of stories of political events that happen in one province or the other, or in Lahore or in Peshawar or in Karachi, but reports on provincial political party alliances or policy initiatives by provincial governments seem much less common than they are in India. This raises the question of just what sort of systematic politics is significant in each province, including the social and economic linkages of leaders and parties. There seem to be few in-depth scholarly analyses of provincial politics in Pakistan (one is White 2008b), even in Katherine Adeney's recent book on federalism in India and Pakistan (Adeney 2007).

My suspicion is that, although there is undoubtedly interesting and significant politics going on in the provincial arena in Pakistan, it is probably closely controlled by the government of Pakistan, taking its character largely from the bureaucratic–military command-state experience of most of Pakistan's history, in which the autonomy of the province-level arenas was often undermined. In the provinces other than the Punjab, Islamabad would need only the army and the bureaucracy to guide or control political activity – political-party- and civil-society-led opposition is fairly easily controlled or if necessary crushed in most areas (FATA being the exception). The Punjab is potentially in a different class, given its size and centrality; the bureaucratic–military partnership needs to play politics there. One indication of this is that the military, making use of the Directorate for Inter-Services Intelligence (ISI), saw fit to create the IJI, a party alliance led by Nawaz Sharif, to contest the 1988 election. The idea was to deny Benazir Bhutto her expected victory nationally by opposing the PPP in the Punjab. According to Vali Nasr (1992: 526): "[The] PPP failed to wrest control of Punjab, the country's largest and most populous province, from the IJI. The inability to win Punjab, crucial to the stability of any government, it can be argued, sealed Benazir's fate then and there."

Ian Talbot (1999: 294) notes the importance of "*biraderi* [clan], tribal and *piri–muridi* [saint–disciple] allegiances in political mobilization" in Punjab, and that "in Lahore itself rivalries between Kashmiris and Arains lay beneath party rivalries." Talbot (1999: 294) also points to family rivalries and patronage, which "has always been the stuff of Punjab politics." This continues to be true: consider the role of the Chaudhrys of Gujrat under Musharraf's regime. My impression is, however, that there is a personalist, patronage-based system in the Punjab as well as in the other provinces, and the patterns of cooperation and competition are rooted in class and community identities, but without much in the way of formal organization. The parties that emerge are tools of those interests, with only a thin veneer of ideological difference – with the major exception, of course, of the Islamist parties. This neo-patrimonial pattern at the provincial level can work with both autocratic and democratic systems at the national level, but is more likely to undermine the legitimacy of a democratic than an autocratic regime.

## Ruling classes in local arenas

In local arenas in India – at the "village" level particularly[11] – there are often dominant groups, mainly labeled with a caste name, with the power and will to make democratic institutions and processes something of a joke (see C. Jeffrey 2000). Yet there are also important examples of cooperative action in the "traditional" village (see Wade 1988 for a particularly insightful description of managing irrigation). There are undoubtedly other villages where democratic processes, especially elections, have broken the power of the dominant castes; and, though the consequent empowerment of the marginalized may not be great, or according to fixed rules, it is significant (see Chakravarti 1975; M. Robinson 1988; Krishna 2002). In my own research sites – in the old city of Delhi, where I studied municipal government, and in the villages of Western UP, where I studied land consolidation (Oldenburg 1976, 1990) – and in a few more recent trips into the north Indian countryside (in 1991–2 and 1998), I found situations in which powerful propertied interests were successfully challenged through the democratic political system in order to gain significant benefits, albeit not to the point of seriously modifying the socio-economic power structure of that area. From their superb study of governance in districts of Bihar, Jharkhand, and West Bengal, Corbridge et al. (2005: 198) are able to say that "political society has diversified and even democratized from its previously narrow base."

There have been comparatively few recent, detailed studies of how politics works in the establishment (i.e. non-NGO) sector at the grassroots, still less in cities and towns. No village, no cluster of villages, no town and no city is representative of India as a whole, or even of the immediate region of which it is a part. Just how many such localities in India, and what percentage of ordinary citizens, could be said to have a façade of democratic institutions as their government in daily life is probably impossible to discover, or even to guess at. On the other hand, it is probably true that whatever power elite exists locally does not determine election results – otherwise it would have been impossible, for example, for the BSP to come to power in UP in 2007.

We do not have positive evidence of, say, a preponderance of a day-to-day working democracy in the countryside, or in city and town neighborhoods. We can be skeptical about how democratic even the new institutions of local self-government are – especially since the provisions of the constitutional amendments entrenching them that require significant transfer of financial resources to such bodies have not been implemented, except in one or two states (see G. Kumar 2006). Yet there are studies of *panchayati raj* in practice that point to the genuine empowerment of at least significant numbers of citizens, including many of the women elected to reserved seats. There is also evidence that in state and national elections the majority of voters cast ballots without interference, and (according to surveys) without relying entirely on the advice – let alone the command – of husbands, caste elders, and the like.

On the other side of the ledger, it seems clear that the modal pattern of social, political, and economic power at the grassroots is one of fragmentation, countervailing pressures, and cross-cutting cleavages. Elite and powerful men mobilize dependent workers with benefits and not just threats in order to confront other elite and powerful men – who are not infrequently their brothers or fathers or other kin. That happens more often than joining in an alliance of landlords to suppress the demands of those beneath them. Citizens, even the desperately poor, often maneuver and manipulate those in power over them, these days making full use of the formal political arena. If things get really bad, they leave.

The middle segment of the rural population has grown over the last fifty or so years, as measured by their share of operational holdings area.[12] Possibly many sons who now typically survive into adulthood divide their patrimony, reducing the numbers of large landlords, while the landless more frequently leave for the cities in search of unskilled work in factories or construction or informal-sector services. Many holders of uneconomic holdings – too small or of too poor quality to support a family – earn their living by labor in the fields, or in the informal sector, or by commuting or migrating to towns or cities (see the fine study by Sharma and Poleman 1993). They lease out their land to their richer neighbors, who may well have capital but need land in which to invest, to make farming a viable occupation. Such farmers may also lease some land from neighbors' holdings, especially if it is a plot at some distance from the large farmer's main holding, and thus difficult to farm well, owing to higher irrigation and labor-supervision costs.

The leverage of this "middle" group in dealing with the state certainly depends on the number of votes they represent, so they have a vested interest in supporting elected officials, who in turn are expected to intervene when things like fertilizer, or irrigation water, or health and education services are allocated. In one village in Meerut district that I studied, for example, the traditional headman, whose caste fellows controlled one-third of the village lands, had been deposed in a village council election by an alliance of the holders of most of the remaining land, the middle-caste *malis* (gardeners) and the formerly untouchable *jatavs*. To the extent that anyone had the upper hand in the land-consolidation process I observed (see Oldenburg 1990), it was the two leaders of this "middle–lower" alliance.

As it happens, a description of the exception to this picture, one of overwhelming village-level political power by a "big man," comes from West Bengal in 2006, in which the "big man" is a member of the CPM, a landlord, a middle peasant Muslim:

> The Comrade had to practice a sort of vernacular do-it-yourself hegemony to maintain the complete dominance of the Communists at the local level: no one was allowed to air critiques of the government openly, and no single person was able to build a following of any significance in opposition to the Comrade's. He used the resources of the Party and the government strategically to achieve this.
>
> (Banerjee 2008: 84–5)

Yet, five years before, there had been a serious challenge to the Comrade's power, from a young man campaigning for the Trinamul Congress (Banerjee 2008: 85–90). The villagers, in Banerjee's convincing account, turn out for elections in "a festive and solemn moment of power and equality that holds out hope and succor for the next [year]. It is a 'ritual of thralldom' to democracy . . ." (Banerjee 2008: 80–1). But Banerjee's (2008: 92) explanation for that enthusiasm is that the CPM is "the most responsive of all parties [making use of] a liberal mix of cynical handouts and ideological programs," combined with the Comrade's "hegemony," and that made the voters feel that they could influence policy (see also Ruud 2000).

The major exception to this picture of an uncoordinated and shifting set of powerful men and sometimes groups – but almost never, I would argue, a "class" in a sense stronger than a word meaning "category" – has to do with the position of women and Muslims. Women are denied their full economic rights by an almost airtight patriarchal structure, and most women are indeed severely constrained as far as political activity is concerned. Women now vote almost in the same percentage as men, but their representation as elected officials is clearly overstated by the reservation system in the *panchayats*, which has been subverted by the practice of having wives elected who are the puppets of their husbands or other male family members. Even then, there are significant numbers of women who are truly autonomous, energetic, and effective; enough to puncture for ever the notion that only men can be in government. There are also increasing numbers of women in the administrative services.

Muslims – and other minorities in specific regions – tend to be excluded from power unless they are a substantial percentage of the population of a particular place. In the aftermath of the 1992–3 riots caused by the demolition of the Babri Masjid, the numbers of riots declined significantly in all of India, and the pogrom of 2002 in Gujarat has not disturbed that overall trend (see Varshney 2004: 183 and Table 9.1 below). But that may be less a consequence of more tolerance of Muslims, or a conscious stepping back from the provocations of the years leading up to the destruction of the Babri Masjid (though I suspect that was true in some places), and more a disturbing indication that the *hindutva* partisans had succeeded in putting Muslims "in their place," as second-class citizens. That is, Muslims no longer felt that they had the political and legal protection to protest vigorously and confront those who attacked them.[13] Their lack of advancement in government – in the bureaucracy and in political parties – may be part and parcel of their continuing poor economic and social position (see the Sachar report [India 2006]), but it is probably also a matter of discriminatory exclusion in many cases. The *State of Democracy in South Asia* report (2008: 57), however, found that Muslims have slightly *more* trust in governmental institutions than the mean, and that 37 percent of the "minority" (75 percent of whom are Muslims) felt that their condition has improved, and 18 percent felt that it had deteriorated (SDSA 2008: 271).

It is more difficult to sketch the empirical landscape of the micro-level of Pakistan than it is for India, simply because of the difference in number of scholarly studies (see, however, S. R. Khan et al. 2007). In neither case can we say that there has been even adequate coverage, particularly in this time of rapid change, since studies relying on what the situation was twenty or even ten years ago are of rapidly diminishing value. It is strikingly obvious, though, that there is no evidence in either country for much local power being projected very far upwards – or from the periphery to the center – although there is evidence for the power of the local leadership to resist the penetration of power and authority from above. There is no evidence for any theory that supposes that the lessons of democratic or autocratic behavior and ideas developed in local arenas affect the democratic or autocratic practices in higher arenas, and little evidence for the reverse flow: ideas and practices learned in the high councils of the state percolating down.[14] In countries as gigantic as India and Pakistan, where the literal distance between peripheral arenas and the ones at the core is so enormous – as is the cultural, linguistic, and other social distance – the numbers of translations (literal and metaphorical) that would need to be done make such simple chains most unlikely. Nor would there be any way of distinguishing their degree of impact from more general influences of mass culture. By way of illustration: it would be impossible to measure convincingly whether people in a village become "more demo-cratic" from participating in a well-functioning "village assembly" or from being exposed to an intense election campaign for national office. In any case, no one has tried to do any measurements of this kind.

The best we can say is that the more widespread and the more intense democratic institutions are – from civil-society organization activist actions to village-level (free and fair) elections, to vote-mobilizing parties, to mass-contact election campaigns – the more likely the higher levels of national (and provincial) system are to favor democracy. But our data do not reveal what really goes on in those arenas – and the best studies we have of village-level politics, for example, reveal all sorts of complexity and ambi-guity and (again) fairly rapid change over time. "Adding them up," as it were, is probably a fool's game.

None the less, it is worth doing a superficial survey. Looking at Pakistan's historical experience, Wilder (1999: 16) notes:

> An important aspect of the bureaucratic legacy, especially in the Punjab, was the tradition of district politics. This involved containing politics at the district level by co-opting local influentials whose power was based on their leadership of religious, tribal or kinship groups, and/or on their control of land. Colonial administrators provided patronage to these local notables in the form of land grants, pensions, and honorary titles, and were provided revenues and political stability in return. A political system was thus institutionalized that was based on patron–client relationships. [After independence], unlike the Congress Party in India,

Waseem [1994: 12] notes, the Muslim League "failed to offer itself as a rival source of patronage to the local elite which, therefore, continued to look towards the district bureaucracy for influence and security."

The largely landlord leadership of the Muslim League in UP in the 1930s never got the chance of office, but their instincts would have likely been the same. In any event, whether landlord or lawyer, Muslim League refugee leaders freshly arrived in Pakistan would have probably been attracted to the possibility of building an instant political base through patronage of the old sort. There were, for example, evacuee properties to distribute (see Waseem 1989: 111–12).

Clive Dewey's (1991) important article on the "rural roots of Pakistani militarism" focuses on the strength of support of the military in at least very significant parts of Pakistan, a support that could fairly be said to grant *legitimacy* to army rule. As he says:

Political scientists working on Pakistan have systematically ignored the possibility that tribes with codes of honour prefer military rule *on ideological grounds* [emphasis in the original]. Yet all the locally-dominant castes in the great Punjabi recruiting grounds have value systems comparable with the *Pukhtunwali* of the Pathans: value systems which hold the warrior up to admiration as the finest sort of man. The martial castes are conscious of their martial traditions, and go to great lengths to transmit them from one generation to another.

(Dewey 1991: 262)

Dewey outlines the great historical depth of this culture, and adds that "self-government only strengthened the martial castes' influence. . . . [They] constituted a majority of the electorate throughout the heavily-recruited zones; and the leaders of the martial lobby became the leaders of the Punjab Unionist Party" (Dewey 1991: 265). Ultimately, in post-independence Pakistan, Dewey argues (1991: 270), "it is possible to see the military . . . as a paternalistic employer, a development agency, a force for order and a moral community, all rolled into one."

The evidence for this assertion rests firmly on local-arena foundations. On employment, he notes, "individual families, as well as entire tribes, satisfy their socio-economic aspirations through military service" (Dewey 1991: 271). The army's food-supply system has helped modernize agriculture even as it gives a very large number of Punjabi farmers a direct stake in the system. And the army "creates a pool of skilled and disciplined labour on an unprecedented scale," as well as promoting literacy and technical training more effectively than other government institutions (Dewey 1991: 273). As for "order," he points out that "if villagers left the maintenance of order to the only agencies supplied by the state – the courts and the police – they would live under conditions of anarchy" (Dewey 1991: 274). So "they enforce their own norms. Disputes are inhibited and resolved by informal means: through the authority of village bosses and the threat of retaliation" (Dewey 1991: 274). Then, "each time the army intervenes, half a million disciplined men are added to the overstretched police force," and "the army supplies the peasantry with potential adjudicators: the retired officer class" (Dewey 1991: 275).[15] Finally, up until 1971, "the army ... held out the possibility of a more appropriate morality [than the politicians could offer]. It attempted to impose self-discipline and self-sacrifice for the sake of a great patriotic/religious cause: the defense of Pakistan, which was also the defense of Islam" (Dewey 1991: 277). That moral community, Dewey maintains (1991: 278), was undermined by the defeat by India, and thus its changed external mission, and creeping corruption.

These factors clearly apply to a limited segment of Pakistani society: the core rural areas of the Punjab that constitute the recruiting ground for the army.[16] The other branches of the military recruit their soldiers from all over the country, and the officer corps draws on the entire range of Pakistanis (including a few women). Urban areas clearly are far less affected by these things. But the army's increasing economic and societal power – to be discussed below – is not simply a matter of spreading money around, and exercising force from time to time. It rests significantly on a foundation of legitimacy – that is, those immediately dependent on it and perhaps the next layer of indirect beneficiaries provide a large pool of citizens who easily grant the army a *right* to rule, as well as seeing the practical value of its ruling. That would give it authority far superior to that of the bureaucracy and most politicians (who continue to rely largely on patron–client political ties, at least in the countryside) to go along with its obviously superior firepower. It is the army rather than its competitors for power that is deeply rooted in a very crucial part of the country, and it has effectively leveraged that power to govern against forces arrayed in the provinces on the margins, and the middle-class-dominated towns and cities.

In India, too, it is at the local level that the political beliefs of citizens and the foot-soldiers of political parties and movements are probably most powerfully shaped, by the patterns of domination, control, and resistance, and the explicit and implicit legitimation of those patterns.[17] But India has had a much longer and more significant experience of local self-government than Pakistan, as well as a much more active and effective set of civil-society organizations, though not very numerous in absolute terms, nor firmly based in terms of funds and personnel (see Alsop and Kurey 2005). Local-level non-state actors are more powerful vis-à-vis the bureaucracy – the military not being a factor, generally, at this level – in India than they are in Pakistan, mirroring the balance of power at the national level that favors politicians.

Noting the contrast of Ludhiana District in India and Sialkot District in Pakistan as extreme cases, Holly Sims (1988: 165) says of the two post-independence Punjabs:

Extensive state involvement in the Indian Punjab led to the establishment of new institutions which disturbed a pre-existing status quo and
offered new channels of social and economic mobility. Cooperative
societies, political parties, and schools have all served to undermine local
power structures. . . . In the Indian Punjab, local power structures were
leveled by the rise and expansion of the state. . . . In Pakistani Punjab,
large landowners hold vast powers due to their grip on sources of
employment, food and protection.

Although Sims suggests that neither country changed the elite civil services
or even the district administration very much, she argues that the political
environment mattered. Unlike the Pakistani leaders, "Indian leaders
re-designed institutional structures and their jurisdictions, and established a
parallel system of local government" (Sims 1988: 135). She describes how
that difference plays out, as both countries, with US help, set up community development programs and extension services (Sims 1988: 140–60). This
contrast shows up in responses to a survey Sims conducted:

Farmers . . . [were] asked what they would do if faced with an agricultural
problem involving red tape. . . . More than half of the Indian farmers
said they would try to solve the problem through direct individual
action, by either seeing the concerned officer or bribing him. Only 16
percent of Pakistani respondents gave either response. The majority said
they would act in an indirect fashion, through intermediaries, such as
Malik Sahib [in Sialkot].

(Sims 1988: 168–9)

The difference between the two Punjabs becomes significant when one
remembers that Pakistan Punjab holds some 60 percent of Pakistan's
population, while India's Punjab has only 2.3 percent of India's. True, the
Indian Punjab's influence is greater than that would suggest, owing to its
disproportionate contribution to India's foodgrain supply and share both in
the military and in the ranks of entrepreneurs. But it is in no way comparable to the significance of Pakistan's Punjab.

Corbridge et al. (2005), in the conclusion of a study saturated with
subtle empirical analysis of grassroots governance in substantial part in the
state – Bihar – *least likely* (in the conventional wisdom) to have good, or
perhaps even *any* governance, agree with a statement in the World Bank's
*World Development Report 2004* (p. 18) that "despite the urgent needs of the
world's poor people, and the many ways services have failed them, quick
results will be hard to come by. Many of the changes involve fundamental
shifts in power – something that cannot happen overnight." But they add:

James Scott is right to suggest that poorer people are rarely empowered
in the long run by governments which claim to see all on their behalf.

We can add to this that poorer people are rarely empowered by political movements that claim to see the future in utopian terms. Poorer people instead need to be supported in their diverse and discontinuous efforts to bring agencies of the state more firmly under their gaze and control. These efforts will often take shape in political society, with the help of local mediators.

(Corbridge et al. 2005: 262–3)

Anirudh Krishna (2002, 2006) describes one set of "local mediators" – young men he calls *naya neta* ("new leaders") – in Rajasthan and Madhya Pradesh. The importance of equivalent but differently named local mediators has been noted as well in South India, by Manor (2000) and Reddy and Haragopal (1985). Circumventing the "traditional" leaders drawn from dominant castes, these men, newly educated but unable to find employment commensurate with their skills, serve as a bridge between the bureaucracy and the villagers. Their ability to get things done for the less powerful villagers does not come from their wealth or their traditional social status, but from their knowledge of how government works, and their standing as autonomous citizens in an overtly democratic set-up. Councilors of the municipal government of Delhi, whom I interviewed in 1969–70, spoke eloquently and, I think, accurately of the value of democracy at the local level in diverting government benefits to the larger number of citizens, avoiding state capture by the rich and well placed (see Oldenburg 1976).

Local self-government functions poorly in India, even in the wake of the seventy-third and seventy-fourth amendments to the constitution (passed in 1993 and 1994) that "entrenched" local government in the constitution. There have indeed been frequent and significant elections, but the other critical feature of those amendments has not been implanted: most important, there has not been a significant reallocation of financial resources to the lowest tiers, except in Kerala. Still, the new system has permitted the exercise of *some* more power by, or on behalf of, the greater mass of the citizenry. While that has not exactly made the bureaucracy accountable to any serious extent, it has probably served to change attitudes, so that even the poorest challenge bureaucrats' decisions, and those in the middle and at the top can influence those decisions (sometimes aided by corruption), not infrequently through collective action. Though I have no direct evidence, I believe that when citizens develop a belief that they *can* affect what government does that can contribute to a genuine commitment to democracy at the "higher" levels of government (see Yadav 2000).

Is the situation different in Pakistan? Zaidi (2005c: 15–16), reviewing decentralization of government over the decades, claims that, despite the emergence of a powerful "middle farmer" category along with the green revolution, "when the military's local government is confronted with representation, the artificial system set up by the military comes undone. The military and participatory or democratic politics, despite the military's attempts, do not go together." Under Ayub Khan's "Basic Democracies" scheme, it was the bureaucracy that was the "controlling authority," and so "the Basic Democracies scheme [was] not, in reality, democracy, for it [did] not represent control by the people over government power except in an extremely limited manner" (Friedman 1960: 114; quoted in Zaidi 2005c: 15). Under Bhutto, "there was no implementation of any sort of local government, and . . . the unrepresentative structure of doing government at the local level – largely through the bureaucratic structure – remained" (Zaidi 2005c: 17). Under Zia, according to Zaidi (2005c: 25), "urban and rural councilors were the only elected representatives of the regime, and were responsible and accountable, given their limitations, to the needs and demands of the electorate" and "a very large number of individuals who had been trained, for the first time ever in politics, through the Local Bodies, emerged later as members of the National and Provincial assemblies in 1985 and in the elections held after that." Yet when, in 1988, a national government elected on a party basis took over "local government was dispensed with" (Zaidi 2005c: 28).

Almost as soon as he came to power, General Musharraf instituted a new system of decentralized government, though "it is noteworthy that local government is still not part of the Constitution" (Zaidi 2005c: 34). Despite some major innovations – including reserving one-third of the elected positions for women – *"there has been no decentralization of any federal level powers, duties or responsibilities to either the provincial or district level"* (Zaidi 2005c: 34; his emphasis). According to the International Crisis Group report on decentralization, the elected women in fact have no power, and that is only one of the many problems with the program (International Crisis Group 2004a). In summary:

> The scheme was to strengthen local control and accountability and, according to President Pervez Musharraf, "empower the impoverished." In practice, however, it has undercut established political parties and drained power away from the provinces while doing little to minimize corruption or establish clear accountability at local level. The reforms, far from enhancing democracy, have strengthened military rule. . . . The misuse of local government officials during the April 2002 presidential referendum and the October 2002 general elections has left little doubt that these governments were primarily instituted to create a pliant political elite that could help root the military's power in local politics and displace its traditional civilian adversaries.
>
> (International Crisis Group 2004a: i)

There is a well-done study by Sharukh Rafi Khan, Foqia Sadiq Khan, and Aasim Sajjad Akhtar (2007) of the on-the-ground impact of the local government initiative. They cite studies for the Pattan Development

Organization, Islamabad, done in 2000 and 2001 by S. Bari and B. H. Khan that found that "councilors were for the most part not wealthy or from politically influential backgrounds, but that the apex officers, the *nazim* and *naib* [deputy] *nazims*, were" (S. R. Khan et al. 2007: 58). In their sample villages in Punjab and Sindh, S. R. Khan et al. (2007: 78–9) find that indeed the *nazims* were both from the landed elite and from the locally powerful *beradari* (clan). In some of the places studied in Balochistan and the NWFP, however, the power of the landed was on the wane, replaced by money, though *beradari* and *quom* remain important (S. R. Khan et al. 2007: 105–6, 112, 120).

It is unlikely that participants in local government during any of these schemes of decentralized local government, including the elected representatives, were believers in democratic activism. They certainly did not challenge the rule of the bureaucracy. A comparison with the experience of political actors in India would suggest – no empirical studies exist, as far as I am aware – that local-level politics, and the beliefs of political actors at that level, has been on balance supportive of democracy at the upper levels in India, and of autocratic rule in Pakistan. But the contribution of this to the different regime paths is unlikely to be large.

The differences in the answers to the question "who (really) governs" in the two countries may contribute something to the solution of our puzzle, but not much. Gender inequality is probably greater, especially in local arenas, in Pakistan than in India, but it is "most true" that it is men who run things in both countries. Caste inequality, and the marginalization of the "lower orders" is probably greater in India, particularly in local arenas, but "feudal" relations are more prevalent in Pakistan. Economic and social classes are so fragmented in both countries that it is hard to argue even that a "coalition of dominant classes" runs things in either place. The state has a great deal of autonomy in both countries. After decades of democratic practices in India, it is probably true that Indian citizen attitudes favor democracy more than Pakistan's – i.e., that the data from the *State of Democracy in South Asia* report reflect a durable difference, rather than a snapshot of views as of 2004 – but it is not clear how much influence that has on the persistence of democracy in India and autocracy in Pakistan.

We cannot settle who the ruling class or classes were, or are, in either country. We can perhaps least inadequately deal with the issue by carefully taking into account, in both day-to-day governance and in times of crisis, the extent to which "the people" in whole or in part played a decisive role in setting national agendas if not particular laws and policies and programs, and to what extent they were opposed by "vested interests" within the state or outside it. In this, the contrast is clear. In India, the people could count on a full set of democratic freedoms and build on a democracy-friendly nationalist movement to exercise power through elected representatives. In Pakistan, the people were excluded from decision-making in part because they were not trusted in times of crisis to do the right thing, and because they had the disadvantage of a too-short and too-narrow nationalist movement, and a fatal lack of legitimate linkage to the Muslim League, even in the first days of freedom.

The first thirty years of independence posed severe challenges to the very existence of the two new countries, not to speak of the political system each had adopted. Pakistan was unable to manage the enormously difficult tasks that immediately confronted it in 1947. Its leaders had to maintain the country's independence while completing a nation-building that seemed to require bringing Kashmir in, with India the adversary, and making Urdu the sole national language, against Bengali opposition. Although popular as the against-all-odds creators of the new country, they found themselves to be a political minority, with little chance to legitimize their rule through democratic means, since Muslim League supporters and leaders had been separated by partition. At the same time they had to resolve the constitutional issues that East Bengal's majority population, and the commitment to having an "Islamic" state when those with power, Jinnah's followers in his liberal interpretation of the proper place of religion, were members of the civil and military wings of the state. Jinnah's "viceregal system" proved useful, when legitimation by election proved impossible, and the outcome was the indirect and then direct seizure of power by bureaucrats and then the army.

These contradictions persisted even after the acceptance of the compromise of parity, the addition of Bengali as a national language, and the minimal agreement on Islam as a passive principle for the state, because the army, strengthened by its ties to the US alliances, and secure in its own ideas of "guided democracy," denied its East Wing citizens anything like their full rights and influence. The consequence was not only the perpetuation of military rule, but also ultimately the break-up of the country. The rise to power of a popularly elected leader in the aftermath of that disaster did not succeed in making Pakistan a democracy, partly because of Zulfiqar Ali Bhutto's own character, and partly because of Pakistan's seriously precarious security situation that did not allow the politicians fully to control the bureaucracy and the military.

In India, by contrast, the launching of the new democratic regime was comparatively smooth, resting on the solid foundation of a deeply rooted and broadly popular nationalist movement, with a rich array of experienced politicians, able and willing to assert their power over the state apparatus. Nehru's unbroken long tenure as a towering leader of government and party, and his commitment to, and understanding of, democratic institutions, especially elections and parliament, was invaluable. The momentum of the first twenty years carried India through economic and political crises, until it slipped into a quasi-authoritarian regime with Mrs Gandhi's Emergency, in which, however, the civilian and politics-schooled leaders never relinquished their control over the state apparatus.

In March 1977, both India and Pakistan held elections. It was immediately clear that India's marked a cathartic rededication to the ideals of democracy that the nationalist movement and then Jawaharlal Nehru had fostered. The crowds that came into the streets to celebrate the Janata Party victory were reminiscent of those in 1947, crying "freedom." In Pakistan, a rigged election brought the crowds into the streets in protest, in this case reminiscent of those that had brought down President Ayub Khan, another leader whose claims for the value of guided democracy had proved hollow. Another iteration of what Kennedy (2005) has called the "Military-Governance paradigm" soon ensued.

In the thirty years after the 1977 elections, those portents of revived democracy versus repeated army rule have been accurate. India and Pakistan seem to have more vividly than before taken very different paths. India as a whole has not slipped into anything like the Emergency of 1975–7, and Pakistan has not strayed far from the military-directed polity instituted by Zia ul Haq in 1977. There have been challenges that arguably threaten the established regime in both countries: from Hindu nationalism and from the state's reaction to separatist movements, especially in Punjab, Kashmir, and the northeast in India; and from elections and popular movements in Pakistan. Since these challenges have been, on balance, less severe than those they faced in their first thirty years of independence, it is not surprising that they have not shaken the foundations of either regime, in the thirty years plus since the two countries' paths so clearly diverged.

## Notes

1 Electoral constituencies in India were recently delimited on the basis of new census data after a gap of thirty-five years, but even then only within states. Delegation numbers to parliament have been frozen at their 1977 level, despite very different population growth rates. The ideal of "one person, one vote" is certainly not even approached.

2 There has been some empirical exploration of this "lower" (constitutive?) level in India (see Frankel and Rao 1989; Baru 2000; Jenkins 1999; Harriss 2003; Heller 2000; Sinha 2005, among others), but very little in Pakistan.

3 "The industrial capitalist class has *not yet* [my emphasis] been strong enough to undermine the economic importance of the class of rich farmers or absorb them in giant capitalist agro-business enterprises; nor has it succeeded in colonizing the bureaucracy and moulding it to suit largely capitalist goals" (Bardhan 1984: 60).

4 For a more recent view of Bardhan's analysis, see Herring and Agarawala (2006: 339). Bardhan himself (2003) may have a different view of present-day India: the word "classes" appears only twice in his lecture on "Political-Economy and Governance Issues in the Indian Economic Reform Process," and without the word "dominant". Indeed, he reports (2003: 5–6): "Cynics may even argue that the retreat of the state, implied by economic reform, is now more acceptable to the upper classes and castes, as the latter are losing their control over state power in the face of the emerging hordes of hitherto subordinate groups, and they are opting for greener pastures in the private sector and abroad."

5 Those are arguably also inappropriate units for analysis, as there are typically regions within states (or straddling state boundaries, particularly in the Hindi belt), defined by geography or dialect or culture within which one finds "locally" dominant groups.

6 There is a dearth of scholarly work on institutions and forces at this level, to the point that even good cases are hard to find, let alone empirically solid broad-scope analyses. For a probably representative sample, see the bibliographies of chapters of Jayal et al. (2006). Himmat Singh (2001: 230–57) writes of the "urban–rural continuum" of the Punjab and shows how rural–urban disparities have lessened, slowing urbanization. See also the excellent short discussion centered on a particular Rajasthan village in Mendelsohn (1993: 819–30).

7 A useful introduction, and corrective view, is Herb (2003). See also Herb (2005).

8 Most taxes can be hidden in the prices charged for goods at retail, since most revenue comes from excise taxes and customs duties and other indirect levies, and fees for services. Land revenue and property tax are for most a small burden (land revenue in India has been reduced almost to zero, and property taxes are easily evaded through corruption), so it is only price increases of goods that citizens know well the government controls – diesel, kerosene, food grains – that bring popular protest. I suspect that most country dwellers in India literally do not know that they pay significant taxes.

9 See Herring (1979); Noman (1990); I. Talbot (1999): 233–4.

10 A term I use to call attention to the extent to which in small countries, or in countries with a very small governing class, the relationships between the players are both personal and formal, in that everyone typically knows both political supporters and opponents personally, and often their families as well. It is derived from Bayart's concept of "intimate repression" in small countries of Africa: "In [small countries] a ruler who has been in power for one or two decades would in all probability know personally every instance of personal aggrandizement, whether of wealth or influence. . . . In these countries there is, to varying degrees, what one can call intimate repression, sometimes good natured and paternalist but sometimes wholly unbearable. Examples abound . . . in Guinea, prisoners leaving the torture chamber to take a telephone call from Sékou Touré" (Bayart 1986: 114).

11 I put "village" in quotes because of the ambiguity of the term (see Hill 1986: 45–6). It usually refers to the "revenue village," which often is comprised of several settlement areas that inhabitants would call "their" village. Villagers frequently own land in (revenue) villages other than their own, including "uninhabited" (revenue) villages.

12 See, e.g., India, Ministry of Agriculture (n.d.), reporting survey 1991–2 data: "both the number and area of operated holdings increased in the case of sub-marginal, marginal and small size groups of holdings and a decrease of number and operated area of holdings in the medium and large size groups." A press note issued by the National Sample Survey on 31 August 2006 reported results of the 2002–3 survey: the area under "marginal" (less than one hectare) holdings increased "by 6–7%" to "22–23%", thus equaling the area share of "small" (1–2 ha.) and "semi-medium" (2–4 ha.) categories, which remained unchanged. The implication is that the area held in "medium" (4–10 ha.) and "large" holdings decreased by a total of 6–7 percent. In the percentage of the total number of holdings, "marginal" increased significantly, and the numbers of all other categories decreased. The average operational holding was 1.06 ha. in 2002–3, down from 1.34 in 1991–2 and 1.67 in 1981–2.

13 Copland (2005: 203–4) believes that "self-policing" by "subjects who did not belong to the community of the ruler" of the princely states "kept the states in the early twentieth century free from serious communal violence," because they "could expect little sympathy from the authorities if they tried to disturb the hierarchy by challenging . . . [a] system stacked against them."

14 See below, pp. 187–88, for a discussion of the "vernacularization" of democracy in India. Harry Eckstein argues that among other factors contributing to the

democratic culture necessary for democratization, in turn just one of the "lessons" of nineteenth-century European and American processes for present-day countries, "Democratic culture and structure are constituted by substantially *congruent* segments, in which the norms and practices of smaller entities substantially resemble those of national governance, especially those smaller entities that play important roles in political socialization and the recruitment of politicians and leaders. Society in this way can be a school for learning democratic citizenship and governance. From this it follows that political democratization should be accompanied by a good deal of *social democratization* – the democratization of social life in a more general sense" (Eckstein 1996: 16–17; italics in the original).

15 This alliance also benefits the army, according to Dewey (1991: 276), as it is able to recruit men "from tribes with codes of honour [who] already admire the martial virtues – bravery, strength, loyalty, belligerence," thus making military indoctrination easier.

16 Though, echoing Mackinder, one might say: the values and patterns of the military heartland provide the basis of the rule of the Punjab, and he who rules Punjab rules Pakistan, with those values and patterns in place.

17 There is no way yet of measuring the impact of the penetration of standardized educational instruction, and the mass media, into villages and city and town neighborhoods; the "probably most powerfully shaped" is my summary judgment that I would be hard put to defend if challenged. I am hugely impressed by the new textbooks that the National Council for Educational Research and Training (NCERT) has, in 2006, produced in India (see in particular the textbook *Democratic Politics* for Class IX) via the NCERT website: http://www.ncert.nic.in/textbooks/testing/Index.htm. *If and when* that book is universally distributed and effectively taught, it *might* have a significant impact on how Indians think about and practice democracy. But televised political campaigns and news reporting are much more likely to do so, even in the long term.

# Part II

# From 1977 to the present

The year 1977 is not just a convenient marker, roughly the halfway point in the history of India and Pakistan, but also indicates a turning point in their trajectories; we begin this part with a detailed examination of just what happened then. Before resuming our chronological narrative, we examine two other explanations for regime difference that do not rely on historical choices, and patterns of political change.

Religious difference is often used in the analysis of why countries – even more, "civilizations" that might "clash" – are more or less receptive to democratic ideology and practices. Since Pakistan was founded with Islam in mind, with its claims to nationhood referring to Muslim practices as well, it is natural to expect that its Islamic nature should help us understand why democracy has not taken root. Hinduism – the religion of 80 percent of India's people – arguably sets the tone for India's religious culture, and certainly affects ideas about equality and community that are relevant to political practice. Yet in neither country, we find, is religion as powerful an explanation of constitutional and political differences as we might expect.

Another explanation for regime difference has to do with external relations. India was far less influenced by outside forces in its political path than Pakistan. India's sheer size and resource endowments made economic as well as political autarky attractive, and Jawaharlal Nehru shied away from entangling alliances, choosing a policy of non-alignment. Because Pakistan was faced at independence with a more severe national security problem than India, it wound up fairly quickly in an alliance with the United States, an alliance that strengthened its military significantly. That has had a major impact on Pakistan's governmental balance of power, as the military took advantage of its central role in three separate periods: during the first decades of the Cold War, in the Afghanistan *jihad* that contributed to its end with the collapse of the Soviet Union, and in the years after 11 September 2001.

Our chronological narrative then resumes by examining the ways in which military rule became entrenched in Pakistan, as it laid claim to important sections of national security policy and actively interfered with politics during periods of nominal democratic rule. At the same time, in India, the 1977 election galvanized a popular upsurge that brought more and more of the marginalized *dalits* and other "backward" groups, as well as women, into democratic politics. There was also a rise in the numbers and importance of grassroots movements and NGOs. The result was a deepening of India's democracy.

We then turn to examining recent developments. In Pakistan, a relatively free and fair election in February 2008 raised the possibility of politicians extracting the state from the decisive influence of the military. In India, each new election raises the prospect of resolving major crises of Maoist insurgency and the continuing problems of corruption and criminality in politics.

# 6   1977 as a turning point?

Nineteen seventy-seven is the year in which, quite possibly, the paths of India and Pakistan were closest to each other, but after which two very different directions were chosen. It is not difficult to imagine a very different outcome, one in which Pakistan would have moved towards a genuine democracy, while India relapsed into a more ideologically driven and intensely harsh version of Mrs Gandhi's Emergency regime, with her son Sanjay in a starring role. The powers of the bureaucracy could easily have been enhanced, on the excuse of the need to accelerate development, and of the military to bring India to the status of a Great Power on the world stage. Soon, a new generation of politicians with only weak legitimacy – the Congress was already decaying at its roots, with loyalty to the leader in Delhi paramount, and with perhaps less taste for free and fair elections – would quickly lose power to the bureaucrats, or even the military.

Across the border, one can imagine a Zulfiqar Ali Bhutto somewhat in the mold of Jawaharlal Nehru – still an aristocrat with authoritarian tendencies, but also a man who reveled in his magical connection to the masses, who expressed their hopes, and yet was still one of them. A man devoted to Islam but not pious, a man imaginative and bold. Bhutto was fully capable of understanding that the deep causes of Pakistan's tragedy had to do with the early rejection of both a democratic commitment to the rule of the majority, and the absolute necessity of fully free and fair elections, and a federal system built on justice and respect. Had that knowledge been sealed into determination to prevent a recurrence of that tragedy, it is not difficult to imagine him throwing himself into building a democratic system by partnering with the opposition, as Nehru had twenty-five years before, instead of suppressing them. With that comparatively small change, it is quite possible that Pakistan's next thirty years would have been entirely under democratic rule.

The Pakistan People's Party was perhaps too young an organization to have reined in the Bhutto that actually existed, but that it has lasted more than thirty years since Bhutto's death suggests that it had genuine strengths that could have allowed it to play the role the Congress had in India after independence. The new Pakistan of 1972, considering the relative power of politicians and state apparatus, was one in which the army and the bureaucracy were responsible, and seen to be responsible, for the shameful loss of half the country, and so a party and a leadership banking on the legitimacy that came from winning Pakistan's first free and fair election ever could well have altered the balance of power in their favor.

So it was not inevitable that India would be boosted to a higher democratic trajectory after 1977, and Pakistan returned to an autocratic regime that gradually dug itself in deeper and deeper. To understand what choices were made, we need to look carefully at the governments of both countries in the years before 1977, as Pakistan came to grips with its loss of its East Wing, and India chose a period of Emergency rule.

## Pakistan

After the trauma of the break-up of the country in 1971, Pakistan had a swift and quiet handover of power from a military regime to a democratically elected government. It was truly a reprise of 1947 in some ways: the 1970 election, like that of 1946, had been for a constituent assembly for a united country, but the country split before the assembly could meet. Bhutto's mandate from the election was to keep Pakistan united – *the* issue of the campaign was the Awami League's six-point program – and, although the PPP's slogan pledged them to "Islam . . . democracy . . . socialism," it is not clear how much weight any of those had in the minds of voters. Bhutto was not quite Jinnah's equal in stature, but he was head and shoulders above any other West Pakistan leader in charisma and experience. After Pakistan's partition, there was the same need to create a new country with new borders in a situation of threat from India, and to legitimize political rule (see LaPorte 1973: 188).

But this time, the politicians should have had the advantage over the state apparatus. Bhutto and his PPP had won five-eighths of the seats in West Pakistan in the free and fair, universal-suffrage election of 1970, in which the turnout was 54 percent, with a 40.7 percent vote share. Bhutto himself, though a "feudal" landlord, had the populist credentials and talent to break away from the economic and social power structure in Pakistan, and make a significant effort to change it. Yet the politicians were unable to build on their initial leverage to establish a qualitatively different balance of power.

The military and its bureaucratic allies had been humiliated by defeat at India's hands, and could be blamed for the mismanagement and worse that resulted in the dismemberment of the country. Forty-three "top officers" of the armed services were retired in the first four months (H.-A. Rizvi 2003a: 144), and 1,300 civil servants were dismissed (LaPorte 1973: 189). Haqqani (2005: 91), however, notes that

> except for a handful of Yahya's colleagues, most military officers . . . kept their jobs, and, in fact, they gained from vacancies at the top. Bhutto's left-wing lieutenants argue, with some justification, that Pakistan's

intelligence services helped the return of civilian rule at this stage primarily to maintain their, and the military's, institutional primacy.

The military as a corporate institution was not touched; it retained control of its internal recruitment, training, and promotion.

The crushing defeat provoked a justifiable need to augment Pakistan's security, and that would have to mean the development of nuclear weapons, of necessity done under military auspices. Pakistan could not but feel threatened.[1] It would have been very difficult, even if Bhutto had wished it, to make significant changes in the ethos, personnel, and strategy of the military.

The shame of losing half the country was perhaps justified in some minds by the notion, impolitely put, of "good riddance to bad rubbish." The Bengalis had never been fully accepted as equal by the West Pakistanis, particularly since many of them were Hindu. East Pakistan's jute crop had been a major source of revenue for West Pakistan's development, but that was changing. The replacement of jute by artificial fiber for carpet backing, and the replacement of burlap sacks with shipping containers, meant that East Pakistan was rapidly losing its economic value. Its lack of other resources and continuing poverty was likely to be a drain on Pakistan's progress. Quite possibly some in West Pakistan saw the loss of a Hindu-influenced economic "basket case" (Kissinger's infamous characterization of post-independence Bangladesh) as a silver lining of the black cloud of defeat.

Although Bhutto may have had a fantasy that the Bengalis would think better of their independence and reunite with Pakistan,[2] he decided, in effect, to turn Pakistan's back to South Asia, to face the Middle East. Pakistan would be the easternmost and largest, and in many ways most advanced country of the Middle East, rather than a peripheral, and comparatively small and weak country of the South Asian subcontinent. Pakistan's membership in the Organization of the Islamic Conference was used to good effect; and, in the post-1973 renaissance of oil-price-fueled power in the Middle East, Pakistan fitted right in.

Middle Eastern money started to flow into Pakistan, replacing to some extent the flow of US aid, thus changing the character of resources from abroad. The money was no longer coming to gain support for a US-directed global strategic security system, in the context of an alliance with the US. It rather came as a consequence of Pakistan's involvement in a regional system in which it could play an important role as a Muslim country. This was supplemented by the remittance-flow mainly from unskilled workers. After the second oil shock of 1979, these flows increased; in 1982–3, Middle East remittances were $2.4 billion, close to 10 percent of Pakistan's GDP (Gilani and Addelton 1985: 52–3; see also Gilani et al. 1981).

The military was also strengthened by this turn away from South Asia. After the Iranian Revolution, Pakistan and Saudi Arabia, with the encouragement of the US, worked out military cooperation deals in which the Saudis gave Pakistan aid for providing military personnel, particularly technical people desperately needed to service American aircraft, and possibly some army units to serve as an active part of the Saudi security system (see Safran 1985: 363; Cordesman 1984: 348).

In striking contrast to the post-1947 period, the Pakistan Constituent Assembly rapidly completed work on a new constitution. Bhutto had the National Assembly meet to approve an "interim constitution" on 21 April 1972, which essentially "re-established the [British] viceregal system," with Bhutto as president (Burki 1980: 91). A new constitution was inaugurated on 14 August 1973, twenty months after Pakistan's re-emergence in its new form (see Hamid Khan 2001: 448–508 for a complete description of the process and outcome). Bhutto wanted to retain a presidential system; but, in accordance with the PPP's platform and the views of other founding leaders, Pakistan reverted to a parliamentary system (see Burki 1980: 92–5).

When Bhutto took over in December 1971 it was as chief martial law administrator. He kept that title until August 1972, and continued to act in that role even afterwards, when it came to drawing up the constitution. While he was president, Pakistan was governed under the state of emergency declared in November 1971, which was immediately replaced by the declaration of an emergency under article 232 of the new 1973 constitution.[3] According to Ardeshir Cowasjee (2007):

> Bhutto had already jailed his friends of the Awami National Party, Wali Khan & Co., and various other political nuisances, and to keep them safely behind bars and out of his hair he needed to prolong the state of emergency and to suspend certain of our guaranteed fundamental rights (they remained imprisoned until President General Zia ul Haq freed them after throwing out Bhutto).[4]

In Gerald Heeger's (1977: 259) contemporary account (written well before the regime fell): "Buttressed by Bhutto's personal support, those in office were seldom reluctant to harass not only members of opposition parties, but their opponents within the PPP as well. Arbitrary jailings, bogus criminal charges, physical intimidation by the police – all became common."[5] The interim constitution adopted in April 1972 had retained the position of an executive president, and a strong executive was a major feature of the 1973 constitution. One telling provision was that "for a no-confidence vote to be accepted, a majority of the prime minister's party had to cast votes of no-confidence" (Kennedy 2005: 41). While this new regime was not formally the same as the "viceregal system" inaugurated by Jinnah, it certainly gave the head of government equivalent powers, and Bhutto did not hesitate to use them.

A Sindhi-language movement had emerged in 1970, and riots between supporters of Urdu and Sindhi occurred in January 1971 and then again in July 1972. The election promise of the PPP chief minister of Sindh to restore Sindhi to its official status provoked a violent reaction, and Bhutto had to step in with a compromise formula that gave roughly equal status to both languages for conducting government business (T. Rahman 1995: 1012–14). Bhutto forcibly put a stop to the Baloch starting down what he might have interpreted as the Bangladesh path a year later.

Bhutto set out to bring the state apparatus under control (see Shafqat 1997: 165–81). He had dismissed the senior military officers who had forced Yahya Khan to step down, and may well have expected those who then rose more rapidly than they would have otherwise to be grateful to him. He poured resources into the military and gave them an additional role in helping to develop a nuclear weapon. He founded the paramilitary Federal Security Force (FSF), in order to relieve the army of its "aid to the civil" duties (International Crisis Group 2008a: 4, citing Jalal 1995: 82), which it saw as contrary to its mission and discipline. According to a former inspector-general of police interviewed by the International Crisis Group, the FSF included "some of the worst elements of the other law-enforcement agencies and was accountable only to the prime minister" (International Crisis Group 2008a: 4). It ended as "Bhutto's private military arm" (Nawaz 2008: 338). Yet, in Richter's (1980: 98) interpretation, "Bhutto's five years in office were a concerted but ultimately unsuccessful attempt to break the 'vicious circle' of recurrent military rule."

Bhutto transformed the bureaucracy by breaking the monopoly of the highest positions held by the Civil Service of Pakistan (CSP) officers, and bringing in, via "lateral entry," "committed" administrators (to use Indira Gandhi's term). LaPorte (1992: 105) provides some rough estimates: "[Bhutto] also conducted two purges of the civil service, one in 1972 when 2,000 civil servants were dismissed and another in 1976. Through lateral entry, over 5,000 individuals were appointed to civil service positions." Waseem (1989: 318) points out, however, that "essentially it was an exercise in shifting officers to another, more privileged, service cadre. Thus, of all the 514 lateral entrants between 1973 and 1975, 90 percent were already government officers."[6] Bhutto's reforms resulted in the politicization of the civil service that continues "to the extent that it has all but destroyed the concept of a neutral and competent civil service" (Wilder 2009: 22). Bhutto sought to make the state apparatus a reliable and powerful instrument in prime ministerial hands.

The Pakistan People's Party, which Bhutto had founded in 1967, also was likely to be a reliable instrument of rule. It had been forged in the struggle against Ayub Khan in 1968–9 and in the triumphant election campaign of 1970. And, in the initial years of Bhutto's government, progressive if not socialist programs were proposed and implemented: the nationalization of certain industries, a land reform program, etc. However, the initial programmatic thrust of the party was blunted, and Bhutto turned increasingly to strong-arm tactics to keep even his supporters in line. He revived the anti-Ahmadiyya feeling that had been put into play in 1953 by having them declared "non-Muslim" in 1974, and he instituted certain other "Islamic" measures, such as changing the weekly holiday from Sunday to Friday and the banning of alcohol. The Federal Security Force was also used to pursue Bhutto's objectives, through intimidation and possibly murders, notably the one that ultimately resulted in Bhutto's hanging.

That is, although Pakistan looked like a functioning democracy, with a popularly elected prime minister governing under the rule of law, not very far beneath the surface one could find the autocratic strand that had characterized Pakistan governance since its beginning. In Paula Newberg's summary (1995: 161): "Until 1977, the People's Party government gradually took on the character of martial law. . . . By the time of the elections, however, blatant power rather than delegated authority had governed political life for too long." Waseem (1989: 353–61) presents a balanced appraisal of whether Pakistan under Bhutto was "fascist," or "Bonapartist," or just "populist," or "patrimonialist." Whatever its name, the regime most certainly had very significant autocratic tendencies.

Bhutto called the 1977 election a year early, expecting an easy victory; and, although an effective opposition alliance had formed, it seems likely that Bhutto would have won his majority in the new parliament (see Sharif al Mujahid 1980 for a detailed discussion). Hamid Khan (2001: 548) claims that

> it is, by all accounts, certain that Bhutto was dissatisfied with the parliamentary system. . . . He was unhappy with the 1973 Constitution and the constraints that it imposed on the executive. . . . His message was loud and clear. Bhutto was going back to the people to seek a mandate for bringing about a change in the country's political and constitutional structure.

For that he would have needed a two-thirds majority, and perhaps for that reason (and not necessarily as the result of direct orders from Bhutto) there was a significant amount of rigging in the election.

The opposition movement took to the streets in a demand for a fresh election, and ultimately invited the army to take over to see that the new election was free and fair. Zia's claim that the army was only interested in having a fair election within ninety days might have been an honest one,[7] but the army may well have been intending to intervene all along (Richter 1980). When Bhutto emerged from jail with greater and more enthusiastic support than before, making it likely that he would win the election, the ninety days seemed too short a time. Indeed, it stretched to eleven years of military rule even though Bhutto had been executed.

## India

In the meantime, there were certain parallel developments in India. True, Mrs Gandhi stood as a triumphant warrior and humanitarian in 1971, and followed that with a sweeping victory in the state elections of 1972, with a totally loyal party to command. The "second liberation" from the military threat from Pakistan (Chopra 1974) was reinforced by India's green revolution achievement of becoming self-sufficient in food-grain production, liberating India from its humiliating dependence on US food aid. There was also the promise of the Bombay High offshore oil field, with other finds expected to follow, seemingly making it possible to hope for energy independence as well.

But economic developments to a large extent beyond India's control stalled the economy and provoked high levels of inflation in 1973–4. Coupled with the failure of the nationalization of the wholesale wheat trade, this forced Mrs Gandhi to step back from her "progressive" identity – she famously broke the railwaymen's strike in 1974. At roughly the same time, India conducted its "Peaceful Nuclear Explosion." Like Bhutto, Mrs Gandhi seemed to be moving towards a "hard state" "committed bureaucracy" future, with the Congress Party her utterly dependent instrument of popular mobilization.

Mrs Gandhi, when faced with the JP movement in Bihar, and with Morarji Desai's effective mobilization of the Gujarat Congress(O) against her dismissal of its government, with the trigger of the adverse judgment of the Allahabad court, imposed the Emergency. And then, nineteen months later, she called for an election.

In a way, Mrs Gandhi's turn to autocracy was as flawed as Bhutto's "democratic" rule. By global standards of dictatorship, it was pretty mild. The worst day-to-day abuses of coerced sterilizations, arbitrary slum clearances, and the locking up of opponents happened mainly in Delhi, Haryana, and Western and Central UP. Mrs Gandhi also attempted to institutionalize her rule within the legal and constitutional system. She obtained favorable rulings from the Supreme Court and she had constitutional amendments passed by parliament. Admittedly, most of the opposition was in jail; but, had they been in parliament, they would not have been able to prevent those amendments from passing. She apparently stepped back from a plan to introduce a presidential system when the opposition to that became clear. While the press was censored, and the right of assembly abridged, there was plenty of information flowing freely, and (unreported) protests were in fact underway, even in Delhi.[8]

There are a host of explanations for Mrs Gandhi's calling the election, though the most convincing one is that she believed she would win handily (see Narain 1978; Mayer 1984). The Emergency had been visibly popular at its outset, as corruption came down and the government operated with heretofore unknown efficiency. There had been a number of programs that had brought benefits to the poor, such as house construction in villages (see Schlesinger 1977). All the normal advantages of incumbency were in place, and the opposition was fragmented, with some leaders still in jail, until just a few weeks before election day.

It was only midway in the campaign that Jagjivan Ram took himself and his group out of the Congress. It became clear that the opposition had used its time in jail to forge bonds – as had happened in the jails in the 1930s – that were strong during the campaign, though they weakened later, in the Janata government. It is also likely that the channels of information upwards to Mrs Gandhi had been blocked by people's understandable unwillingness to be the bearer of bad tidings, so it took time for the depth of the resentment of the family planning campaign to emerge.

In the event, an anti-Indira "wave" built fairly suddenly towards the end of the campaign – which to Mrs Gandhi's credit had been conducted freely and fairly (if one can ignore the fact that there were leaders still jailed), with the Election Commission in charge, and the press largely uncensored. The Congress was soundly defeated. (The best account is Weiner 1978.) What was most remarkable was the demonstrable commitment of a broad range of citizens to "democracy" in some abstract way (see Narain 1978: 107). Many of the Delhi intelligentsia, mainly of the upper classes, discovered during the Emergency that freedoms, though perhaps "bourgeois," were something to be valued, and worth fighting for. They took part in the campaigning with unprecedented enthusiasm. The poor and otherwise completely powerless received an object lesson in the power of the vote.

India's near-brush with long-lasting authoritarian rule fits the generalized pattern Juan Linz presents in his *Breakdown of Democratic Regimes: Crisis, Breakdown, and Reequilibration* (Linz 1978). According to Linz, a political crisis ripens to the point at which the elected leadership proclaims a state of emergency, which can result in either regime change or re-equilibration. Elements of the crisis include a "disloyal opposition," unsolvable problems, inappropriate and ineffective use of the military, and some sort of "environmental" crisis – economic depression, military defeat, etc. This leads to a governmental crisis, featuring difficulty in forming coalitions, party fragmentation, and the like (Linz 1978: pp. 50 ff.). The political crisis in India was nowhere near the magnitude of the crisis in Weimar Germany (which is Linz's paradigmatic case), but there was, for example, a "disloyal opposition" traceable in Jayaprakash Narayan's call for the army to disobey commands; and there certainly was a "governmental crisis" of the sort Linz describes.

Linz describes the possible outcomes of a "state of emergency" that a failing government declares. Most common is regime change (Linz 1978: 81–4), including a military coup or a takeover by bureaucrats, and civil war. One explanation for why that did not happen in India is provided by D. A. Low, in an unpublished 1975 paper summarized by Mayer (1984: 141), who places the Emergency in the context of British operations in the 1930s and 1940s in which there were "no deliberate political killings; no dramatic political trials; no suspension of the Constitution; no dismissal of the legislatures; no employment of the army." Low predicted elections would follow, because "whatever its defects . . . these two mechanisms for dealing with parliamentary crises ['declaring what one British official engagingly called

"*civil* martial law"' and the post-independence President's Rule] largely
explain why the military has not hitherto moved to take control of India's
political system."

Instead of regime change, what happened in India is what Linz calls a
"re-equilibration" after the state of emergency. Linz (1978: 87–8) suggests
certain "requisites" that indeed we find in the Indian case: the "uncomprom-
ised leadership" (Jayaprakash, Morarji Desai, and other leaders locked up
during the Emergency); "accepted by regime loyalists" (accepted by the
Congress – especially those who had come to oppose Mrs Gandhi); in which
the "deposed leadership accepts the transfer of power"; "confidence in new
democratic leadership"; and the "indifference of the bulk of the population
to the final dénouement." The confidence in the new democratic leadership
was of course demonstrated in the election itself, which also, paradoxically,
indicated the "indifference" of at least a substantial part of the population,
when one notes that the Congress did quite well in South India, and when
one considers that a short three years later Mrs Gandhi came back to
power. After a moment of exhilaration, politics as usual – with citizen indifference at best, and dislike at worst – kicked back in.

Linz (1978: 48–9) also provides an important insight into the support
from the intelligentsia that Mrs Gandhi originally had, and then forfeited
during the Emergency, which I myself found in seemingly endless discussions
during my time in Delhi in 1969–70 and then in 1975–6. Noting that "the
paradox of the ambivalence of intellectuals toward liberal democracy is not
easy to explain," Linz points to factors such as

> the elitism of intellectuals and their hostility to the average man, who
> is, after all, the average voter; their dislike for politics based on self-
> interest rather than on ideas of a better society; [and] their dislike for
> the professional politician, whom they often consider their inferior.

The intelligentsia, he continues, are not prepared to join mass parties, where
their influence is less than people like leaders of interest groups, and some
have a "bitter hostility against other intellectuals ready to serve those in power."
Moreover, the "literati . . . tend to become indignant with the banality of the
routine political process [which] contrasts with the potential for great historical transformation realized in other societies that serve as utopian points
of reference." Finally, Linz points out:

> The ambivalence of many intellectuals toward competitive pluralistic
> liberal democracy has perhaps an even more profound origin. It is the
> basic moral ambiguity of a political system that legitimizes decisions on
> the basis of formal, procedural, legal correctness without distinction of
> content except respect for civil liberties and the equality before the law
> of all citizens, with no reference to substantive justice and no link to a
> system of ultimate values. In societies suffering from serious injustices

and deep cultural cleavages, it is difficult to accord intellectual justification to a system in which the will of the electorate, the technicalities of the law-making process, and the decision of the courts can serve to maintain a social order that rouses moral indignation or, conversely, can allow a reformist majority to question an inherited value system.

We can see beliefs like these reflected to some extent even in the scholarly work of non-Indians. Francine Frankel, for example, writes "there were many other deep-rooted problems behind the Emergency that went beyond Mrs Gandhi's personality," and says that P. N. Haksar "got at the fundamental cause of the Emergency, by relating it to the 'maturing of the crisis in our entire social, economic, political, cultural and value system which became increasingly incapable of solving the structural problems of building a new India'" (Frankel 2005: 651, using Austin 1999: 298 as the source of Haksar's quote [1979: 228]). During the Emergency, the intelligentsia discovered that their ideas – often supportive of the regime's avowed principles – were suddenly kept from the general public because of censorship by bureaucrats. Even worse, their connections to the elite and their ability to make their arguments directly to those in power were curtailed, often by bureaucrats who were demonstrably loyal to Mrs Gandhi and her son and their inner circle of politicians. When their opportunity came to express their frustration, in the election campaign, they seized it, and many of them became committed to political activism on behalf of democracy. As journalists and other writers, community organizers and lawyers, academics and religious leaders, the intelligentsia contributed significantly to the support democratic institutions received in the following years.

It took only months after the 1977 election before the triumphant Janata coalition began to fall apart. It proved to be impossible to bring Mrs Gandhi herself to justice, or even to roll back entirely the Emergency constitutional amendments or institute an autonomous broadcasting system and other such reforms. Scholars began to wonder whether it was the Emergency that was the aberration in India's democratic history. Instead, perhaps the democracy upsurge of the 1977 election was the aberration. Peter Mayer (1984: 128) introduces his masterful discussion and evaluation of the various explanations for imposing the Emergency by pointing out (calling it a "grave error") that "the more complacent of our colleagues [conclude] that, deplorable and disturbing though it was, in its quintessence the emergency was an exceptional event, a statistical freak." Myron Weiner (1983: 56) writes:

That one person or a handful of persons can take [measures to end the democratic process] indicates how powerful the state is, how easy it is for a small group to dominate the state, and how fragile are the political institutions within the society. India's brief authoritarian interlude is a reminder of how vulnerable India's democratic system remains.

And Ainslie Embree (1983: 66–7) concludes his essay "The Emergency as a Signpost to India's Future" with:

> It can certainly be argued that the loss of such institutions as a free press is undoubtedly regrettable, but that this must be balanced over against the greater good of the greater number who will profit from the benefits of an authoritarian government, free to use all resources for the benefit of the masses. It is the seductiveness of such an appeal that, combined with the weight of India's historical experience, suggests to this observer that authoritarian rule, even if it is no more successful than the old forms, is the likely path to India's future.
>
> (Embree 1983: 66–7)

It is striking that Embree, a mere five years after the transformative 1977 election and twenty-five years after independence, echoes Phillips Talbot's 1947 assessment (quoted above, pp. 33–4). It was certainly not self-evident that India's democratic rule would persist.

After Mrs Gandhi's defeat, the new government, hampered by the need to accommodate the Congress, whose votes in the Rajya Sabha were needed for any change, re-amended the constitution to get rid of some of the executive-strengthening measures Mrs Gandhi had rammed through her rump parliament. Particular policies like coercive family planning and slum demolitions were withdrawn or put into cold storage, but few of the instruments of oppression – the use of the police to spy on opponents, for example – were discarded.

And yet the Emergency did mark a turning point, perhaps coincidentally linked to profound changes in India's society, economy, and polity, for which other signposts include: the green revolution; the beginnings of a shift away from a command economy; the emergence of a substantial urban middle class; and the like. The euphoria of the 1977 election was productively transformed into support for a far more vigorous and professional media. The media reporting on what the Emergency had meant for India was independent of the Shah Commission and other official inquiries, and provided a foundation for the development of first-rate investigative journalism. Yet it has taken a long time for that print media revolution to spread to the electronic media; radio is still not liberated.

Intellectuals revived organizations such as the People's Union for Civil Liberties to provide oversight to the judicial system, and a new generation of activist judges fostered the development of public-interest litigation. The new government moved decisively away from large-scale industrial enterprise, in both the public and the private sector, quite deliberately to constrain the power of the bureaucracy and the large business houses. And the government appointed the Mandal Commission in 1979, which proposed legal accommodation of what becomes what Yogendra Yadav (2000) has called the "second upsurge."

Mayer makes the argument that "the destruction of the historical Congress Party and its replacement by Indira's Congress . . . was the essential transformation which made the emergency possible in 1975 [while it would not have been possible in 1965 or 1970]" (Mayer 1984: 145).

Perhaps the most important outcome of the Emergency was the changed party landscape. The Janata Party, of course, did not have much staying power. It was, however, the first version of the national-level "third force" collection of state-based parties – Lohia socialist and OBC-based parties, and remnants of a democratic-socialist Congress – that emerge as the "National Front" in 1989 and the "United Front" in 1996. Being part of the Janata coalition and party allowed the Bharatiya Jana Sangh to shed some of its explicit Hindu nationalist skin, to become the secular-surfaced Bharatiya Janata Party, which had a substantial number of the seats within the Janata. The Congress continued to come apart after its 1969 split – during the 1977 election itself, when Jagjivan Ram came out, and again in 1978, when the Congress (Indira) was formed. It was reduced even more clearly to being Indira's Congress; and, though it remained the strongest party in India, it had begun a long decline.

It is not far-fetched to argue that, had Sanjay Gandhi not died, he would have tried to use the "shouting brigade" Youth Congress MPs that had been elected in 1980, and the blunt instruments of the state, to replay the Emergency and parlay it into a right-wing autocratic regime. It is unlikely that would have survived an opposition challenge built on new and thus still vigorous parties. Yadav's "Third Electoral System," which he dates from this time, has its roots in these parties (see Yadav 1999a, 1999b). Indeed, all three of the elements of the transformed politics of the 1990s in India – "Mandal, Market, and Mandir" in the widely used phrase – have their origins in the aftermath of the Emergency. Whether they have contributed to a genuine "deepening" of democracy, or only to a greater routinization of the system, remains to be seen.

Let me propose a metaphor for what happened in 1975 through 1977 in India and Pakistan. When space probes are launched to the outer planets of the solar system, they are sent via one of the inner planets, so that, passing close by, they will accelerate (owing to the gravitational pull of the planet) and be slung into the trajectory to their destination with added speed. India's democratic system received just that sort of boost from its close encounter with the Planet of Autocracy in 1975–7, moving towards a consolidated and mature democracy at a different level and speed. Pakistan's political system, already on an unsteady trajectory, was captured by that planet and became a moon, albeit with a highly elliptical orbit (with Zia's period close in, and the 1988–9 period quite distant).

There was a turning point also within the balance-of-power framework at this time. In India, Mrs Gandhi's requirement of a "committed" bureaucracy and judiciary ensured that her rule and the rule of those parts of the state apparatus (the military had been left unpoliticized) were conjoined in the mind of citizens. Very few, if any, bureaucrats resigned rather than carry out the policies of the Emergency that were later recognized to produce "excesses" (the sterilization campaign especially); and, indeed, there were many who publicly relished their newly renewed power to command; accountable to no one other than, ultimately, Mrs Gandhi. It is likely that those who continued to serve under the leaders, fresh from jail, who had thrown out the Congress, had once again to prove their acceptance of the role of public *servant*. Even more important, the judiciary had to redemonstrate their autonomy from the legislative-executive; indeed, they had an incentive to expand it, which they very quickly began to do. The intensity of the democratic experience of the election of 1977 – something that helped energize civil-society activity in the decades ahead – renewed the advantage politicians and voters (whose grievances the courts would seek to resolve directly in the following years) had over the state apparatus.

In Pakistan, Zulfiqar Ali Bhutto's rigged election indicated a descent in the legitimacy of the elected politician. His early success in reducing the power of the superior civil service, and the installation of a "committed" bureaucracy of his own, weakened the bureaucracy so much that ever since it has been the visibly junior partner to the army in the bureaucratic polity Pakistan became. The army was able to regain the legitimacy it had lost in the comprehensive defeat of 1971, but not by winning a war against external enemies. It was the opposition politicians who had invited the army to intervene, and so Zia could pose as a savior of a democratic regime – who then was "forced" to put the system to rights by purging it of corrupt and criminal politicians, including Bhutto himself. Zia did not restore the superior civil service to its earlier pedestal; instead of allowing lateral entry into the bureaucracy by civilians, he gave that opportunity to military officers (Wilder 2009: 23–4). The army thus became a political player opposed to the PPP (a party with genuine popular roots) and allied with the right-wing opposition – a pattern that continues to the present. While Zia's Islamization project undoubtedly came from his deep belief in its validity, it did not hurt that embracing and promoting Islam might be a way to provide a popular base and perhaps cement the legitimacy of the military's guidance of the state, as the ultimate guarantor of the nation's existence.

Before we resume the narrative of the political choices made in the years after 1977 – in Chapters 9 and 10 – we need to examine two major explanations of why the two countries have diverged, especially after 1977: one has to do with religion, the other with external influences. We have considered both of these briefly in the course of the narrative of events of the first thirty years of independence, but the following chapters provide a more systematic view. Mrs Gandhi, even while in opposition, had begun to weaken parties that had opposed the Congress, including the Akali Dal in Punjab, a party that was "Sikh" both in composition and in support, and in its thinly disguised religious base. There she played the "religion card," making use of an extremist Sikh religious leader, Sant Bhindranwale. The consequences ultimately were a full-scale separatist movement in the Punjab that lasted until the early 1990s, and Mrs Gandhi's assassination at the hands of her Sikh bodyguards. In the late 1980s, a separatist movement emerged in Kashmir, also with a significant religious element. More important, at roughly the same time, a Hindu nationalist movement led by the "*Sangh parivar*" gathered momentum, leading to the climax of the demolition of the Babri Masjid in December 1992.

In Pakistan, it was not long after Zia ul Haq took over that he introduced the first of his Islamization measures, the Hudood ordinances. Very soon thereafter, two external events that were to influence Pakistan strongly occurred: the Iranian Revolution and the Soviet invasion of Afghanistan. Both of these strengthened Zia's effort to make Pakistan more of an Islamic state. Yet the fervor of support for the new order in Iran – even though only 20 percent or so of Pakistan is Shi'a, the clerical takeover in Iran was widely welcomed – rested on the foundation of increasing religiosity in Pakistan, perhaps derived from the vastly increased movement of Pakistanis to and from the Gulf countries in the aftermath of the 1973 Israel–Egypt war, and the "oil shocks" that followed. The external influence on Pakistan's governance had been greater than on India's even before 1977; after India had established itself as a dominant power in South Asia, in 1971 and then with its "Peaceful Nuclear Explosion" in 1974, the difference in degree of vulnerability each country felt increased, and the impact of outside powers with it.

## Notes

1 India, though victorious over Pakistan, paradoxically felt an *increased* vulnerability, because of the near-total lack of support in the UN for its taking military action to help Bangladesh emerge, and the gunboat diplomacy of the US. So India very quickly set out to strengthen further *its* military capacity, by developing a nuclear weapon among other things.

2 In an interview with Oriana Fallaci (1976: 198) in April 1972, he said: "I think that within ten or fifteen years Pakistan and Bangladesh can be reunited in a federation."

3 *The Gazette of Pakistan*, Extra, 15 August 1973, Islamabad: No. F24 (1)/73-Pub. As quoted in Cowasjee (2007); see also Cowasjee (2009).

4 Heeger (1977: 259) discusses what was done to Wali Khan and others. See Hamid Khan (2001: 456–73) for the details of the state of emergency.

5 See Ardeshir Cowasjee's (2009) scathing description of the restrictions on fundamental rights introduced by Bhutto literally hours after the constitution came into effect, and the partisan nature of the first seven amendments in the following years. See also Ahmed (2001): 47.

6 See also International Crisis Group (2008a: 4) for how this affected the police. See also Burki (1980): 98–103.

7 See Ardeshir Cowasjee (2008a) for testimony of his contemporaneous skepticism – remarkably expressed to Zia ul Haq himself twenty days into his rule.

8 As someone who spent October 1975 to December 1976 in Delhi and Lucknow, I can personally testify to quite a few open discussions. I happened to witness one large anti-government demonstration – a lawyers' protest at the Tis Hazari courts in Delhi – that was not in the next day's newspaper.

# 7   Religion as an explanation

The role of religious belief and practice in explaining the emergence and stability of particular political regimes in general is too large a subject to be discussed here (instead, see Anderson 2006a). Nor is there any need for me to consider Samuel Huntington's "clash of civilizations" argument – as almost all writing on this topic these days seems to do (see Stepan 2000). The question of whether Islam and democracy in general are compatible has been written about mainly in the context of the Middle East, and with the implicit or explicit comparison with Christianity.[1] Whether Hinduism is compatible with democracy receives almost no attention at all, even in comparative studies (Anderson 2006a: 197; Stepan 2000).

There seems to be no absolute contradiction between Islam and democracy theoretically, according to Fattah and Butterfield (2006: 75):

> In sum, Islamic thought regarding politics and (in particular) democracy is no less diverse than any other culturally or religiously informed view of the matter. The cultural entrepreneurs – the intellectuals and ulama – who interpret Islam for the masses are hardly of one mind. Distinctions are not subtle, nor are they a matter of degree; significant qualitative differences separate them into widely divergent camps. Orientalist assumptions about a specific Islamic interpretation of democracy or that resort to generalizations about the compatibility of Islam and democracy rely either on a single interpretation or on the fact that most Islamic societies (and virtually all Arab ones) are not very democratic. Our examination of Islamic intellectual and scholarly thought suggests that such assumptions do not have the predictive power their adherents advocate.

Nor is there evidence that in practice the situation is different. In Minkenberg's (2007: 903) summary:

> Norris and Inglehart (2004) analyze, among other things, the approval of democratic values and performance and find more evidence which refutes the claim that Islam and democracy are incompatible. After

controlling for economic development and social factors, their results show that "contrary to Huntington's thesis, compared with Western societies, there were no significant differences between the publics living in the West and in Muslim religious cultures in approval of how democracy works in practice, in support for democratic ideals, and in approval of strong leadership" (Norris and Inglehart 2004: 146).

Or, in a study that relies on multiple regression analysis of Muslim, Catholic, and Eastern Orthodox respondents in eight countries, Hofmann (2004: 654) concludes:

The results of the study lend support to scholarly works that stress possible points of fusion between Islam and democracy. The sources and patterns of democratic support are not found to systematically differ between Muslim and Christian respondents in the countries included in the study. . . . The model also suggests that in the countries included in the study, religion may play a fairly minimal role in shaping individuals' attitudes concerning democracy.

Anderson (2006b: 193, 203), "taking on board" arguments of this sort, none the less wants to argue that "religion is not entirely irrelevant to understanding the evolution of democratic experiments" and asks "is there any sense in trying to factor religious traditions, as opposed to the actions of specific religious organizations, into explanations of democratic outcomes?" His answer is, of course, a "yes," but hardly a full-throated one: "it might still be argued that there remain elements within 'actually existing Islam' – within the tradition as presently constituted and realized in the world – that are problematic for democratic development. . . . [And] at the ideological level there remain features of contemporary Islam that may be unhelpful for processes of democratization" (Anderson 2006b: 209). In literally the final sentence of the book, Anderson (2006b: 214) says: "Religious tradition cannot determine outcomes, but when the factors working for or against democratization are finely balanced, then whose God is prevalent may just make a difference."

## Islamization, Hindu nationalism

Religion was an important part of both Indian and Pakistan nationalist movements, and the constituent assemblies of both countries had to wrestle with how to define "secularism" in India and the "Islamic state" in Pakistan. The ultimately successful effort to declare the Ahmadiyya "non-Muslim" certainly affected Pakistan's politics, though it was treated as a symbolic gesture by those who cynically made use of it. By extension, the principle conceded has continued to disturb the relations between Shi'a and Sunni, first during Zia's Islamization campaign in the 1980s, and then in the emergence of sectarian warfare in the 1990s. Although Zia was himself a deeply religious man, he did not claim to be acting as a religious leader, and all other Pakistani leaders have been far more secular than he was. The various laws that have been put in place that can be called Islamic have not affected the core structure of the Pakistani state.

When General Zia seized power in July 1977, with the encouragement of the parties opposed to Bhutto's PPP, his announced goal was to hold fresh elections. Once he discovered – to his horror, he claimed – how deeply corrupt the Bhutto regime had been, he proposed to clean up the mess and then restore democracy. But very quickly he shifted to a transformative project, the centerpiece of which was Islamization.

This involved most prominently changes in the legal system. Charles Kennedy (1990: 62) effectively proves this bold contention that he makes at the outset of his paper:

> It has been a decade since the late President Zia-ul-Haq promulgated his Islamic reforms (Nizam-i-Mustapha) in Pakistan. I contend that these reforms have had only a minor impact upon the political, legal, social, and economic institutions of the state. . . . Admittedly, the politicization of the process of Islamization has played a very significant role in the political environment of Pakistan during the 1980s. . . . Zia's government portrayed the reforms as leading Pakistan in the direction of becoming "truly Islamic," and promised rapid and thorough implementation of the reforms. Opponents of the reform also argued that the reforms were being implemented rapidly although they deemed aspects of the reforms as misguided, reactionary, antidemocratic, and/or discriminatory to women. I contend, however, that such rhetoric, despite its strident nature, was primarily "political noise," signifying little in regard to implementation or public policy.

In the two decades since, the situation of Islamic rhetoric overstating the extent of the enforcement of Islamic law remains much the same. In its 2006 report on religious freedom, the US State Department noted that "no successful cases have been brought under [the Hudood Ordinance standard that decrees that] Muslim and non-Muslim and male and female testimony carries different weight, and harsh Qur'anic punishments can be applied."[2] The Musharraf government did enact some change:

> According to human rights monitors, 80 percent of the female prison population was awaiting trial on adultery-related offenses under the Hudood Ordinances. However, with the enactment in December 2006 of the Women's Protection Bill, women are not supposed to be arrested under the Hudood Ordinance nor required to produce four witnesses to prove a charge of rape, as required under the zina laws (laws regarding extramarital sexual intercourse). Family members had previously used

the Hudood Ordinances to control their children from making their own choices in marriage. Abusive husbands sometimes invoked the ordinances, or neighbors invoked the ordinances to settle personal scores. After the passage of the Women's Protection Bill, authorities released from prison approximately 300 to 500 women due to the less-harsh guidelines in the bill. In July the president promulgated the Law Reforms Ordinance, allowing women held under the Hudood Ordinance to be eligible for bail. According to the Progressive Women's Association, approximately 1,300 to 1,500 additional women were released upon the passage of the Law Reforms Ordinance.[3]

Other serious human rights violations remain, especially in the enforcement of strictures against the laws on blasphemy, against the Ahmadiyya, and in so-called "honor killings."[4]

Islamization also meant measures to enforce some of the core practices of Islam, such as the payment of *zakat* (a tithe) and the banning of *riba* (usury). Laws intended to do the first had to be amended when the Shi'a protested strongly that, according to their interpretation, *zakat* could not be levied by the state (see J. Malik 1996: 85–119). According to Malik: "The diverse tendencies of Islam in Pakistan suggest that a single uniform policy of Islamization as envisaged under the regime of Zia ul Haq in collaboration with fundamentalist forces was doomed to failure from the start" (1996: 8). This was true not only at the elite level. Richard Kurin (1987: 127) concludes his analysis of the impact of Islamization in one Punjab village with this observation: "vocal and articulate [villagers view Islam] . . . as a core symbol, and not as a specific theology, philosophy, body of practice, set of moral injunctions or legal doctrines, and certainly not as a social order promulgated by the [Zia ul Haq] government." Banning of *riba* remains in abeyance – despite a decision by the *shariat* court requiring the banking system to conform – while the government tries desperately to find a way of doing "Islamic banking" that will not slow down Pakistan's recent economic growth (see Kennedy 1993).

Indeed, Martin Lau (2006: 210), in the conclusion to his book *The Role of Islam in the Legal System of Pakistan*, writes:

> Pakistan's higher judiciary has confounded the perception that the relationship between human rights and Islam is as of necessity best described as a "clash of civilisations." . . . Pakistan's superior courts have been able to use Islam to expand the scope of fundamental rights and even to add rights like a fundamental right to justice to those human rights expressly protected by the 1973 Constitution. . . . [Even more surprising], throughout the 1980s the Federal Shariat Court and the Shariat Appellate Bench of the Supreme Court formulated an approach to the Islamisation of laws which replicated to a large extent the existing fundamental rights. Statutes which infringed the right to equality, the right

to be heard or which accorded the state excessive discretionary powers were declared repugnant to Islam.

He quickly points out that this "sits uneasily" with other cases that tend in the other direction – on land reforms, social reform, women's rights, and the freedom of religion. But it suggests that a critical institution of the state, the autonomy of which is crucial for democracy, has not been captured by the religious establishment. Indeed, this may be true also even in local environments. Pakistan – unlike Bangladesh – has not, it would seem, been plagued by local clerics issuing *fatwas* that enforce penalties that violate the rule of statutory law. (The tolerance of the enforcement of local moral regimes is another matter, when one thinks of the "honor killing" issue, especially in the frontier areas.)

Zia's Islamization policies aimed to purify social customs, so that, among other things, women appearing on television had to wear a headscarf, and women were not allowed to participate in sports with men in the audience. Alcohol was banned, though it continues to flow freely – at least among the elite. It was no accident that the most significant opposition to Zia's rule began with elite women organizing protests, including some in the streets, and their suffering at the hands of the police probably enhanced anti-Zia public opinion significantly. Most of these restrictions have not survived, and in 2006 four women fighter pilots graduated from the Pakistan Air Force Academy.[5]

Much more significant has been the adoption of an Islamic struggle ideology, in the Afghanistan *jihad* and the Kashmir *jihad* that followed. There were visible signs – more young men with beards in the Islamic style – and the numbers of *madrassas* increased substantially (International Crisis Group 2002a, 2007a). All of this occurred with the active encouragement of the state. Pervez Hoodbhoy (2008), a careful observer of Pakistan's society and culture, sees a dark future:

> The immediate future of Pakistan looks grim, as increasing numbers of mullahs are creating cults around themselves and seizing control over the minds of their worshippers. . . . In the long term, Pakistan's future will be determined by the ideological and political battle between citizens who want an Islamist theocratic state, and citizens who want a modern Islamic republic. It may yet be possible to roll back the Islamist laws and institutions that have corroded Pakistani society for over 30 years, and defeat the "holy" warriors. However, this can only happen if Pakistan's elected leaders acquire the trust of the citizens.

Waseem (2004: 33) notes that the "army-dominated state apparatus" has given Islamic organizations "a relatively free hand" compared to others of civil society, and particularly those of the Left, in "providing social, cultural, economic and political space."

The religious parties were given certain advantages in the 2002 elections – Islamic-institution degrees were counted as equal to the Bachelor degrees others had to have in order to contest, for example – and a spectrum of parties, some of whose followers had been literally murdering each other, managed to form an alliance. But these "Islam-favoring" (*Islam-pasand*) parties only managed to get 11 percent of the vote. Since they captured power in the NWFP and had considerable support in Balochistan as well, their support in the Punjab heartland of Pakistan must have been only in single digits (see Grare 2006). In the February 2008 elections, the Muttahida Majlis-e-Amal (MMA) was virtually wiped out as a force in the national assembly and reduced to ten seats (of ninety-six declared as of 15 March 2008) in the NWFP provincial assembly.[6] On the other hand, according to a public opinion survey conducted by the International Republican Institute in March 2009, at the time when the government had agreed to a Taliban demand to restore *shariat* courts in Swat, 56 percent of respondents said "yes" to the question "In the future if the Taliban demand *sharia* in other parts of Pakistan like Karachi, Multan, Quetta or Lahore for instance? Would you support their demand?"[7] We need to assess the importance of belief in Islam by leaders and followers in Pakistan in possibly reinforcing the choices favoring autocracy, and whether there were not other elements of the Islamic tradition that might have supported democracy there.

In India, the RSS element in the Janata Party (and then the BJP when the Janata split) strove to hang on to its opening to the moderate and secular middle, explored in jail during the Emergency and during their 1977–9 term in government. Mrs Gandhi apparently saw the opportunity of taking yet another piece of the program of the *Sangh parivar* – to go along with the hard state-and-discipline perspective, in effect stolen from them during the Emergency and soon to be revived in the 1984 election campaign – namely, religious nationalism. This took the form of encouraging Zail Singh in Punjab to play "divide and rule" by supporting the radical Sant Bhindranwale against the Akalis. Corbridge and Harriss (2000: 109) spell out the consequences:

> Not only did the Congress Party, under Mrs Gandhi, fight religious fire with religious fire, thereby breaching one of her father's rules for the management of Centre–State relations, it also created a leader/ monster (Bhindranwale) who refused to do the bidding of his mistress/ Frankenstein. . . . [S]he chose in June 1984 to deal with the growing terror and violence in Punjab by authorizing an army assault on the Golden Temple . . . [securing] the deaths of Bhindranwale and many of his supporters, but at a terrible price.

That price was not only her assassination and the pogrom in Delhi in which thousands of Sikhs were murdered, but also eight years of Khalistani violence and police repression in a hideous vicious circle. That put the

Congress firmly on the "Hindu" side, with the Sikhs playing the role of the "other."

Within a year of her assassination, fortuitously, Rajiv Gandhi chose to balance the concessions given to the traditionalist Muslims in the Shah Bano affair by allowing the reopening of the shrine to Rama inside the Babri Masjid, attempting to take credit for a step to assuage allegedly hurt Hindu feelings. Combined with the drubbing they had received in the 1984 election (two seats and 7.4 percent share of the vote), this provoked the BJP to outbid the Congress in the Hindu nationalism contest, replacing Vajpayee with the more hard-line Advani as the party leader, and embarking on *yatras* (public pilgrimage), *shilanyas* (laying temple foundation-stones), and the like. In the meantime, as the 1980s came to a close, the Congress resumed its earlier practice of rigging Kashmir elections, in a place where the Islamization wave from the west reinforced the grievance of an aborted autonomy. Violent resistance to Indian rule began after the 1989 election brought V. P. Singh to power with BJP support.

The rising curve of communal rioting, and *Sangh parivar*-led provocative Ayodhya-centered Hindu nationalism, was fueled in part by the popularity (sic) of V. P. Singh's acceptance of the Mandal Commission report (see Oldenburg 1991: 31–5). After the Congress victory in the 1991 election, in which Hindu nationalism did not play much of a part, but with a BJP government in power in UP, the Babri Masjid was destroyed. Bombay and a few other places suffered severe communal riots, though it was also true that barely noticed but notable Hindu–Muslim peace initiatives took place in Bihar and West Bengal.

Two months later, the Bombay stock exchange and other buildings were bombed, with Muslim gangsters believed to be the perpetrators. There was a great loss of life, but no rioting. Some eight months later, midway through the campaign in the elections in the states that had been taken over from the BJP in the Babri Masjid destruction aftermath, the BJP had to drop its Hindu nationalist program. Even so, they lost in all those states. The BJP soon handed leadership of the party back to Vajpayee, who developed electoral alliances with parties that were opposed to core *hindutva* ideas. The victories of the BJP-led alliances in 1998 and 1999 occurred because Hindu nationalism was *not* on the agenda. Indeed, the years in between December 1992 and 1998 had been some of the least marked by Hindu–Muslim rioting in India's post-independence history.

Even so, the fifteen years or so of virulent religious nationalism certainly put Indian democracy under severe stress. But it is not clear whether that was because possibly autocratic-minded leaders made use of Hindu symbols and sentiments, as well as setting Hindus against Muslims and Christians as "the other" to mobilize followers for political ends. Did they take advantage of some resonance of Hinduism as a belief system with their political goals? And, before – and possibly after – this *hindutva* phase of Indian politics, did other aspects of Hinduism help reinforce democracy?

## Hinduism and Islam as systems of belief, and the effect on politics

The overall argument here is that *neither* Hinduism nor Islam, either in philosophy or in practice, is particularly favorable to democracy, though both religious traditions have elements that are available to those who wish to legitimate democratic rule. The picture does not change all that much if we consider their relationship to autocracy: those for, and against, an autocratic system can find justification in each religion.

Some argue that Islam is antithetical to democracy because in Islam God is sovereign – and therefore the people only make and enforce laws on God's behalf. Just who is capable of acting as God's intermediary is a crucial argument for Muslims – is it the *ulama*, pious Muslim men, or someone else? Strictly speaking, Muslims ought not to be content to live in a country where non-Muslims rule, and should struggle to bring that country under Muslim rule, even when Muslims are in a minority. This legitimates special laws for non-Muslims. On the other side, there are Islam's strong traditions of equality in matters of worship, albeit with separation of men and women, requiring Muslims to welcome believers into the community (the *umma*) no matter what their race or other superficial markers of identity. These elements should reinforce democratic norms.

Particular elements of Hinduism as a religion that are seen to be antithetical to democracy include its designation of kingship as the ideal system of rule and its legitimation of a caste system and discrimination against women. Elements thought to be conducive to democracy include (comparatively) high toleration of heterodox beliefs, and a focus on the individual as moral actor. In terms of practice, the crucial feature of Hinduism is that it has no "church" remotely comparable to the Catholic Church or Protestant denominations. Hindus, by and large, do not operate as congregations, and the core of the practice of Hinduism is located in the home, for those who are "of the world," and literally in the open for those who are "renouncers."

Since in Hinduism there are no foundational texts that are the "word of God," containing rules and laws of behavior, there are no religious courts. There are no *fatwas*, although in local arenas caste *panchayats* often order punishments – including death – for perceived moral transgressions. Traditionally, practitioners of other religions have tended to be incorporated into the caste system, in a subordinate position, and not persecuted.

The ideal political system in classical Hindu belief is kingship, in which the ruler – necessarily of the Kshatriya (warrior) *varna* (caste category) – partners with the Brahmin priest. In Brian K. Smith's summary:

> Hinduism . . . condones and legitimates political power verging on the dictatorial. . . . But Hinduism also tempers these absolutist powers. . . . The ruler . . . should be a kind of this-worldly *yogin* whose rule over

others is predicated on his rule over himself (2003: 187). . . . [The conundrum] inherent in the Hindu view of political rule [lies in] the problematic alliance between the king and his Brahmin priest. . . . By virtue of the very fact that the Brahmin has formed such a relationship with the king, his power to legitimate the king's rule is thereby compromised.

(B. Smith 2003: 208; see Mehta 2004: 114)

This belief has no direct influence on Indian politics: no one is advocating a return to a monarchy or rules that would limit political positions to Kshatriyas and Brahmins. Gandhi and others have spoken of "Ramrajya" (Rama's Kingdom) as something of an ideal political state; some refer to incidents in the Ramayana for legitimation of democracy – Rama's bowing to the will of his subjects in exiling Sita, for example. But there is no evidence that these particular beliefs have had any serious influence on what politicians or bureaucrats do.

Hinduism's caste system in theory and practice – and the practice is echoed in the *biradari* (clan) system in Pakistan – enshrines a hierarchy of groups defined by who can marry whom, but which has in the past implied assigned occupations, and a position on a scale of purity and pollution. Individuals thus have an inescapable group identity, and mobility in the caste hierarchy – which does occur, often in the process labeled by M. N. Srinivas "Sanskritization" – is by group. Those who have a right to rule are supposedly only those in the duumvirate of the top two *varnas*, the Brahmins and the Kshatriyas. And, indeed, in India's post-independence history, political leaders have come disproportionately from those *varnas*, including some from upwardly mobile *jatis* (castes) that have succeeded in making themselves Kshatriyas when they were once thought to be Sudra (the lowest *varna*). Women also are in a subordinate position in Hindu belief, and have in practice been kept out of political roles, with only a few exceptions.

Those exceptions matter, however. Gandhi – himself neither Brahmin nor Kshatriya – was able to bring women into the nationalist movement as active participants, paving the way for Indira Gandhi to serve as prime minister. She served for a long time (1966–77, 1980–4), exercising real power, as does her Italian-Indian daughter-in-law, Sonia Gandhi. Dr B. R. Ambedkar, who was the major leader of the untouchables, fought bitter political battles with Gandhi as a near-equal. He later served as Nehru's law minister, chairing the drafting committee of India's constitution, and playing a major role in shaping it and defending that document. In 2007, an untouchable woman, Mayawati, was elected chief minister of India's largest state, Uttar Pradesh, and she also exercises power; she is not anyone's puppet.

More important, there are traditions within Hinduism which are anti-caste. The *bhakti* (devotional) movement that spread from South to North India over centuries, reaching a peak some 500 years ago, claimed devotion to God as *the* path to liberation, and often welcomed all castes and both genders into the fold, as worshippers and even saints. Liberation itself – the ultimate spiritual goal for a Hindu – is very much a matter of individual choice and practice. Spiritual leaders are "gurus" – teachers – who (in theory) do not dictate what one must do to be liberated.

In practice, in family and village and urban neighborhood, the caste system has been a powerful structure underpinning local autocrats, and its religious sanction has been used as a tool, as when upper-caste landlords pursue their factional disputes by having their economically dependent untouchable farmworkers beat up their rivals, thus adding the insult of being ritually polluted to the humiliation of being beaten (M. Robinson 1988: 263). Caste has been used as a justification for keeping lower castes uneducated and out of positions of power, but there is little evidence that such use has made much difference: what has mattered is the economic and social strength of the upper castes, and that has been eroding – and, by world historical standards, quite rapidly.

Tolerance of others' beliefs seems to follow from the fact that one can believe in any god, or none at all, and still be a good Hindu. That certainly may help explain why so many very different religious communities have found safe haven in India over the centuries. It is also true that there have been sectarian battles among Hindus. Hindus have not been particularly tolerant of practices that they feel are contrary to Hindu belief – in recent centuries, people killing cows and eating beef, for example.

Hinduism as belief system certainly influences the conduct of democratic politics – often appearing in decidedly non-democratic garb, as "the other" (lower castes, Muslims) are demonized and then beaten or even killed. Identity politics is to a significant extent caste politics. And "hurting religious feelings" – an offense that is in fact a part of the criminal code – has been used to justify censorship and intimidation. Hindu symbols – supposedly not allowed to be used for politics, according to the law and the rules of the Election Commission – are none the less widely deployed in political movements and election campaigns. There is little evidence, though, that the impact on elections or governance more generally has been very great.

Hindus do not have a country-wide church, let alone an "established" one. There are a handful of what even Indians call "holy men," some with independent followings, and a few with the institutional base of the *math* (monastery) system established by Shankaracharya. From time to time they throw their weight behind particular political movements or issues. But the center of gravity of Hinduism's spiritual practice is firmly in the household, where men and women spend time in prayer, and organize the rituals on special occasions. Temples in South India, particularly, form an important social, economic, and at times political force, but typically only in their immediate neighborhood – which often contains rival temples (Mines and Gourishankar 1990). There is nothing remotely like Protestant church denominations in the US, with their organized networks of congregations, some with a hierarchy. While from time to time a particular guru will hold well-attended public discourses on a sacred text like the Bhagavad Gita, and draw contemporary political lessons from it, the impact is not great. On the occasions when literally millions of Hindus gather – the *kumbh melas* – there are no sermons to speak of, and little political impact. While politicians, including some wearing the saffron robes of "holy men" or "holy women," make a great deal of use of religious symbolism and identity, religious leaders have only a marginal impact on politics, compared even to others in civil society.

The national-arena politicians who have used Hinduism to make a significant impact are almost entirely those who promote *hindutva*, and their Hindu beliefs are very far from those of the classical tradition (see Hansen 1999; Jaffrelot 1994; Jaffrelot 2000). Pratap Mehta (2004: 120) ends his essay on Hinduism and democracy with the insight that the best antidote to the *hindutva* focus on a Hindu identity that he labels "collective narcissism" is for Hindus to rely on the "wealth of positive possibilities that reside within the self, including its capacity to transcend the egotistical 'I'. . . . Hindus have nerved themselves for the last half-century and more to follow democracy's lively allure. . . . Now Hindus must keep their nerve by turning away from the blind alleys and dead-end roads of identity politics." Descending to a more mundane level, and returning to our analytic framework, it is hard to argue that the balance of power between politician and the state apparatus is affected in any way by Hindu beliefs or practice.

Muslims in Pakistan live in a similarly diffuse religious-institutional landscape. The schools of belief – "Barelvi," "Deobandi," "modernist," etc. – are far from primary identity words for almost all Pakistanis.[8] Not only are there belief communities totally outside this largely Sunni set, such as the Shi'a and Ahmadiyya, and belief communities that encompass various schools, such as the Tablighi Jamaat, but also there is a stubbornly persistent sufi strand of Pakistani Islam. In politics, it is the sufi that have been most significant, as several *pirs* have been prominent politicians, mobilizing their quite large followings in the countryside, particularly in Punjab and Sindh (see Ewing 1983). The essentialist-modernist Jamaat-i-Islami is both religious movement and political party, and other parties have Deobandi or Shi'a direction, but none has been very successful in elections. There are local congregations in Islam – in the form of those who typically worship on Fridays and on festival days at a local mosque – where political sermons are preached, and political actions mobilized. But the day-to-day practice of Islam is the responsibility of the individual, who must pray five times a day, fast during Ramadan, and so on. Most religious practice occurs in private, in the home, and on an individual basis, as in ordinary visits to shrines. There is no group of religious leaders, let alone a single one, who can make a call to political action that would necessarily be obeyed by more than his own mosque's or shrine's following, and none has much ideological presence, even when given free rein on television, as in Zia's time.

All of Pakistan's leaders have had to deal with how Islam should be linked to the country's politics.[9] Jinnah (2000: 125) famously said:

> I do not know what the ultimate shape of [Pakistan's] constitution is going to be, but I am sure that it will be of a democratic type, embodying the essential principles of Islam. Today, they are as applicable in actual life as they were 1,300 years ago. Islam and its idealism have taught us democracy. It has taught equality of men, justice and fairplay to everybody. . . . In any case Pakistan is not going to be a theocratic State – to be ruled by priests with a divine mission.[10]

Ayub Khan was notably a moderate who wanted no part of the Islamist agenda of the Jamaat-i-Islami and others, but argued that an authoritarian system was sanctioned by Islam (Sayeed 1967: 170). Zulfiqar Ali Bhutto, in a speech in Karachi in January 1970, using words repeated often in the months leading to the December 1970 election, says:

> As I have explained, Islam is our first principle, then comes democracy. We have struggled for democracy. The people of Pakistan have struggled for democracy. In democracy the people are represented and their opinion carries weight. That is why the people of Pakistan want democracy and we have struggled for it. This struggle was not against our religion. There is no conflict between our religion and the principles of democracy.
>
> (Bhutto 1973?: 4)

It is hard to decide, though, whether Bhutto truly believed either in democracy or in Islam: his practice of democracy was deeply flawed, and the measures he introduced – forcing the "Red Cross" to become the "Red Crescent," and establishing (but not enforcing) a ban on alcohol, for example – were not very significant.

According to Ian Talbot (1999: 256), "Zia [ul Haq] was of the opinion that a Western-style democracy was unsuitable for Pakistan," and apparently agreed with his advisory Council of Islamic Ideology that "a presidential form of government was 'nearest to Islam' " and that "political parties were non-Islamic." There is no doubt, of course, that Zia was a pious Muslim, and that his efforts to move Pakistan towards institutionalizing the *nizam-i-mustapha* (rule according to the Prophet) suggest that democratic arrangements were but temporary expedients. Under Zia, the 1973 constitution was amended to require that a Muslim is qualified to be a member of parliament if "he has adequate knowledge of Islamic teachings and practices obligatory duties prescribed by Islam as well as abstains from major sins" (section 62[e]). Suffice it to say, there is no indication that this provision has ever been enforced.[11]

Zia's views and policies were perhaps helped by a trend in Pakistan of taking Islam as practiced in the Gulf as a norm, perhaps a consequence of Bhutto's turn to the Middle East. It is possible that the millions of

Pakistanis who went to the Gulf countries for work were also carriers of Wahhabi Islamic practices they saw practiced there. As Pervez Hoodbhoy (2008) imaginatively puts it:

> For three decades, deep tectonic forces have been silently tearing Pakistan away from the Subcontinent and driving it towards the Arabian Peninsula. This continental drift is not geophysical but cultural, driven by a belief that Pakistan must exchange its Southasian identity for an Arab-Muslim one. Grain by grain, the desert sands of Saudi Arabia are replacing the alluvium that had nurtured Muslim culture in the Indian Subcontinent for over a thousand years. A stern, unyielding version of Islam – Wahhabism – is replacing the kinder, gentler Islam of the Sufis and saints.

During the Afghanistan *jihad*, Pakistanis fought along with Saudis and other Arabs with Wahhabi beliefs, and the Saudis and others were also pouring money into Islamic education.

It should be noted that the causal relationship between Islamic education, particularly education in *madrassas*, and a *"jihadi"* culture is not clear (for the connections in the 1980s, see Malik 1996: 202–9). Most assume that it is in the *madrassa* that young men are indoctrinated with ideas that *jihad* is the duty of the Muslims of Pakistan (see International Crisis Group 2002a). Marika Vicziany (2007: 68, 73), however, argues persuasively that the arrow of causality – to begin with at least – went the other way:

> Ironically, it is these *government* texts that are imported into the *madrassas* and private schools of Pakistan by *reform-minded* teachers wanting to expand the curriculum in *modern* directions. . . . During the last three decades, [*government*] curricula have assiduously promoted military values and *jihad*. In raising religious–military heroism to national prominence, the government-controlled school curricula of Pakistan have created their own communal monster.
>
> (Vicziany's italics)

In the period of the Benazir Bhutto and Nawaz Sharif governments, and even under Musharraf's government, the Zia Islamization measures could not be reversed. And even with thirty years of the spread and strengthening of "fundamentalist" Islamic political ideas – from the Iranian Revolution to the *jihad* movements in Afghanistan and elsewhere – support for the *Islampasand* (favoring Islam) parties did not increase all that much: as noted above, they got only 11 percent of the vote in the biased 2002 elections. That percentage was cut in half in the relatively free and fair 2008 election, with the discriminatory rules still in place. Pakistanis rank at the bottom of South Asians when it comes to the percentage who participate in the activities of any religious organization – only 15 percent, compared to the South Asia average of 33 percent (*SDSA* 2008: 100, 269–70).

Islamists, however small in number, can act as a "disloyal opposition," in Linz's terms, that "question the existence of the regime and aim at changing it" (Linz 1978: 27). The regime they want would not be a democracy. As Linz (1978: 28) notes: "No regime, least of all a democratic regime, which permits the articulation and organization of all political positions, is without a disloyal opposition." But despite the fact that "such oppositions cannot be repressed or isolated; in a crisis they can mobilize intense effective support; and by a variety of means they can take power or at least divide the allegiance of the population, which can lead to civil war" (Linz 1978: 27). It is the semiloyal opposition, according to Linz (1978: 28) that can have the decisive role in democratic regime breakdown. Linz (1978: 32–3) argues that "an indicator of semiloyal behavior" is:

> A willingness to encourage, tolerate, cover up, treat leniently, excuse, or justify the actions of other participants that go beyond the limits of peaceful, legitimate patterns of politics in a democracy. . . . Political violence, assassination, conspiracies, failed military coups and unsuccessful revolutionary attempts provide the test situations for semiloyalty.

The Islamists in Pakistan have indeed directly supported the authoritarian regimes of Zia and Musharraf; and, as important, many in Pakistan's political society act as a semiloyal opposition, when they see virtue in the actions of Islamists – not just when they are fighting in Kashmir, or setting up an Islamic regime in Afghanistan, but even when they murder Christians or others they believe are blasphemers, and when they justify the illegal application of Islamic punishments on women, in "honor killing" cases and otherwise.

The recent increase of violence by "*jihadi*" groups, including suicide bombings of innocent bystanders as well as attacks on the police and the military, has perhaps brought more Pakistanis to consider how to strike a new balance between Islam and politics. Vali Nasr (2005: 20) concludes his argument on the rise of "Muslim Democracy" (on the model of "Christian Democracy" in Europe after World War II), in which he draws heavily on the Pakistan case, by suggesting that "the values of Muslims . . . can interact with practical elections strategies to play the main role in shaping political ideas and driving voter behavior. . . . The future of Muslim politics is likely to belong to those who can speak to Muslim values and ethics, but within the framework of political platforms fit to thrive in democratic settings." This is not a call to separate Islam from politics, and such a "secularist" move might not be possible in Pakistan. S. Akbar Zaidi's (2005b: 5180) assessment is persuasive:

> [W]hile there is a noticeable drift towards conservatism and even towards appropriating Islamic symbols and following rituals, this need

not translate into the electoral triumph of Islamic parties. . . . It must also be emphasized, that Islam is very much part of the cultural and social milieu of Pakistan and Pakistan will not move towards becoming a secularised state for years to come, if ever. Yet Islam is neither a problem nor a constraint towards any move towards a possible democracy.

Farzana Shaikh (2009: 209), in the epilogue of a book that explores the "damaging political, economic, and social consequences [for Pakistan]" of Islam in the formation of Pakistan's identity, suggests an alternate route: "by recasting its enduring quest for religious consensus in terms of a cultural heritage rooted in the discourse of Indian Islam, [Pakistan] may yet salvage a pluralist alternative consistent with democratic citizenship" (Shaikh 2009: 211–12). This might be seen by many in Pakistan as an extreme solution to the tension between Islam and the state. But there is no indication that the other extreme is viable: there is very little likelihood of an "Islamic revolution" in Pakistan, or of a collapse of state authority that would allow religious leaders to expand the de facto "Islamic emirates" that exist in some parts of the Pakistan–Afghanistan frontier, as in the case of the one in Swat that lasted for a few weeks in 2009, into the rest of Pakistan's territory.

The very diversity of Islamic groups has also set limits on popular support, since each "fundamentalist" or "essentialist" movement seems to require almost a conversion of those not in the core or activist community. Zia ul Haq's Islamization project, which continues under the guidance of the Jamaat-i-Islami and others, could hope to convert or eliminate the Ahmadiyya, because of the small size of the community, but cannot do the same to the Shi'a. One alternative is to emphasize a lowest common denominator of Islamic belief, one that will accommodate all sects and schools of law, but that looks too much like "secularism" to the committed Islamists, who continue to try to convert and indoctrinate people or at times enforce their beliefs with violence. The paradox is that an Islam that directs political choices towards conformity with the *sharia* cannot unite all or even most of Pakistan's Muslims, while an Islam that could encompass them all would have been shorn of all specific political "Islamic" programs, though not goals and policies for them as part of the *umma*.

A similar situation exists in India, made even more complex by the presence of so many Muslims. The activists of the *Sangh parivar*, in their search for a common denominator to make the word "Hindu" equal "Indian," claim that there should be no problem for Muslims to think of themselves as "Muslim Hindus." All they need do is worship Ram – no need to have more than one of the Hindu gods – in the same way that Hindus are prepared to worship "Allah" as another god. They seem literally not to understand why Muslims find that impossible. They also have not been able to "convert" more traditional Hindus, who worship other gods and worship in different ways from the stripped-down, modernized Hinduism of the Arya Samaj and Vivekenanda traditions that the *Sangh parivar* favors – worship that is congregational, aniconic, not recognizing caste, compressed to save time, etc. Perhaps Minkenberg (2007: 902) is correct to warn that one can

> go too far in assuming a complete interchangeability of particular religions and in postulating that the "multi-vocality" of all religious traditions is up for grabs for any interpretation and political use. Against this view, it has been argued that democracy has core meanings which some religions may have problems in accepting, that at any point in time religions have dominant discourses which constrain some of the many voices within a particular tradition, and that religion is not completely irrelevant to political outcomes.

But, for India and Pakistan, the case for the differing religious traditions of the two countries directly determining to any great extent the differing political trajectories remains weak.

However, has there been a differential impact on the balance of popular political forces versus the state apparatus? Did Islam give an advantage to the latter in Pakistan, and Hinduism to the former in India? Up to 1971 in Pakistan, the state apparatus did not favor Islamists, nor did its bureaucratic and military leaders draw on Islam for legitimacy. Islamic movements and parties tended to oppose autocratic rule, willing to ally with more secular parties, and compromise – for example, on the candidacy of a woman, Fatima Jinnah, to be head of state – for the sake of gaining power democratically.

On the other hand, Zia ul Haq built on the concessions Zulfiqar Ali Bhutto had made to Islamic sentiment to push his Islamization program, without much help from the bureaucracy, but co-opting the major Islamist party, the Jamaat-i-Islami. Since then, the Jamaat and other Islamist parties have tended to join with the military and its allied political formation of the moment (the IJI, the PML-Q, the PML-N) in support of autocratic rule, but not so much because of "Islam" per se as because of the links to the Muslim world centered in the Middle East. But those Islamist parties have not added that much to the preponderance of power the military wields by virtue of its institutional strength, external links, and, more recently, economic interests. General Musharraf could credibly position himself as the standard-bearer of a program of "enlightened moderation" for Pakistani Islam without undermining his authority, even though he could not enforce the relevant policy initiatives, such as reforming the blasphemy law, or the *madrassas* (as formulated in his speech of 12 January 2002, which at the time was hailed as a worthy successor to Jinnah's speech of 11 August 1947). The army continues to claim, though not overtly, the right to determine policy with regard to Pakistan's near neighbors, especially India, and, even more, the right to absolute autonomy within the state – and the right to veto political decisions that it sees as jeopardizing those rights. "Islam" seems irrelevant to those claims.

In India, political Hinduism has clearly been a feature of the active civil society and political-party landscape, and barely visible in the state apparatus. True, the parties and movements that have adopted *hindutva* have tended to be internally autocratic – though hardly more so than the CPM – and have at times verged on being a disloyal opposition, but they have not taken steps to dismantle democratic institutions (or, perhaps more accurately, have not been more zealous than the Congress or other parties). While communal violence has been used to political advantage in some areas, and at certain times, the BJP was forced to retreat from its militant nationwide fanning of Hindu–Muslim difference in the aftermath of the demolition of the Babri Masjid, and has not returned to that strategy since, except in certain places – like Gujarat. Hinduism as such, or even Hindu culture, much less India's pluralistic religious landscape, has had no obvious role in strengthening politicians, or weakening the state apparatus's claims to a right to rule.

## Notes

1  See *inter alia* Afsaruddin (2006); Fattah and Butterfield (2006); Hofmann (2004); Minkenberg (2007); Stepan and Robertson (2004); Tezcür (2007); H. Yilmaz (2007). Donno and Russett (2004), expanding and critiquing Fish (2002), provide an important quantitative test.
2  US Department of State, *Pakistan International Religious Freedom Report 2006*; available at: http://www.state.gov/g/drl/rls/irf/2006/71443.htm; accessed 19 June 2007.
3  US Department of State, *Country Reports on Human Rights Practices – 2007: Pakistan*; available at: http://www.state.gov/g/drl/rls/hrrpt/2007/100619.htm; accessed 4 June 2008.
4  See International Crisis Group (2003); Baxi et al. (2006); Rais (2007: 121).
5  See the BBC report of 30 March 2006; available at: http://news.bbc.co.uk/1/hi/world/south_asia/4861666.stm; accessed 19 December 2009.
6  Only one of the five component parties of the MMA participated in this election.
7  The International Republican Institute (Pakistan), *IRI Index: Pakistan Public Opinion Survey March 7–30, 2009*, p. 25; available at: http://www.iri.org/newsreleases/pdfs/2009%20May%2011%20Survey%20of%20Pakistan%20Public%20Opinion,%20March%207–30,%202009.pdf; accessed 12 May 2009. A Pew survey of May–June 2009 has similar results; 83 percent of respondents favored stoning to death of adulterers, and 71 percent favored giving power to Islamic judges. See the Pew Global Attitudes Project, *Pakistani Public Opinion: Growing Concerns about Extremism, Continuing Discontent with US*, p. 3; Available at: http://pewglobal.org/reports/pdf/265.pdf; accessed 16 August 2009.
8  There is a large literature on the various schools and other Islamic groups in Pakistan. See, e.g., Waseem (2004: 24–7); Nasr (2002); Irfani (2004).
9  There is an enormous literature on this. See *inter alia* Binder (1963); M. A. Syed (1995); Cohen (2004: ch. 5); Shaikh (2009).
10  This statement clearly is the source for a clause of the preamble to the 1956 constitution: "Whereas the Founder of Pakistan, Quaid-i-Azam Mohammad Ali Jinnah, declared that Pakistan would be a democratic State based on Islamic principles of social justice."
11  See Jahangir (2009), in which she underlines the possible unfortunate consequences of the Supreme Court's judgment in the National Reconciliation Ordinance case (December 2009) relying on another qualification of membership, in clause 62(f) of the constitution, which reads: "he [must be] sagacious, righteous and non-profligate and honest and ameen [trustworthy]."

# 8    External influences

The foundations of government in the Indian subcontinent were built by an external power, the British Empire. India and Pakistan became independent as democracies as the result of a progression in the "Indianization" of representative institutions, and the struggle for independence with the British, in which both the Congress and the Muslim League chose to play by British rules. They petitioned parliament, organized legally, joined in governing councils, and – after Gandhi – generally respected the law even as they broke it. Parliamentary democracy in its British form was happily accepted. There was no discussion of the possibility of adopting an alternate form of regime. Although this limiting of choice of regime seems to have been based on endogenous forces, it is also true that British decolonization was intended as liberation of the citizenry of the colony as a whole.

While the British did say that paramountcy over the Indian princes would lapse on their leaving, there was little doubt that the on-the-ground reality of more than a century of British rule – namely, that the princes had lost their de facto sovereignty – would mean that princes could only choose to join one of the successor dominions, and that dreams of independence were just that, dreams. Monarchy would not survive (Bhutan and Sikkim were constitutionally special). In the event, there were serious difficulties with integrating only three of the hundreds of princely states: Junagadh, Hyderabad, and Kashmir. In the first two, India's forcible takeover (through a mass movement in Junagadh, and a "police action" in Hyderabad) was ratified by a plebiscite that allowed the state's Hindu majority to choose to join India. India at least claimed that it was ready to accept the results of a plebiscite in Kashmir as well.[1]

It is possible that this choice of democracy was also influenced by the idea of a "free world," to use the term favored in US rhetoric during World War II and after – with "freedom" meaning not only liberation from tyrannical (outsider's) rule but also having a democratic system. The decolonization process begun in the prewar period by the US in the Philippines, and by Britain in India and Ceylon, assumed that democratic regimes would emerge. As the Cold War began, however, security policies such as the drive to "contain" a communist "world" that had expanded through military occupation in Europe and through revolutionary struggles in China, Indochina and elsewhere transformed the "free world" into a set of US allies, whether or not their domestic system was democratic. The speed with which this occurred makes one doubt the depth of the US and European commitment to democracy as an end in itself.

There followed a period in which newly freed countries, as well as some long-independent Latin American ones, were turned into military or party dictatorships, not infrequently with the approval, if not the actual aid, of the US and other democracies.[2] It was only with the onset of democracy's "third wave" (dated from the Portuguese revolution of 1974 [Schmitter 1996: 37]), and possibly with the help of President Carter's human-rights focus and the development of the European Union as a political entity, that the "mature" democracies began to encourage democratization, even when there were strong socialist political parties or other things that made the US uncomfortable. But there were also exceptions in the post-1974 period – Pakistan notable among them – for which the old pattern of supporting a military dictatorship was justified by some perceived greater goal. In the case of the influence on Pakistan, it was resisting and defeating the Soviet Union in Afghanistan, and then waging the "war on terror."

## Pakistan

Analyzing the early years of Pakistan's independence, Ayesha Jalal (1999 [1990]: 123–4) makes a startling claim:

> The "Rawalpindi Conspiracy" dispels any notion of the Pakistan military possessing a superior edge over an inefficient civil service and a hopelessly disorganized political party. The inescapable conclusion is that some four years after the establishment of the state, no single institution was either stable or solid enough to command a clear monopoly of power – not the military, not even the well-oiled civil bureaucracy and certainly not the main political party. While an alliance between certain members of the defence and civil establishment had begun pushing the pendulum of power away from the political leadership, it was the skilful manipulation of international connections that eventually cleared the ground for the development of the institutional imbalances that have plagued Pakistan's history.

It was this that provoked Ayub's reorganization of the Pakistan army, and the link to the United States (Jalal 1999 [1990]: 125), which since then (roughly 1951) has been an informal and formal ally.

Paradoxically, at present, Pakistanis are more anti-American than almost any people in the world, let alone Indians, who are more pro-US than even Europeans.[3] In recent years, this has had a great deal to do with US support of Israel and a perceived (Christianity-related) bias against Islam.

But there is also a long-standing belief that the US has failed to honor what Pakistan believed the alliance commitments were, particularly during the India–Pakistan wars of 1965 and 1971, and after the Soviet Union was defeated in Afghanistan. In 1965 the government said that it was India that had attacked Pakistan, and the treaty terms required the US to aid Pakistan against aggression. The argument was that "Operation Gibraltar" and Pakistan army actions in support were *within* Kashmir, crossing only the ceasefire line, and it was *India* that crossed the India–Pakistan border first (Kux 2001: 160–1). In 1971 the US government certainly made its "tilt" of support to Pakistan clear, accusing India of aggression. But that was backed up only with a UN resolution against the use of force to resolve the dispute, and the useless gunboat diplomacy of sending USS *Enterprise* into the Bay of Bengal. Anti-American feeling is indicated – to give a few examples – by the attack on the US embassy in 1979; the popularity of the Iranian Revolution; the protests when the US cut off aid once the Afghan *jihad* had succeeded in humiliating the Soviet Union (because Pakistan had developed a nuclear weapons capability); popular (but not governmental) support of Saddam Hussain in the first Gulf War; and protests against the "U-turn" on Afghanistan and the Taliban that General Musharraf was forced to make.

The US–Pakistan linkage, then partnership, then alliance began shortly after independence, when the Pakistan military sought aid from the United States to bolster Pakistan's security vis-à-vis India. With the alliances of the 1950s – membership in SEATO and CENTO included – the military began its on-again, off-again relationship. The Pakistanis wanted US ties for obtaining military hardware, training and exchange programs, and as an ultimate guarantee against Indian aggression. In the Cold War era, the US wanted to have Pakistan as an ally because it was a strategically placed country on the frontier with the Soviet Union and China, and not coincidentally a country with well-sited airfields. In the 1980s, there was an active partnership to get the Soviets out of Afghanistan by joining with the Saudis in backing the *mujahidin*. After 9/11, Pakistan was needed in the struggle against *jihadi* Islam, and in particular provided a necessary platform for US actions against the Taliban regime and al-Qaeda in Afghanistan, again with well-placed airbases and road access. The US military aid cut-off mandated by US law imposed after Musharraf's coup was quickly reversed by using some creative wishful thinking (see Shah 2006: 60).

The extent to which the US has actually participated in, and perhaps even at times dictated, Pakistan government decisions is a live issue. Zaidi (2008b: 11) writes: "Whether it was the military in office or some form of electoral democracy, Pakistan has always been a client state of the US, except possibly for the brief period [of Zulfiqar Ali Bhutto's rule]." Particularly at the time of active US–Pakistan military collaboration (in 1971, during the Afghan *jihad*, post-9/11), some Pakistanis have referred to the American ambassador as a "viceroy." That reveals a bitterness that makes this more than a joke. There were accusations that Pakistan was just a "banana republic" (for example, Amir 2002). Even when there was an elected government in place, the US and international institutions such as the IMF could also count on "the active collaboration of a powerful authoritarian coalition (comprising technocrats, civilian bureaucrats and the military) contemptuous of consent-driven, partisan politics" (Shah 2006: 63).

But the perspective can be reversed, to argue that in those same periods it was the Pakistan government that in one way or another managed to shape US policy. The US could not protest over the genocidal crackdown in March 1971 – as urged by senior Dhaka consulate officers – because Pakistan was facilitating the US–China opening. Pakistan was needed as an ally during the Afghan *jihad*, so the US turned a blind eye to the continuing development of Pakistan's nuclear-weapons program, which made Pakistan subject to US non-proliferation laws – even after its "architect," A. Q. Khan, boasted that Pakistan had a bomb, in the mid-1980s. Pakistan and its ISI determined which *mujahidin* received US aid, and what groups could exist. General Musharraf got US support even though he rigged elections and continued to serve as chief of the army staff while he was president, at a time when the US was trying to install a democracy in Iraq. When Pakistan followed US "dictates" it was as the result of an arm-twisting exercise, as when Richard Armitage on 12 September 2001 allegedly underlined his "with us or against us" choice with an "or else" of severe bombing. The Pakistan leadership has employed the full panoply of the "weapons of the weak" James Scott (1986) describes (for a very different context), of foot dragging, slander, and sly sabotage.

Has that US tie strengthened the tendency towards autocracy in Pakistan? Although the US has condemned each of Pakistan's military coups, there were no serious consequences, and the US government happily worked with all four military governments. Perhaps because of the belief that the US had reneged on its alliance assurances to Pakistan – a belief that may well have been encouraged by the deceptive arguments of military governments in power at those times – it is likely that being anti-American would bring more political rewards to democratic politicians. That was true during Bhutto's rule and from 1990 to 1999, when aid was cut off because of the nuclear program.

Certainly, military governments have generally replaced governments that were less friendly to the US than army-led governments. Those governments did accommodate US interests, and have received significant US political support to go along with military and economic aid.[4] US economic aid helped Ayub launch his superficially successful "decade of development;" Musharraf's 2001 U-turn solved Pakistan's immediate economic problems. That in turn arguably enhanced the popular support for those governments, since military governments tend to require economic success as one of the pillars of their legitimacy, along with maintaining internal and external security. In addition, material support was directly significant, to the extent that US aid paid for new weapons and other things that would have been impossible for the Pakistan government to have paid for out of domestic resources (see Kux 2001: 364). That helped the Pakistan army pursue its professional duty to protect the country without having to concern itself very much about which particular government was in power.

In general it may be true that "US military assistance appears to be a contributing factor in undermining civilian elements and increasing the incidence of praetorianism in the less developed areas of the world" (Rowe 1974: 253),[5] but Dennis Kux is undoubtedly correct when he writes, in the concluding chapter of his very careful study of Pakistan–US relations, "it is hard to see that events in Karachi would have unfolded very differently if the Eisenhower administration had decided against extending military aid in 1954" (Kux 2001: 363).

Here the beliefs of the political activists are significant. Perhaps, for some in the elite, the de facto imprimatur of "the world's oldest democracy" somehow allowed them to excuse at a minimum periods of military rule, but that is hardly likely to have been much of a factor. At present, military training for foreign officers in the US includes "the proper role of the military in a civilian-led democratic government."[6] We do not know whether in all those military-to-military relationships over the decades the value of civilian control of the military in a democracy, or the limitations of military rule, was communicated from the US side. Particularly for the first decade of the alliance, the military in power in Pakistan was most often a fact on the ground, and no purpose would have been served by embarrassing them or insulting them by implying that they were acting improperly, by insisting on the necessity of having a democracy.

Economic aid was channeled through the bureaucracy of course, and it worked closely with an array of American advisors in the 1950s who contributed to Ayub's development plan (see Rosen 1985; Shah 2006). But, if that strengthened the civil wing of the state apparatus, it was not by very much, and after the mid-1960s even that aid disappeared. The level of aid was high – for example, aid from all sources from 1960 to 2002 totaled US$73 billion (2001), of which 30 percent was US bilateral aid (Anwar and Michaelowa 2006: 196). US military and economic aid was most significant during Ayub's regime, peaking in 1962. Starting in the 1970s, significant additional funds came to the Pakistan state via some portion of remittances by workers in the Middle East and elsewhere, to the extent that they came in through official channels and not via *hawala*. It would be nice to have an estimate of the extent to which, over time, the Pakistan state was able to rely on these sources rather than raising resources domestically through taxation, a sort of "rentier state" index. We do not have this data, but it is certainly true that, if we did have a reliable "rentier state" index, Pakistan would have a higher number – probably a much higher number – than India.

As noted above, Bhutto in the 1970s turned Pakistan's face towards the Middle East, where there were not only the traditional Islamic monarchies of the Gulf but also countries ruled by leaders and parties with ideologies not so different from Bhutto's – Egypt, Syria and Iraq, Qaddafi's Libya, and even the Shah's Iran. These were not democratic regimes. The Pakistani elite might well have developed a belief in the value of a fused military–party-leader autocratic system in a Middle Eastern brotherhood of countries. When the Middle Eastern wind became "Islamic," with the rising power of the Gulf countries and then, most dramatically, with the Iranian Revolution, it is likely that non-elite citizens as well would have had favorable views of those autocratic regimes, and perhaps internalized a belief in either Islamic or secular-welfarist autocracy. Throughout the last decades, Pakistani public opinion, both of secularists and of Islamists, has strongly favored the (autocratic) regimes of the Middle East as they have come under attack by Israel and the United States.

Public opinion in Pakistan also favored the Afghan *jihad*, even though there was never a goal of establishing a democracy in Afghanistan once the Soviet Union and the Najibullah regime had been defeated. When it suited Pakistan's security interest to nurture and support the Taliban takeover in the mid-1990s, the issue of what sort of regime it was – an ideologically committed autocracy, if not a tyranny – did not arise. To be sure, there was an impact on Pakistan's own regime from these policies, as Weinbaum and Harder (2008: 37) explain:

> Pakistan's Afghan policies over the past 30 years, whether pursued for domestic political or strategic reasons or under US and international pressures, have come at the expense of the country's political stability and social cohesion. These policies . . . have affected the balance of political power within Pakistan, most of all by reinforcing military ascendance.

Nearly four decades after Bhutto reoriented Pakistan, to join the Middle East, as it were, Pakistan's autocratic regime history makes it fit right in, and that is not without popular support.

Still, India looms large on Pakistan's eastern border; and Pakistanis in general, not to speak of government officials and politicians, are acutely aware of what happens there. They literally speak the languages India uses most (colloquial Hindi, English); and many, with relatives in India, have gone there. Has India's democratic practice influenced, pro or con, the beliefs of Pakistanis about the value of democracy? To some extent, it would seem, Pakistan has indeed defined itself *against* India, from the time of the competing nationalist movements against the British and against the Congress. The two countries chose different paths of economic development, Pakistan accepting the Western-influenced development paradigm rather than India's non-alignment and aggressive "Third Worldism."

The typical Pakistani view of India's democracy, for good reasons, often focuses on the discrimination Muslims in India suffer, especially when they hear it from Indian relatives. When Pakistanis visit, since both India and Pakistan are similarly open as societies – there is certainly little restriction of private speech – they probably do not find India's politics unfamiliar when there is some sort of elected government in Pakistan. There may be a tendency to assume that, even as Indian and Pakistani culture and customs (food, dress, music, and so on) are often identical, political customs are also the same. Pakistanis might well assume, for example, that elections in India are rigged just as they are in Pakistan. They would also have no difficulty learning of the experience of day-to-day discrimination, if not oppression, at the hands of the police and the bureaucracy that far too many Indian Muslims experience.

Even now, Pakistanis rationalize their lack of democracy by pointing to the comparable economic performances of the two countries. From shortly after independence to the mid-1990s, Pakistan outperformed India economically, and Pakistanis could feel that India's much trumpeted democracy had brought few development benefits. There were hundreds of millions of desperately poor people in India, and far fewer in Pakistan. This rationalization has come under some strain recently, as India's economic growth rate has surpassed Pakistan's.

It is worth proposing that this reflects a much deeper issue: the fear of Indian influence in all fields overwhelming Pakistan if the two countries were somehow to come closer together. We can construct a far-fetched paradoxical variation of the "democratic peace" argument that countries that are both democratic tend not to go to war with each other. If a certain degree of hostility keeps the borders closed, that would prevent Pakistan from being swamped by things ranging from India's much stronger economy to Bollywood movies, and thus from betraying the 1947 liberation. If having a democracy like India's would lower that hostility, and even promote "friendship," then it is incumbent to deny the value of democracy, at least in its Indian version. Since India's democracy is significantly flawed, there is no reason to adopt it as a model, or even learn lessons from Indian practice. The most trenchant critics of Pakistan's autocratic rulers, enthusiastic supporters of introducing real democracy into Pakistan – people like the columnist and politician Ayaz Amir come to mind – are quick to react to India's periodic falls from democratic grace (the Gujarat pogrom of 2002, for example) with sweeping denunciations of the whole Indian political system.

The international community has not put much pressure on Pakistan to restore democracy, nor does it offer powerful incentives such as the requirement of having a democracy in order to join the European Union, which has served its purpose for Eastern European countries. Pakistan was suspended from the Commonwealth after Musharraf's coup, but remained a member in good standing of any number of international organizations, and has enrolled many peace-keeping forces under UN auspices. It is hard to believe that black marks from Freedom House, or exhortations from abroad about democratic practices, have had much impact on Pakistan's democracy. It is quite possible that the democracy situation would have been even worse in their absence, but also possible that they have had little or no effect.

It is politically difficult for serious pressure to be applied. In November 2009, the Obama administration's pairing of Pakistan with Afghanistan as a problem area for defeating terrorism and encouraging democracy may have produced a more active US role vis-à-vis Pakistan, if a clause in the Kerry–Lugar aid bill is any guide. That requires the secretary of state to report every six months, giving

> an assessment of the extent to which the government of Pakistan exercises effective civilian control of the military, including a description of the extent to which civilian executive leaders and parliament exercise oversight and approval of military budgets, the chain of command, the process of promotion for senior military leaders, civilian involvement in strategic guidance and planning, and military involvement in civil administration.[7]

Although this language – not uncommon in such agreements, it later appeared – had been inserted with the full knowledge of Pakistan's civilian government, the Pakistan military and a significant segment of elite opinion apparently strongly objected to this "interference," and to other similar provisions for oversight.[8] The bill was passed with the language in it, but an explanatory note was attached that reduced even further the chance that the assessments would have any impact, at least for the life of the program.

In recent years, the US and European governments have established institutions to spread or strengthen democracies, and there are also "First World"-based non-governmental organizations with similar goals.[9] In addition to focusing on helping countries to conduct free and fair elections, these institutions have promoted the strengthening of political parties and the media. Pakistan has welcomed many of them, having allowed the National Democratic Institute and the International Republican Institute to establish offices that sponsor programs aimed at democracy development. Pakistan – unlike India – allows election monitoring by a range of foreign institutions, most importantly the European Union parliament.

Other international institutions are active in Pakistan, including the World Bank, the Asian Development Bank (ADB), the Asia Foundation, the Friederich Ebert Stiftung, and the International Crisis Group (ICG), among others. In 2002 the ADB allocated funds for two four-year programs, under the rubric "governance reforms": $300 million for a "Decentralization Support Program" and $350 million for an "Access to Justice" program.[10] The Brussels-based ICG regularly publishes some of the best and most detailed analyses of political developments and human-rights issues, with recommendations for strengthening Pakistan's democracy. These programs, between them, work with the Pakistan state, political parties, and civil-society organizations; it is of course impossible to judge just how much impact they have had.

Both Pakistan and India have substantial numbers of people living abroad, who presumably have attitudes shaped by the countries that they are in, which can be communicated or perhaps transmitted or brought back to their country of origin. Both countries have recent temporary workers in the Gulf. India's more recent export of persons to other places has been largely to the US and mainly of professionals; while Pakistan's has been to England and the Middle East, and much more likely to be working class. That might mean that the content of what they communicate to their friends and family is different, but it would be a real stretch to think that this has more than a minor impact on regime difference.

## India

India is far more autonomous a country than Pakistan when it comes to external influences on its governance. The factors that might have had some material or ideological influence in Pakistan – US military aid, other sources of economic support to the state – do not apply to India. Whatever positive reinforcement it receives internationally from having a democracy is vitiated by the accompanying caveats about the major blemishes – insurgencies and state repression in Kashmir and the northeastern states, corruption, violence, etc. The major economic sanctions India has endured have been the result of India's non-compliance with the international nuclear-weapons regime, and thus have not been directed to change or preserve the political system in general. Nor does India see itself in a "democratic camp" to the extent that its foreign policies are altered, even in its immediate neighborhood. For example, there was a period when India provided a base for Burmese opposed to the military regime in their country, and supported that with rhetoric about the suppression of democracy by the Burma military government. But, when China seemed to reap the benefit of good relations with Burma, India soon followed suit and, among other things, shut down opposition radio broadcasts.

The Indian military has since independence taken pains to be as self-reliant as possible in its training, ordnance supply, etc., and has been at pains to make deals for weapons that include provisions for gradual "Indianization" of the supply of spare parts, if not the manufacture of the weapons themselves. Since much of India's weaponry came from the Soviet Union, Indian officers certainly went in significant numbers to the Soviet Union, but there is no indication that any of them influenced what are still, at their core, British-style armed forces. For many decades some Indian military officers have attended British and US military training and education institutions, and US officers have joined Indian military institutions for extensive courses, but it is only recently that extensive US–India joint training exercises have been conducted. These contacts – and those with other countries, such as Australia – may have served to reinforce an Anglo-American view of civil–military relations, but there is no evidence of any major impact. India's long experience in UN peace-keeping has had no obvious influence, positive or negative, on its military's political ideas. It would not be surprising if an important factor in the military's acceptance of its role subordinate to civilians and elected politicians would be its view of the experience of the Pakistan army in taking over its country. Worst of all was the overwhelming defeat of 1971, but also its loss of prestige in recent years and its privileges and corruption would be something to avoid. The Pakistan army's seizure of power would be seen as an object lesson of what not to do.

India no longer seeks advice from abroad on how to strengthen its administrative apparatus – as it did in the immediate post-independence years – and it is unlikely that the handful of bureaucrats and military officers who go abroad for academic training or study have increased their power or authority vis-à-vis the politicians as a result. India has been the recipient of a great deal of foreign aid from international sources, and from the Ford Foundation and other foreign-based foundations. Most of that aid has been channeled through the government, and in the early years was a major factor in certain policy and programs, especially those that came to usher in the "green revolution." Some of these, in all probability, served to encourage the professionalism of the bureaucracy, increasing its capacity while following the norm of deference to elected politicians. Indians serving in those organizations abroad have also returned to positions of influence, especially the economists (Prime Minister Manmohan Singh and his close partner in economic policy-making, Montek Singh Ahluwalia, most notably). Recently, the state governments have been able to negotiate directly with the World Bank and other international lenders, and the chief ministers have played an important role in implementing projects that would meet international standards. Successful chief ministers would depend on high-quality administrators under them.

International organizations also support, and sometimes partner, Indian NGOs, and thus have influenced slightly the shape of civil society, and strengthened certain elements in it. The Indian government has actively regulated that activity, most importantly by requiring that NGOs register with the government in order to receive donations from abroad. Educational institutions and think-tanks are required to obtain permission to invite foreigners for conferences, or to give lectures, although that provision is often ignored. Given the huge numbers of NGOs and the small numbers concerned with directly empowering citizens who receive support from them, the impact of external actors is minimal.

The US brings politicians to the US to see, among other things, American democracy in action; but that, too, is unlikely to have much impact. The Indian elite, including many of its politicians, now has literally many of its children resident in the US (in 2009, for example, the daughter of Prime Minister Manmohan Singh was in the headlines as a leading American Civil Liberties Union lawyer), and that must have some effect on their ideas of the value of democracy. Although India has had significant, and at times powerful, anti-democratic intellectual currents, both on the left and on the right, there is no evidence of major foreign direct influence, let alone control. RSS ideology and practices may have been influenced by fascism and by Hitler (see Jaffrelot 1994: 50–64), but there has been little if any connection with present-day authoritarian parties or movements outside India. Communists in India have at times justified authoritarian rule in the Soviet Union and China; but their leadership has, except to some small extent in the 1940s and 1950s, followed a "line" from Moscow. There is no significant influence by those few who have studied in the Soviet Union.

Ayesha Jalal's (1995: 124) assertion quoted at the beginning of this chapter needs to be re-emphasized: "it was the skillful manipulation of international connections that eventually [produced] the institutional imbalances that have plagued Pakistan's history." It was not simply that at the beginning of Pakistan's independent existence the scope and character of its military and security links with the United States in particular bolstered the leverage of the Pakistan military, and probably also reinforced and legitimated the army's penchant to serve as the political guardian of the nation. Each military leader of Pakistan received wholehearted US support: Ayub Khan for his "decade of development" economic policies; Zia ul Haq for his part-nership in the Afghanistan *jihad* (at a time when "*jihad*" had a positive spin for the US government); and General Musharraf in the aftermath of 9/11. Pakistan's efforts to institutionalize democracy have been supported by the US and by European organizations. Pakistan is also open to influence from the countries of the Middle East and even – in certain ways – from India, but those efforts do not come close to matching the support the military has received.

India's experience was starkly different, because its initial military endow-ment and security situation was so very different. India pursued a policy of maximum feasible autarky in defense matters, staying clear of alliances until 1971, when it entered into something more of a partnership with the Soviet Union, in a treaty that was finalized only when India was shocked by the announcement of the US opening to China. While the United States has served as an enemy figure in security matters, particularly when Mrs Gandhi was in power and while Mrs Gandhi was supported by a Communist Party that probably received financial and other support from the Soviet Union, it is unlikely that the Soviet Union or its Eastern European allies had any signifi-cant impact on the course of India's political history. Nor have military-to-military contacts with the British and the Americans had any notable influence on India's civil–military relations. There is no way of measuring how significant foreign government, foundation, and NGO aid programs have been in strengthening the capacity either of the bureaucracy or of political parties and leaders. Some decades ago, when institutions such as the Ford Foundation had a massive presence, and actively sought to mold Indian insti-tutions, that influence was something of a political issue. The World Bank and various United Nations organizations have grown in size and reach, in terms of sponsoring governance initiatives; but, again, it is not clear that their impact has been felt at all. Indians returning from studying and working in Europe and the US have played a much larger role, but that hardly counts as direct external influence.

India's great size and endowments of natural resources and people, its deeply rooted and continuous civilization, and its nationalist-movement-inspired determination never again to come under imperial rule have insulated India to a far greater extent than Pakistan from direct foreign pressure and indirect influence, in culture as well as politics and economics. India's democratic ideas and institutions have an obvious relationship to those of Britain and the United States, but that does not mean that the military, or the bureaucracy, or politicians and political parties have seen their choices as in any way molded or determined by outsiders. There are no formal or informal relationships with other countries or organizations that have significantly affected India's democratic path.

Pakistan, in contrast, while having as keen a commitment as India to maintaining real independence in a post-colonial Cold War world, was early on forced by its security situation to seek an alliance with the United States – an alliance twice renewed, in the 1980s Afghanistan *jihad* and the post-2001 war in Afghanistan. That alliance and the relationships with countries of the Middle East that developed after 1971 strengthened the military as a legitimate locus of power within the Pakistani state. Given the importance of the Punjab and its martial heritage, and its record in fighting India to a standstill over Kashmir before any alliance was formed, it is quite possible that the military would have staged coups welcomed by the public and claimed a right to rule even without the US alliance and the turn to the Middle East. But it is probably less likely that they would have been as successful a domestic political player as they have been.

## Notes

1 It is obviously impossible to deal with the Kashmir problem here, since almost everything about the history of Kashmir's accession to India is contested even by third-party scholars. It is not clear that Pakistan has ever repudiated its acceptance of Junagadh's accession to Pakistan in 1947. It is curious that Junagadh ("Junagadh & Manavadar") is shown as part of Pakistan on the Physical map (but not on the Administrative map) in the Survey of Pakistan's (1986) *Atlas of Pakistan*. 1st edition, reprinted with corrections. Rawalpindi: Survey of Pakistan.

2 See Muller (1985) for a provocative analysis of the impact of US economic and military aid on the "anti-communist" coups of Latin America in the first decades after World War II.

3 For a general summary of the view of the US, see Kux (2001: 365–8). In a (disproportionately urban) survey released in December 2007, the Pew Global Attitudes Project reported that 15 percent of Pakistanis had a favorable view of the United States, up from 10 percent in 2002, and down from a peak of 27 percent in 2006. Those with unfavorable views went from 69 percent (2002) to 68 percent. In 2002, 54 percent of Indians had a favorable view of the US; the number was

59 percent in June 2007 (28 percent unfavorable) (Richard Wike, "The View from Pakistan," 28 December 2007; available at: http://pewresearch.org/pubs/674/view-from-pakistan-before-bhuttos-assassination-public-opinion-was-increasingly-opposed-to-terrorism and "Global Unease," 27 June 2007; available at: http://pewresearch.org/pubs/524/global-unease-with-major-world-powers-and-leaders.

4 Things might have gone not so swimmingly in 1979, with Jimmy Carter in office, after a mob attacked the US embassy in Islamabad, while General Zia was taking a bicycle tour of neighboring Rawalpindi and somehow did not send timely help. But the Soviet Union invaded Afghanistan, and a new Republican administration quickly climbed into bed with Zia, after President Carter's offer of aid had been dismissed as "peanuts."

5 This is the concluding sentence of an article based on quantitative analysis of military aid and coups.

6 US Department of Defense *Security Assistance Management Manual*, as described on the website of the Federation of American Scientists: http://www.fas.org/asmp/campaigns/training/IMET2.html#top; accessed 17 June 2007.

7 Text of the bill as passed by the Senate, section 302, clause 15; available at: http://www.govtrack.us/congress/billtext.xpd?bill=s111-1707; accessed 7 October 2009.

8 An 8 October 2009 press release from the Committee, responding to the "myth" that the bill requires US oversight of the Pakistan military, notes that, while the Secretary of State is to report on civilian control of the military, it does not require such control, nor does it place any restriction whatsoever on Pakistan. This benchmark, like all benchmarks in the monitoring reports, is informational. It presents a datapoint on which US policy-makers can base decisions. See: http://kerry.senate.gov/cfm/record.cfm?id=318845; accessed 9 October 2009.

9 In the US, these would include the US Institute of Peace and the National Endowment for Democracy; the National Democratic Institute; and the International Republican Institute; the Carter Center; Freedom House; etc. See Youngs (2008); and a *Journal of Democracy* panel discussion on "A Quarter-Century of Promoting Democracy" (vol. 18, no. 4; October 2007).

10 See http://www.adb.org/Documents/Others/PRM_Supplement/ADB_PAK_Governance_Reforms.asp?p=prmnews; accessed 24 November 2009.

# 9 Clearly diverging paths

In the years since the turning point of the 1977 elections, the choices made in both countries seem to have placed India and Pakistan on clearly diverging paths. While the degree of divergence should not be overstated, it is fair to say that Pakistan's political history since Zia's coup has seen the increasing entrenchment of the military in political power, and the deepening of democracy in India. The entrenchment of the military in Pakistan has paradoxically been accompanied by an increase in the openness of its society, even as it is both transformed by modernization and subject to the increased tension of religion-based violence. In India, a similar strengthening of democratic forces in society has also surfaced contrary forces of exclusionary and oppressive nationalism in the form of *hindutva*, and violent separatist and revolutionary movements that have been met by strong state suppression in certain parts of the country.

The two paths are not as far apart as many other possible pairs of countries – one with a Freedom House rating of a closest-to-democracy "1" on both civil and political rights, and the other with a closest-to-full-autocracy "7" on both. Although the scores on the Freedom House index for the years 1978–2008 show India with an average of civil and political rights scores of 2.7 and Pakistan with 4.9, there is one period of three years (1993–5) when their graphed scores coincide (see Figure 1.3, p. 13). Pakistan's worst scores were left behind, in the Zia era. There are many democratic countries with scores in the 1–2 range, on the one hand, and autocratic ones with scores in the 6–7 range, on the other; for example, in 2008, in the twenty-four largest countries (with populations of more than 50 million), six were in the former category and five in the latter. Pakistan has never been near the bottom in its scores, and India needs to improve a great deal to match fully consolidated democracies.

The nearly flat lines of the graph for almost the last decade suggest that the paths – preserving the metaphor – may have become ruts. The small moves towards democracy in Pakistan – the relative freedom of the media discussed above, the active political parties and periodic elections, and democratic decentralization – can only go so far, and that limit is set by the military. The military has moved from being able to make and break governments as it did in the 1990s, while keeping elected leaders from "interfering," as it were, in security policy, including relations with India. It has expanded its interests in economic enterprise, and has taken up positions in educational institutions and the like. This expanding base of power has allowed the military to permit those small moves towards democracy; ultimate control remains firmly in the military's hands, with the bureaucracy as junior partner.

In India, the seemingly frozen level of the path towards even more democracy is explained by the inertia of governmental institutions, including the courts, the bureaucracy, and even the political parties, which have so far not reflected the changes happening deeper down in political society. The *State of Democracy in South Asia* report (2008: 226–7) data show that the belief in democracy is directly correlated with class: 32 percent of the lowest-class respondents are "strong democrats," as are 54 percent of the upper-class respondents; for "weak democrats" the figures are 49 percent for the lowest class, and 31 percent for the upper class. The education dimension confirms this: 26 percent of the non-literate are "strong democrats" compared to 53 percent of secondary-school graduates, while 56 percent of the non-literate are "weak democrats," as are 33 percent of the secondary-school graduates. Since wealth and education have on average been increasing substantially in the last decades, these figures suggest that belief in democracy has probably been increasing and will continue to increase. It should only be a matter of time before that is reflected in improvements in day-to-day politics and holding government accountable.

## Entrenching military rule in Pakistan

It was the Zia ul Haq regime that intensified the process of entrenching the military as an autonomous power in the polity. Zia had himself "elected" president by a referendum worded in such a way that a "no" vote would have been one to reject Zia's Islamic initiatives. Even then few Pakistanis bothered to cast a ballot, so the regime inflated the turnout figures (see Kennedy 2005: 55 for a thumbnail comparison of this referendum with Ayub's and Musharraf's). Then, having held a "partyless" and foregone-conclusion "election" to a revived parliament, Zia amended the 1973 constitution by ordinance – the eighth amendment. That amendment "immunized" the military government from prosecution for what it had done, and made ordinances, in particular the Hudood ordinances, into a constitutional amendment rather than a law that could be reversed by a simple majority in parliament. More important, it gave the president the power to dismiss parliament even when the government had the confidence of the House. Until that provision of the eighth amendment was repealed in 1997, this meant that the president could, in principle, dismiss a government before it could go through the cumbersome impeachment proceedings to get rid of him or her. In practice, whichever person – president or prime minister – had the confidence of the army could win any major struggle for power.[1] And, indeed, it is clear that it was the army that decided that the elections would proceed as scheduled in the aftermath of Zia's death in 1988, and it was the army that had the final say in the decisions of the president to dismiss the governments of Benazir Bhutto in 1990, of Nawaz Sharif in 1993, and of Benazir Bhutto again in 1996.

The "non-party" election of February 1985 brought Muhammad Khan Junejo to power as prime minister, though he remained clearly subordinate to Zia, but the politics did change significantly. Once martial law was lifted by the end of the year, political parties were allowed to reappear. Benazir Bhutto was able to return to Pakistan within months, and famously drew an overwhelmingly enthusiastic public response, as it took many hours for her to travel from the Lahore airport to the Minar-e-Pakistan, in April 1986. Zia dismissed Junejo after he acted autonomously to investigate the April 1988 accidental explosion of arms and ammunition meant for the Afghanistan *jihad.* These were stored in the Ojhri army camp right next to a residential area in Rawalpindi, so hundreds died. Zia scheduled another "partyless" election for August 1988, but was killed in a mysterious plane crash, along with a large contingent of his senior officers, and the American ambassador.[2]

The Supreme Court ruled that the election could proceed with parties contesting. Despite an army-led effort to organize and support an "Islamic" alliance centered on the revived Pakistan Muslim League, Benazir Bhutto's PPP won. Bhutto did not have much chance to accomplish any PPP programs since she was saddled with an army that did not cede her much power, linked to an unsympathetic president, and had to deal with a newly minted opposition leader, Nawaz Sharif, as chief minister of the Punjab. When the army had her dismissed in 1990, a caretaker government was appointed. While that government instituted a biased "accountability" process that targeted Benazir and left Nawaz Sharif alone, it conducted a reasonably free and fair election, which saw Sharif's alliance win handily (see Blood 1994).

The caretaker government of 1990 was headed by the erstwhile leader of the opposition, G. M. Jatoi, but he did not then develop a neutral stance, to put it mildly. When the Nawaz Sharif government was dismissed in 1993, the president appointed another caretaker government, led by Moeen Qureshi, a non-partisan technocrat employed by the World Bank. He used the opportunity – reminiscent of the first months of Ayub's military government, and foreshadowing Musharraf's – to appoint a government of experts, with an eye especially to putting Pakistan's economy back on track. The caretaker government's apparent success arguably made it more difficult for the democratically elected successor to measure up: such governments pick the low-hanging fruit, as it were, and retire in a blaze of approbation, leaving the hard problems behind. Whether Benazir's 1993–6 government would have been less corrupt and ineffective had the PPP been able to gain momentum from the contrast with the Nawaz Sharif government is an open question.

Let us pause to consider, given this innovation of caretaker governments, whether there has been a greater belief in having "experts" as governing authorities in Pakistan, compared to India. The *State of Democracy in South Asia* report survey question on "experts" provides contrary evidence (*SDSA* 2008: 236–7). The question – one of a series – was: "There are different ways in which a country may be governed. . . . [Do you agree/disagree with the idea that] All major decisions about the country should be taken by experts rather than politicians?" In India, 51 percent of "elite" respondents "strongly" agreed; in Pakistan, the figure was only 21 percent. In India 29 percent of the "mass" respondents strongly agreed; in Pakistan it was 16 percent.[3] Eighty percent of the elite "strongly agreed" or "agreed" in India; in Pakistan, only 55 percent did.

One could argue that this reflects the Indians' lengthy experience of having politicians make decisions, and Pakistanis' having seen the fruits of bureaucratic and military expertise. Looking at who the economic-policy decision-makers have been, for example, it is fair to say that, with the exception of Manmohan Singh's tenure as finance minister in the Narasimha Rao government (1991–6) and present stint as prime minister (2004– ), India has had pure politicians in direct charge. In Nehru's time expert ministers and advisors like Mahalanobis, though very influential, were not, ultimately, in charge. Some of the most important economic-policy decisions are associated with other politicians: C. Subramaniam, Indira Gandhi, Mohan Kumaramangalam, V. P. Singh *inter alia.* When Ayub and Zia ruled in Pakistan, professional economists – including Mahbub ul Haq in both governments – took charge. Musharraf used the Citibank executive Shaukat Aziz first as finance minister and then as prime minister. A similar pattern appears in foreign policy. From independence to the end of the Z. A. Bhutto government, the foreign minister was a politician, often the prime minister. After that, many foreign ministers have been expert former diplomats – Yaqub Khan and Agha Shahi, for example. In India, Natwar Singh is the only former diplomat who has served as external affairs minister, and then only briefly, and long after he had resigned from the foreign service.

Resuming our historical narrative, Prime Minister Nawaz Sharif, elected with a two-thirds majority in 1997, set about enhancing the power of the prime minister in a series of moves to amend the constitution. (It is doubtful that he was disinterestedly working to establish the superior power of parliament itself rather than seeking more power for himself.) First, parliament repealed the president's power to dismiss the government at will. Then Sharif intimidated the Supreme Court, literally sending in thuggish political party workers to do the job. Then he tested his power to dismiss the chief of the army staff (COAS) by firing General Jahangir Karamat for having proposed, even though quite informally, the setting up of a National Security Council to give the army "a permanent, constitutional role in the decision making" (Lodi 1998). Then he attempted to control the press by measures from denying newsprint supply to throwing editors in jail. In both cases he tackled highly visible and powerful persons and institutions, with mixed results. And after Pakistan's nuclear tests of May 1998 he imposed a state of emergency that "enabled [him] to amass more power," used "to interfere in provincial governmental affairs" (Rizvi 2000: 231). When Nawaz Sharif tried again to exercise his constitutional control over the military by dismissing COAS General Pervez Musharraf to forestall a widely expected coup he was himself overthrown, with insult added to injury in being charged with treason. His departure was generally welcomed by the Pakistan citizenry.

On taking power, General Musharraf reassured a global audience that there was nothing to worry about with respect to the control of Pakistan's newly demonstrated nuclear weapons, thus admitting that the army had held control of them since the beginning of the program. The Legal Framework Order of August 2002, which was mainly focused on setting the rules for the upcoming elections, established a National Security Council, in which one-third of the membership would be the serving heads of the armed services.[4]

General Musharraf, first "chief executive" and then president (after a sham referendum reminiscent of Zia's in 1984), retained his position as chief of the army staff, having that innovative duality ratified by a parliament elected in an election that was not free and fair. The seventeenth amendment to the constitution restored to the president the power of dissolving parliament at his own discretion, though that can be vetoed by the Supreme Court. Thus the de facto fusing of the powers of the president and of the military that had obtained from 1985 through 1997 was made constitutional under Musharraf.

Although the judiciary was nominally independent – and might have been so for a while after independence – each military intervention was followed by efforts to force judicial approval. When General Musharraf took over, echoing what Zia had done in 1981, he required superior-court judges to swear a new oath to the Provisional Constitutional Order he had dictated. Five of the seventeen Supreme Court judges refused and were dismissed (International Crisis Group 2004a: 5). In the summation of the International Crisis Group report on judicial independence:

> Since Pakistan's first decade . . . [its] constitutional jurisprudence, rather than being characterized by inquiries into the validity of executive action, is a series of elaborate jurisprudential efforts to vindicate and facilitate military interventions into democratic politics. . . . Often cast aside or illegally amended the Constitution of 1973 barely qualifies as a rule of law, as opposed to a discretionary guideline that executive officials can follow if and when it is convenient.
>
> (International Crisis Group 2004a: 3)

The Supreme Court crisis of 2007, to be discussed below, certainly served to underline the limits of the rule of law in Pakistan.

Throughout this period, the military kept direct or indirect control of major governmental functions. In the security area – apart from the near-total independence in most matters of strategic doctrine; military training, recruitment and promotion, and other day-to-day activity – the most significant thing has been its total control over the nuclear program (see Ahmed 1999). The army has made use of its intelligence agency to enter the political arena even when it is not formally in charge. The (Directorate for) Inter-Services Intelligence (almost always referred to as the ISI) is an integral part of the army, staffed by serving officers, who rotate in and out (see Stepan 1988: 13–29 for a discussion of the comparable organization in Brazil). Its duties have been expanded well beyond intelligence-gathering. It coordinated support for the Pakistan-based resistance to the Soviet invasion of Afghanistan. Then it helped to bring the Taliban to power in Kabul, and provided support for its rule. It has more and more been used as a force in domestic politics, to manipulate elections. It is doubtful that in the near future, even under a democratic regime, Pakistan would be able to follow the example of the United Kingdom, France, and the United States, countries that "have crafted mechanisms for the democratic management, monitoring, and oversight of their intelligence systems" (Stepan 1988: 140); in 2008, an effort to bring the ISI under the interior ministry of the newly elected PPP government was scotched by the military.

The military has set up a recruitment-to-grave social security system for both officers and men (see Nawaz 2008: 576–7 on the army's perks). The cantonment is a different world from the rest of Pakistan when it comes to things like cleanliness and to more important things like the quality of education and healthcare (Lancaster 2002). At retirement, ordinary soldiers hope for employment in one of the many military foundation enterprises, and officers can expect to do well out of the real-estate deals they can make quite legally (see Siddiqa 2007). As a startling example, consider the family real-estate holdings that General Musharraf, acknowledged as a non-corrupt officer, publicly declared: "five housing plots (two in Karachi, including one in which his house was being built, one each in Rawalpindi, Peshawar, and Lahore). He also listed agricultural land in Bahawalpur, his parents' house in Islamabad, his daughter's house in Karachi, and two other plots (one in Eastridge, Rawalpindi, and one in Gwadar" (Nawaz 2008: 530, citing *Dawn*, 3 November 1999).[5]

While the military still remains economically dependent on the government budget for its current account and capital expenditure, it has, under military regimes, gradually taken on more management positions in a wide array of non-military arenas. In one summary: "Today, military officers dominate education and training institutions in the civil sector. All the major civil service training establishments, for example, are now headed by army officers. They also head universities and state-owned corporations" (Nawaz 2008: 577). They have also had appointments as ambassadors in important countries, including the United States.

According to Shuja Nawaz (2008: 532), when Musharraf took over, "More than 1,000 [military] officers were brought into senior positions in the civil administration, academia, foreign service, and even civil service training institutions."[6] As the foremost scholar of the Pakistan military, Hasan-Askari Rizvi (2003b), puts it:

> The repeated military intervention in politics in Pakistan has led to what is often described as the militarisation of Pakistani state and society. The military and its retired and serving officers have penetrated the institutions of the state (government and semi-government), the civil society, the economy and business and other civilian sectors in such an overwhelming manner that Pakistan's civilian and political institutions can never become autonomous of the military. *Democracy in Pakistan may never come out of the shadow of the military* [my emphasis]. Civilian institutions can hardly afford to disregard the sensitivities of the military on key foreign policy and domestic-political and economic issues. The military sets the tone of the political institutions and processes and the operational norms emphasise management of the political affairs rather than participation of the people, regions and interests.

The evidence for this sweeping assessment is fairly clear as far as the exercise of political authority is concerned.

There are no firm data on just how many companies are controlled by serving or retired military officials in the interest of the armed forces (see Siddiqa 2007 for the richest set of data we have; see also Mazhar Aziz 2008: 97–8; Gregory and Revill 2008: 42; and, for a critique of Siddiqa that marshals empirical evidence, Cloughley 2008: ch. 6). One of the major organizations involved is the Fauji Foundation, set up to enhance the welfare of retired servicemen. A simple listing of its interests (embedded in a story on the alleged plans for the takeover by the military of "Pakistan's only Fortune 500 company") is indicative:

> The Fauji Foundation is currently running the Fauji–Jordan Fertilizer Company, the Fauji Fertilizer Company, the Fauji Cereals, the Fauji Corn Complex, the Fauji Polypropylene Products, the Foundation Gas, the Fauji Oil Terminal and the Distribution Company Limited, the Mari Gas Company Limited and the Fauji Kabirwala Power Company Limited. The Pakistan Army-run Army Welfare Trust (AWT), separately, runs an empire of business projects that also includes banks, insurance companies, and pharmaceutical and cement plants.[7]

As S. Akbar Zaidi (2008d: 3) puts it: "The image of soldiers fighting to defend the motherland changed to one of serving military generals who were acting as corporate bosses, soldiering over tonnes of sugar, cement, and steel." It has long been a tradition that serving military officers head powerful parastatals, most importantly the Water and Power Development Authority (WAPDA), and there is little doubt that the corporate interests of the military have been well served as a result.

This is not without the support of significant parts of the population, who see in the military an institution that is more honest and efficient than those who run state or even private enterprises. The Pakistan military, in control of the state and inserting itself into the economy, has given itself an autonomy that makes it a rentier institution *within* the state. The military is typically not as accountable to the state as it ought to be, and not only when it constitutes the government. Right from the days of Ayub, the military bypassed the foreign ministry in negotiating for military aid, and that continued significantly during the Afghanistan *jihad* and in the "war against terror" after 9/11. It can maintain its own personnel after they retire, providing healthcare, and schooling, and urban land for officers and rural land for ordinary soldiers. Siddiqa (2007) presents a fairly convincing account, however, of how inefficient military enterprises other than real estate have been: they consistently make losses, while providing employment and the opportunity to embezzle or otherwise skim money from the enterprise. Whatever the balance sheet might show (it is carefully hidden), military enterprises are not going to make the army independent of foreign military aid or Pakistan government support, attractive as that prospect might be.

The implication of this entrenchment for our Riggsian analysis is clear: the military – and its bureaucratic allies, though they are not so prominent now – has gradually occupied more and more of the high ground of control of state-derived economic and managerial resources, leaving the politicians to fight an uphill battle. We shall discuss this further in the context of the 2007 Supreme Court crisis – or perhaps the "Musharraf's future" crisis would be a better label – that follows in the next chapter. The post-1977 thirty years of gradual diminution of the influence – not to speak of the power – of politicians has only periodically been broken by episodes of popular enthusiasm and support for them. No towering leader has emerged, commanding broad-ranging respect, on the model of a Nelson Mandela, or even a Zulfiqar Ali Bhutto, though several have offered themselves in that role (Imran Khan, Benazir Bhutto). Nor have non-political, civil-society-based movements or people filled the political vacuum (see Islam 2001: 1343–4; Zaidi 2008c), though the response of organizations and individuals to the Kashmir earthquake of 2005, and the lawyers' movement of 2007 might indicate a change. Otherwise, it would seem that only a crisis on the scale of 1971 would transform the balance of power in favor of politicians. A crisis of that magnitude might well put the entire state into desperate straits.

## Deepening democracy in India

It is worth emphasizing at the outset of this section that I am retaining the "proceduralist" definition of democracy. I shall argue that, *taking India as a whole*, elections have become increasingly free and fair, with voters given a more significant array of parties and politicians to choose from; that the concomitant freedoms of speech, press, and association have been, on balance, strengthened; and that the rule of law has also been improved. Most important, there is little evidence that the military and civil administrative branches of the state have gained any power at the expense of elected representatives. Nor has any international force or domestic extra-governmental institution. At the same time, the foundation of this deepening has been both institutional and socio-economic. Important changes to the constitution and the laws have been made, with certain critical institutions such as the Election Commission strengthened. More important, there has been an expansion in the number and significance of civil-society organizations and social movements (see Katzenstein et al. 2001). Groups heretofore on the margins of power – the lower castes and women, in particular – have as a result increased their political weight.

In the introduction to his edited volume, *The Success of India's Democracy*, Atul Kohli notes that "over the past five decades, democracy in India has not only taken root but . . . spread wide and deep" (Kohli 2001: 14). But "the struggle for democratic deepening is an ongoing one. Here, one wants to analyze the processes whereby India's unkempt [sic] masses are actually inaugurated into the democratic system, that is, come to feel some loyalty to it, participate in it, and hope to benefit from it" (Kohli 2001: 4). The implication of the volume as a whole is that the deepening is occurring.

Patrick Heller (2000), on the other hand, has made a strong argument for attending to the *lack* of success in India as a whole, coupled with a very useful insistence that our analysis must take seriously the geographic variation in India's political system, and a persuasive account of Kerala's comparative success. He claims that there are "degrees of democracy," or (citing Guillermo O'Donnell) "differences in the intensity of citizenship." Heller minces no words in his overall appraisal:

> Fifty-three years of almost uninterrupted democratic rule has done little to reduce the political, social, and economic marginalization of India's popular classes. . . . In India the increasing incidence of caste and communal violence, the criminalization of politics, the spread of corruption, and the rise of ethnic-chauvinist and communitarian parties all point to a crisis of the democratic state. . . . The failure of Indian democracy to give effective voice to substantive demands has locked in a vicious cycle that is eroding the very legitimacy of democratic governance.
>
> (Heller 2000: 485, 496)[8]

In Kerala, according to Heller (2000: 519), "the logic of class politics has strengthened civil society. It has done so not through the small group dynamics of trust and reciprocity emphasized by many civil society theorists, but rather through the emergence of broader social solidarities that were forged from a history of conflict."

This idea about conflict is at first glance disturbing. But it is worth recalling Rustow's insight, in his seminal article on transitions to democracy: "the basis of democracy is not maximum consensus. It is the tenuous middle ground between imposed uniformity (such as would lead to some sort of tyranny) and implacable hostility (of a kind that would disrupt the community in civil war or secession)" (Rustow 1970: 363). Rustow argues that, although consensus is needed in the recognition of the community, in establishing the rules of democracy, and in citizens not only believing them but also becoming habituated in their practice, conflict is crucial:

> [N]ew issues will always emerge and new conflicts threaten the newly won agreements. The characteristic procedures of democracy include campaign oratory, the election of candidates, parliamentary divisions, votes of confidence and of censure – a host of devices, in short, for expressing conflict and thereby resolving it. The essence of democracy is the habit of dissension and conciliation over ever-changing issues and amidst ever-changing alignments. Totalitarian rulers must enforce unanimity on fundamentals and on procedures before they can get down to other business. By contrast, democracy is that form of government that derives its just powers from the dissent of up to one half of the governed.
>
> (Rustow 1970: 363)

Rustow clearly does not equate "conflict" with "class conflict," and that leads us to ask whether Heller's judgment of Indian politics outside Kerala might need to be modified. Is it indeed true that "the failure of Indian democracy to give effective voice to substantive demands has locked in a vicious cycle that is eroding the very legitimacy of democratic governance" (Heller 2000: 496)?

I shall leave aside the difficulties of measuring the incidence – and thus increase or decrease – in corruption, criminalization of politics and the rest. Heller provides no empirical evidence, and I have reason to be suspicious.[9] An enormously experienced India scholar, James Manor (2002: 235–6), states flatly:

> The common assertion that India has witnessed a steadily rising tide of corruption over the last two decades or so is demonstrably false. The overall level of corruption in the country *may* be somewhat higher today than ever, although this is difficult to measure. But it is clear that within individual Indian states, the incidence of corruption has fluctuated – upward but also downward, moderately or often markedly.

Manor produces solid evidence for this assertion, and also presents evidence for a fine, nuanced discussion of "criminalization" (Manor 2002: 234–5).

Have those usually described as "marginalized" – women, tribal peoples, religious minorities, and the lowest castes and classes – been unable to make "substantive" demands that are met by the Indian state? Is there indeed a "vicious cycle" threatening the legitimacy of India's democracy? The empirical evidence, I submit, does not support Heller. As Yogendra Yadav (2000: 140), writing more or less at the same time as Heller, puts it:

> The story of contemporary Indian politics is often recounted, in popular and academic versions, in terms of an impending catastrophe: it is a story of the decline and collapse of the democratic edifice, of growing apathy and widespread indifference, and of a resultant loss of popular legitimacy for the political system. The evidence presented in this paper does pose serious difficulties for this popular reading.

Yadav uses very high-quality survey data to show that those Heller calls "marginalized" have increased their voting participation significantly: "with the partial exception of Muslims, then, we can say that the second democratic upsurge has a bahujan [majority, mass] character. . . . The odds of an OBC, dalit or adivasi voting are much higher than in 1971" (Yadav 2000: 133). Voters also believe in the efficacy of their vote. In a 1971 survey, 48.5 percent said their vote has an effect; in 1996, the figure had gone up to 58.6 percent (Mitra and Singh 1999: 141); and in 2005 it was 61.7 percent (Jaffrelot 2008: 51).[10] While illiterates, scheduled tribes people, and the very poor were the least likely to say their vote made a difference (47.0 percent, 47.8 percent, 50.4 percent) and the upper class (62.1 percent), males (66.2 percent) and the college-educated (79.6 percent) among the most likely to say so, that 58.6 percent is a fairly impressive absolute figure.

Powerful leaders of the other backward classes (OBCs) and even the *dalits* have emerged as chief ministers and important ministers in Delhi: Mayawati in UP, Lalu Prasad Yadav in Bihar and Delhi (2004–9) are only the most visible. The most impressive evidence of the significant reduction in the *political* marginalization of these groups is the change of the caste profile in the legislative assemblies of the states (Jaffrelot and Kumar 2009; see also Yadav and Palshikar 2008: 19–20). Selecting here the largest states (with the exception of Orissa), with 80 percent of India's population, the percentage of legislators (MLAs) who are upper caste has declined significantly from the 1950s. In UP, Bihar, Madhya Pradesh, Gujarat (35.1 percent of India), the OBCs have increased; in Rajasthan (5.5 percent of India) it is the "intermediate/dominant"-caste MLAs who have increased. In Maharashtra, Andhra Pradesh, and Karnataka (21.9 percent of India), "intermediate/ dominant"-caste MLAs have been the largest contingent throughout, with very few upper-caste legislators. In Tamil Nadu (6.1 percent of India) it has been the OBCs that have always held sway. Only in West Bengal and Kerala (10.9 percent of India) have the upper castes retained a dominant position in the legislature (Jaffrelot and Kumar 2009: 15–22).

Votes have made a difference in social practices as well (see Krishna 2006; M. Robinson 1988). For a small example from one of the very few longitudinal village studies we have, consider T. S. Epstein et al. (1998: 174–5), writing about a place – not in Kerala – that in 1955 had displayed "severe caste discrimination":

> The council spent about 30 percent of its total expenditure . . . between 1990 and 1996 on improving low caste housing. There did not seem to have been any attempt made by the dominant Peasant caste to oppose these housing improvements or to sidetrack the JRY funds for other purposes.

This is not an isolated case. Price (2006: 315), in Michelutti's (2008: 21) summary, "reports how since the 1970s 'low caste informants spoke of experiencing independence in their lives' and 'being rulers of their own lives.'"

In between, as it were, this village snapshot and Yadav's all-India data, we have the conclusion of Michelutti's study of the Yadavs of north India, and in particular Mathura:

> At first glance the post-independence nationalist elite's efforts of creating an equal and casteless society look like miserable failures. But, as this book shows, the idea of equality (at least social if not economic) has made important inroads in popular consciousness and paradoxically, it has been precisely the working towards equality and freedom through democratic means (particularly through voting) which has, and is, promoting the political use of caste and its social reinvention into quasi-ethnic communities. . . . The ethnography presented in this book shows that when caste re-enters politics as "*samaj*" [literally, "society" in general, and commonly "community" or "association"] mobilized by caste-based political parties, rather than weakening the democratic process it generally strengthens it, and by deepening it, gains more and more vitality and produces new social relations and values which in turn help democracy to ground itself further into society.
>
> (Michelutti 2008: 7, 8)

The Yadavs are of course more likely to be a large and dominant community than a small and marginalized one. Certain large and previously marginalized communities – the UP *dalits* variously named *chamar* or *jatav*, for example – have used votes to leverage themselves into positions of real power at the state level. Others, most importantly Muslims and *adivasis*, have not. If those groups similarly "make it" into the "ruling-groups" category, which is not difficult to imagine, the numbers of Yadav-like communities might add up to as much or more than the combined totals of the highly fragmented small-and-marginalized castes.

In the survey data of the *State of Democracy in South Asia* report, it is clear that India's religious and ethnic minorities (except for the Sikhs) only differ slightly in their perceptions from Indians as a whole. This is true of their general support of democracy (*SDSA* 2008: 20) and in their trust in government institutions.[11] Thirty-seven percent of minorities in India felt their conditions had improved, while 18 percent felt they had deteriorated (*SDSA* 2008: 74).

Yadav (1999b: 38; see also Yadav 1999b: 30) underlines the extent to which the previously marginalized have done even more:

> The journey of the idea of democracy in India has not only changed the lives of the millions it has touched, but it has also changed the idea of democracy itself in more ways than one. Call it "creolization" or "vernacularization" of democracy, this transformation is at the heart of whatever success democracy has achieved in India. The serious attempt to marry the democratic idea to popular beliefs, to develop shared protocols with the preexisting language of the people, is what has distinguished India from other countries where the democratic enterprise never took off. And that is also what can continue to maintain this distinction in the future.

Michelutti (2008: 217) agrees that through the "vernacularization of democratic politics [the 'process through which ideas and practices of democracy become embedded in particular cultural and social practices, and in turn become entrenched in the consciousness of ordinary people'] . . . popular politics thrives in North India." And "vernacular idioms have been paramount in making democracy part of the Indian political imagination and in informing the political upsurge of the *bahujan samaj* (the common folk)." This outcome is also to be found in eastern India, according to Corbridge et al. (2005: 198–9): "Political society has become domesticated in the minds of many villagers. The careers of political activists are linked from the outset to ideas of reciprocity, obligation and proper conduct which are constructed in part through vernacular idioms. . . . Voting, or showing up to a public meeting, is in part a social obligation."

Michelutti (2008: 222–9) argues that this process exists in communities other than Yadavs, and that the earlier ideas of a yawning gap between "elite" and "mass" cultures in Indian politics is at least no longer there (if it ever was). She concludes (Michelutti 2008: 227):

> The hypothesis developed from the case of the Yadavs – a low caste (traditionally marginalized both in ritual and economic terms) that through vernacularization has achieved high levels of politicization and assertiveness – provides an alternative way to look at popular politics. It shows that faith in democracy and deepening of democracy is not only dependent on what states fail or succeed to deliver. In India, for example, poverty, illiteracy, corruption, disregard for law and order, and political violence coexist with a commitment to the "idea of democracy" among the poor.

There is a cautionary lining to the tale of Yadav self-assertion, which, emphasizing the importance of the Yadav "wrestler/politicians," has as "an outcome . . . the emphasis given by young Yadavs to their muscular bodies and to the creation of a strongman reputation within their neighborhood and town" (Michelutti 2008: 66). We need to ask whether "vernacularization" might also be linked to the politics of (violent) exclusion – the deliberate sharpening of communal identities by demonizing the "other," in particular the Muslims of India.[12]

The dark side of the upsurge of the *bahujans* (the masses; literally, the majority) is a staple of media reporting and commentary, undoubtedly influenced by the perceptions of those more comfortable with regulated and orderly politics. Throughout India's post-independence history there have been outbreaks of caste and communal violence, and revolutionary activity. The issue we need to examine is whether they constitute a deep threat to India's democracy, by undermining the legitimacy of politicians or enhancing the capacities and inclination of the police and army to increase their share in governance.

Caste violence – typically, attacks by upper-caste land-owners in the countryside on *dalits* – continued at high levels through the 1990s (see Corbridge and Harriss 2000: 203–16), but seems to have decreased or stabilized in the last decade (if newspaper accounts of atrocities are any guide), or been transformed in the context of revolutionary counter-violence in the "red corridor" of central and eastern India.[13] While the causes of the increase are far from settled, the decrease seems to be directly linked to the emergence of *dalit* movements and, even more significantly, the Bahujan Samaj Party (BSP) and the Lok Janshakti Party (LJP) into positions of real power. In the villages, the conflict between OBCs and those below them continues, but the resolution of that problem will perhaps lie more in the transformation of India's economy into one in which an increase in jobs outside agriculture will open up opportunities for exit to both sets of people.

In recent years the number of Hindu–Muslim riots seems to have decreased significantly (see Table 9.1), in contrast to the situation in the 1980s and early 1990s (see *inter alia* Akbar 1988; Brass 1996, 2003; Varshney 2002; Wilkinson 2004, 2005).

*Table 9.1* Hindu–Muslim communal incidents in India

|           | 2002  | 2003  | 2004  | 2005  | 2006  | 2007  | 2008  |
|-----------|-------|-------|-------|-------|-------|-------|-------|
| Incidents | 722   | 711   | 640   | 779   | 698   | 761   | 656   |
| Killed    | 1,130 | 193   | 129   | 124   | 133   | 96    | 123   |
| Injured   | 4,375 | 2,261 | 2,022 | 2,066 | 2,170 | 2,117 | 2,272 |

*Source*: Ministry of Home Affairs, Government of India, Annual Reports 2003–4 to 2008–9.

There is good reason to doubt the accuracy of this data, but even if they understate the incidence by a large amount there are, on average, two or three "incidents" per day. The numbers of killed and injured are also not large, when one considers that ten people a day are killed in the Mumbai train system (mainly, one assumes, by falling off outrageously overcrowded carriages). Although these incidents tend to occur in particular riot-prone cities, or parts of cities, the all-India death rate of 10 per 10 million people (the 2002–3 figure, which includes the Gujarat pogrom and riots), let alone 1 per 10 million people (the 2008–9 figure), does not give us a picture of continuous violence, with an ever fearful population.

Indeed, there is some evidence on the level of fear. The *State of Democracy in South Asia* report has a chapter on "freedom from fear," in which it is reported that 6 percent of Indian respondents said that "they, their family members or acquaintances faced physical assault in the last year" (*SDSA* 2008: 111), and 5 percent felt "unsafe" where they lived (*SDSA* 2008: 114). The breakdown by marginal community for this question was: Hindu Dalit 5 percent; Muslim 4 percent; Adivasi 4 percent; Christian 7 percent; and Sikh 5 percent. Of those with an opinion on the sources of feeling "insecure" – four degrees of "insecurity" were specified – 45 percent felt "not at all insecure" from riots or mob violence, compared to 32 percent feeling "not at all insecure" from theft or robbery and 49 percent feeling "not at all insecure" from "police/army/security forces" (calculated from *SDSA* 2008: 279–80). The threat of mob violence was felt by 36 percent of Sikhs and 23 percent of Muslims. Women and men feel "safe" and "a little unsafe" in equal proportions (75 and 76 percent, 16 and 17 percent), a lack of gender difference that carries through situationally: while going out after sunset, in the workplace, at home. The major variation among those who felt "safe" (an average of 76 percent) were lower figures (69 percent, 67 percent) for the east and the Northeast, and higher for the west and the south (86 percent, 81 percent) (*SDSA* 2008: 272). Also, 45 percent of Indians felt "more safe than a few years ago" (*SDSA* 2008: 112).

It is fair to say that Indians in general, and minorities and women in particular, certainly do not live in fear of severe violence, even though domestic violence is commonplace. And, at the same time, their feeling of insecurity when it comes to everything from riots to the security forces is certainly significant. But there is no indication that things have become very much worse, if worse at all.

It is possible that the earlier increase and current levels of violence against Muslims and *dalits* are the result of the upward mobility of a previously entirely powerless group of people such as the *dalits* (M. Robinson 1988: 264). In the case of the Muslims, this might happen when they acquire new sources of money – from remittances from the Gulf in the 1970s, for example – to set up in business on their own and thus challenge members of the majority who had been exploiting them economically. The current decline in violence, in one interpretation, would be the result of the "upper" communities coming to terms with, and even accepting, the loss of their power over groups previously subservient. But it could also be true that the violence has succeeded in forcing *dalits* and Muslims to "know their place," particularly in local arenas. The rise of *dalits* to positions of rule would favor the first interpretation; the relative quiescence of Muslim leadership since the Babri Masjid killings and the 2002 Gujarat pogrom would suggest the latter interpretation.

The other major blemish on India's democracy concerns the areas of the country that are in effect ruled by a combination of the martial law authorities and armed insurgents' local diktat. This has been the situation in at least part of the Northeast for more than fifty years, in the Kashmir valley since 1989, and sporadically in the east-central tribal belt – the contiguous parts of Maharashtra, Madhya Pradesh, Chhattisgarh, Bihar, Jharkhand, West Bengal, Orissa, and Andhra Pradesh – with the most recent threat from what have been labeled "Naxalite" or "Maoist" groups.[14] According to the South Asia Terrorism Portal's *India Assessment – 2007*:

> [Of the] 2,765 people [who] died in terrorism-related violence in India during year 2006 . . . nearly 41 per cent of all such fatalities occurred in Jammu and Kashmir (J&K); 27 per cent resulted from Left Wing Extremism (Maoism/Naxalism) across parts of 14 States; [and] 23 per cent . . . in the multiple insurgencies of India's Northeast. . . . At least 231 of the country's 608 Districts are currently afflicted, at differing intensities, by various insurgent and terrorist movements.[15]

These figures match those provided by the government of India's Home Ministry (Table 9.2).

But just what the figures mean is a matter of dispute when it comes to assessing how great a threat this activity is. There does not seem to have been a great increase in violence over the past five years, merely some shifts in which states are most affected – most notably the decline of incidents in Andhra Pradesh. A recent report (Pradhan 2009) notes that Andhra Pradesh had only thirty-five incidents, with twenty-six people killed in 2009 (up to 13 December). Yet Prime Minister Manmohan Singh, speaking to the directors-general of police of the states on 15 September 2009, "reiterated his contention that left wing extremism was the 'gravest internal security threat' confronting India" (Sahni 2009; see Sundar 2007: 266–70 for a critique of that judgment). Shivraj Patil, home minister from 2004 to 2008, pointed out in a television interview in February 2008 that the units of analysis used are important (see Table 9.3):

> If you say 10 states are affected, it is 30 per cent of the country affected. If you say 180 districts are affected, you are saying that nearly 25 per cent of the country is affected. If you go by the statistics relating to the police stations affected, it comes down to three per cent. That means

*Table 9.2* Naxalite violence in India, 2004–8: selected states arranged by number of incidents in 2008

| State | 2004 | | 2005 | | 2006 | | 2007 | | 2008 | |
|---|---|---|---|---|---|---|---|---|---|---|
| | *I* | *D* | *I* | *D* | *I* | *D* | *I* | *D* | *I* | *D* |
| Chhattisgarh | 352 | 83 | 385 | 168 | 715 | 388 | 582 | 369 | 620 | 242 |
| Jharkhand | 379 | 169 | 312 | 119 | 310 | 124 | 482 | 157 | 484 | 207 |
| Bihar | 323 | 171 | 186 | 96 | 107 | 45 | 135 | 67 | 164 | 73 |
| Orissa | 35 | 8 | 42 | 14 | 44 | 9 | 67 | 17 | 103 | 101 |
| Andhra Pradesh | 310 | 74 | 535 | 208 | 183 | 47 | 138 | 45 | 92 | 46 |
| Maharashtra | 84 | 15 | 94 | 53 | 98 | 42 | 94 | 25 | 68 | 22 |
| West Bengal | 11 | 15 | 14 | 7 | 23 | 17 | 32 | 6 | 35 | 26 |
| India* | 1,533 | 566 | 1,608 | 677 | 1,509 | 678 | 1,565 | 696 | 1,591 | 721 |

* There were thirteen states in which Naxalite violence occurred; incidents were in the single digits in the remaining states (Haryana, Kerala, Karnataka, Madhya Pradesh, Tamil Nadu Uttar Pradesh).

I = no. of incidents; D = no. of deaths.

*Source*: Ministry of Home Affairs, Government of India, Annual Report 2008–9, Annexure IV; http://www.mha.nic.in/pdfs/AR(E)0809.pdf; accessed 30 December 2009.

*Table 9.3* Naxalite violence 2003–7, by number of police-station areas affected: selected states*

| | 2003 | 2004 | 2005 | 2006 | 2007 | *Total stations in state* |
|---|---|---|---|---|---|---|
| Andhra Pradesh | 183 | 149 | 188 | 93 | 59 | 1,635 |
| Bihar | 100 | 106 | 80 | 69 | 71 | 834 |
| Chhattisgarh | 57 | 68 | 66 | 81 | 71 | 307 |
| Jharkhand | 96 | 101 | 79 | 85 | 99 | 310 |
| Total of 13 states | 491 | 482 | 460 | 395 | 361 | 10,027 |

* States selected from a list of thirteen affected by Naxalite violence.

*Source*: Ministry of Home Affairs, Government of India, Annual Report 2007–8, p. 143.

from 30 per cent, you are coming down to three per cent [T. N. Ninan (2009) uses the figure of 2,000 police stations of 14,000]. And if you are giving this kind of statistics, are we not creating fear psychosis in the country?[16]

But of course it is what "affected" means that makes the difference. Whether the distortion in the normal conduct of government in a democratic context is greater than that in places where, for example, large landlords still have sway, or places where there is in effect one-party dominance bordering on tyranny, and so on, is something that we probably shall never be able to measure.[17]

As was memorably pointed out by James Scott (1976), given the conditions of most Third World countries – and India is emphatically almost a paradigm – the mystery is why everyone is *not* up in arms against their oppressors, whether they be local landlords, exploiting factory-owners, or an oppressive state. Scott's answer is to consider the peasant's sense of justice, and for that we must turn to an understanding of the "moral economy" in which people live. The same question applies in India. Why are some parts of the country perennially in revolt? The fight against the Indian state in Kashmir is easy to understand, as it has very clear historical roots, and clear international-actor explanations, to go along with some consideration of ethno-political dynamics. Independence movements in the Northeast also have fairly obvious historical explanations (see Baruah 2001, 2005).[18] "Revolutionary" movements, on the other hand, seem more complicated.[19]

The great danger to democracy from revolutionary and separatist movements probably comes less from the insurgencies directly than from the legitimation of a repressive policy by the state. This can take the form of sponsoring counter-insurgency groups of local strongmen whose use of torture, summary execution, and other techniques mirroring the insurgents' is implicitly justified, even as the connection with state policy is denied (see Sundar 2007). Or it can take the form of flooding an insurgent-affected area with massive numbers of armed police and paramilitary, with the almost inevitable use of constant surveillance, disruptive checking of identity, and the use of indiscriminate force in conducting raids and apprehending suspected terrorists, which rapidly cross the boundaries of the rule of law.[20]

There is also a danger from an increase in the semiloyal opposition (Linz 1978) – those who make excuses for groups that deny the legitimacy of the constitution and the state, and typically adopt violent methods, like those of the Naxalites and the virulently anti-Muslim Bajrang Dal (see Jaffrelot 2009). Citizens and political parties and courts, as well as the police and other state authorities, may be prepared to ignore the violence of these groups, or make compromises that in effect allow them autonomy. They may treat Bajrang Dal members who demolished the Babri Masjid or trashed M. F. Husain's paintings (Jaffrelot 2009: 208–18) as people overwhelmed by patriotic feelings, or agree that extreme denial of justice and the predations of armed oppressors justifies killing landlords and police. The pressure on the center from an increasingly militant Right and revolutionary Left would be enhanced by a penumbra of generally law-abiding citizens who justify delegitimation of the political system. So far, in India, the system has managed to co-opt and incorporate many extremists (see Jaoul 2009), and the semiloyal opposition – at least those visible in party politics – have not increased to dangerous levels.

The "deepening" of democracy – perhaps another way of saying "placing procedural democracy on a broad social and economic foundation" – must go beyond the inclusion of the marginalized and relatively powerless in the ranks of an active citizenry committed by belief and practice to democracy. In addition to the politically active elite, or the recent popular upsurge of the "bahujan" classes, we must focus on the great middle range: in the countryside the "middle peasants" and in the urban areas the "middle class." There is of course a political-theory tradition stretching back to Aristotle that sees democracy as requiring a substantial middle category of citizen. This sees the middle class in terms of property-holding citizens who have a vested interest in stability and rules set by the polity as a whole. They cannot afford to muster private protection, as the rich can, and are still vulnerable to the demands, perhaps backed by force, of citizens who have nothing.

Donald Attwood (1992: 291–319), analyzing rural political economies in Maharashtra, West Bengal, UP, and India more generally, describes what he calls a "revolution from the middle," by which he means:

> that India is dominated mainly by its "intermediate classes:" that is, by the educated, urban middle class, on the one hand, and by the large and middle peasants (including commercial peasants) on the other. . . . The sheer size of these intermediate classes has major effects on the character of the political system. . . . Being so huge, these classes are regionally and ethnically heterogeneous. They are also open to mobility. They have kept India's government reasonably stable and democratic, since political leaders are required to seek broad coalitions and compromises in order to satisfy the interest of these classes.
>
> (Attwood 1992: 311)

The Rudolphs (1987: 49–55) coined the term "bullock capitalists" (small-scale self-employed farmers) to highlight the changed character of one category of farmers, arguing that they are part of an "ascendant agrarian political class that strengthens the prospects of centrism" (Rudolph and Rudolph 1987: 52). The "status aspect" of that class, overlapping but not congruent, is the "backward" castes – the Rudolphs mention the Yadavs (Ahir), Kurmis, Koeris, Vokkaligas by way of example (Rudolph and Rudolph 1987: 54). Then there are the "most backward castes" which are included in the core – along with the *dalits* – of those whose rise Yogendra Yadav (2000) calls the "second upsurge." The Rudolphs conclude that "the sectoral politics of the new agrarianism accepts the [democratic] system but calls for changes within it; that is, it is incremental rather than either status quo or revolutionary" (Rudolph and Rudolph 1987: 392).

Events in the last twenty years have tended to confirm that analysis. Even in West Bengal, the CPM "drew strength from the existing balance of political forces by conducting what has been described as the 'politics of middleness'" (Bhattacharyya 1999: 296). There has been an enlargement of the domain of those occupying the middle ground between the utterly powerless – those with no economic foothold and no strength even in numbers – and those whose power derives from disproportionate wealth in land that enables them to employ people or develop a set of clients to use force rather than numbers to prevail. They may well constitute a majority in many parts of rural India, although they are far from a united class in most places. Djurfeldt et al. (2008), using panel data from 1979 and 2004 in Tamil Nadu, find that family farms have increased in proportion, and inequality of income has come down. These groups may not be the equivalent of the Jeffersonian yeoman farmer that was to be the bulwark of a developing American democracy; but in their comparative autonomy, and in their demand for dignity and respect, in an environment in which the majority of Indians still reside, they are well suited for their role as core democratic citizens.

It is not just in the countryside that a possibly democracy-committed class has emerged. In the mid-1980s, reflecting perhaps the emergence of Rajiv Gandhi and his coterie at the center of Indian politics, some analysts focused the role of a middle class (alternately, "the bourgeoisie") in providing the bulwark for liberal democracy (see Palshikar 2001). The critical factor here was the emergence of an industrial and modern services capitalist economy for which a property-rights-guaranteeing rule of law was seen to be necessary. The middle class, typically identified (for measurement of its size as well) by the durable goods it owns – house or flat, motor vehicle, refrigerator, television, and air conditioner – is perceived to have a stake in the political economy that fits well with democracy (see *inter alia* Dubey 1992; Varma 1998; Sheth 1999; I. Ahmad and Reifeld 2001; Sridharan 2004). The middle class was also an educated class that read newspapers and magazines that also catered to their consumerism. This seemed to fit the model of the citizen informed on issues and policies and programs, who would choose political leaders accordingly. Some expected that the old-style politicians, with their patronage and corruption and inefficiency, would be rejected in favor of the disciplined, honest, and policy-competent ones (Palshikar 2001: 177–9).

The overwhelming majority of political and state officials in office have been middle class at least in terms of education, consumer tastes, and economic autonomy. And the middle class also staffs the upper levels of significant civil-society associations – not only the professional societies (like the Bar) and the businessmen's associations, but also the NGOs. As Madsen (1996: 265–6) argues:

> These NGOs [that Madsen has studied] involve themselves in complex processes of interaction with the state in order to influence policy and legal codes and methodologies. Such NGOs are not spontaneous grassroots organizations, but elite brokers and innovators with links to power centers as well as the grassroots. To a considerable extent, their process of "NGO-ing" consists of *penetrating a number of villages (or towns and cities) and building up support there in order to demonstrate to significant others in positions of power and influence that justice in a particular case would be better served if those significant others use their power and influence to support the case as defined by the NGO* [emphasis in the original].

Ignoring for the moment Madsen's caveat about generalizing from the NGOs he studied (Madsen 1996: 264), it can be said that it is a rare NGO that "comes up" from a non-middle-class group of people; and not a few have connections, including funding of course, with international NGOs, which are also decidedly middle class in character. True, there is a Gandhian segment of NGOs in India that are not quite as middle class as the rest, but they are distinctly in a minority. Similarly, even working-class movements, farmers' movements, and trade unions typically have leaders – often lawyers – who are middle class. Despite the generally middle-class nature of the leadership of grassroots movements, the majority of participants understand well what the movement is about (see Palshikar 2001: 180–2). They are not passive objects of "mobilization." And they have played an important role in stabilizing and deepening democracy, as Katzenstein et al. (2001: 268) observe:

> Social movement activism has been a largely unacknowledged bulwark against the materialization of the conditions that so often propel authoritarian responses. . . . [I]t appears likely that interest-based social movement activism along with the courts and the bureaucracy have played a significant role in safeguarding against such an eventuality in India. It is unlikely that electoral practices alone would have been able to secure a similar outcome.

Even as the middle class expanded in the 1980s, many of its members, particularly in northern and western India, moved to an identity politics centered on *hindutva* (see Palshikar 2001: 182–4), providing an expanding electoral support-base for the BJP (V. B. Singh 2004: 321–2).[21] Adherents tended to practice a modernized religion with a focus on a single god-king, Rama, who was more human than other gods (no extra limbs, monogamous, etc.). This also involved the demonization of non-Hindus even as it mirrored Christian and Muslim belief systems, and ultimately supported a movement of direct action that climaxed with the destruction of the Babri Masjid (see Pollock 1993). There is little doubt that elements within that movement could be labeled "fascist,"[22] but that has been true of many movements in "mature" democracies as well. And of course Germany in the 1930s was already a middle-class country, with a vibrant associational life. That suggests that the middle class will not resist, and will accept an authoritarian regime, as the lack of resistance and indeed joyful welcoming by the middle class of each major military coup in Pakistan attests.[23] The middle class perhaps acts as stabilizing base for whatever regime can give it reliable rules, efficient and effective government (keeping the streets clean is the paradigmatic task), with no violence, while allowing it to maintain its standard of living (i.e., its consuming habits), and some autonomy in family and social decision-making.

We must not lose sight of the very serious weaknesses that remain in India's democratic institutions. Yadav himself (1999b: 33–6) sets out the indictment:

[T]he achievements of democracy as a set of institutions or as a regime do not, of course, satisfy the deeper ethical impulse associated with the idea of democracy. . . . [T]he promise of a community of equals has been a false one. . . . The liberty [the politicized social community] offers, at least formally, is distributed in extremely unequal measure. The power it brings to the people as an abstraction is rarely, if ever, exercised by the real people. And there are still many people – full citizens of the republic of India – who feel as powerless under this democracy as they did under British rule. The performance of Indian democracy in achieving national integration has left much to be desired. . . . The promise of social revolution that the democratic invitation has always contained has been realized only in parts and in fragments. . . . The single biggest failure of democratic politics lies in the nonfulfilment of the promise of material well-being.

But, in the conclusion of his essay, Yadav (1999b: 38) writes : "The serious attempt to marry the democratic idea to popular beliefs, to develop shared protocols with the preexisting language of the people, is what has distinguished India from other countries where the democratic enterprise never took off. And that is also what can continue to maintain this distinction in the future." For India, then, the "deepening" of democracy is most clearly the case at the "bahujan" level of society. That deepening has been at times messy, and even violent, but it has also meant the acceptance of belief in democracy and its practices.

Pakistan has not had the same class profile – there are a handful of very rich at the top, but very few also of the desperately poverty-stricken, and those largely in very remote areas. Pakistan's middle class is probably less wealthy than its Indian counterpart. Pakistan's statistics for female literacy are far behind India's, and in general its educational system is probably much weaker. All of this is reflected in the small number and comparative weakness of civil-society organizations (see Candland 2007a; Weiss and Gilani 2001; Zaidi 2008c). There is nothing comparable to what Yadav calls the "second upsurge" visible: those at the margins of power and status and wealth have not been seriously involved in political activity, even voting. In a survey circa 1999, 44 percent of the women said that the reason for voting was "men of the house told me to vote that way" (Shaheed 2002: 129), and very few women were able to name members of the national or provincial assemblies (Shaheed 2002: 135). The Islamist movements, though drawing on a vast reservoir of believers, have not been able to mobilize a mass following that comes out in the streets, or even casts votes for them.

The Indian citizen whose day-to-day experience of government is mainly that of an inefficient and often callous and corrupt bureaucracy has little incentive to support an increase in the power of the state apparatus over politicians, except in times and places of crisis, where security and order are necessary. Those crises have been rare for the overwhelming majority of Indians in the last decades, so the balance established by the victory for democracy in the 1977 elections has remained in place.

Citizens in Pakistan have spent a total of twenty years since 1977 under direct military–bureaucratic rule, albeit not of a particularly harsh variety compared to others in the Third World. The remaining time has seen weak political parties in power, with leaders tarnished by accusations of corruption, with the military keeping control of significant areas of government policy, and continuing to enhance its economic and social power. While the Pakistan military has held on to ultimate power and enhanced its strength, the emergence of *jihadi* culture and the developments in Afghanistan after 9/11 have forced it to fight armed enemies, terrorists, and others who have established islands of authority in the borderlands, as well as maintaining the country's security against India. As it has turned its attention to that battle, and withdrawn from day-to-day control of most of civilian governance, allowing first the return of Pakistan's former prime ministers, Benazir Bhutto and Nawaz Sharif in 2007, and then a free and fair election in February 2008, its respect among the citizenry, as measured by public opinion surveys, has increased enormously. There are few signs, however, that the army will dismantle any of its economic activities, or give up its veto over national security policies, still less its claim to be the ultimate judge of how Pakistan should be governed.

## Notes

1 Strictly speaking, "the military," but even now it is the army that made and broke governments in Pakistan, not the the navy or the air force.
2 For possible solutions to the mystery of this crash, see Coll (1994); and, for a wonderful and wildly inventive fictional account, Hanif (2008).
3 This set of questions generally was answered by almost all the "elite" respondents, but (in this case, for example) 38 and 40 percent of "mass" respondents had "no opinion." It is not clear, of course, just how the respondents interpreted "experts" – whether, for example, that would include "management experts" (and thus civil-service officers).
4 "The President shall be the Chairman of the National Security Council and its other members shall be the Prime Minister, the Chairman of the Senate, the Speaker of the National Assembly, the Leader of the Opposition in the National Assembly, the Chief Ministers of the Provinces, the Chairman Joint Chiefs of Staff Committee, and the Chiefs of Staff of the Pakistan Army, Pakistan Navy and Pakistan Air Force." According to an insider at the time, Nasim Zehra (2008): "Three days into the Oct 12 [1999] coup, in a background discussion Musharraf had rebuffed the idea of a National Security Council because 'it was unthinkable to put an unelected body on an elected one.'" Prime Minister Gilani announced the dissolution of the NSC on 29 November 2008.
5 To which list one more house should apparently be added: when Musharraf resigned, in August 2008, he returned to Army House, awaiting, it was said, the completion of the construction of his new house in Islamabad.
6 His source is an article by Nasir Iqbal in *Dawn* (3 October 2003), which gives vivid details:

> The range of fields [where military officers are in civilian posts includes] communications, education, diplomacy, water and electricity management, information, post office, jails, local bodies, think-tanks, industrial production, shipping, minority affairs, population welfare, health, agriculture, railways, highways, housing, labour and manpower, social and women development, law and justice and sub-sectors of sports from cricket to hockey.

7 "Pakistani Generals Prepare to Take Over Billion Dollar State-Owned Oil Company," *South Asia Tribune* (web edition) 59, 14–20 September 2003. See also M. Zaidi (2003).

8 This assessment is often to be heard from members of the broader intelligentsia in India; for example, in the writings of activist-analyst Arundhati Roy (2008: viii):

> Every day, every week, every month, more and more people are rising up in myriad ways, massing into a colossal wave of resistance – all kinds of resistance, violent, non-violent, revolutionary and criminal – that threatens to engulf the country, fill the prisons, and for better or for worse shatter the almost pornographic contentment of India Shining [an election slogan in 2004, referring to India's high growth and modernization]. . . . Before our very eyes, our hollow-to-begin-with democracy has begun to devolve into an elaborately administered tyranny.

9 In Oldenburg (1987) I consider the case of corruption; in Oldenburg (2005) I deal briefly with the data on communal riots. Transparency International's India chapter's 2005 survey study of the incidence of corruption is a much better guide to what goes on than that world-wide organization's annual ranking of countries by level of corruption. Available at: http://www.tiindia.in/data/files/India%20Corruption%20Study%202005%20in%20PDF.pdf; accessed 19 July 2008.

10 Those who said it "makes no difference" also increased, from 16.2 percent to 21.3 percent, and the "don't know" category shrank from 35.3 percent to 19.1 percent.

11 *SDSA* (2008: 59). An index was computed from responses to questions about the central government, provincial government, local government, civil services, police, army, courts, parliament, political parties, and the Election Commission. In India, the overall index number was 64 (with 100 being highest trust). In Pakistan, provincially and linguistically defined groups also do not differ much from the overall index number of 44, with Urdu-speakers, Punjabis, and Sindhis having slightly less trust, and Pukhtuns and Saraiki-speakers somewhat more trust.

12 It is important to note that Michelutti shows clearly that this is not the case in the Mathura she studied, where the Samajvadi Party of the Yadavs very explicitly brought Yadavs and Muslims together – indeed, with the normally vegetarian Yadavs on occasion sharing meat meals with Muslims (Michelutti 2008: 147).

13 The home ministry's National Crime Records Bureau annual publication *Crime in India* reports total crimes against scheduled castes of 31,440 in 1996, which dipped to 25,093 in 1999, and increased to 33,507 in 2002 and 30,030 in 2007. The number of cases registered under the Prevention of Atrocities Act increased from 8,054 in 1997, shot up between 2000 and 2001, to 13,113, and then came down to 9,795 in 2007 (again with a large increase between 2006 and 2007). Since it is likely that there is significant under-reporting of these crimes, it is not clear whether changes in the numbers reflect the actual crime rate, as opposed to the willingness of the police to register cases or of persons to complain.

14 See D. K. Gupta (2007) and Guha (2009) for recent comprehensive accounts with extensive references; Jaoul (2009) for a fieldwork-based study of the Bihar situation; and Kunnath (2006) for an insightful participant-observer's perspective.

15 Available at: http://satp.org/satporgtp/countries/india/index.html; accessed 29 November 2009. The South Asia Terrorism Portal reports the number of civilians, Maoists and other "terrorists," and security forces people killed on a weekly basis in each state, and summarizes that data in an annual "assessment" that also covers Kashmir and the states of the northeast. The data collected are "compiled from news reports," but in an organization headed by K. P. S. Gill, one of India's most senior and most prominent ex-policemen, one can assume some government sources have also been consulted, if only for cross-checking.

16 See http://ibnlive.in.com/news/naxal-threat-has-not-become-worse-patil/59198-3-p1.html; accessed 19 December 2008. "Police station" means here a demarcated area, not a building. See the attack on Patil's point of view by Ajai Sahni, the editor of *Faultlines*, in the foreword to volume 19 (2008); available at: http://satp.org/satporgtp/publication/faultlines/volume19/Foreword.htm; accessed 24 July 2008.

17 That the areas most affected by Naxalite activity have been for a very long time – if one looks at the record of "peasant" revolts that occur in just those areas as long ago as the nineteenth century – in some sense "tribal" is suggestive. It is likely that these are conflicts fueled not by a radical ideology, but rather by exploitation of one ethno-cultural group by another (see Guha 2009; Calman 1985).

18 See Baruah (2009) for an important new perspective.

19 Relevant works include Brass and Franda (1973); Bouton (1985); D. K. Gupta (2007).

20 For a summary of these issues, see the stories in *Frontline*, 24 (18) of 21 September 2007; available at: http://www.flonnet.com/fl2418/stories/20070921500400400.htm; accessed 1 January 2010.

21 It should be emphasized that this is indeed a matter of class rather than ("upper") caste support. Drawing on extensive survey data, V. B. Singh (2004: 322) concludes: "more than any other indicators, be it caste hierarchy or level of education, it is the economic status which plays a determining role in influencing one's vote preference, especially in the case of the BJP."

22 The definition used in India encompasses movements that are violent, authoritarian (anti-democratic), favoring a "hard" state, hyper-cultural-nationalist, demonizing Muslims and left-wing movements. See Datta-Choudhury (1976); Shourie (1978).

23 The Rudolphs (1964: 7), discussing the possibilities of military rule in India, note (in a passage quoted on p. 51):

> The authoritarian character created by the traditional family, the attraction of cultural fundamentalism to the urbanized lower middle classes, and the appeal of order, discipline and efficiency to the professional classes, now marginal features of Indian political life, are susceptible of mobilization by military leadership under the right circumstances.

# 10 Prospects for path convergence in the next decades

Thirty years after independence, in 1977, India took a giant leap forward towards a consolidated democracy, while Pakistan embarked on a path of enhanced and entrenched military rule. India seems well set in its democratic ways, but it has not crossed the threshold level of economic development that seemingly guarantees its future as a democracy (see Przeworski and Limongi 1997), and it will undoubtedly face crises of some sort in the next thirty years, whether a war- or a climate-change-produced catastrophe, or something else. So we need to assess how strong its democratic foundation is.

After another thirty years, Pakistan has possibly made another turn, with General Musharraf being dislodged from office by the lawyers' movement, ratified, as it were, by the results of the reasonably free and fair February 2008 election. The new, democratically elected government in Pakistan is a more hopeful outcome than the military takeover that followed the equally broad and intense popular movement against Ayub Khan's rule in 1968–9. But the military still remains in place as a political player of great significance, with much more power than it had in the immediate post-independence period. We need to assess the likelihood that Pakistan in the next decades – a generation or so – will consolidate its democracy and establish a balance in which democratically elected leaders will be decisive in the balance-of-power struggle with the military and the rest of the state apparatus.

## Pakistan

The Pakistan military has been gradually digging itself into a permanent position of power in government, and into institutions of civil society. It has been directly or indirectly in control of the country for almost all of Pakistan's lifetime, and has exercised an effective veto over major government decisions in most of the period of civilian rule. Civilians were in complete control only from 1947 to 1958, and from 1972 to 1977. From 1954 to 1958 the "civilians" in ultimate control were bureaucrats, not politicians, and Bhutto's reign was, arguably, an authoritarian democracy. In the period after the 2002 elections the military refused to act as if parliament had any oversight role, even in the most harmless and symbolic ways (see Mazhar Aziz 2008: 61–3).

Importantly, all of Pakistan's coups have preserved the chain of command: power has been handed to the head of the army, and its decisions under "civilian" rule have followed that disciplined pattern. Two coup attempts by radical junior officers were easily detected and crushed (see Schofield and Zekulin 2010).

The pattern of military rule has been neatly and provocatively outlined by Charles Kennedy (2005), who analyzes General Musharraf's first four years of rule as a case of Pakistan's ten-step "military governance paradigm." He comes to a "reluctant conclusion" that

> Pakistan's failure to develop a stable constitutional regime is the fault of both Pakistan's military and civilian leadership. . . . Clearly, constitutional stability can only be achieved if there is an accommodation between the interests of the two sets of actors. . . . What is needed are untidy constitutional accommodations, accommodations in which neither the military nor the political parties "wins" or "loses."
>
> (Kennedy 2005: 72–3)

And he proposes a system resembling that operating during the 1988–97 period (until the Nawaz Sharif government passed a constitutional amendment to remove the power of the president unilaterally to dismiss the national assembly):

> Ideally, in such a system the president would be a duly-elected civilian; the superior courts would be free from political interference in undertaking their responsibilities as referees of the process; the president would be loath to exercise his authority except in extreme cases. However flawed such a system may be, it seems preferable to the continuance of Pakistan's military-governance paradigm.
>
> (Kennedy 2005: 74)

As we shall see below, Kennedy's suggested constitutional compromise may well emerge out of the constitutional discussions that began after the February 2008 election.

One effort to institutionalize military rule has apparently failed. This was the establishment of an old idea, a National Security Council. Musharraf's predecessor, Jahangir Karamat, had been in effect fired by Nawaz Sharif for publicly suggesting that such an institution be formed (see H.-A. Rizvi 1999: 181). In the Legal Framework Order of 2002, as part of the bargain with the Islamic parties, Musharraf decreed and then had accepted by parliament a National Security Council that gave the military a "legitimate" veto power over the government. According to H.-A. Rizvi (2005: 9):

> President General Pervez Musharraf maintains that, as a consultative body, the NSC is not superior to the Parliament and that it serves as

a "check on the office of the President;" he cannot exercise his powers in disregard to the views of the NSC. He argues that the NSC averts the possibility of imposition of martial law because the Army Chief can use this forum to voice his opinion on the policies, governance and political management.

When Musharraf declared the state of emergency and issued the provisional constitutional order on November 3, 2007, however, there was no mention of the NSC playing any role whatsoever. Musharraf, *qua* chief of the army staff (COAS), did not object. Indeed, Rizvi (2005: 19) had pointed out that

> the establishment of the NSC in Pakistan is understandable against the backdrop of the gradual expansion of the role of the military in the non-professional fields, its expanding professional and corporate interests and the top commanders' perception of their critical role to political stability, economic development and external and internal stability. However, this does not necessarily mean that the military will limit itself to the NSC to pursue its guardian role and expanded interests.

When Prime Minister Yousuf Raza Gilani announced the dissolution of the NSC on 28 November 2008, it hardly caused a ripple.

None the less, the military not only retains its power to limit what the government decides with respect to India (and particularly Kashmir) and nuclear weapons; it also has not lost any of its autonomy. Even though the COAS, General Kayani, backed away from overt intervention in civilian matters – importantly during the February 2008 election – the army did not relinquish its political role. According to Hasan-Askari Rizvi (2009), for example, "in December 2008, the civilian bureaucrat holding the top administrative slot (Secretary) in the Ministry of Defence was replaced with a retired lieutenant-general on the recommendation of the army headquarters. This revived the practice of appointing retired senior army officers to this position."

The power of the military was, until the spring of 2007, linked directly to the power of the president, General Musharraf. It was then that Musharraf sacked the chief justice of Pakistan, provoking a crisis that led to Musharraf's exit from power, and also from Pakistan – at least temporarily. The sacking led to an unprecedented "lawyers' movement" that ended with the chief justice's reinstatement, but the crisis continued. In quick summary, major steps included the declaration of a state of emergency and a "provisional constitutional order" on 3 November 2007; the cleansing of the Supreme Court and provincial high courts of judges opposed to the regime; the return of Benazir Bhutto and Nawaz Sharif, and Musharraf's "taking off" his army uniform along with his position as chief of the army staff; the assassination of Benazir Bhutto; the elections of 18 February 2008 and the defeat of Musharraf's party; the coming together and then unraveling of the coalition of Zardari's PPP and Nawaz Sharif's Pakistan Muslim League (Nawaz) (PML-N); the selection of Asif Zardari as president; and, coming full circle, as it were, the restoration of Chief Justice Chaudhry and other senior judges in March 2009.

Musharraf's 2007 moves constituted a pre-emptive coup against the judiciary, since it was becoming clear that not only would the Supreme Court rule on the legitimacy of Musharraf's claim to serve as both president and COAS; it would probably also rule against his continuation in both offices, and might have ruled against his re-election as president by the existing national and provincial assemblies. Musharraf tried to avoid that by threatening the chief justice in order to secure his resignation, but that backfired. The eruption of anti-Musharraf action by the lawyers, coupled with humiliating incompetence in dealing with Islamic militants in the Red Mosque in Islamabad, ultimately brought about a behind-the-curtain deal with Benazir Bhutto (with US pressure in all likelihood) that allowed her to return to Pakistan from self-imposed exile. The anticipated difficulties with the Supreme Court then provoked the declaration of quasi-martial law on 3 November 2007, which in turn was so unpopular that Musharraf was finally forced to step down as chief of the army staff, appointing General Ashfaq Kayani to replace him (see Fair 2009).

The state of emergency was soon lifted, and an election scheduled for January 2008. Benazir had returned in triumph in October, surviving an assassination attempt as she took part in a mammoth procession in Karachi, reminiscent of her triumphal Lahore procession of 1986. But in the course of a vigorous campaign she was assassinated on 27 December 2007 in Rawalpindi. The election was rescheduled for February.

Nawaz Sharif, first making use of the Supreme Court, and then with the help of the Saudis (as rumor had it), had managed to return to Pakistan before his ten years of exile were up, in order to lead his party in the elections or confront the regime. It is worth recalling that Nawaz Sharif, after his 1997 installation as prime minister with a two-thirds majority in parliament, apparently began to act from motives not entirely congruent with democratic values, and was seemingly attempting clumsily and brutally to collect all the threads of power into his hands. His was the first attempt both to exercise and to underline the prerogative of the government of the day to dismiss the army chief (see Wilke 2005: 184–5). He succeeded in getting General Karamat to resign; but when he tried again, ordering the dismissal of General Musharraf, the army revived and carried through its plan – apparently given up a few months before owing in part to US pressure – to overthrow the government.

The turmoil of emergency rule, the assassination of Benazir, and the postponement of the election ended in the sweeping election victory of the parties opposed to Musharraf, and the formation of a "grand coalition" government of the PPP, the PML-N and the Awami National Party (ANP) in March 2008. News reports suggested that there was probably some rigging, especially in Karachi in favor of the MQM, but it seemed that the last-minute decision of the army not to interfere in any way brought Pakistan probably its best election – in terms of being free and fair – since 1970. However, a report submitted some months later by the Free and Fair Election Network on a large and seemingly highly credible election-monitoring effort provides a much darker picture (FAFEN 2008: 8):

> [In a sample of constituencies, problems included:] polling officials, polling agents, or others stamping ballot papers; voters being openly pressured inside polling stations to choose a particular party or candidate; polling stations "captured" by armed men, polling agents, or others; physical violence against voters, polling officials, polling agents, or election observers; showing and use of firearms inside polling stations; and closure of women's polling booths. In total, significant problems in polling stations were documented in 129 out of 194 constituencies (66% or two-thirds).

About half of these polling stations had close outcomes. In addition: "In 49 of 194 constituencies (25%), one or more polling stations in the sample had voter turnout rates equal to or exceeding 100% of the number of registered voters published by the ECP [Election Commission of Pakistan] the week preceding the election" (FAFEN 2008: 9). Ballot-box stuffing resulting in overstated turnout was obviously likely in many more polling stations. In Karachi the situation was worse: half of the constituencies had polling stations with more than 100 percent turnout; "turnout in some polling stations in Karachi reached as high as 735%, 631%, and 471% in NA-242" (FAFEN 2008: 33). This had some impact: "When the polling stations with greater than 100% turnout are included in the average turnout for Karachi, overall voter turnout for the city is 53.9%. When these exceptional stations are omitted from the analysis, voter turnout is reduced to 46.5%" (FAFEN 2008: 34).[1]

Since we do not have comparably detailed observations for earlier elections – FAFEN mobilized 16,000 observers to conduct a parallel vote tabulation and report on voting problems – it is hard to judge whether this election was an improvement on previous ones, as the news reports had it. That said, the results of the election are reported in Table 10.1.

It is not clear how much of the swing in seats in favor of the PPP and PML-N was due to informal seat-sharing arrangements. Although the improvement in the vote share of the PML-N is impressive, it falls short of that of the Pakistan Muslim League (Quaid-e-Azam) (PML-Q), a party that has disappeared from public view since the election. It is likely that PML-Q supporters have shifted to the PML-N, if the shift of opinion in favor of Nawaz Sharif is any guide. Only one of the parties of the MMA of 2002 contested the 2008 election, leaving one of the stronger parties of the

*Table 10.1* Pakistan national assembly results, 2002 and 2008: major parties

| | 2002 | | 2008 | |
| --- | --- | --- | --- | --- |
| | Vote share (%) | Seats | Vote share (%) | Seats |
| Pakistan Peoples Party Parliamentarians | 28.4 | 62 | 30.6 | 88 |
| Pakistan Muslim League (Quaid-e-Azam) | 26.6 | 76 | 22.9 | 43 |
| Pakistan Muslim League (Nawaz) | 12.7 | 14 | 19.9 | 70 |
| Muttahida Majlis-e-Amal | 12.3 | 51 | 2.3 | 6 |
| Mohajir Qaumi Movement | 3.6 | 13 | 7.2 | 19 |
| Awami National Party | 1.0 | 0 | 2.0 | 10 |
| Independents and other parties | 15.4 | 53 | 14.8 | 36 |
| Total | | 269 | | 272 |

*Sources*: Vote share, 2002: Election Commission of Pakistan; from website: http://www.ecp.gov.pk/Seats, 2002: *Dawn*, 12 October 2002.

alliance, the Jamaat-e-Islami, on the sidelines. The precipitous decline in their vote share and seats thus overstates the extent of their loss of support. But news accounts suggest that their loss in the national election, reflected in their losses in the NWFP provincial assembly election, does mean that voters turned against them, in part also because of an "anti-incumbency" vote on the MMA's record of governing. The lack of a major protest by any of the parties suggests that, even with the rigging and distortions of particular results, the election was recognized, as the media generally agreed, as by and large free and fair. It counts as a major step forward in Pakistan's quest for a democratic regime.

The election produced a government in which the PPP ruled with the support of the PML-N and others; but, although a prime minister (Yousuf Raza Gilani) was chosen, it was Asif Zardari, the head of the PPP and Benazir Bhutto's widower, who ran the government. The alliance with the PML-N almost immediately came close to breaking when Zardari evaded fulfilling the crucial promise of reinstating Chief Justice Chaudhry and other judges removed in November. The PML-N ultimately withdrew from the coalition but continued to support the government.

The PPP's popularity plummeted, in both the country as a whole and even more in Punjab, between January and October 2008, while that of the PML-N correspondingly increased enormously, reaching 89 percent support in Punjab in March 2009, and 62 percent in the country, according to public opinion polls conducted by the International Republican Institute (see Table 10.2).[2]

It is not surprising that Nawaz Sharif is seen as the leader "able to handle the problems facing Pakistan most effectively" by 51 percent of Pakistanis, compared to 13 percent who favor Asif Zardari – a division of opinion that has also remained roughly the same since October 2008 (International

*Table 10.2* Support of PPP and PML-N in Pakistan and Punjab, percentage of survey respondents

|  | Pakistan | | | | |
|---|---|---|---|---|---|
|  | *January 2008* | *June 2008* | *October 2008* | *March 2009* | *July 2009* |
| PPP | 50 | 32 | 19 | 17 | 22 |
| PML-N | 22 | 36 | 35 | 62 | 57 |
|  | Punjab | | | | |
| PPP | 44 | 24 | 8 | 4 | 6 |
| PML-N | 32 | 51 | 54 | 89 | 82 |

*Source*: International Republican Institute (2009: 45–6).

Republican Institute [IRI] 2009: 37–8). Zardari seems to have inherited Musharraf's unpopularity: in the five polls from September 2007 to October 2008, when Musharraf was president, 60–75 percent disapproved of "the job the President is doing"; in the two polls since he was made president, Zardari's disapproval went from 67 percent to 62 percent (IRI 2009: 39). In answer to another question, 66 percent said they "disliked" Zardari, compared to 27 percent who disliked Prime Minister Gilani (35 percent answered "neither like/dislike" or "don't know"); Gilani's approval steadily increased over three polls from October 2008 to July 2009, to 45 percent, while Zardari's approval stayed steady, at just under 20 percent (IRI 2009: 41–2).

The parties agreed in August 2008 to impeach President Musharraf, who then resigned, although not in disgrace as far as the army was concerned. The coda of Musharraf's resignation speech was a departure via a guard of honor, which was immediately denounced by some. An editorial on 20 August 2008 in the *News International* sets out the issue:

> Many of those who saw General Musharraf take his farewell guard of honour as president of Pakistan must have surely wondered why a man who had twice mangled the constitution of the country, launched a vicious attack on the country's judiciary and independent media and who allowed intelligence agencies under his watch to pick up Pakistani citizens and hold them incommunicado at will was being given such a respectable send-off.

It concludes with a crucial point:

> We need to break with the past, a past where the misdeeds of many a dictator were brushed under the carpet, hidden from public view, with the people conveniently told that bygones should be bygones. That is precisely [why] democracy has not taken root in Pakistan and why we

have seen a stream of military interventions and their accompanying "saviours" – surely we should have learnt some lessons from this and now is the time for our collective atonement.

On 9 September 2008, Asif Zardari was sworn in as president.

President Zardari continued resisting the demand to restore the judges, and only after the retirement of the chief justice that Musharraf had appointed to replace him was Chief Justice Iftikhar Chaudhry (and more than one hundred other senior judges) restored to office, on 22 March 2009. The Supreme Court declared on 31 July 2009 that Musharraf's acts of 3 November 2007 were "void, illegal and unconstitutional."[3]

In the meantime, both politicians and the army were forced to deal with two major security crises: the first erupted when a dozen terrorists armed and directed by the Lashkar-e-Taiba attacked Mumbai in late November 2008, leading India to put a great deal of pressure on Pakistan to shut down its (undeclared) policy of supporting bombings and other attacks by such groups on Indian soil. Shortly after, a "Pakistan Taliban"-linked group in Swat reached an agreement with the ANP government of the NWFP, and with Islamabad, which they interpreted as allowing them to impose *shariat* courts (without appeal to the provincial courts). They then attempted to extend their rule into neighboring territory, a short distance from the capital. That was apparently too much for the army and the PPP leadership. Perhaps encouraged by the US and others concerned about the effort to contain the Afghan Taliban and the safety of Pakistan's nuclear weapons, the government reacted with a massive military intervention. Millions of inhabitants had to flee their homes, and it took months to restore some semblance of order in Swat. This action was followed up by the army going after elements of the "Pakistan Taliban" in Waziristan in the fall of 2009.

It remains to be seen whether the 2006–7 lawyers' movement will have an added impact at some later point, and whether lawyers – *qua* principled judges or just as ordinary practitioners – will be seen as powerful and attractive agents of change. Have these recent developments altered Pakistan's underlying political trajectory in any way? Have elected politicians managed to improve their position vis-à-vis the military and the bureaucracy, and by how much? Is there, indeed, some prospect of extracting the military from its entrenched positions of power, so that its dominance, either open or recessed, is ended? At the other end of the spectrum, is it possible that Pakistan could end up as a failed state?[4] Or could the present regime, instead of democratizing, succumb to a different kind of authoritarian rule, of an Islamic cast?

Let us begin by considering these last questions, which imply Pakistan moving on to a very different path from the one in which the military and the politicians play the crucial roles. No scholar or Pakistani analyst expects Pakistan to collapse into anarchy, a state-less society (on the Somalia model), although some do not discount the possibility entirely. Ahmed Rashid (2008: xliii), who at the beginning of his book mentions the possibility that a "perfect storm of circumstances and events . . . could undermine Pakistan's very existence," stops far short of an apocalyptic vision of the future. Hasan-Askari Rizvi (2008) agrees that "Taliban-type elements constitute the main threat to Pakistan's existence as a coherent and effective state," and worries that "religious fanaticism and violent enforcement of a narrow interpretation of Islam will tear apart Pakistani society to such an extent that it will not be able to sustain itself as a collective social entity." However, we should remind ourselves of the reach and power of the institutionalized state in Pakistan: the law-and-order system is weak but pervasive and can still function; taxes are collected, and educational and health services are provided, however inadequately. The government is able to conduct country-wide elections. The daily carnage in recent years – bombings and assassinations and battles between security forces and terrorists – while certainly making headlines and causing considerable insecurity, still does not have a massive impact, if one considers Pakistan's size. The 6,715 deaths in 2008 (as reported by the South Asia Terrorism Portal),[5] equals thirty-eight killings per million of Pakistan's population. The odds against a Pakistan citizen being caught up in terrorist violence, let alone killed, are very large.

There is no doubt that the war in Afghanistan, the actions of *jihadi* groups (suicide bombings, the takeover in Swat, etc.) have persuaded Pakistanis that there is a genuine threat from the Taliban. The July–August 2009 poll of the International Republican Institute (2009) finds that 90 percent of the respondents see religious extremism as a serious problem (IRI 2009:14), even though 50 percent of the respondents think that religion should play a "dominant" role in politics (IRI 2009: 50).

A threat is not necessarily an existential threat, and it is hard to find scholars or op-ed analysts who feel that Pakistan could in any way be taken over by the Taliban or another Islamic group (see Schofield 2009). None of the possibilities seems likely: there will be no victory in battle for Islamic groups, no victory in a democratic election, and no Islamic revolution, either by religious leaders backed by a mass movement or from within the state by a coup of Islamist army officers. The Taliban are almost entirely based in Pakhtun areas, though they have developed some support in the southern Punjab; they are fine, perhaps nearly invincible fighters in their own homeland, given their current weaponry. But they are not at all likely to be able to defeat the modern, disciplined, and far better-equipped Pakistan military on its home ground, the Punjab plains. The *jihadi* groups that have formed to support fighters in Kashmir, such as the Lashkar-e-Taiba, depend too heavily on the tolerance of the military, and have shown no inclination to turn their attention from India to confront the Pakistan government (see Tankel 2009). There are other groups pursuing sectarian agendas, who, like the Taliban, conduct suicide bombings or other attacks in Pakistan cities. These feed on economic and social dislocation, and the willingness of believing Muslims to excuse their behavior because their goals are seen to be pure, and are difficult to defeat through policing, particularly as innocent lives will be lost in the process. But their impact can be contained.

The Islamists, whether organized as a diffuse movement, perhaps focused on the Tablighi Jamaat or a similar group, or as movement-parties such as the Jamaat-i-Islami, have never generated significant support among the mass of citizens.[6] Islamic parties, some of which have anti-democratic agendas (a wish to establish the *nizam-i-mustapha*, for example), lost support in the February 2008 election. And, of course, they have never been widely supported. On the other hand, they benefit from the willingness of other parties – particularly the PML-N and the PML(Q) in recent times – to overlook their ideology and program, and ally with them against the more secular parties, these days the MQM, the ANP, and the PPP. All significant Islamic provisions in the law, both liberal (the Family Laws Ordinance) and Islamist (the Hudood Ordinances), have been imposed by military regimes, but most of those provisions have not been enforced, even when the military was ruling directly. That suggests a deep-rooted if silent resistance to an Islamic agenda of a fundamentalist kind. Pakistan is too open and modernized a country for an Islamist dictatorship to be installed via an election, as was a genuine threat in Algeria, for example.

Pakistan also has no religious leaders to mobilize the masses in an Islamic revolution of an Iranian kind – the sectarian divisions in the country are the major obstacle. Nor are their traditional leaders of a "tribal" kind – like the Saudi royal family – that could challenge politicians and military alike for the allegiance of Pakistanis. There is little evidence of a significant increase in Islamists within the army itself, or likelihood that an Islamic revolution would originate there, and be imposed from above, although Abbas (2005: 153) claims that "Pakistan was . . . within an inch of becoming a radical Muslim state," as the result of a coup planned for September 1994. Shaikh (2009: 153) argues that, because of the army's weakening professionalism and criticism of the officers' "secular ways" after 1971, there was intensified pressure for an "Islamically informed military identity" which, under Zia, equated "military professionalism with Islamic piety and the display of religious beliefs as a pre-requisite for advancement within the ranks." Shaikh (2009: 154–8) goes on to suggest how Zia's approval of the formally a-political Tablighi Jamaat and a shift to thinking of the army as a protector of a Muslim nation that perhaps stretched beyond Pakistan's borders influenced the officer corps.

The question then becomes: How strong has that identity become in the army, in terms both of spread and of intensity, and is it sufficient to serve to justify a military–Islamist regime far more revolutionary than anything Zia ul Haq was able to do? The military, in many ways a thoroughly modern organization, is not a natural prospect for conversion. Cloughley (2008: 169) spends only a paragraph on this issue, but does quote at second hand a general saying "the percentage of religious zealots in [the] PAF [Pakistan Air Force] is alarmingly large." Shuja Nawaz (2008: 572) notes that army officers who joined in Zia's time, and are thus the most likely to have Islamist leanings, "will take over the running of the Pakistan Army" in the next few years (around thirty-five years after recruitment), and are a group that was "deprived of advanced overseas training during its formative years . . . [whose officers were] denied exposure to the world outside till late in their careers, by which time their worldview had been formed." Nawaz (2008: 585) concludes that the army "is not *yet* [my emphasis] a breeding ground for large numbers of radical Islamists that many fear." The implied window of danger of a radical Islamist cohort taking over the army and thus ultimate control of government will open soon and last at least twenty years, if one believes that Musharraf's easing out of those generals who opposed his U-turn in 2001 changed the Islamist biases conveyed to new recruits. But it is probably larger, given the more general atmosphere of wanting to resist perceived attacks on Islam in Palestine, Iraq, and Afghanistan, ever closer to Pakistan, that shows no sign of dissipating. To the extent that "prodemocracy" activism by Western governments is seen as "anti-Islam" by Pakistan army officers, the chances of them resting their claims to legitimate political influence on their Islamic beliefs would increase. Just what those beliefs are, however, is certainly not self-evident. That none of the regular armies of Islamic countries from Algeria to Indonesia has so far formed a ruling partnership with radically fundamentalist Islamists is perhaps significant.

Another indicator of state weakness, if not of failure, is the prevalence of corruption and criminal and terrorist violence. The Pakistan chapter of Transparency International commissioned studies of the perception of corruption, its cost, and practice in 2002, 2006, and 2009 (see Transparency International – Pakistan 2009 [hereafter TIP 2009]). The template and methodology is similar to the India survey (see above, pp. 198n9), with a marketing firm responsible for doing the actual survey of 5,200 households (in 2009).[7] Ninety percent of the 27 percent who interacted with the police – perceived to be the most corrupt of the nine "sectors" covered – in the previous year had faced corruption. Respondents said that money was demanded directly (52 percent of the cases) or indirectly (22 percent), and was offered (and presumably accepted) directly in 15 percent of the cases, and indirectly in 10 percent. (The largest number of cases – 30 percent – had to do with traffic violations.) This was typical of all the experiences reported, in other government departments as well.

It is not at all clear, however, how much this undermined citizens' belief in the legitimacy of government, much less the democratic system. Political parties were perceived to be the most corrupt (by around 28 percent of respondents), compared to public officials/civil servants (22 percent), parliament/legislatures (17 percent), business/public sector (14 percent), the judiciary (9 percent), and the media (6 percent),[8] but respondents were not specifically asked about bribery of politicians. Asked "which government has done more to harm the country on account of corrupt practices?", 54 percent of the respondents answered civilian government, and 46 percent said military government (TIP 2009: 35). In the International Republican Institute poll of July 2009 (IRI 2009: 11), it must be noted, "corruption" was the answer of only 5 percent of the respondents, to the question "What is the single most important issue facing Pakistan?"[9] Corruption in Pakistan may be endemic, but it is far from a fatal affliction.

That even fewer people (3 percent) chose "law and order" as an answer in that poll, and only 13 percent chose "terrorism," even though more than two-thirds expressed a sense of insecurity (IRI 2009: 10), suggests that even the rapid-fire suicide and truck-bombings of markets, government offices, policemen, clerics, and politicians that became everyday events in the second half of 2009 are likely to be weathered by a populace that had suffered such things – although less frequently – in the years before. Moreover, there are not that many young men and women prepared to become suicide bombers, and a determined and ruthless military and government can eradicate them, as happened in Sri Lanka in mid-2009. The problem is very serious, however: according to the Pak Institute for Peace Studies (hereafter PIPS) (2009: 4), terrorist incidents increased by 746 percent between 2005 and 2008, with 2,267 people killed and 4,558 injured in 2008 (see PIPS 2009: 16–18 for a comprehensive summary of "Pakistan's security landscape"). Even so, the heartland of Pakistan – particularly rural Punjab – remains largely untouched by these incidents, and citizens literally pick up the pieces after a bombing and resume their normal lives. They seem to treat the terrible carnage as akin to a natural calamity, like a flood or an earthquake (which take far, far more victims). It is clear that most support the government's efforts to deal with this threat; the state's authority is far from breaking down.

We must return to our "balance of forces" question to assess the prospects of elected leaders and parties being able to reduce the dominance of the military and persuading it to accept a position of inferior authority in the political system. In Najam Sethi's (2008) view, "The real issue is the 60 year old civil–military imbalance in Pakistan. The civilians must establish their credentials for responsible democracy and functional governance before they can safely and effectively tame the military." The weakness of the government elected in February 2008 is evident. In one telling incident, not long after it assumed power, the new PPP government was forced publicly to reverse a decision to place the ISI under the interior ministry (removing it from the military chain of command) within twenty-four hours of issuing the official notification.[10] If a government elected by a substantial majority, and with widespread popular support, replacing a military leader whose popularity had shrunk precipitously,[11] could suffer so public a humiliation at the hands of the military, its underlying weakness is evident. The elected PPP government, like every predecessor since Zulfiqar Ali Bhutto's, lacked a powerful leader and party with followers that the military might fear.

The party system is not an alternate framework of legitimacy in Pakistan, in part owing to the general lack of institutionalized parties. As Dewey (1991: 256) bluntly put it: "Political parties in Pakistan are temporary expedients which pick up the pieces after the generals fail to reconcile internal conflicts. Their main function is to pave the way for the restoration of military rule." The institutional weakness of the PPP, the more institutionalized of the two major parties, was brought into tragic relief with the assassination of Benazir Bhutto on 27 December 2007. Although it was clear to everyone that her life was in extreme danger – she had barely survived an assassination attempt when she returned to Pakistan in October (an attack in which around 150 people died) – there was no provision made for succession to her as leader, chairperson of the PPP "for life," other than a "will" she gave her husband, which designated her college-aged son, Bilal, as her successor. Bilal was duly appointed, with his father as co-chair, in the days after the assassination. The party will indeed be forced to rely for votes not on the charismatic leader – for the first time in its history – but on its ideology and record, as, ironically, a party in a parliamentary system is supposed to do.

The situation is no different with any of the other parties, with the possible exception of the Jamaat-i-Islami. It will remain to be seen whether the PML-N can survive the departure of Nawaz and Shabaz Sharif, or the MQM the departure of Altaf Hussain, or the various Islamic parties designated by their leaders' names. Imran Khan's party – it is hardly ever referred to by its name (Tehreek-e-Insaf) – is essentially a one-person operation. Dynastic succession seems almost inevitable in those cases. No civilian leader with any support or competence has emerged outside the party system. It is notable that Shaukat Aziz, a prime minister brought in from afar (he was a senior Citibank executive in the US), who was allowed by General Musharraf to run the government, and who did so competently, was not even given a ticket in the 2008 elections, and has vanished from public view since.

It is possible that as the opposition parties weaken, or are marginalized by the regime in some fashion, the PML-Q (officially it is simply the "Pakistan Muslim League") will continue as a "king's party," where the "king" means the military. This would be not unlike the pattern of Egypt under Mubarak, a regime that has lasted for more than a quarter of a century. There a government party rules, according to Mustafa and Norton (2007: 39–40), with some other parties allowed for "cosmetic purposes"; the Islamist parties have "privileged access to the political system"; and the political elite "is restricted to those who are well connected to the bureaucratic-security apparatus, [excluding] almost all genuine liberals."[12]

To the extent that the military exercises political authority, it is perhaps more valid to treat it as being simultaneously a part of the state apparatus and a political party. Barnett Rubin (2008), analyzing the situation in Pakistan in the context of the crisis following the assassination of Benazir

Bhutto, provides a vivid and compelling conceptualization of the army-as-political-party. It is worth quoting him at length:

> As Chief of Army Staff, Musharraf occupied a role similar to that of head of the ruling party in a one-party dominant system. His party, the military, unlike the other parties, is a disciplined cadre organization which, along with its fellow travelers (civilian allies of the military) controls all the key levers of power, including the civil administration and the judiciary. . . . Musharraf needed new political allies to run institutions. But he did not want political allies to negotiate a transition to democracy: he wanted political allies to legitimate continued military rule. The Islamist parties were willing to partner with the military on that basis, because it was their only way of acceding to power. But the PPP and the PML-N (Nawaz Sharif's party) could actually win elections. . . . [The military] could not allow a party that actually aspired to rule to come to power. Enter the PML-Q (Musharraf's party, aka the King's Party). The military assembled this party out of notables of various sorts to represent those civilian allies that supported military rule.

This is a useful way of looking at the military's role, but it should not be taken too far: it is probable that the military remains, most importantly in its self-perception, an integral, even central element of the state-nation, and not a political party with a civilian façade.

Clearly, parties strong enough to confront the military cannot be expected now to emerge, as parties elsewhere have done in the past, out of some sort of nationalist or revolutionary movement, on the lines of the Congress in India or the PRI in Mexico. Apart from somehow mobilizing and institutionalizing support from the top down in the aftermath of an election – which, on past form, seems extremely unlikely – the only alternative would seem to be to have parties as the outgrowths of powerful classes in society. Landed notables in Pakistan, including those whose power base comes from their religious status, such as the major *sufi pirs*, are no longer numerous or powerful enough. What remains is the possibility of parties coming out of civil society institutions or movements, with leaders most likely from the middle classes, professionals and businessmen.

There are few signs that this will happen. One of the more important NGO leaders, Omar Ashghar Khan, was co-opted by the Musharraf government (see Zaidi 2008c: 38). There was a remarkable mobilization by a broad range of middle-class citizens willing to spend money, time, and effort in the relief of victims of the Kashmir earthquake of 2005, but no permanent organizations of significance emerged. The lawyers' movement of the first half of 2007 was impressively inclusive and visible, but has seemingly broken into factions to the point where it was not a factor in Pakistan politics in 2009. There are no business federations or labor unions or any other interest groups with

*Table 10.3* Support for democracy in India and Pakistan, by economic class and education (percentages)

| | Strong democrats | | Weak democrats | | Non-democrats | |
|---|---|---|---|---|---|---|
| | India | Pakistan | India | Pakistan | India | Pakistan |
| *Class* | | | | | | |
| Lowest | 32 | 5 | 49 | 46 | 20 | 49 |
| Lower | 39 | 8 | 48 | 56 | 13 | 36 |
| Middle | 47 | 10 | 36 | 47 | 17 | 43 |
| Upper | 54 | 11 | 31 | 52 | 15 | 37 |
| Highest | 43 | 18 | 44 | 45 | 13 | 37 |
| *Education* | | | | | | |
| Non-literate | 26 | 4 | 56 | 53 | 18 | 43 |
| Below primary | 41 | 13 | 44 | 50 | 15 | 37 |
| Middle | 44 | 9 | 40 | 48 | 16 | 43 |
| Secondary | 53 | 16 | 33 | 45 | 14 | 39 |
| Graduate+ | 62 | 25 | 24 | 42 | 14 | 33 |

Source: *State of Democracy in South Asia: A Report* (2008), appendix table 1.1, pp. 226–7.

any political weight. The women's movement that led the popular upsurge against the Zia regime in the mid-1980s has not played a similar role since.

One explanation for the absence of the middle class as a political force is to be found in the conclusion of S. Akbar Zaidi's (2005b: 5180) essay on "the future of democracy in Pakistan":

> [The urban and rural middle classes] who have the most to gain from establishing democratic institutions in the country, in order to access the state and its actors, already have access to the state and to the nexus of power. Thus they do not have the need for either messy democracy, participation or even, accountability. . . . Whichever way one looks at it, with regard toward their antagonistic disposition towards democracy, Pakistan's urban middle classes [classes that are now dominant in Pakistan] reflect trends which seem to be against the norm found in other countries . . . and are perhaps unique to Pakistan.

There is indirect evidence for this assertion in the data from the *State of Democracy in South Asia* report (2008); see Table 10.3. The high absolute number of "non-democrats" and the very low number of "strong democrats" for Pakistan is striking. The more literate and the higher the economic class – measures which clearly overlap to a considerable extent – the stronger the commitment to democracy. But the highest "strong democrat" figure, 25 percent for graduates plus, is lower than the lowest "strong democrat" figure for India, 26 percent for non-literates. And if we set "middle class" to mean those with the two higher levels of education, then "non-democrats" in Pakistan would be around 36 percent, while only 14 percent in India.

If the balance of power will not change owing to the strengthening of civilian political institutions, then democratization will have to be the result of the weakening of the military's will or capacity to rule. This would perhaps require a "transition to democracy" process that political scientists inductively discovered in the democratization of Southern Europe and Latin America in the 1970s and 1980s (see O'Donnell and Schmitter 1986). The focus in that analysis is on cracks appearing within the ruling military, with "hard-liners" and "soft-liners" differing on the value of negotiating with leaders, some of whom are "exemplary individuals," in the context of a popular upsurge in which powerful institutions, such as the Catholic church in Latin America and the Philippines, play a leading role.

When asked "How much power is the military going to relinquish and how?" a month after the election, Husain Haqqani (just before being appointed ambassador to the US) replied:

> The military has a significant role in helping determine national security policy. . . . But the military is never trained to do big picture political analysis. They are trained in tactical matters and in military strategy. I think the military will gradually move in that direction. Of course given Pakistan's recent history and the residual impact of the military's deep involvement in politics, there will still be some people in uniform who will continue to think politically. But the global environment – in which Myanmar and Pakistan are the only two countries run by men in uniform until a few weeks ago – is making the Pakistani military rethink its role. . . . I think there's going to be a gradual withdrawal of the military from politics. But the days when the military had an opinion on everything and that opinion prevailed are now over.[13]

However, the military seems not to have learned that it is a bad idea to be involved in politics, with the army's senior officers blaming Musharraf for the problems of Musharraf's government, rather than pointing to "the structural problems inherent in their institution's old and deep-seated habits of meddling in politics and behaving as a 'state within a state'" (Goodson 2008: 13). In addition, as Stepan (1988: 136–7) warns, "to the extent that the military have a near technical monopoly concerning military expertise, the capacity of a democratic government to exercise a monopoly over the management of force within the state apparatus is extremely limited." The minister of defence in the PPP government after March 2008, Ahmad Mukhtar, as best one can tell from searching the Pakistan press, seems only to attend some ceremonial functions, and make statements to the press about terrorist attacks on military facilities. It is hard to see any indication of global pressure that will have any effect on the Pakistan military. Nor are they likely to trust the politicians to maintain a posture of strength and distrust vis-à-vis India.

It is possible that the military's effort to eliminate the "Pakistan Taliban" that began after the fiasco of the Swat agreement in early 2009 will reinforce the point of view that the military cannot simultaneously rule the country, even indirectly, and protect it by fighting the enemy. The military would then be open to a gradual shifting of its role, perhaps achieving a more institutionalized ultimate right to intervene, in something like the now-dissolved National Security Council, perhaps following the Turkish pattern (see H.-A. Rizvi 2005: 17–19 for a descriptive comparison). That would mean that the military would retain a veto over political policy initiatives or the participation of certain players, in order to allow it to retreat from day-to-day governance. Such a scenario would allow Pakistan to maintain its relatively open society, permit the repression of extremist groups and others of a "disloyal opposition", and, with luck, move gradually to shifting the balance of power slowly to favor civilian rule. In the meantime, economic and social transformations, brought about in part by globalization, and perhaps even India's or Bangladesh's example, might help develop a democratic culture built on civil-society organizations, and change the character of underlying forces.

## India

India held its fifteenth parliamentary election in April–May 2009. In something of a surprise, the Congress-led United Progressive Alliance (UPA) coalition again won and was able to form a government (see the "National Election Study 2009," *Economic and Political Weekly*, 44 (39), for a comprehensive first-cut analysis). The constituencies had been given a new delimitation, for the first time since the 1971 election, some new leaders emerged and others were eased out, and there were some changes in the pattern of results, but in almost everything it was a business-as-usual election. The Congress increased its vote share by only a few points (28.6 percent as opposed to 26.5 percent in 2004), while the BJP lost vote share (at 18.8 percent, down from 22.2 percent). The Left parties taken together received 7.5 percent, continuing their slow decline, while the BSP increased its share to 6.2 percent. Regional parties retained nearly one-third of the vote. There seemed to be no one issue or even factor that explained the results (see Yadav and Palshikar 2009).

The defeat of the BJP-led National Democratic Alliance, despite earlier encouraging results in some state elections and the expectation that it would reap the benefit of an "anti-incumbency" swing, also seemed to suggest the continuing decline in *hindutva* (Hindu nationalism). Hindu nationalism has been seen as a serious threat to India's democracy. And yet, after its triumphant demolition of the Babri Masjid on 6 December 1992, and the terrible riots and pogroms that followed the disproportionate killing by the Mumbai police of Muslim demonstrators, its fortunes changed. When the BJP set out to reclaim the states from which it had been unceremoniously removed, it was forced, midway through the campaign in the November 1993 elections, to drop its triumphalist rhetoric, and was soundly defeated. In the following years, it turned to moderate leadership, and sacrificed its principles to fight elections in a coalition with partners who forced it to put aside its *hindutva* agenda, much to the disgust of the core activists of the *Sangh parivar*. The victory of the BJP as the core party of an alliance in 1998 and 1999 was not a victory for *hindutva* as much as it was a victory for a disciplined party perceived to be less corrupt than others, and a group of state-based parties that shared mainly a position of opposition to the Congress in their own states (see Basu and Roy 2007: 9; V. B. Singh 2004: 309).

Despite the subtle arguments of Basu and Roy (2007: 7–8), that "Hindutva's war of position" has produced a state of "democratic bankruptcy" as a democratic constitutional order and a vibrant civil society coexisted with and indeed encouraged extreme violence, it can be argued that the Gujarat pogrom of 2002 was the death rattle of *hindutva* as a major political force in India as a whole. Even in Gujarat, despite Chief Minister Modi winning the December 2002 election by flaunting his government's actions of February, and embracing the demonization of the Muslims, the election of 2007 was fought on Narendra Modi's leadership and the BJP government's economic achievements, not on Modi's *hindutva* agenda. It is easy to imagine a different result with a different leader of the opposition.[14] In any case, if *hindutva* in the form of an ideology that inspires autocratic solutions and the semi-tyranny of a majoritarian democracy was ever a serious threat to India's democracy, it is no longer so (see Swamy 2004). A disturbing new development, however, is the apparent emergence of *hindutva*-inspired terrorists, mimicking *jihadi* terrorists, in the September 2008 Malegaon bomb blast (see Jaffrelot 2009: 224–7).

Terrorist attacks by *jihadis*, whether domestic or inspired and organized in Pakistan, have become a regular feature of India's daily life, spurred by the post-Ayodhya riots and the Gujarat pogrom of 2002. They include the bombs set off in multiple locations in Bombay in March 1993; the attack on the Indian parliament in December 2001; the bomb blasts on Mumbai commuter trains in 2006; and the attack on the main railway station and hotels in Mumbai in November 2008. While the organizers of these and other attacks may believe that India will come apart with *ek aur dhaka* ("one more shove"), there is absolutely no indication that the state or the social fabric has frayed, let alone come under unmanageable strain because of them; quite the reverse. The possible threat to India's democracy, rather, lies in the state's reaction to those attacks: war-footing mobilization of the armed forces (as in 2001–2); religious profiling and discrimination against Muslims, including deportation of alleged illegal Bangladeshi migrants with only a semblance of legal due process; and similar actions.

The less spectacular threats to the system are to be found in other arenas, and some if not all of these might grow worse in the next decades. These include:

- the slowly increasing economic inequalities that have accompanied India's new economic-reform-driven growth trajectory;
- the autocracy of the "hard state" actions against nationalist movements in Kashmir and the Northeast, and "revolutionary" tribals and others in the east-central belt from Andhra to West Bengal;

- a paralysis in the party system, reminiscent of what happened in Italy in the 1950s, where constantly changing coalitions eroded political authority, and left the state apparatus – the civil bureaucracy – to carry on, and basically govern;
- the continuing debilitating weaknesses in the rule of law, as the legal system, especially at the lowest levels, seems unable to emerge from the nineteenth century, let alone the twentieth. The "criminalization" of politics is a special part of this, as is the continued "disease" of political corruption.

Yet all of these challenges are certainly manageable to the democratic system.

If India continues on its accelerated economic growth path, there is little doubt that sufficient benefits for the poor will be generated to draw the sting of increasing inequality. In particular, the provision of public goods will also keep citizens believing in "the system" – things such as public transport like the Delhi Metro for the lower middle class; higher-quality and broader-based schooling, with an enhancement of tertiary education; improved public-health systems; a better electricity supply; and so on. If economic growth and globalization produce, as a side-effect, a shift away from the "black" economy to a "white" one, then there will be a shift from indirect to direct taxation, which would be helped along by democratic politics, as politicians see their way clear to tax those who benefit most from the new economy.

The pattern of state governments competing with each other in development-friendly programs, rather than via political connections and cash payoffs in Delhi, and buttressed by necessary human capital investment, is likely to persist. The picture is not all bright, as James Manor (2002: 256; see also Manor 2007) notes:

> While . . . some state governments [have] become more corrupt and brutish, more of them have sought – with mixed but sometimes impressive results – to become more responsive. So on balance, we can say – rather tentatively, and with no assurances that the trend will continue – that responsiveness has outweighed brutishness in India's recent history. This is true even though the latter has received more attention in the Indian and international media.

There is no sign that the party system that has in part resulted from this pattern of state competition – one in which the center of gravity has shifted to state arenas from one centered on the national government – is fundamentally unstable, or liable to decay. If anything, the stability of a system with two to three opposing parties and/or coalitions seems assured. Parties have managed to transfer leadership to new generations – in the Congress, in the CPM, but not quite yet in the BJP. India remains a democratic system that works. It seems likely that civil society will also strengthen, with organizations from residents' welfare associations in the city, to anti-corruption

NGOs in the countryside. If at some point – as seems inevitable, given global trends – the central government relinquishes control over radio broadcasting, as it has over television, the last blemish on the freedom of the press will have been removed.

The conflicts in Kashmir, in the Northeast, and in the desperately poor *adivasi* (tribal) belt have persisted since 1947. In all these places there have been both periods of relative calm, and shifting of the geographic areas of conflict over time. There is no indication that the state apparatus – bureaucrats, police, the paramilitary (and occasionally the army) – has modified, let alone given up on, the strategy of severe repression. This includes terrible violations of human rights, and is paired with political concessions to leaders, involving the sharing of power and spoils. The law-and-order bureaucracy perhaps feels that it is safe to ignore critics, who are rarely practicing politicians, because the dire predictions of the past, when insurgencies were particularly strong – for example, Kashmir in the 1990s – have been "solved" by yet more armed men, killing and dominating outside the public's gaze. The strategy apparently succeeded, most notably in Punjab.[15] It is true that India's police strength, measured by numbers of men per 100,000 citizens, is much less than that of other countries, including consolidated democracies (Maquire and Schulte-Murray 2001: 91–2; see Swami 2008 for graphic detail of this problem and the consequences in Orissa).

At the end of 2007, according the ministry of home affairs annual report, 474 battalions were sanctioned for the five major paramilitary forces. According to the International Institute for Strategic Studies, the twelve central government forces totaled 851,000 persons, and the State Armed Police another 450,000 (International Institute for Strategic Studies 2008: 345). It is likely that the large number in four of these (340,000; in 289 battalions) – Border Security Force, Assam Rifles, Indo-Tibetan Border Police, and the Sashastra Seema Bal – are in fact posted on the borders and in the northeastern states.

The percentage of India's population that is directly "under" the hard control of either the security forces or various insurgents, or both (depending on the time of day), is not that high. The threat to stability, from the point of view of the state apparatus, is manageable. In India as a whole, 22 percent of the police are armed, but in the seven states of the Northeast the median percentage is 54. Similarly the median number of police per 100,000 people is 558 in the Northeast, and a mean of only 126 for India as a whole. Outside the Northeast, only Kashmir has such high numbers.[16]

It is not difficult to imagine India's democracy being undermined by the deficiencies in the rule of law, and in particular the criminalization of politics and political corruption. The problem in assessing the threat comes from our lack of fine-grained data. We must not assume that just because Mumbai houses a mafia or mafias (see the novel *Shantaram*), and that organized crime has recently spread to Hyderabad (see Manor 2002), that organized crime is a common feature of Indian cities, or towns, or the countryside. That does not appear to be the case. "Criminals," on the other hand, are clearly widely distributed, and some of them have joined politics, with quite a few winning seats in state legislatures and parliament.[17] The Election Commission now requires candidates to declare their criminal cases as well as their financial assets; but, as the respected columnist Swaminathan Anklesaria Aiyar (2008) says:

> In India, we have spending limits on elections that are ignored by all. We have laws barring the participation of criminals in elections, which are ineffective since the judiciary and police seem incapable of convicting anybody important beyond all appeals. Indeed, many criminals have joined politics to better sabotage cases they face. In the absence of a police–judicial system that works, all political parties have welcomed musclemen and moneybags who can influence outcomes through violence and bribery.

When the criminal acts involve – as they allegedly did in the July 2008 vote of confidence, and in another vote of confidence fourteen years earlier – the purchase of an MP's vote and allegiance in an effort to bring the government down, or prop it up, then this has a serious impact on India's democracy. Yet the actual number of criminals is (not yet?) so great as to color the day-to-day functioning of legislatures or parliament.

This problem clearly points to the inadequacies of the legal system. Aiyar's (2008) solution would require changes:

> We need a new law that will truly discourage criminals from contesting elections. This should postulate that cases against legislators will be given top seniority in hearing by the courts, will be heard on a day-to-day basis, and be disposed of within one year at most, by shortening and guillotining the legal procedures if necessary to meet the deadline. This will greatly dissuade criminals from contesting elections, since getting elected will hasten their prosecution. Indeed, many criminals in legislatures will, hopefully, resign in order to escape early prosecution. That will certainly transform the quality of politics.

The legal system at the lower-court level, however, is weak and corrupt, so in order to be effective it is likely that special courts would have to be established, as they have been to try people accused of terrorism.

Criminality and corruption are clearly intertwined, though in the Indian context "criminals in politics" tends to conjure up images of violence rather than of money. The problem of corruption in India is constantly discussed in the media and in private conversations, but is rarely studied seriously, as I discovered when I investigated the reputation for corruption in the land consolidation program in UP in the early 1980s (Oldenburg 1987). The situation has not changed in twenty-five years, but it is also true that the predictions of a total collapse of the political system into a putrid mess because of corruption have not turned out to be true. My essay argued that the "folk-lore of corruption" has to be distinguished from its actual practice, and that the smoke-to-fire ratio may be much larger than most believe. I remain some-thing of a skeptic, not of the existence of endemic corruption, particularly in certain departments, but of its alleged spread and growth and impact.

Fortunately, the India chapter of Transparency International has produced a survey of corruption (Centre for Media Studies 2005). This is at least better than the often-cited ranking of India in Transparency International's global survey, which relies too much on the country's reputation for corruption among foreign businessmen and other outsiders. There are many problems with this survey – see the note at the bottom of Table 10.4 – which make it difficult to use its index of corruption or trust the monetary "impact" that it reports. Table 10.4, which I put together from the report's data, does give an

*Table 10.4* Centre for Media Studies/Transparency International India Survey 2005: percentage of respondents who paid a bribe directly for public services, twenty states

| Department | Median | Range |
| --- | --- | --- |
| *"Need based"** | | |
| Rural financial institution | 16 | 1 (Kerala)–49 (Bihar) |
| Income tax (individual assessees) | 26 | 15 (Himachal)–89 (Karnataka) |
| Municipal services (including building plan approval) | 29 | 9 (Himachal)–76 (Kashmir) |
| Lower judiciary | 58.5 | 10 (Kerala)–97 (Karnataka) |
| Land administration | 58.5 | 29 (Kerala)–94 (Rajasthan) |
| Police (crime/traffic) | 54 | 32 (West Bengal)–79 (Assam) |
| *"Basic services"** | | |
| School (to 12th standard) | 8.5 | 2 (Kerala)–36 (Bihar) |
| Water supply | 15.5 | 3 (Gujarat)–77 (West Bengal) |
| PDS (ration card/supplies) | 11.5 | 2 (Himachal)–67 (Kashmir) |
| Electricity (consumers) | 19.5 | 8 (Himachal)–49 (Kashmir) |
| Government hospital | 18.5 | 1 (Himachal)–45 (Bihar) |

*Source*: Centre for Media Studies (2005): Part III – State-wide Report.

* "Need based" and "Basic services" are the terms used in the report. The difference between "need based" and "basic services" is that, for the latter, there are alternate, private providers; for the former, the government has a monopoly.

*Note*: An explanation in table 1.3 of part I of this report ("80% of those who had interacted with the Police Department paid a bribe") suggests that these percentages are those who interacted (an unreported percentage of the sample), not the entire "sample of households interviewed" (which range in the twenty states from 527 to 960, for a total of 14,405). There is no reporting of the actual questions, so we do not know whether there was a clause like "in the last year" or other specified period for interaction. For some questions, we do not know who in the household was the "respondent" (with a perception of corruption), or whether "respon-dent" equals "anyone in the household" who paid a bribe. There is no indication of whether bribes were paid because the bribe-giver wanted an illegal benefit, versus being paid to get a service to which he or she was entitled.

indication of the incidence of corruption, which by any standard is high, and in some areas extraordinarily high. The experience of ordinary citizens is certainly one of needing to pay bribes (often called "fees" or a "commission") to get things done for many transactions, or to avoid paying the price for an illegal action. But it should be emphasized that it is not true that one needs to bribe for "everything" (see Oldenburg 1987).[18]

Corruption most certainly also affects the formulation of policies and the implementation of projects, particularly those involving construction, where huge "commissions" are paid and shared between administrators and politicians, and the transfers and promotion of officers to and from "lucrative" posts (see Wade 1982 for the best description). The continuation of this system depends on there being severe scarcities of government services, on the lack of transparency, and, most of all, on the corruption of the judicial system itself (in the Transparency International Survey, the 10 percent who bribed the lower judiciary in Kerala was an outlier; the next-lowest number was 43 percent who bribed in Himachal Pradesh). It has been very difficult to convict politicians, administrative officers, and bribe-givers in the lower courts, even for gigantic bribes of tens of millions of rupees. This is not only because lower-court officials are corrupt when it comes to things like getting documents, setting dates for a court hearing, etc., but also because of the perfectly legal ways of delaying a case, and the fact that in many cases the ultimate choices about investigation and prosecution lie with politicians and administrators who are part of the corruption system. It is possible that legal reforms – and especially reforms of the functioning of the district courts and the grassroots-level police system – will happen, albeit gradually, perhaps under pressure from newly emerging modern industrial- and commercial-sector organizations anxious to have reliable contract-enforcing institutions and, ultimately (as scarcities retreat), "clean" government.

A democratic system that works is led by politicians – including some even patently corrupt ones – who control the bureaucracy at all levels. If and when the changes listed above occur, and politicians become increasingly accountable to both the electorate and the legal system, the claim of bureaucrats of a right to rule will be eroded further. In the meantime, India will continue to grow economically and, in the not too distant future cross the threshold of wealth that seemingly guarantees a consolidated democracy to those countries that are democratic (Przeworski and Limongi 1997), provided that inequality is kept moderate or low (Boix and Stokes 2003).

## Notes

1 See the editorial by Najam Sethi, and the article by Raheel Asghar Ginai, in the *Friday Times*, 28 December 2007–3 January 2008, both written before Benazir Bhutto's assassination, for prescient accounts of how the elections would be rigged. The relevant websites are: FAFEN (Free and Fair Election Network; http://www.fafen.org/); PACFREL (Pakistan Coalition for Free, Fair and Democratic Election; http://www.pacfrel.com/); European Union Election Observer Mission: http://www.eueompakistan.org/.

2 The percentage of respondents naming Nawaz Sharif as the "one leader [who can] best handle the problems facing Pakistan" went from 23 percent to 38 percent between January and June 2008. They report also that 83 percent of respondents supported the reinstatement of the old Supreme Court.

3 *News International*, 1 August 2009. See also Sethi (2009); on the politics of this judgment, see Gazdar (2009). For a more detailed summary and interpretation of events up to late 2008, see Fair (2009); Adeel Khan (2008); and Nelson (2009).

4 See Call (2008) for a critique of the concept of a failed state.

5 Available at: http://www.satp.org/satporgtp/countries/pakistan/index.htm; accessed 2 October 2009.

6 The Tablighi Jamaat does attract very impressive numbers to its gatherings. See Aijazuddin (2007: 144–6).

7 However, the respondents were hardly representative, even though selected from urban and rural areas in four provinces. They were overwhelmingly middle class (only 15 percent illiterate, only 15 percent farmers and 6 percent laborers). The results are not very clearly reported, and so should be treated with a great deal of caution.

8 My estimates of percentages from the bar graph (TIP 2009: 3).

9 The other answers were: "inflation" (40 percent); unemployment (20 percent); terrorism (13 percent); electricity and water (11 percent); poverty (8 percent); law and order (3 percent); and education (1 percent).

10 *Dawn*, 28 July 2008.

11 The International Republican Institute (2008) poll reported that "The vast majority of Pakistanis want Musharraf out of office, with 75 percent wanting his resignation and 16 percent opposed."

12 See also Albrecht and Wegner (2006); Rutherford (2006) on the Islamist constitutionalism; and El-Gobashy (2006) for the role of judges and electoral rules.

13 Husain Haqqani interview with *News International*, 16 March 2008.

14 See Linz et al. (2007: 104–6, footnote 42) for a discussion of why the "Gujarat Model" is "not bound to be successful in India's twenty-seven other states."

15 See Mahadevan (2008) for a strongly positive assessment, written with the help of K. P. S. Gill and his organization, with reports at the South Asia Terrorism Portal (SATP). The lessons, according to others writing on the SATP site, have been used in Andhra against the Maoists; see, e.g., Ajai Sahni, "Maoists: Creeping Malignancy"; available at: http://www.satp.org/satporgtp/sair/Archives/5_51. htm#assessment1; accessed 24 July 2008.

16 India, Ministry of Home Affairs, National Crime Records Bureau, *Crime in India 2007*, table 17.5.

17 Six Members of Parliament who were actually serving jail terms, for such crimes as murder, were brought from jail to Delhi to vote in the confidence motion of July 2008.

18 In Pakistan, according to a Pew Research Center survey of August 2009, "when asked how often in the past year they had to do a favor, give a gift, or pay a bribe to a government official to get services or a document that the government is supposed to provide, a majority (58%) volunteers that they have never had to do it and another 16% say they have not had to do it in the past year" and 19 percent said they have given a bribe, with 11 percent of them giving it "often or somewhat often" (Pew Research Center 2009: 34).

# 11  Conclusion

This volume is by no means the first to attempt to solve the puzzle of why India and Pakistan wound up with such different regimes.[1] Our answers all focus on similar factors: the legacy of colonial rule and the nationalist movements; the links of citizenry to government provided by political parties and leaders; the social structure, particularly ethnic divisions; and the differing external security positions. It seems that the best explanation of the current regime each country has is that it was the regime they had yesterday, and last month, and for the last thirty years. The military in Pakistan, only under the unambiguous control of civilian politicians for the first four years of Pakistan's existence, has formed a partnership with a junior, the bureaucracy, and is now in its own self-image firmly and permanently ensconced as the guardian of Pakistan's existence, with a right to intervene in politics, shape the constitution, and directly control some critical economic and civil-society institutions. In India, both military and bureaucracy have stayed where they were at independence – under the rule of elected politicians, held accountable by an active electorate, and by a largely autonomous judicial system and a vigorous independent media.

The paths of the two countries diverge decisively in 1977. The counterfactual history we conjured up earlier (pp. 131–32) is important. A more democratically minded Zulfiqar Ali Bhutto, in his five years of power, would have strengthened the PPP and the parliament as an institution, and would have used parliament and the courts to bring the bureaucracy and the military under democratic control. A very public commission of inquiry into the causes of the tragedy of 1971 could have been part of that. Bhutto could have respected the opposition's role, and seen that it was not necessary to be able to command constitutional changes. There is no evidence that the absence of other alleged "requisites" of democracy – equality, homogeneity, high levels of economic development, democracy-friendly religious belief systems – would have necessarily undermined the progress towards democracy of the sort that India made in the same period, where the same correlates were also absent.

To a significant extent, of course, the crucial players of 1977 were constrained by what had gone on before, as well as by their own personal character, beliefs, and history. An enlightened Prime Minister Bhutto probably would not have been able to get the military–bureaucratic partnership that bore much of the blame for Pakistan's collapse into civil war to recognize the extent to which it was the lack of popular accountability, and the poison of ethnic arrogance, that was to blame. Bhutto himself – in actuality not enlightened, and a prime mover in the effort to keep Pakistan united using ethnic cleansing if not genocide – was a product of what had become a guided democracy system.

But it is not hard to imagine a different scenario of party-building in opposition to the Ayub regime, perhaps with a spell in jail for the PPP and other opposition leaders, after which a cross-party partnership would have seemed more natural than one with the state apparatus. It is harder, though, to imagine our way out of the critical initial conditions of Pakistan's constitution-making and politics that helped sabotage democracy: the shallow roots of the Muslim League in the areas that were to become Pakistan, and a political leadership claiming a right to rule because of its role in gaining the country's freedom, rather than from the citizenry of the place it found itself in. (Again, a contributory factor was the fatal choice of Urdu.) Nor can we imagine away the loss of Jinnah, though we would also need to reimagine him as having a more Nehruvian commitment to democracy. Liaquat's early death was also certainly important; but, again, it is not clear that he would have worked hard to institutionalize democracy. It is much harder to assume away the position of extreme vulnerability to an India not reconciled to partition, and the severe internal-order problems in Pakistan that came with that partition, which led to a necessary reliance on the army and the bureaucracy for the preservation of the new country. The role of the US in providing economic and military aid (and advice) was also significant.

For India, it is not difficult to image a very different outcome if Mrs Gandhi had not called the election of 1977, or had handed real power to her son Sanjay, and had he not died in 1980. By 1977, India had resolved some crucial issues, putting in place a legitimate federal system and a language formula that was acceptable to almost all. Yet it is not hard to imagine that its "fissiparous tendencies" would have proven too hard to tame, and that Selig Harrison's (1960) surmise (not prediction) that an authoritarian regime would be needed to prevent a break-up would have turned out to be accurate. The five free and fair general elections (to Pakistan's one), and the institutionalization of a working parliament might have happened without Nehru – and it is certainly not hard to imagine an assassin – but those things would have been far more difficult to do. The largely pernicious transformation of the institutionalized Congress Party by Indira Gandhi, had it occurred ten or fifteen years earlier, might have done much greater damage to the system. It might not have been true that in 1977 the citizenry had become so accustomed to democratic freedoms, and the ability to hold government accountable, at least through the press and demonstrations and access via politicians with long-developed links to them, that it made their choice of democracy over guided democracy crystal clear in that year's election.

I shall not move back beyond 1947 in this speculation, but it is worth saying that India's great democratic momentum rested on what had been developed during the history of the nationalist movement, which was far older and sent roots far deeper than Pakistan's. Perhaps that in turn depended on something of a miracle – the fact of Gandhi, and the willingness of the movement to put itself under Gandhi's direction, even when its leaders did not seriously share his most important beliefs.

The foundations of India's democracy are strong, even though the structures built on it have weakened in some ways, while being strengthened in others. The current trends of economic development, increased equality (ultimately) from a transformed class and economic base, the global winds favoring democracy but, most of all, continuing to work the system in mainly democratic ways will only make its democracy seem more and more natural.

Pakistan, on the other hand, though likely to develop at a relatively rapid pace, may find it difficult to escape the embrace of a deeply entrenched state apparatus, with the military at the center of power. It will require starting from where it was when the British ruled, and painstakingly building political movements to challenge the state, and, with luck, peacefully produce a redressing of the balance between political authority and the state.

Is the comparison of India and Pakistan useful for understanding regime change and persistence elsewhere? At present, the questions, in Third World countries with less than the threshold income, concern either consolidation of democracies, or transitions to democracy. The India–Pakistan comparison suggests that poor, inegalitarian, and ethnically and religiously diverse democracies, once inaugurated, *can* set themselves firmly on the path to consolidation, at a minimum. The prevalence of a particular religion or political culture – Islam, or the "Asian value" system – is of less significance than other factors. Quite possibly, major land reforms or class transformations are not prior conditions.

It is not helpful for the chances of maintaining a fragile democracy, the Pakistan case tells us, to be enmeshed in a global security system in a position that brings military aid and partnership to any government in the country, including a military dictatorship. What seems to have made the most difference in India and Pakistan is having a political society with a thick layer of institutions and leaders who have forged their identities and capacities in some sort of struggle for democracy, and have then been able to maintain and develop the citizen–politician link, typically through a vigorous party system, once the democracy begins to function. Politicians with that base of legitimacy can win the critical battles for authority with the state apparatus, in its bureaucratic and military form.

These factors also matter for transitions from authoritarian rule. Pakistan came closest to being on the road to democratic consolidation during the 1972–7 Bhutto regime, when the party in power had been formed in a struggle with the previous dictatorship, and military rule itself had been delegitimated by defeat in war and the loss of half the country. Given a not-too-difficult-to-imagine difference in international links and leadership, Pakistan could have achieved a strengthening democracy, in parallel to India. Yet the path Pakistan took after 1977 saw the military increasing its hold on the political system, the society, and the economy – acting, as Barnett Rubin says, more as a dominant political party than as a branch of the state apparatus. It is likely that a far deeper and longer-term economic and social transformation will have to occur in Pakistan, with a very different international security environment, before democratic politicians would be able to establish dominance vis-à-vis the bureaucracy and the military.

These lessons can be illustrated by looking at other South Asian countries. Bangladesh, as a successor country to the united Pakistan, had certain India-like advantages when it began in 1971. Its nationalist movement was more than twenty years old, and had more than one generation of leaders. It had won independence by drawing on the support of a cross-religious and cross-class alliance of Bengalis, organizing mass demonstrations, and spending time in jail – and then by fighting a civil war. Its unquestioned leader, Sheikh Mujibur Rahman, had been in jail, under threat of conviction for treason, during the war, and returned as the "Bangabandhu" (literally "friend of Bengal" but meaning "father of the nation"), who began his leadership of the new country with overwhelming legitimacy and popularity. The military began with internal divisions, between those who had fought in the liberation army, and those of the regular army, trapped in Pakistan in 1971, who had been unable to do so. To some extent, that division had an ideological dimension: radicals versus establishment professionals. So the politicians began in a position of strength vis-à-vis the army.

Unfortunately, Bangladesh followed the post-colonial pattern of a charismatic liberator-leader with little taste for the nitty-gritty of governing, faced with enormous economic and other problems, choosing to deal with challenges to his political position by moving to a single-party regime. By the time of the military coups of 1975, Bangladesh had a quasi-authoritarian regime. It took fifteen years, and several military governments later, and the removal by assassination of many of the important 1971-era leaders, before the first free election took place in 1991. The political parties that contested were headed by the personal heirs of their founders: the daughter of Sheikh Mujib, and the widow of General and then President Zia ur Rahman. Those parties, with those two women, have contested elections in 1996, 2001, and 2008 – the last one after a quasi-coup and a caretaker government had postponed elections by two years. The balance of power favored the politicians after Ershad's military government, because it was so corrupt and ineffective that it lessened the military's authority. That authority was possibly inherently weaker than that of the Pakistani military because, while Pakistan has a real use for an army to protect its borders, Bangladesh does not. At present the bureaucracy is comparatively strong in the power relationship with politicians, supported with an alliance of convenience with the very large and well-functioning set of NGOs. Bangladesh, in terms of our analysis, looks like a weak version of Pakistan: its emergence on a path leading to stable and consolidated democracy seems more likely than Pakistan's.[2]

Sri Lanka's history has come up from time to time in my argument. I have speculated that its current problems in consolidating its democracy may be in part due to not having had to struggle as much to achieve independence as either India or Pakistan. Constitutional reforms happened almost before they were requested by the Sri Lankans. At independence, the offices of government were transferred to leaders of the English-speaking elite, both Tamil and Sinhala; and it was only then that political struggles on the basis of language, religion, and ethnicity began in earnest. Whether that would help us understand better the success of Bandaranaike's "Sinhala only" campaign and the ultimate inability to solve the problem of accommodating the Tamils, which led to the recently ended civil war, is an open question. Elected Sinhalese politicians have maintained control over the bureaucracy and the military – there was an unsuccessful coup attempt in 1962 – and managed to suppress a "revolution" in 1971, but they have also presided over extremely violent repression of alleged revolutionaries and Tamils. Still there continue to be free elections, with a reasonably free press in much of the country, and an active civil society that has worked to hold the politicians accountable. Sri Lanka thus seems to be a weak version of India in its political system. That it has chosen majoritarian rather than federalist solutions as a way of accommodating the Tamils is probably a function of the two-person-game nature of the Sri Lanka polity.

It seems clear, even from looking at these two countries, closest to India and Pakistan on a number of dimensions – civilizational, socio-economic, and historical – as well as being subject to India's gravitational mass, as it were, that the India–Pakistan case comparison cannot be turned into "factors" susceptible to statistical analysis. The outcome of my argument, if it is convincing, does support the "contingency school" approach (Waterbury 1997: 383) – as opposed to the structural-factors (class structure, for example) or basic-forces (clash of civilizations, for example) approaches – to understanding why some countries become and remain democratic. And that requires great sensitivity to the unique characteristics of particular countries' society and history and position in the world.

The puzzle of India's and Pakistan's divergent regime paths is a *puzzle* for political scientists because of these two countries' broad similarities in characteristics that they have used to predict which countries are likely to become democracies and remain democracies. Their level of economic development, most memorably identified as *the* factor by Seymour Martin Lipset in 1959, was roughly the same, and has indeed, while growing significantly, remained largely the same ever since. Their high level of inequality, extreme ethnic and religious fragmentation, etc., was thought to militate against reaching and retaining democratic status. "Culture" theories of democratization like Huntington's would also not permit their believers to predict the paths actually taken. India in particular remains a massive exception (see McMillan 2008; Doorenspleet and Mudde 2008); but Pakistan, as a "partial" democracy (adopting for the moment the term favored by D. L. Epstein et al. 2006) for much of its history, is also problematic for most of these generalizations.

In recent years, these theoretical approaches to explaining why countries of the world wind up as democracies or autocracies or somewhere in between, and why they transit from one to the other regime, have been revived, typically using much more highly developed quantitative tools. Lipset's "requisites of democracy" ideas have been reimagined and tested by a roster of eminent political scientists.[3] "Cultural" theories have been addressed by others.[4]

Leaving aside the rich nuances of these works, and the critiques each make of their predecessors, particularly on methodology and conceptualization,[5] the most salient issues concern what effect levels of development, measured by GDP, have on the process of democratic transition and consolidation. Przeworski and Limongi (1997) show that "wealth has no effect on democratization but instead promotes consolidation" (Houle 2009: 589). In other words, "the impact of economic development is to make democracies endure, once established through other means" (Hadenius and Teorell 2005: 88).

Boix and Stokes (2003: 539), having extended the time-frame for regime-change cases back to 1850, show that "development causes dictatorships to fall to democracy and causes democracy to last", and explain that result by arguing that "as countries develop, incomes become more equally distributed." Houle (2009: 590), using a much larger set of countries, shows that "inequality harms consolidation but has no net effect on democratization."[6] Houle (2009: 611) states flatly that "democracies with sufficiently low levels of inequality are nearly immune from breakdowns;" and, having illustrated the point by contrasting the probability of breakdown faced by India, Peru, and Nigeria, concludes that "income distribution is a leading candidate in explaining why some poor democracies, such as India, have been remarkably stable, while others, like Peru and Nigeria, have not" (Houle 2009: 613). According to the Human Development Report measures of inequality, inequality has been significantly greater in India than in Pakistan throughout the last twenty years, with not much change in either country over time, reminding us that these demonstrated correlations cannot explain individual cases.

Hadenius and Teorell (2005: 100–1), having extended the time period to the 1990s and using Freedom House ratings, show that economic development has a beneficial effect even on countries that are "partly free" – the category in which Pakistan falls. D. Epstein et al. (2006: 566) claim that "the middle category – the partial democracies – [are] critical to the understanding of democratic transitions. More volatile than either straight autocracies or democracies, their movements seem at the moment to be largely unpredictable." Pakistan's regime transitions do not display the extreme volatility of some other countries; rather, they transit from a "soft" autocracy to a "hard" democracy, and back. There is no general theory that might help us predict whether never falling into "full" autocracy provides a brake on moving towards full democracy – because it is endurable: the people's voice is not suppressed, and can even be effective; repression is not as harsh as in a typical authoritarian place; civil society is, by and large, civil. Svolik (2008: 164) finds that, as of 2001, the odds were 70 percent that India is a consolidated democracy (despite its low GDP), because of its longevity. India is not yet a full democracy, however, and might even now break down, but almost certainly not completely.

At various points in my argument, I have drawn on the concepts and generalizations of the "breakdowns" and "transitions" literature.[7] The final volume of that set of studies is titled "Tentative Conclusions about Uncertain Democracies," and the final section of that volume is titled "Concluding (but not Capitulating) with a Metaphor." This indicates an admirable sense of the fruitfulness of modest generalization. That tradition has in recent years focused on the consolidation of democracies, rather than on their breakdown.[8] Becoming "free" does not mean that a country's democratic regime is "consolidated," nor does it mean that it is immune to breakdown. Linz and Stepan (1996: 5), crediting Guiseppe di Palma, famously provide a succinct definition of consolidation: "a political situation in which . . . democracy has become 'the only game in town.'" Schneider and Schmitter's (2004: 62) complex formal definition begins with a statement that underlines how chancy a process it is: "Regime consolidation consists in transforming the accidental arrangements, prudential norms and contingent solutions that have emerged during the uncertain struggles of the transition into institutions . . ." Although the quasi-field of "consolidology" has encompassed many empirical studies, mainly focused on the arena of the original "breakdowns" and "transitions" literature – Southern Europe and Latin America – and added the post-communist countries of Eastern Europe, it does not seem to have made much progress in generating theories about why some countries, at least for the time being, have consolidated their democratic regimes.

Croissant and Merkel (2004: 3) point out that many countries mix democratic and autocratic rules, and "may take a third direction: the path into the 'grey zone' between open autocracy and liberal democracy." Schmitter (1992: 429) notes that some regimes that enter into a transition will "regress to autocracy," but "more are likely to get stuck in a sort of purgatory." Pakistan would be a paradigmatic case. Some of these are what they call "defective democracies" (those that are closer to the autocratic pole might, one supposes, be called "defective autocracies"), but it is not clear from the analysis (e.g. Croissant 2004) that the reasons for their intermediate status, and for persistence in that status, derive from a special understanding of transitions and breakdowns; the familiar explanations of GDP, inequality, etc., are instead brought to bear, mainly for descriptive purposes.

Gandhi and Przeworski (2007: 1280) provide one explanation for the comparative longevity of certain military autocrats:

> when [autocratic rulers] need to neutralize threats from larger groups within society and to solicit the cooperation of outsiders, autocrats frequently rely on nominally democratic institutions. Specifically, partisan legislatures incorporate potential opposition forces, investing them with a stake in the ruler's survival. By broadening the basis of support for the ruler, these institutions lengthen his [from the footnote: "the gender is not accidental"] tenure.

They provide a convincing quantitative test of a large number of cases, considering the number of parties and other factors. They show also that autocrats who institutionalize with a single party survive significantly longer than others. What they do not do, unfortunately, is extend the analysis to autocrats who rule from behind the scenes, as the Pakistan military has done, having followed the pattern of sharing spoils, conceding certain policies, and allowing partisan politics that Gandhi and Przeworski predict. Since the Pakistan military has maintained its corporate integrity, with coups always led by the head of the army, it has solved to a considerable extent the succession problem that bedevils other autocratic rulers.

Schmitter (1992: 425) reviews the difficulties in analyzing how and why consolidation occurs, and argues that "*the core of the consolidation dilemma lies in coming up with a set of institutions that politicians can agree on and that citizens are willing to support*" (his italics). He suggests that it would be better to think of democracy not as a regime but as a composite of regimes, in which citizens *qua* "parties, associations, movements, localities, and various *clientele* would compete and coalesce . . . to capture office and influence policy" (Schmitter 1992: 427). This would have advantages for empirical research, and would allow us to examine a range of types of democracy more effectively. Ultimately, Schmitter's (1992: 429) "hunch is that the role of different representative organizations and, with it, the type of democracy that will emerge, is determined to a significant degree by the timing and sequencing of accomplishing [the tasks of holding elections, forming parties and other social groups, setting up the administration, writing the constitution, etc.]" (see Schmitter and Santiso 1998 for an elaboration of this point). Our analysis of the cases of India and Pakistan would seem to provide firm support for this idea.

Sequencing of this sort is at the heart of an early but still enormously influential approach to the problem of understanding what regime paths countries take, in Robert Dahl's *Polyarchy* (1971).[9] The regime types he identifies – closed hegemonies, inclusive hegemonies, competitive oligarchies, and polyarchies – are conceptualized as lying on dimensions of inclusiveness (participation) and liberalization (public contestation), and the actual historical experience of democratization has been one of change over time along paths which need not go in one direction (see Dahl 1971: 9–11). Dahl (1971: 202–3) sets out the seven sets of "complex conditions" on which the chances of a country being a polyarchy depend. These are: historical sequences (whether competition precedes inclusiveness or vice versa); the socio-economic order (access to violence, economic sanctions; agrarian or commercial–industrial economy); the level of socio-economic development (measured by GNP per capita); equalities and inequalities (objective and subjective); subcultural pluralism (amount and degree of markedness); domination by a foreign power; and six elements of beliefs of political activists. Dahl refuses to attempt to test the impact of these factors empirically, mainly because of the quality of the data available then. He points out that the availability of data on socio-economic levels "exaggerates the importance of this factor and obscures the importance of others" (Dahl 1971: 206); and that the bulk of recent theorizing on this topic relies on just those data, albeit analyzed with increasing statistical sophistication, should give us pause. Although other factors have been added to Dahl's list, the ones he identified are arguably still the most important (see for example the control variables used by Houle 2009: 603–4).[10] Finally, Dahl (1971: 206) points out "the weaknesses in the data impose another serious limitation": the impossibility of assigning weights to the various conditions.

We have been considering a small sample of theoretical analyses of why some countries become and remain democratic, while others do not, and have used them to illuminate the cases of India and Pakistan. The India–Pakistan comparison will obviously not contribute to proving or disproving these theoretical propositions, let alone settle any of these arguments.

But there are perhaps features of our argument on India and Pakistan that may contribute some useful caveats and add something to these theoretical perspectives. We can begin with the problem of weightage of Dahl's seven conditions. Historical sequences seem far more important than any of the other sets of conditions. Dahl argues that the chances of polyarchy increase if competition precedes inclusiveness. In India, the long history of the nationalist movement allowed that to happen: Congress and other party members took office when the franchise was very limited, and only in very constrained arenas. It was thirty-five years after its founding that the Congress, under Gandhi, began to include many more activists, but even in 1945–6 – by which time the arenas for political competition had expanded to the provincial level – the franchise had expanded to only 15 percent of the adult population, and the quarter of the population who lived in the princely states did not vote at all. The adoption of universal franchise, along with full-scale competition, with the first elections of 1951–2 was not a great shock to the system. In Pakistan, on the other hand, the Muslim League participants were few in local bodies and provincial councils before the 1937 elections, and they were in competition in both Punjab and Bengal with parties that included

Hindus and Muslims. The mass mobilization of Muslims in 1945–6, and then of Bengalis in 1948–52, took place before the (mainly rigged) elections in the new country. The competition of the 1950s, the early 1970s, and the decade 1988–99 followed the participation of citizens in anti-government movements. Thus our cases would provide support for Dahl's surmise.

In the "socio-economic order" cluster of conditions, India and Pakistan are much the same – with both in the middle range between "dispersed or neutralized" and "monopolized" violence and socio-economic sanctions (in all of the pairs quoted from Dahl 1971: 203, the first is "most favorable to polyarchy" and the latter "least favorable to polyarchy"). India's agrarian economy is now closer to "free farmers" than to "traditional peasant" than Pakistan's, though both are to be found towards the "traditional peasant" end. Pakistan's commercial–industrial economy has been closer to the "decentralized direction" pole, though, again – despite India's initial attempt to control the "commanding heights" of the economy – given the very small formal sector there, both countries are midway on this dimension. Both countries are in much the same position when it comes to the fourth cluster, level of socio-economic development. Perhaps some measure of volatility should be added to this factor: India's GDP has steadily grown, at first very modestly, then more recently quite fast, but with only a few years of mildly negative growth. Pakistan's has had several serious interruptions. India's more stable pattern should give it some advantage in democratization.

In Dahl's fourth cluster, "equalities and inequalities," Pakistan has indeed somewhat more equality (as measured by the Gini of consumption) than India, and both are closer to "low." When it comes to "subcultural pluralism" (the fifth cluster) both come out as "high" (which is seen by Dahl to be least favorable to polyarchy), but in his further deconstruction, "if marked or high," India's position is more favorable than Pakistan's, especially before 1971. Although Hindus are a majority in India, they are divided by caste, language, and region, and no group is "indefinitely out of government." Pakistan's language issue was the key to the trauma of the break-up of the country, and the dominance of the Punjab has proved problematic for democratic bargaining since. India's advantage in this, if it exists, must be weighted as less than that from the "historical sequences" cluster.

The final two clusters of conditions are "foreign domination" and "beliefs of political activists." India's case is one in which the dominance of the colonial power was comparatively mild, allowing for considerable political and intellectual freedom, and after independence Dahl's "weak or temporary" domination describes the situation well. Pakistan, sharing India's colonial experience, was, however, drawn into a close relationship with the United States, at a time when that country was prepared to justify, and even encourage, autocratic rule as long as the country remained part of the "free world." The US partnering with the Ayub, Zia, and Musharraf military dictatorships did not come close to Dahl's "strong and persistent" domination (unfavorable to polyarchy), but was certainly much closer to that situation than India's with the Soviet Union or anyone else.

Dahl (1971: 200) notes that "In India . . . in the years preceding independence there was an astonishing degree of agreement among leaders and activists on the proposition that India must be a democracy in the Western sense." When independence came, there was no barrier to maintaining that belief. A similar belief – though less widespread, if only because the Muslim League had gained mass support only just before independence – existed in Pakistan, but it was quickly contradicted by the Muslim League leaders' claim to have the right to shape the country's future on the matter of a national language, and on federalism, despite their not commanding the support of a majority of Pakistan's population. That belief, and the belief of senior bureaucrats and army generals that the need to maintain state stability had to take precedence over democratic procedures, justified the suppression of those who wanted democracy. The democratic beliefs of Bengali activists in this period sat comfortably with their political goals, but it is likely that even those opposed to the Muslim League in West Pakistan, as overwhelmingly drawn from the "feudal" land-owning class, may have had some doubts about the idea that (in Dahl's first "belief" in his list) "institutions of polyarchy are legitimate." That difference in belief persists to the present, if we can rely on the opinions in the *State of Democracy in South Asia* report. There is no evidence of which I am aware for measuring the other beliefs listed by Dahl, such as "compromise necessary and desirable," but I suspect that the differences between Indian and Pakistani political activists are not very great. We have also suggested that it would be hard to show that either country had an advantage (in achieving polyarchy) derived from the content or practice of their differing (majority) religions.

The conditions that our study suggests should be weighted most heavily – historical sequences, (part of) subcultural pluralism, foreign domination, and political activists' beliefs – are not necessarily the ones that will be most important in other countries. Indeed, that would be unlikely. It is not at all clear how one could systematize the weighting process, however. The search for evidence for theoretical proposals like Dahl's must therefore rely on the careful work of scholars who know particular countries very well indeed – those like Juan Linz and Alfred Stepan, in Schmitter's review of their book (Linz and Stepan 1996), who "plow through an immense amount of raw and processed material (in several languages), order it loosely according to a broad set of interpretive categories, compile a rich narrative full of complex linkages and sequences, and then proceed to draw insightful conclusions" (Schmitter 1997: 168).

### Notes

1 See in particular Adeney and Wyatt (2001); Mushirul Hasan (2001); Stern (2001); Christophe Jaffrelot (2002); D. A. Low (2002); and Meghnad Desai (2005); not

to speak of relevant additional work focusing on one country or the other – e.g., Kothari (1988); Waseem (1989); Varshney (2000); Manor (1990); Zaidi (2005b); McMillan (2008) – or calling into question the comparison itself (Jalal 1995).

2 On the other hand, a "prominent writer" quoted by the International Crisis Group (2008b: 11) in its report on the upcoming election, said: "Why would the military want to run the country, in the traditional sense – through martial law – when it has officers in almost every branch of the government, running private businesses and heading up civil society organizations? What we have here is an embryonic Pakistani military."

3 I do not pretend to command this literature, and so select a few illustrative studies: Przeworski and Limongi (1997); Boix and Stokes (2003); Hadenius and Teorell (2005); D. L. Epstein et al. (2006); Houle (2009). For a recent summary of the other interpretation of the correlation, the issue of whether democracy promotes economic growth, see Gerring et al. (2005).

4 For example, Ingelhart (2003); Hadenius and Teorell (2005).

5 For example, both Przeworski and Limongi (1997) and Boix and Stokes (2003) dichotomize the regime dimension (democracy/autocracy); while Hadenius and Teorell (2005: 100) "measure democracy on a semi-continuous scale," and use Freedom House categories. D. L. Epstein et al. (2006) trichotomize the regime dimension, using Polity IV numbers, which Hadenius and Teorell (2005: 95) reject because they make "no reference to civil liberties." Houle (2009) without fuss adopts the Przeworski and Limongi dichotomization.

6 He uses capital share of the value added in the industrial sector as the indicator of inequality, and uses several other measures of inequality in imputing 15 percent of the observations.

7 Linz (1978); O'Donnell et al. (1986).

8 That is not a function of the absence of breakdowns. Although the number of persons living in "Not Free" countries, according to Freedom House, has remained roughly the same (around 35 percent of the world population, with China contributing 20 percent) since 1992, the number living in "Free" countries has doubled (to around 45 percent), with the remainder in "Partly Free" countries. This suggests that the trend is away from breakdowns (*Freedom in the World 2008*: 4).

9 Dahl has written a great deal more on this topic since *Polyarchy* but, as best I can gather, without affecting the discussion offered here.

10 In the postscript, Dahl (1971: 208–27) makes an argument that applies eerily to developments in post-9/11 Afghanistan and Iraq, on how the US "might facilitate the transformation of countries [with a 'mixed profile'] into polyarchies." (The answer in a word is: Don't try.) He also has words of wisdom for an "Innovator" in such a country.

# Bibliography

Abbas, Hassan (2005) *Pakistan's Drift into Extremism: Allah, the Army, and America's War on Terror.* Armonk, NY/New Delhi: M. E. Sharpe/Pentagon Press.

Abbott, Freeland (1966) "Pakistan and the Secular State." In Donald Eugene Smith (ed.) *South Asian Politics and Religion* (Princeton, NJ: Princeton University Press): 352–70.

Adams, Norman (1973) "Historical Presentation Analysis of Pakistan's Export Trade with the United States, and Suggestions for Augmenting Its Total Export Earnings." PhD dissertation, Karachi University; available at: http://eprints.hec. gov.pk/731/01/526.html.htm; accessed 19 June 2007.

Adeney, Katharine (2007) *Federalism and Ethnic Conflict Regulation in India and Pakistan.* New York: Palgrave Macmillan.

Adeney, Katharine and Andrew Wyatt (2001) "Explaining South Asia's Uneven Democratic Career." In Jeff Haynes (ed.) *Towards Sustainable Democracy in the Third World* (Basingstoke: Palgrave Macmillan).

Afsaruddin, Asma (2006) "The 'Islamic State': Genealogy, Facts, and Myths." *Journal of Church and State,* 48 (1): 153–73.

Ahmad, Imtiaz and Helmut Reifeld (eds) (2001) *Middle Class Values in India and Western Europe.* New Delhi: Social Science Press.

Ahmad, Riaz (preparer), Sharif al Mujahid and Yousuf Saeed (eds) (1981) *Quaid-i-Azam Jinnah: A Chronology.* Karachi: Quaid-i-Azam Academy.

Ahmed, Samina (1999) "Pakistan's Nuclear Weapons Program: Turning Points and Nuclear Choices." *International Security,* 23 (4): 178–204.

Ahmed, Samina (2001) "The Fragile Base of Democracy in Pakistan." In Amita Shastri and A. Jayaratnam Wilson (eds) *The Post-Colonial States of South Asia* (Richmond, Surrey: Curzon Press): 41–68.

Ahsan, Aitzaz (2005) "Why Pakistan Is Not a Democracy." In Meghnad Desai and Aitzaz Ahsan, *Divided by Democracy* (Delhi: Roli Books): 75–144.

Aijazuddin, F. S. (2007) "The Shifting *Qiblah*: Islamization under General Zia ul Haq and Secularism under General Pervez Musharraf – the Pakistani Experience." In T. N. Srinivasan (ed.) *The Future of Secularism* (Delhi: Oxford University Press): 124–55.

Aiyar, Swaminathan Anklesaria (2008) "How to Check Money in Politics." *Economic Times,* 24 July.

Akbar, M. J. (1988) *Riot after Riot: Reports on Caste and Communal Violence in India.* New Delhi: Penguin.

Alavi, Hamza (1972) "The State in Post-Colonial Societies: Pakistan and Bangladesh." *New Left Review*, I (74): 59–81.

Alavi, Hamza (1983) "Class and State." In Hassan Gardezi and Jamil Rashid (eds) *Pakistan: The Roots of Dictatorship. The Political Economy of a Praetorian State* (London/Delhi: Zed Press/Oxford University Press): 40–93.

Alavi, Hamza (1987) "Ethnicity, Muslim Society, and the Pakistan Ideology." In Anita Weiss (ed.) *Islamic Reassertion in Pakistan: The Application of Islamic Laws in a Modern State* (Syracuse, NY/Lahore: Syracuse University Press/Vanguard): 21–48.

Albrecht, Holger and Eva Wegner (2006) "Autocrats and Islamists: Contenders and Containment in Egypt and Morocco." *Journal of North African Studies*, 11 (2): 123–41.

Ali, Imran (2004) "Historical Impact on Political Economy of Pakistan." *Asian Journal of Management Cases*, 1 (2): 129–46.

Ali, Shaheen Sardar (1999) "The Rights of Ethnic Minorities in Pakistan: A Legal Analysis." *International Journal on Minority and Group Rights*, 6 (1–2): 169–95.

Ali, Shaheen Sardar and Javaid Rehman (2001) *Indigenous Peoples and Ethnic Minorities of Pakistan: Constitutional and Legal Perspectives.* Nordic Institute of Asian Studies Monograph Series No. 84. (Richmond, Surrey: Curzon Press).

Alsop, Ruth and Bryan Kurey (2005) *Local Organizations in Decentralized Development: Their Functions and Performance in India.* Washington, DC: World Bank.

Amin, Shahid (1984) "Gandhi as Mahatma." In Ranajit Guha et al., *Subaltern Studies 3: Writings on South Asian History and Society* (New Delhi: Oxford University Press): 1–61.

Amir, Ayaz (1996) "The Myth of Feudalism." *Dawn* (10 June); reprinted as app. 2.2 in S. Akbar Zaidi, *Issues in Pakistan's Political Economy* (Karachi: Oxford University Press, 1999): 24–5.

Amir, Ayaz (2002) "A Banana Republic without the Bananas," *Dawn*, 1 February.

Amir, Ayaz (2008) "The Road to Hell: Paved with Good Intentions." *News International*, 1 August.

Amir, Ayaz (2009) "Who's More Powerful, Taliban or the Sugar Barons?" *News International*, 11 September.

Anderson, John (ed.) (2006a) *Religion, Democracy, and Democratization.* London: Routledge.

Anderson, John (2006b) "Does God Matter, and If So Whose God? Religion and Democratization." In John Anderson (ed.) *Religion, Democracy, and Democratization* (London: Routledge): 192–217.

Anwar, Mumtaz and Katharina Michaelowa (2006) "The Political Economy of US Aid to Pakistan." *Review of Development Economics*, 10 (2): 195–209.

Attwood, Donald W. (1992) *Raising Cane: The Political Economy of Sugar in Western India.* Boulder, Colo.: Westview.

Austin, Granville (1966) *The Indian Constitution: Cornerstone of a Nation.* Oxford: Oxford University Press.

Austin, Granville (1993) "The Constitution, Society, and Law." In Philip Oldenburg (ed.) *India Briefing 1993* (Boulder, Colo.: Westview): 103–29.

Austin, Granville (1999) *Working a Democratic Constitution: The Indian Experience.* Delhi: Oxford University Press.

Aziz, K. K. (1976) *Party Politics in Pakistan, 1947–1958.* Islamabad: National Commission on Historical and Cultural Research.

Aziz, Mazhar (2008) *Military Control in Pakistan: The Parallel State.* London: Routledge.

Balagopal, K. (1987) "An Ideology for the Provincial Propertied Class." *Economic and Political Weekly,* 22 (36–7): 1544–6.

Banerjee, Mukulika (2008) "Democracy, Sacred and Everyday: An Ethnographic Case from India." In Julia Paley (ed.) *Democracy: Anthropological Approaches* (Santa Fe, Calif.: School for Advanced Research Press): 63–96.

Bardhan, Pranab (1984) *The Political Economy of Development in India.* Oxford/New York: Basil Blackwell.

Bardhan, Pranab (2003) *Political-Economy and Governance Issues in the Indian Economic Reform Process.* 2003 K. R. Narayanan Oration. Canberra: Australia South Asia Research Centre, Australian National University; available at: http://rspas.anu.edu.au/papers/narayanan/2003oration.pdf.

Bari, S. and Khan, B. H. (2001) "Local Government Elections." Islamabad: Pattan Development Organization.

Baru, Sanjaya (2000) "Economic Policy and the Development of Capitalism in India: The Role of Regional Capitalists and Political Parties." In Francine Frankel, Zoya Hasan, Rajeev Bhargava and Balveer Arora (eds) *Transforming India: Social and Political Dynamics of Democracy* (Delhi: Oxford University Press): 207–30.

Baruah, Sanjib (2001) *India against Itself: Assam and the Politics of Nationality.* Delhi: Oxford University Press.

Baruah, Sanjib (2005) *Durable Disorder: Understanding the Politics of Northeast India.* Delhi: Oxford University Press.

Baruah, Sanjib (ed.) (2009) *Beyond Counter-Insurgency: Breaking the Impasse in Northeast India.* Delhi: Oxford University Press.

Basu, Amrita and Srirupa Roy (eds) (2007) *Violence and Democracy in India.* Calcutta: Seagull Books.

Baxi, Pratiksha, Shirim M. Rai and Shaheen Sardar Ali (2006) "Legacies of Common Law: 'Crimes of Honour' in India and Pakistan." *Third World Quarterly,* 27 (7): 1239–53.

Baxter, Craig (1977) "Some Aspects of Politics in the Punjab, 1936–1945." In Lawrence Ziring, Ralph Braibanti and W. Howard Wriggins (eds) *Pakistan: The Long View* (Durham, NC: Duke University Press): 40–69.

Bayart, Jean-François (1986) "Civil Society in Africa." In Patrick Chabal (ed.) *Political Domination in Africa* (Cambridge: Cambridge University Press): 109–25.

Bayly, Christopher (1998) *Origins of Nationality in South Asia: Patriotism and Ethical Government in the Making of Modern India.* Delhi: Oxford University Press.

Belkin, Aaron and Evan Schofer (2003) "Toward a Structural Understanding of Coup Risk." *Journal of Conflict Resolution,* 47 (5): 594–620.

Berg-Schlosser, Dirk (2007) "Concepts, Measurements and Sub-Types in Democratization Research." In Dirk Berg-Schlosser (ed.) *Democratization: The State of the Art,* 2nd revised edn (Opladen/Farmington Hills, Mich.: Barbara Budrich): 31–43.

Bhattacharyya, Dwaipayan (1999) "Politics of Middleness: The Changing Character of the Communist Party of India (Marxist) in Rural West Bengal 1977–1990." In Ben Rogaly, Barbara Harriss-White and Sugata Bose (eds) *Sonar Bangla? Agricultural Growth and Agrarian Change in West Bengal and Bangladesh* (New Delhi: Sage): 279–300.

Bhatti, Amjad (2008) "The Colonial Burden of Pakistan's Judiciary." *Himal Southasian*, January; available at: http://www.himalmag.com/The-colonial-burden-of-Pakistan-s-judicary_nw2045.html; accessed 7 January 2008.

Bhatti, Zubair Khurshid (2006) "Citizens, Courts, and Police: Fictions and Facts." Government of Pakistan, Access to Justice Program website; available at: http://www.ajp.gov.pk/articles/zubair_k_bhatti_01_citizens_courts_and_police.asp; accessed 7 August 2008.

Bhutto, Zulfiqar Ali (1973?) *Marching towards Democracy: A Collection of Articles, Statements, and Speeches 1970–1971.* PDF copy accessed from www.bhutto.org; 31 May 2008.

Binder, Leonard (1963) *Religion and Politics in Pakistan.* Berkeley: University of California Press.

Blair, Harry (1980) "Mrs Gandhi's Emergency, the Indian Elections of 1977, Pluralism and Marxism: Problems with Paradigms." *Modern Asian Studies*, 14 (2): 237–71.

Blood, Peter (ed.) (1994) *Pakistan: A Country Study.* Washington, DC: GPO for the Library of Congress available at: http://countrystudies.us/pakistan/76.htm; accessed 5 May 2010.

Boix, Carles and Susan Carol Stokes (2003) "Endogenous Democratization." *World Politics*, 55 (4): 517–49.

Bouton, Marshall M. (1985) *Agrarian Radicalism in South India.* Princeton, NJ: Princeton University Press.

Braibanti, Ralph (1963) "Public Bureaucracy and Judiciary in Pakistan." In Joseph LaPalomabara (ed.) *Bureaucracy and Political Development* (Princeton, NJ: Princeton University Press): 360–440.

Brass, Paul R. (1990) *The Politics of India since Independence.* Cambridge: Cambridge University Press.

Brass, Paul R. (1994) *The Politics of India since Independence.* 2nd edn. Cambridge: Cambridge University Press.

Brass, Paul R. (ed.) (1996) *Riots and Pogroms.* New York: NYU Press.

Brass, Paul R. (2003) *The Production of Hindu–Muslim Violence in Contemporary India.* Delhi: Oxford University Press.

Brass, Paul R. and Marcus F. Franda (eds) (1973) *Radical Politics in South Asia.* Cambridge, Mass.: MIT Press.

Burki, Shahid Javed (1969) "Twenty Years of the Civil Service of Pakistan: A Reevaluation." *Asian Survey*, 9 (4): 239–54.

Burki, Shahid Javed (1980) *Pakistan under Bhutto, 1971–1977.* London: Macmillan.

Call, Charles T. (2008) "The Fallacy of the 'Failed State.'" *Third World Quarterly*, 29 (8): 1491–507.

Callard, Keith (1957) *Pakistan: A Political Study.* London: George Allen & Unwin.

Calman, Leslie J. (1985) *Protest in Democratic India: Authority's Response to Challenge.* Boulder, Colo.: Westview.

Candland, Christopher (2007a) *Organized Labor, Democracy, and Development in India and Pakistan.* Abingdon: Routledge.

Candland, Christopher (2007b) "Workers' Organizations in Pakistan: Why No Role in Formal Politics?" *Critical Asian Studies*, 39 (1): 35–57.

Centre for Media Studies (New Delhi) (2005) *India Corruption Study (2005).* Delhi: Transparency International India available at: http://www.prajanet.org/newsroom/internal/tii/ICS2k5_Vol1.pdf; accessed 5 August 2008.

Chakrabarty, Bidyut (2006) "Jawaharlal Nehru and Administrative Reconstruction in India: A Mere Imitation of the Past or a Creative Initiative?" *South Asia: Journal of South Asian Studies*, 29 (1): 83–99.

Chakravarti, Anand (1975) *Contradiction and Change: Emerging Patterns of Authority in a Rajasthan Village.* Delhi: Oxford University Press.

Chandoke, Neera (2007) "Negotiating Linguistic Diversity: A Comparative Study of India and the United States." In K. Shankar Bajpai (ed.) *Democracy and Diversity: India and the American Experience* (Delhi: Oxford University Press): 107–43.

Chandra, Kanchan (2004) *Why Ethnic Parties Succeed: Patronage and Ethnic Head Counts in India.* Cambridge: Cambridge University Press.

Chaudhuri, Nirad C. (1953) "Subhas Chandra Bose – His Legacy and Legend." *Pacific Affairs*, 26 (4): 349–57.

Chopra, Pran (1974) *India's Second Liberation.* Cambridge, Mass.: MIT Press.

Chowdhury, G. W. (1974) *The Last Days of United Pakistan.* Bloomington: Indiana University Press.

Clapham, Christopher (1986) *Third World Politics.* Madison: University of Wisconsin Press.

Cloughley, Brian (2008) *War, Coups and Terror: Pakistan's Army in Years of Turmoil.* New York: Skyhorse Publishing.

Cockroft, Anne, Neil Andersson, Khalif Omer, Noor Ansari, Amir Khan and Ubaid Ullah Chaudhry (2003) *Social Audit of Governance and Delivery of Public Services. Baseline Report 2002: National Report.* Government of Pakistan, National Reconstruction Bureau and Community Information Empowerment and Training International (CIET) available at: http://www.ciet.org/en/documents/projects_library_docs/2006224174624.pdf; accessed 7 August 2008.

Cockroft, Anne, Neil Andersson, Khalif Omer, Noor Ansari, Amir Khan, Ubaid Ullah Chaudhry and Sohail Saeed (2005) *Social Audit of Governance and Delivery of Public Services. Pakistan 2004/05: National Report.* Devolution Trust for Community Empowerment (DTCE) and Community Information Empowerment and Training International (CIET) available at: http://www.ciet.org/en/documents/projects_library_docs/200622417568.pdf; accessed 7 August 2008.

Cohen, Stephen P. (1963–4) "Subhas Chandra Bose and the Indian National Army." *Pacific Affairs*, 36 (4): 411–29.

Cohen, Stephen P. (1973) *Arms and Politics in Bangladesh, India, and Pakistan.* Special Studies No. 49. Council on International Studies, State University of New York at Buffalo.

Cohen, Stephen P. (1988) "The Military and India's Democracy." In Atul Kohli (ed.) *India's Democracy* (Princeton, NJ: Princeton University Press): 99–143.

Cohen, Stephen P. (1990 [1971]) *The Indian Army: Its Contribution to the Development of a Nation* revised edn. Delhi: Oxford University Press.

Cohen, Stephen P. (1998) *The Pakistan Army: With a New Foreword and Epilogue.* Karachi: Oxford University Press.

Cohen, Stephen Philip (2004) *The Idea of Pakistan.* Washington, DC: Brookings Institution Press.

Cohn, Bernard S. (1959) "Some Notes on Law and Change in North India." *Economic Development and Cultural Change*, 8 (1): 79–93.

Coll, Steve (1994) *On the Grand Trunk Road: A Journey into South Asia.* New York: Times Books/Random House.

Collier, David and Steven Levitsky (1997) "Democracy with Adjectives: Conceptual Innovation in Comparative Research." *World Politics*, 49 (3): 430–51.

Copland, Ian (2005) *State, Community and Neighbourhood in Princely North India, c.1900–1950.* Basingstoke: Palgrave Macmillan.

Corbridge, Stuart and John Harriss (2000) *Reinventing India: Liberalization, Hindu Nationalism, and Popular Democracy.* Delhi: Oxford University Press.

Corbridge, Stuart, Glyn Williams, Manoj Srivastava and René Véron (2005) *Seeing the State: Governance and Governmentality in India.* Cambridge: Cambridge University Press.

Cordesman, Anthony H. (1984) *The Gulf and the Search for Strategic Stability.* Boulder, Colo.: Westview.

Cowasjee, Ardeshir (2007) "States of Emergency." *Dawn*, 18 November.

Cowasjee, Ardeshir (2008a) "Little Time Left." *Dawn*, 27 January.

Cowasjee, Ardeshir (2008b) "No 'Goonda-gardi.'" *Dawn*, 11 May.

Cowasjee, Ardeshir (2008c) "A Date Etched in Memory." *Dawn*, 14 September.

Cowasjee, Ardeshir (2009) "Spirit of the 1973 Constitution." *Dawn*, 28 June.

Croissant, Aurel (2004) "From Transition to Defective Democracy: Mapping Asian Democratization." *Democratization*, 11 (5): 156–78.

Croissant, Aurel and Wolfgang Merkel (2004) "Introduction: Democratization in the Early Twenty-first Century." *Democratization*, 11 (5): 1–9.

Daechsel, Markus (1997) "Military Islamisation in Pakistan and the Spectre of Colonial Perceptions." *Contemporary South Asia*, 6 (2): 141–60.

Dahl, Robert A. (1971) *Polyarchy.* New Haven, Conn.: Yale University Press.

Dahl, Robert A. (1989) *Democracy and Its Critics.* New Haven, Conn.: Yale University Press.

Das, Gurcharan (2008) "Deceits of Our Political Class." *Times of India*, 15 June.

Datta-Chaudhuri, Mrinal (1976) "Fascism." *Seminar 197: India 1975* (January): 29–32.

Desai, Meghnad (1993) "Constructing Nationality in a Multinational Democracy: The Case of India." In Roger Michener (ed.) *Nationality, Patriotism and Nationalism in Liberal Democratic Societies* (St Paul, Minn.: Professors World Peace Academy): 225–38.

Desai, Meghnad (2005) "Why Is India a Democracy?" In Meghnad Desai and Aitzaz Ahsan, *Divided by Democracy* (Delhi: Roli Books): 13–74.

Deshpande, Satish (1993) "Imagined Economies: Styles of Nation-Building in Twentieth Century India." *Journal of Arts and Ideas*, 25–6 (December): 5–35.

deSouza, Peter Ronald, Suhas Palshikar and Yogendra Yadav (2008) "The Democracy Barometers: Surveying South Asia." *Journal of Democracy*, 19 (1): 84–95.

Dewey, Clive (1991) "The Rural Roots of Pakistani Militarism." In D. A. Low (ed.) *The Political Inheritance of Pakistan* (New York: St Martin's Press): 255–83.

Dhagamwar, Vasudha (2006) *Role and Images of Law in India: The Tribal Experience.* New Delhi: Sage.

Dhavan, Rajeev (2000) "Judges and Indian Democracy: The Lesser Evil?" In Francine Frankel, Zoya Hasan, Rajeev Bhargava and Balveer Arora (eds) *Transforming India: Social and Political Dynamics of Democracy* (Delhi: Oxford University Press): 314–52.

Dhavan, Rajeev (2003) "Law's Magic and Empire Revisited: Public Spaces and Private Lives – the Domain of Law." In Gurpreet Mahajan in collaboration with Helmut

Reifeld (ed.) *The Public and the Private: Issues of Democratic Citizenship* (New Delhi: Sage): 149–80.

Djurfeldt, Göran, Venkatesh Athreya, N. Jayakumar, Staffan Lindberg, A. Rajagopal and R. Vidyasagar (2008) "Agrarian Change and Social Mobility in Tamil Nadu." *Economic and Political Weekly*, 45 (43): 50–61.

Donno, Daniela and Bruce Russett (2004) "Islam, Authoritarianism, and Female Empowerment: What Are the Linkages?" *World Politics*, 56 (July): 582–607.

Doorenspleet, Renske, and Cas Mudde (2008) "Upping the Odds: Deviant Democracies and Theories of Democratization." *Democratization*, 15 (4): 815–32.

Drieberg, Trevor and Sarala Jagmohan (1975) *Emergency in India.* New Delhi: Manas.

Dubey, Suman (1992) "The Middle Class." In Leonard A. Gordon and Philip Oldenburg (eds) *India Briefing, 1992* (Boulder, Colo.: Westview): 137–64.

Eckstein, Harry (1996) *Lessons for the "Third Wave" from the First: An Essay on Democratization.* Paper 96-02. Irvine Center for the Study of Democracy, University of California, Irvine available at: http://escholarship.org/uc/item/6c9087q7; accessed 5 May 2010.

El-Gobashy, Mona (2006) "Egypt's Paradoxical Elections." *Middle East Report*, 238 (Spring).

Embree, Ainslie (1983) "The Emergency as a Signpost to India's Future." In Peter Lyon and James Manor (eds) *Transfer and Transformation: Political Institutions in the New Commonwealth* (Leicester: Leicester University Press): 59–67.

Epstein, David L., Robert Bates, Jack Goldstone, Ida Kristensen and Sharyn O'Halloran (2006) "Democratic Transitions." *American Journal of Political Science*, 50 (3): 551–69.

Epstein, Simon (1982) "District Officers in Decline: The Erosion of British Authority in the Bombay Countryside, 1919 to 1947." *Modern Asian Studies*, 16 (3): 493–518.

Epstein, T. Scarlett, A. P. Suryanarayana and T. Thimmegowda (1998) *Village Voices: Forty Years of Rural Transformation in South India.* New Delhi: Sage.

European Union Election Observation Mission (2002) *Pakistan National and Provincial Assembly Election 10 October 2002: Final Report* available at: http://ec.europa.eu/external_relations/human_rights/eu_election_ass_observ/pak/finalreport02.pdf; accessed 6 January 2008.

Ewing, Katherine (1983) "The Politics of Sufism: Redefining the Saints of Pakistan." *Journal of Asian Studies*, 42 (2): 251–68.

FAFEN (Free and Fair Election Network) (2008) *Pakistan General Election 2008: Election Observation Summary and Recommendations for Electoral Reforms* (June); available at: http://www.fafen.org/admin/products/p4860f3015a25e.pdf; accessed 12 September 2008.

Fair, C. Christine (2009) "Pakistan's Democracy: The Army's Quarry?" *Asian Security*, 51 (January): 73–85.

Fallaci, Oriana (1976) *Interview with History.* Trans. John Sheply. New York: Liveright.

Fattah, Moataz A. and Jim Butterfield (2006) "Muslim Cultural Entrepreneurs and the Democracy Debate." *Critique: Critical Middle Eastern Studies*, 15 (1): 49–78.

Fernandes, Leela and Patrick Heller (2006) "Hegemonic Aspirations." *Critical Asian Studies*, 38 (4): 495–522.

Fish, M. Steven (2002) "Islam and Authoritarianism." *World Politics*, 55 (1): 4–37.

Frankel, Francine (2005) *India's Political Economy, 1947–2004*, 2nd edn. Delhi: Oxford University Press.

Frankel, Francine and M. S. A. Rao (eds) (1989) *Dominance and State Power in Modern India: Decline of a Social Order*, 2 vols. Delhi: Oxford University Press.

*Freedom in the World. 1978–*. New York: Freedom House.

Friedman, Harry J. (1960) "Pakistan's Experiment in Basic Democracies." *Pacific Affairs*, 33 (June): 107–25.

Gandhi, Jennifer and Adam Przeworski (2007) "Authoritarian Institutions and the Survival of Autocrats." *Comparative Political Studies*, 40 (11): 1279–1301.

Gazdar, Haris (2009) "Judicial Activism vs Democratic Consolidation in Pakistan." *Economic and Political Weekly*, 54 (32).

Gerring, John, Philip Bond, William T. Barndt and Carola Moreno (2005) "Democracy and Economic Growth: A Historical Perspective." *World Politics*, 57 (April): 323–64.

Ghosh, Papiya (2007) *Partition and the South Asia Diaspora: Extending the Subcontinent*. London: Routledge.

Ghosh, S. K. (1987) *Law Enforcement in Tribal Areas*. New Delhi: Ashish Publishing House.

Gibson, Edward L. (2005) "Boundary Control: Subnational Authoritarianism in Democratic Countries." *World Politics*, 58 (October): 101–32.

Gilani, Ijaz (2008) *Reflection on the Electoral History of Pakistan 1970–2008: A Dispassionate Analysis of How Elections Are Stolen and Will of the People Is Defeated*; available at: http://www.gallup.com.pk/Gilani/History%20of%20Electoral%20 Rigging%20in%20Pakistan%201970-(2008)pdf; accessed 31 October 2008.

Gilani, Ijaz with Jonathan S. Addelton (1985) *Citizens, Slaves, Guestworkers: The Dynamics of Labour Migration from South Asia*. Islamabad: Institute of Policy Studies.

Gilani, Ijaz, M. Fahim Khan and Munawar Iqbal (1981) *Labour Migration from Pakistan to the Middle East and Its Impact on the Domestic Economy*. Research Report No. 126 (June). Islamabad: Pakistan Institute of Development Economics.

Goodnow, Henry Frank (1964) *The Civil Service of Pakistan; Bureaucracy in a New Nation*. New Haven, Conn.: Yale University Press.

Goodson, Larry P. (2008) "Pakistan after Musharraf: The 2008 Elections." *Journal of Democracy*, 19 (4): 6–15.

Gopal, Sarvepellai (1979) *Jawaharlal Nehru: A Biography*, vol. 2, *1947–1956*. Cambridge, Mass.: Harvard University Press.

Gould, Harold A. (1993) "Mandal, Mandir, and Dalits: Melding Class with Ethnoreligious Conflict in India's Tenth General Election." In Harold A. Gould and Sumit Ganguly (eds) *India Votes: Alliance Politics and Minority Governments in the Tenth General Election* (Boulder, Colo.: Westview): 293–340.

Grare, Frédéric (2006) *Islam, Militarism, and the 2007–2008 Elections in Pakistan*. Carnegie Papers No. 70 (August). Washington, DC: Carnegie Endowment for International Peace.

Gregory, Shaun and James Revill (2008) "The Role of the Military in the Cohesion and Stability of Pakistan." *Contemporary South Asia*, 16 (1): 39–61.

Guha, Ramachandra (2005) "Verdicts on India." *Hindu Magazine*, 17 July.

Guha, Ramachandra (2009) "Adivasis, Naxalites, and Democracy." In Rajesh M. Basrur (ed.) *Challenges to Democracy in India* (New Delhi: Oxford University Press): 167–88.

Gupta, Dipak K. (2007) "The Naxalites and the Maoist Movement in India: Birth, Demise, and Reincarnation." *Democracy and Security*, 3 (2): 157–88.

Hadenius, Axel (1992) *Democracy and Development.* Cambridge: Cambridge University Press.

Hadenius, Axel and Jan Teorell (2005) "Cultural and Economic Prerequisites of Democracy: Reassessing Recent Evidence." *Studies in Comparative International Development*, 39 (4): 87–106.

Haksar, P. N. (1979) *Premonitions.* Bombay: Interpress.

Hanif, Mohammed (2008) *A Case of Exploding Mangoes.* New York: Alfred Knopf.

Hansen, Thomas Blom (1999) *The Saffron Wave: Democracy and Hindu Nationalism in Modern India.* Princeton, NJ: Princeton University Press.

Haq, Noor ul (1993) *Making of Pakistan: The Military Perspective.* Islamabad: National Institute of Historical and Cultural Research.

Haqqani, Husain (2005) *Pakistan: Between Mosque and Military.* Washington, DC: Carnegie Endowment for International Peace.

Harrison, Selig (1960) *India: The Most Dangerous Decades.* Princeton, NJ: Princeton University Press.

Harriss, John (2003) "Do Political Regimes Matter? Poverty Reduction and Regime Differences across India." In Peter P. Houtzager and Mick Moore (eds) *Changing Paths: International Development and the New Politics of Inclusion* (Ann Arbor, Mich.: University of Michigan Press): 204–32.

Hart, Henry (ed.) (1975) *Indira Gandhi's India.* Boulder, Colo.: Westview.

Hasan, Mushirul (2001) "India and Pakistan: Why the Difference?" In Mushirul Hasan and Nariaki Nakazato (eds) *The Unfinished Agenda* (New Delhi: Manohar): 309–43.

Hasan, Zoya, E. Sridharan and R. Sudarshan (eds) (2002) *India's Living Constitution: Ideas, Practices, Controversies.* Delhi: Permanent Black.

Hayat, Sikandar (2008) *The Charismatic Leader: Quaid-i-Azam Mohammad Ali Jinnah and the Creation of Pakistan.* Karachi: Oxford University Press.

Heeger, Gerald A. (1977) "Politics in the Post-Military State: Some Reflections on the Pakistan Experience." Research Note, *World Politics*, 29 (2): 242–62.

Heller, Patrick (2000) "Degrees of Democracy: Some Comparative Lessons from India." *World Politics*, 52 (4): 484–519.

Henderson, Michael (1977) *Experiment with Untruth: India under Emergency.* Delhi: Macmillan.

Herb, Michael (2003) "Taxation and Representation." *Studies in Comparative International Development*, 38 (3): 3–31.

Herb, Michael (2005) "No Representation without Taxation? Rents, Development, and Democracy." *Comparative Politics*, 37 (3): 297–316.

Herring, Ronald J. (1979) "Zulfikar Ali Bhutto and the 'Eradication of Feudalism' in Pakistan." *Comparative Studies in Society and History*, 21 (4): 519–57.

Herring, Ronald J. and Rina Agarawala (2006) "Introduction [to the special issue, *Recovering Class – Observations from the Subcontinent*]: Restoring Agency to Class. Puzzles from the Subcontinent." *Critical Asian Studies*, 38 (4): 323–56.

Hill, Polly (1986) *Development Economics on Trial: The Anthropological Case for a Prosecution.* Cambridge: Cambridge University Press.

Hobsbawm, E. J. (1992) *Nations and Nationalism since 1780: Programme, Myth, Reality*, 2nd edn. Cambridge: Cambridge University Press.

Hodson, H. V. (1968) "The Role of Lord Mountbatten." In C. H. Philips and Mary Doreen Wainwright (eds) *The Partition of India: Policies and Perspectives 1935–1947* (Cambridge: MIT Press): 117–26.

Hofmann, Steven Ryan (2004) "Islam and Democracy: Micro-Level Indications of Compatibility." *Comparative Political Studies*, 37 (6): 652–76.

Hoodbhoy, Pervez (2008) "Pakistan's Westward Drift." *HIMAL Southasian* (September); available at: http://www.himalmag.com/Pakistan-s-westward-drift_nw1947.html; accessed September 2008.

Horowitz, Donald L. (1985) *Ethnic Groups in Conflict.* Berkeley: University of California Press.

Horowitz, Donald L. (1991) *A Democratic South Africa? Constitutional Engineering in a Divided Society.* Berkeley, Calif.: University of California Press; available at: http://ark.cdlib.org/ark:/13030/ft0f59n6zd/; accessed 31 May 2007.

Houle, Christian (2009) "Inequality and Democracy: Why Inequality Harms Consolidation but Does Not Affect Democratization." *World Politics*, 61 (4): 589–622.

Huber, Evelyne, Dietrich Rueschemeyer and John D. Stephens (1997) "The Paradoxes of Contemporary Democracy: Formal, Participatory, and Social Democracy." *Comparative Politics*, 29 (3): 323–42.

Human Rights Watch (2006) *"Everyone Lives in Fear": Patterns of Impunity in Jammu and Kashmir*; available at: http://www.hrw.org/en/reports/2006/09/11/everyone-lives-fear; accessed 7 June 2009.

Human Rights Watch (2009) *Broken System: Dysfunction, Abuse, and Impunity in the Indian Police* (August); available at: http://www.hrw.org/sites/default/files/reports/india0809web.pdf; accessed 4 August 2009.

Hunt, Roland and John Harrison (1980) *The District Officer in India, 1930–1947.* London: Scolar Press.

India, Government of (2006) *Social, Economic and Educational Status of the Muslim Community of India: A Report.* [Report of the Sachar Commission (Prime Minister's High Level Committee)]. New Delhi: Government of India.

India, Ministry of Agriculture, Department of Agriculture & Cooperation (n.d.) "Analysis of Trends in Operational Holdings (Consolidated Report)." Executive Summary; available at: http://agricoop.nic.in/study7.htm; accessed 22 September 2008.

Inglehart, Ronald and Christian Welzel (2003) "Political Culture and Democracy: Analyzing Cross-Level Linkages." *Comparative Politics*, 36 (1): 61–79.

International Crisis Group (2002a) *Pakistan: Madrasas, Extremism and the Military.* Asia Report No. 36.

International Crisis Group (2002b) *Pakistan: Transition to Democracy?* Asian Report No. 40.

International Crisis Group (2003) *Pakistan: The Mullahs and the Military.* Asia Report No. 49.

International Crisis Group (2004a) *Devolution in Pakistan: Reform or Regression?* Asia Report No. 77.

International Crisis Group (2004b) *Building Judicial Independence in Pakistan.* Asia Report No. 86.

International Crisis Group (2005) *Authoritarianism and Political Party Reform in Pakistan.* Asia Report No. 102.

International Crisis Group (2006) *Pakistan's Tribal Areas: Appeasing the Militants.* Asia Report No. 125.

International Crisis Group (2007a) *Pakistan: Karachi's Madrassas and Violent Extremism.* Asia Report No. 130.

International Crisis Group (2007b) *Elections, Democracy and Stability in Pakistan.* Asia Report No. 137.

International Crisis Group (2008a) *Reforming Pakistan's Police.* Asia Briefing No. 157.

International Crisis Group (2008b) *Bangladesh: Elections and Beyond.* Asia Briefing No. 184.

International Institute for Strategic Studies (2008) *The Military Balance 2008.* London: Routledge.

International Republican Institute (2008) *Survey of Pakistan Public Opinion, January 19–29 (2008)*; available at: http://www.iri.org/mena/pakistan/pdfs/2008%20February%2011%20IRI%20Pakistan%20Index,%20January%2019-29,%20(2008)pdf; accessed 3 October 2009.

International Republican Institute (2009) *Survey of Pakistan Public Opinion, July 15–August 7 (2009)*; available at: http://www.iri.org/newsreleases/2009-10-01-IRI_Releases_Survey_of_Pakistan_Public_Opinion.asp; accessed 2 October 2009.

Irfani, Suroosh (2004) "Pakistan's Sectarian Violence: Between the 'Arabist Shift' and Indo-Persian Culture." In Satu P. Limaye, Mohan Malik and Robert G. Wirsing (eds) *Religious Radicalism and Security in South Asia* (Honolulu, Hawaii: Asia-Pacific Center for Security Studies): 147–69.

Islam, Nasir (2001) "Democracy and Governance in Pakistan's Fragmented Society." *International Journal of Public Administration*, 24 (12): 1335–55.

Jacobsohn, Gary Jeffrey (2003) *The Wheel of Law: India's Secularism in Comparative Constitutional Context.* Princeton, NJ: Princeton University Press.

Jaffrelot, Christophe (1994) *The Hindu Nationalist Movement and Indian Politics: 1925 to the 1990s.* New York: Columbia University Press.

Jaffrelot, Christophe (2000) "Hindu Nationalism and Democracy." In Francine R. Frankel, Zoya Hasan, Rajeev Bhargava and Balveer Arora (eds) *Transforming India: Social and Political Dynamics of Democracy* (Delhi: Oxford University Press): 352–78.

Jaffrelot, Christophe (2002) "India and Pakistan: Interpreting the Divergence of Two Political Trajectories." *Cambridge Review of International Affairs*, 15 (2): 251–67.

Jaffrelot, Christophe (2003) *India's Silent Revolution: The Rise of the Low Castes in North Indian Politics.* Delhi: Permanent Black.

Jaffrelot, Christophe (2008) " 'Why Should We Vote?' – the Indian Middle Class and the Functioning of the World's Largest Democracy." In Cristophe Jaffrelot and Peter van der Veer (eds) *Patterns of Middle Class Consumption in India and China* (New Delhi: Sage): 35–54.

Jaffrelot, Christophe (2009) "The Militias of Hindutva: Communal Violence, Terrorism and Cultural Policing." In Laurent Gayer and Christophe Jaffrelot (eds) *Armed Militias of South Asia: Fundamentalists, Maoists and Separatists* (New York: Columbia University Press): 199–236.

Jaffrelot, Christophe and Sanjay Kumar (eds) (2009) *Rise of the Plebeians? The Changing Face of Indian Legislative Assemblies.* London: Routledge.

Jahan, Rounaq (1972) *Pakistan: Failure in National Integration.* New York: Columbia University Press.

Jahangir, Asma (2009) "Another Aspect of the Judgment." *Dawn*, 19 December.

Jalal, Ayesha (1985a) *The Sole Spokesman: Jinnah, the Muslim League, and the Demand for Pakistan.* Cambridge: Cambridge University Press.

Jalal, Ayesha (1985b) "Inheriting the Raj: Jinnah and the Governor-Generalship Issue." *Modern Asian Studies*, 19 (1): 29–53.

Jalal, Ayesha (1995) *Democracy and Authoritarianism in South Asia.* Cambridge: Cambridge University Press.

Jalal, Ayesha (1999 [1990]) *The State of Martial Rule: The Origins of Pakistan's Political Economy of Defence.* Lahore/Cambridge: Sang-e-Meel/Cambridge University Press.

Jaoul, Nicolas (2009) "Naxalism in Bihar: From Bullet to Ballot." In Laurent Gayer and Christophe Jaffrelot (eds) *Armed Militias of South Asia: Fundamentalists, Maoists and Separatists* (New York: Columbia University Press): 21–44.

Jayal, Niraja Gopal, Amit Prakash and Pradeep K. Sharma (eds) (2006) *Local Governance in India: Decentralization and Beyond.* Delhi: Oxford University Press.

Jeffrey, Craig (2000) "Democratisation without Representation? The Power and Political Strategies of a Rural Elite in North India." *Political Geography*, 19 (8): 1013–36.

Jeffrey, Robin (2000) *India's Newspaper Revolution: Capitalism, Politics and the Indian-Language Press, 1977–99.* London: Hurst.

Jenkins, Rob (1999) *Democratic Politics and Economic Reform in India.* Cambridge: Cambridge University Press.

Jenkins, Rob (ed.) (2004) *Regional Reflections: Comparing Politics across India's States.* Delhi: Oxford University Press.

Jinnah, M. A. (2000) *Jinnah Speeches and Statements 1947–48.* Introduction by S. M. Burke. Karachi: Oxford University Press.

Jones, Philip E. (2003) *The Pakistan People's Party: Rise to Power.* Karachi: Oxford University Press.

Kapur, Devesh (2005) "Explaining Democratic Durability and Economic Performance: The Role of India's Institutions." In Devesh Kapur and Pratap Bhanu Mehta (eds) *Public Institutions in India; Performance and Design* (Delhi: Oxford University Press): 28–76.

Katzenstein, Mary, Smitu Kothari and Uday Mehta (2001) "Social Movement Politics in India: Institutions, Interests, and Identities." In Atul Kohli (ed.) *The Success of India's Democracy* (Cambridge: Cambridge University Press): 242–69.

Kennedy, Charles H. (1990) "Islamization and Legal Reform in Pakistan, 1979–1989." *Pacific Affairs*, 63 (1): 62–77.

Kennedy, Charles H. (1993) "Judicial Activism and Islamization after Zia: Towards the Prohibition of *Riba.*" In Charles H. Kennedy (ed.) *Pakistan: 1992* (Boulder, Colo.: Westview Press): 57–74.

Kennedy, Charles H. (2005) "Constitutional and Political Change in Pakistan: The Military-Governance Paradigm." In Rafiq Dossani and Henry S. Rowen (eds) *Prospects for Peace in South Asia* (Stanford, Calif.: Stanford University Press): 37–74.

Khan, Adeel (2008) "Pakistan in 2007: More Violent, More Unstable." *Asian Survey*, 48 (1): 144–53.

Khan, Ayesha (2006) "Déjà vu: The Fantasy of Benign Military Rule in Pakistan." In Naeem Inayatullah and Robin L. Riley (eds) *Interrogating Imperialism: Conversations on Gender, Race, and War* (London: Palgrave Macmillan): 101–27.

Khan, Hamid (2001) *Constitutional and Political History of Pakistan.* Karachi: Oxford University Press.

Khan, M. Sarwar (n.d.; ca 2006) "Reforming the Judiciary – More of the Same." Government of Pakistan, Access to Justice Program website; available at: http://www.ajp.gov.pk/articles/sarwar_khan_01_reforming_the_judiciary.asp?print=True; accessed 7 August 2008.

Khan, Shahrukh Rafi, Foqia Sadiq Khan and Aasim Sajjad Akhtar (2007) *Initiating Devolution for Service Delivery in Pakistan: Ignoring the Power Structure.* Karachi: Oxford University Press.

Khilnani, Sunil (1997) *The Idea of India.* New York: Farrar, Straus, Giroux.

Kohli, Atul (ed.) (2001) *The Success of India's Democracy.* Cambridge: Cambridge University Press.

Kohn, Richard H. (1997) "How Democracies Control the Military." *Journal of Democracy*, 8 (4): 140–53.

Kothari, Rajni (1988) "Why Has India Been Democratic?" In Rajni Kothari, *State against Democracy: In Search of Humane Governance* (Delhi: Ajanta Publications), pp. 154–76.

Kothari, Shanti and Ramashray Roy (1969) *Relations between Politicians and Administrators at the District Level.* New Delhi: Indian Institute of Public Administration.

Kozlowski, Gregory C. (1995) "Loyalty, Locality and Authority in Several Opinions (Fatāwā) Delivered by the Muftī of the Jami'ah Nizāmiyyah Madrasah, Hyderabad, India." *Modern Asian Studies*, 29 (4): 893–927.

Kozlowski, Gregory C. (1997) "Islamic Law in Contemporary South Asia." *Muslim World*, 87 (3–4): 221–34.

Krishna, Anirudh (2002) *Active Social Capital: Tracing the Roots of Development and Democracy.* New York: Columbia University Press.

Krishna, Anirudh (2006) "Poverty and Democratic Participation Reconsidered: Evidence from the Local Level in India." *Comparative Politics*, 38 (4): 439–58.

Krishna, Anirudh (2007) "Politics in the Middle: Mediating Relationships between the Citizens and the State in Rural North India." In Herbert Kitschelt and Steven I. Wilkinson (eds) *Patrons, Clients, and Policies: Patterns of Democratic Accountability and Political Competition* (Cambridge: Cambridge University Press): 141–58.

Kumar, Girish (2006) *Local Democracy in India: Interpreting Decentralization.* New Delhi: Sage.

Kumar, Ravinder (1989) "The Historical Roots of Democracy in India." In Ravinder Kumar, *The Making of a Nation: Essays in Indian History and Politics* (Delhi: Manohar): 229–44. From *Harvard International Review*, May 1985.

Kumar, Ravinder (2002) "India: A 'Nation-State' or 'Civilisation-State'?" *South Asia: Journal of South Asian Studies*, 25 (2): 13–32.

Kundu, Apurba (1998) *Militarism in India: The Army and Civil Society in Consensus.* London: Tauris Academic Studies.

Kunnath, George J. (2006) "Becoming a Naxalite in Rural Bihar: Class Struggle and Its Contradictions." *Journal of Peasant Studies*, 33 (1): 89–123.

Kurin, Richard (1987) "Islamization: A View from the Countryside." In Anita Weiss (ed.) *Islamic Reassertion in Pakistan: The Application of Islamic Laws in a Modern State* (Syracuse, NY/Lahore: Syracuse University Press/Vanguard): 115–28.

Kux, Dennis (2001) *The United States and Pakistan 1947–2000: Disenchanted Allies.* Washington, DC/Baltimore, Md: Wilson Center Press/Johns Hopkins University Press.

Lancaster, John (2002) "Pakistanis Question Perks of Power: Many Say Military Confuses National Interest with Its Own." *Washington Post*, 22 November: A1.

LaPorte, Jr, Robert (1973) "Pakistan in 1972: Picking up the Pieces." *Asian Survey*, 13 (2): 187–98.

LaPorte, Jr, Robert (1992) "Administration." In William E. James and Subroto Roy (eds) *Foundations of Pakistan's Political Economy: Towards an Agenda for the 1990s* (New Delhi: Sage): 102–15.

Larson, Gerald James (ed.) (2001) *Religion and Personal Law in Secular India*. Delhi: Social Science Press.

Lau, Martin (2006) *The Role of Islam in the Legal System of Pakistan*, the London–Leiden Series on Law, Administration and Development. Leiden: Marinus Nijhoff.

Lindsay, Jonathan M. and Richard Gordon (1993) "Reflections on Law and Meaningfulness in a North Indian Hindu Village." In Robert D. Baird (ed.) *Religion and Law in Independent India* (Delhi: Manohar): 361–86.

Linz, Juan J. (1978) *Breakdown of Democratic Regimes: Crisis, Breakdown, and Reequilibration*. Baltimore, Md: Johns Hopkins University Press.

Linz, Juan J. and Alfred Stepan (1996) *Problems of Democratic Transition and Consolidation: Southern Europe, South America, and Post-Communist Europe*. Baltimore, Md/London: Johns Hopkins University Press.

Linz, Juan J., Alfred Stepan and Yogendra Yadav (2007) "'Nation State' or 'State Nation'? India in Comparative Perspective." In K. Shankar Bajpai (ed.) *Democracy and Diversity: India and the American Experience* (Delhi: Oxford University Press): 50–106.

Lodi, F. S. (1998) "General Jahangir Karamat." *Defence Journal* (November); online at: http://www.defencejournal.com/nov98/genjehangir.htm; accessed November 4, 2008.

Low, D. A. (1997) *Britain and Indian Nationalism 1928–1942*. New York: Cambridge University Press.

Low, D. A. (2002) "Pakistan and India: Political Legacies from the Colonial Past." *South Asia: Journal of South Asian Studies*, 25 (2): 257–72.

McGrath, Allen (1996) *The Destruction of Pakistan's Democracy*. Karachi: Oxford University Press.

Maguire, Edward R. and Rebecca Schulte-Murray (2001) "Issues and Patterns in the Comparative Study of Police Strength." *International Journal of Comparative Sociology*, 24 (1–2): 75–100.

McKinsey, Kitty (2007) "The Biharis of Bangladesh." *Refugees* [a UNHCR publication], 147 (3): 12–13 [Box].

McMillan, Alistair (2005) *Standing at the Margins: Representation and Electoral Reservation in India*. Delhi: Oxford University Press.

McMillan, Alistair (2008) "Deviant Democratization in India." *Democratization*, 15 (4): 733–49.

Madsen, Stig Toft (1996) *State, Society, and Human Rights in South Asia*. Delhi: Manohar.

Mahadevan, Prem (2008) "The Gill Doctrine: A Model for 21st Century Counter-Terrorism?" *Faultlines*, 19 (April), available at: http://satp.org/satporgtp/publication/faultlines/volume19/Article1.htm; accessed 5 August 2008.

Mahajan, Sucheta (2000) *Independence and Partition: The Erosion of Colonial Power in India*. New Delhi: Sage.

Malik, Iftikhar H. (2001) "Military Coup in Pakistan: Business as Usual or Democracy on Hold!" *Round Table*, 360 (July): 357–77.

Malik, Jamal (1996) *Colonialization of Islam: Dissolution of Traditional Institutions in Pakistan.* Delhi/Lahore: Manohar/Vanguard.

Manor, James (1988) "Parties and the Party System." In Atul Kohli (ed.) *India's Democracy* (Princeton, NJ: Princeton University Press): 62–98.

Manor, James (1990) "How and Why Liberal and Representative Politics Emerged in India." *Political Studies*, 38 (1): 20–38.

Manor, James (2000) "Small-Time Political Fixers in India's States." *Asian Survey*, 40 (5): 816–35.

Manor, James (2002) "Changing State, Changing Society in India." *South Asia: Journal of South Asian Studies*, 25 (2): 231–56.

Manor, James (2007) "Successful Governance Reforms in Two Indian States: Karnataka and Andhra Pradesh." *Journal of Commonwealth and Comparative Politics*, 45 (4): 425–51.

Markovits, Claude (2002) "Cross-Currents in the Historiography of Partition." In Soofia Mumtaz, Jean-Luc Racine and Imran Anwar Ali (eds) *Pakistan: The Contours of State and Society* (Karachi: Oxford University Press): 3–21.

Mayer, Peter (1984) "Congress (I), Emergency (I): Interpreting Indira Gandhi's India." *Journal of Commonwealth and Comparative Politics*, 22 (2): 128–50.

Mehra, Ajay K. (2003) "Historical Development of the Party Systems in India." In Ajay K. Mehra, D. D. Khanna and Gert W. Kueck (eds) *Political Parties and Party Systems* (New Delhi: Sage): 49–82.

Mehta, Pratap Bhanu (2004) "Hinduism and Self-Rule." *Journal of Democracy*, 15 (3): 108–22.

Mehta, Pratap Bhanu (2005) "India's Judiciary: The Promise of Uncertainty." In Devesh Kapur and Pratap Bhanu Mehta (eds) *Public Institutions in India; Performance and Design* (Delhi: Oxford University Press): 158–93.

Mendelsohn, Oliver (1981) "The Pathology of the Indian Legal System." *Modern Asian Studies*, 15 (4): 823–63.

Mendelsohn, Oliver (1993) "The Transformation of Authority in Rural India." *Modern Asian Studies*, 27 (4): 805–42.

Menon, Kavita (2000) *Pakistan: The Press for Change.* New York: Committee to Protect Journalists, available at: http://www.cpj.org/Briefings/2000/Pakistan_feb00/Pakistan07feb00Br.html; accessed 5 June 2007.

Michelutti, Lucia (2008) *The Vernacularisation of Democracy: Politics, Caste, and Religion in India.* New Delhi/London: Routledge.

Mines, Mattison and Vijayalakshmi Gourishankar (1990) "Leadership and Individuality in South Asia: The Case of the South Indian Big-Man." *Journal of Asian Studies*, 49 (4): 761–86.

Minkenberg, Michael (2007) "Democracy and Religion: Theoretical and Empirical Observations on the Relationship between Christianity, Islam and Liberal Democracy." *Journal of Ethnic and Migration Studies*, 33 (6): 887–909.

Misra, B. B. (1977) *The Bureaucracy in India: An Historical Analysis of Development up to 1947.* Delhi: Oxford University Press.

Misra, B. B. (1986) *Government and Bureaucracy in India, 1947–1976.* Delhi: Oxford University Press.

Mitra, Ashok (1991) *Towards Independence, 1940–1947; Memoirs of an Indian Civil Servant.* Bombay: Popular Prakashan.

Mitra, Subrata K. and V. B. Singh (1999) *Democracy and Social Change in India: A Cross-Sectional Analysis of the National Electorate.* New Delhi: Sage.

Mohammad, Fida and Paul Conway (2005) "Political Culture, Hegemony, and Inequality before the Law: Law Enforcement in Pakistan." *Policing: An International Journal of Police Strategies and Management*, 28 (4): 631–41.

Moog, Robert S. (1997) *Whose Interests Are Supreme?: Organizational Politics in the Civil Courts in India*, Monograph and Occasional Paper Series No. 54. Ann Arbor, Mich.: Association for Asian Studies.

Morris-Jones, W. H. (1957) *Parliament in India*. Philadelphia, Pa: University of Pennsylvania Press.

Morris-Jones, W. H. (1964) *The Government and Politics of India*. London: Hutchinson University Library.

Morris-Jones, W. H. (1988) "'If It Be Real, What Does It Mean?': Some British Perceptions of the Indian National Congress." In Richard Sisson and Stanley Wolpert (eds) *Congress and Indian Nationalism: The Pre-Independence Phase* (Delhi: Oxford University Press): 90–118.

Mujahid, Sharif al (1980) "The 1977 Pakistani Elections: An Analysis." In Manzooruddin Ahmed (ed.) *Contemporary Pakistan: Politics, Economy, and Society* (Durham, NC: Carolina Academic Press): 63–91.

Muller, Edward N. (1985) "Dependent Economic Development, Aid Dependence on the United States, and Democratic Breakdown in the Third World." *International Studies Quarterly*, 29 (4): 445–69.

Mustafa, Hala and Augustus Richard Norton (2007) "Stalled Reform: The Case of Egypt." *Current History*, 106 (696): 39–41.

Nandy, Ashis, Shikha Trivedy, Sail Mayaram and Achyut Yagnik (1995) *Creating a Nationality: The Ramjanmabhumi Movement and Fear of the Self*. Delhi: Oxford University Press.

Narain, Iqbal (1978) "India (1977): From Promise to Disenchantment?" *Asian Survey*, 18 (2): 103–16.

Narayan, Jayaprakash (2001) "Distorted Verdicts." *Seminar 506: Reforming Politics* (October): 42–9.

Narayan, Jayaprakash (2009) "Organized Crime, Corruption, and Democracy." In Rajesh M. Basrur (ed.) *Challenges to Democracy in India* (New Delhi: Oxford University Press): 99–126.

Nasr, Vali R. (1992) "Democracy and the Crisis of Governability in Pakistan." *Asian Survey*, 32 (6): 521–37.

Nasr, Vali R. (2002) "Islam, the State and the Rise of Sectarian Militancy in Pakistan." In Christophe Jaffrelot (ed.) *Pakistan: Nationalism without a Nation?* (Delhi/London: Manohar/Zed Press): 85–114.

Nasr, Vali R. (2005) "The Rise of 'Muslim Democracy.'" *Journal of Democracy*, 16 (2): 13–27.

Nawaz, Shuja (2008) *Crossed Swords: Pakistan, Its Army, and the Wars Within*. Karachi: Oxford University Press.

Nayar, Baldev Raj (1974) "Political Mainsprings of Economic Planning in the New Nations." *Comparative Politics*, 6 (3): 341–66.

Nehru, Jawaharlal (1941) *Toward Freedom: The Autobiography of Jawaharlal Nehru*. New York: John Day Company.

Nehru, Jawaharlal (2007) *The Oxford India Nehru*. Edited by Uma Iyengar. New Delhi: Oxford University Press.

Nelson, Matthew J. (2009) "Pakistan in 2008: Moving beyond Musharraf." *Asian Survey*, 49 (1): 16–27.

Newberg, Paula R. (1995) *Judging the State: Courts and Constitutional Politics in Pakistan.* Cambridge: Cambridge University Press.

Newman, K. J. (1959) "Pakistan's Preventive Autocracy and Its Causes." *Pacific Affairs,* 32 (1): 18–33.

Niazi, Zamir (1986) *The Press in Chains.* Karachi: Royal Book Company.

Niazi, Zamir (1992) *The Press under Siege.* Karachi: Karachi Press Club.

Niazi, Zamir (1994) *The Web of Censorship.* Karachi: Oxford University Press.

Niazi, Zamir (1997) "Towards a Free Press." In Victoria Schofield (ed.) *Old Roads New Highways: Fifty Years of Pakistan* (Karachi: Oxford University Press): 174–95.

Nigam, R. K. (ed.) (1985) *Memoirs of Old Mandarins of India: The Administrative Change as the ICS Administrators Saw in India.* New Delhi: Documentation Centre for Corporate and Business Policy Research.

Ninan, Sevanti (2007) *Headlines from the Heartland: Reinventing the Hindi Public Sphere.* New Delhi: Sage.

Ninan, T. N. (2009) "A Grim Challenge." *Business Standard,* 3 October.

Noman, Omar (1990) *Pakistan: Political and Economic History since 1947,* revised edn. London: Kegan, Paul.

Noorani, A. G. (2001) "Jinnah and Junagadh." *Frontline,* 18 (20 and 21).

Noorani, A. G. (2008) "Army with a Nation." *Frontline,* 25 (14).

Norris, Pippa and Ronald Inglehart (2004) *Sacred and Secular: Religion and Politics Worldwide.* Cambridge: Cambridge University Press.

Ocko, Jonathan K. and David Gilmartin (2009) "State, Sovereignty, and the People: A Comparison of the 'Rule of Law' in China and India." *Journal of Asian Studies,* 68 (1): 55–133.

O'Donnell, Guillermo and Philippe C. Schmitter (1986) *Transitions from Authoritarian Rule: Tentative Conclusions about Uncertain Democracies.* Baltimore, Md: Johns Hopkins University Press.

O'Donnell, Guillermo, Philippe C. Schmitter and Laurence Whitehead (eds) (1986) *Transitions from Authoritarian Rule: Prospects for Democracy.* Baltimore, Md: Johns Hopkins University Press.

Oldenburg, Philip (1976) *Big City Government in India: Councilor, Administrator, and Citizen in Delhi,* Association for Asian Studies Monograph XXXI. Tucson: University of Arizona Press.

Oldenburg, Philip (1985) "'A Place Insufficiently Imagined': Language, Belief, and the Pakistan Crisis of 1971." *Journal of Asian Studies,* 44 (4): 711–33.

Oldenburg, Philip (1987) "Middlemen in Third World Corruption: Implications of an Indian Case." *World Politics,* 39 (4): 508–35.

Oldenburg, Philip (1990) "Land Consolidation as Land Reform, in India." *World Development,* 18 (2): 183–95.

Oldenburg, Philip (1991) "Politics: How Threatening a Crisis?" In Philip Oldenburg (ed.) *India Briefing 1991* (Boulder, Colo.: Westview): 11–44.

Oldenburg, Philip (2005) "Face to Face with the Indian State at the Grassroots." In L. C. Jain (ed.) *Decentralisation and Local Governance* (Delhi: Orient Longman): 132–63.

Overstreet, Gene D. (1970) "The Hindu Code Bill." In Lucien W. Pye (ed.) *Cases in Comparative Politics: Asia* (Boston, Mass.: Little, Brown): 161–88.

Pak Institute for Peace Studies (2009) *Pakistan Security Report (2008),* available at: http://san-pips.com/index.php; accessed 5 October 2009.

Palmer, Norman D. (1975) *Elections and Political Development: The South Asian Experience.* Durham, NC: Duke University Press.

Palmer, Norman D. (1976) "India in 1975: Democracy in Eclipse." *Asian Survey,* 16 (2): 95–110.

Palshikar, Suhas (2001) "Politics of India's Middle Classes." In Imtiaz Ahmad and Helmut Reifeld (eds) *Middle Class Values in India and Western Europe* (New Delhi: Social Science Press): 171–93.

Park, Richard L. (1954) "East Bengal: Pakistan's Troubled Province." *Far Eastern Survey,* 23 (5): 70–4.

Park, Richard L. (1975) "Political Crisis in India, 1975." *Asian Survey,* 15 (11): 996–1013.

Pew Research Center (2009) *Pakistani Public Opinion: Growing Concerns about Extremism, Continuing Discontent with US,* Pew Global Attitudes Project, 13 August.

PIPS *see* Pak Institute for Peace Studies.

Pollock, Sheldon (1993) "Ramayana and Political Imagination in India." *Journal of Asian Studies,* 52 (2): 261–97.

Potter, David C. (1973) "Manpower Shortage and the End of Colonialism: The Case of the Indian Civil Service." *Modern Asian Studies,* 7 (1): 47–73.

Potter, David C. (1979) "The Last of the Indian Civil Service." *South Asia: Journal of South Asian Studies,* 2 (1–2): 19–29.

Potter, David C. (1986) *India's Political Administrators, 1919–1983.* Oxford: Clarendon Press.

Pradhan, Fakir Mohan (2009) "Andhra Pradesh: Maoist Free Fall." *South Asia Intelligence Review,* 8 (23), available at: http://www.satp.org/satporgtp/sair/index.htm; accessed 14 December 2009.

Price, Pamela (2006) "Changing Meanings of Authority in Contemporary Rural India." *Qualitative Sociology,* 29 (3): 301–16.

Pritchard, Iltudus (1900? [1870]) *Chronicles of Budgepore.* London: Richard Edward King.

Przeworski, Adam (1986) "Some Problems in the Study of the Transition to Democracy." In Guillermo O'Donnell, Philippe C. Schmitter and Laurence Whitehead (eds) *Transitions from Authoritarian Rule: Comparative Perspective* (Baltimore, Md: Johns Hopkins University Press): 47–63.

Przeworski, Adam (2006) "Self-Enforcing Democracy." In Donald Wittman and Barry Weingast (eds) *The Oxford Handbook of Political Economy* (New York: Oxford University Press): 312–28.

Przeworski, Adam and Fernando Limongi (1997) "Modernization: Theories and Facts." *World Politics,* 49 (2): 155–83.

Quinlivan, James T. (1999) "Coup-Proofing: Its Practice and Consequences in the Middle East." *International Security,* 24 (2): 131–65.

Qureshi, Salim (2008) "Restoration of Democracy in Pakistan: A Critical Analysis of Political Culture and Historical Legacy." In Veena Kukreja and Mahendra Prasad Singh (eds) *Democracy, Development, and Discontent in South Asia* (New Delhi: Sage): 76–104.

Rahman, Fazlur (1966) "The Controversy over the Muslim Family Laws." In Donald Eugene Smith (ed.) *South Asian Politics and Religion* (Princeton, NJ: Princeton University Press): 414–27.

Rahman, Tariq (1995) "Language and Politics in a Pakistan Province: The Sindhi Language Movement." *Asian Survey,* 35 (11): 1005–16.

Rahman, Tariq (2002) *Language, Ideology and Power: Language-Learning among the Muslims of Pakistan and North India.* Karachi: Oxford University Press.

Rais, Rasul Bakhsh (2007) "Identity Politics and Minorities in Pakistan." *South Asia: Journal of South Asian Studies*, 30 (1): 111–25.

Ram, N. (2000) "The Great Indian Media Bazaar: Emerging Trends and Issues for the Future." In Romila Thapar (ed.) *India: Another Millennium?* (New Delhi: Viking): 241–92.

Ranga, N. G. (1986) [Cited by Austin (1999: 27) as "reminiscence by"] *Journal of Parliamentary Information*, 32 (2).

Rashid, Ahmed (2008) *Descent into Chaos: The United States and the Failure of Nation Building in Pakistan, Afghanistan, and Central Asia.* New York: Viking.

Reddy, G. Ram and G. Haragopal (1985) "The Pyraveekar: 'The Fixer' in Rural India." *Asian Survey*, 25 (11): 1148–62.

Rehman, Inamur (1982) *Public Opinion and Political Development in Pakistan 1947–1958.* Karachi: Oxford University Press.

Richter, William L. (1980) "From Electoral Politics to Martial Law: Alternative Perspectives on Pakistan's Political Crisis of 1977." In Manzooruddin Ahmed (ed.) *Contemporary Pakistan: Politics, Economy, and Society* (Durham, NC: Carolina Academic Press): 92–113.

Riggs, Fred W. (1963) "Bureaucrats and Political Development: A Paradoxical View." In Joseph LaPalombara (ed.) *Bureaucracy and Political Development* (Princeton, NJ: Princeton University Press): 120–67.

Riggs, Fred W. (1981) "The Rise and Fall of Political Development." In S. Long (ed.) *Handbook of Political Behavior* (New York: Plenum), vol. 4: 289–349.

Riggs, Fred W. (1993) "Fragility of the Third World's Regimes." *International Social Science Journal*, 45 (2): 199–243.

Rittenberg, Stephen (1988) *Ethnicity, Nationalism, and the Pakhtuns.* Durham, NC: Carolina Academic Press.

Rizvi, Gowher (1985) "Riding the Tiger: Institutionalising the Military Regimes in Pakistan and Bangladesh." In Christopher Clapham and George Philip (eds) *The Political Dilemmas of Military Regimes* (London: Croom Helm): 201–36.

Rizvi, Hasan-Askari (1999) "Pakistan in 1998: The Polity under Pressure." *Asian Survey*, 39 (1): 177–84.

Rizvi, Hasan-Askari (2003a) *Military, State and Society in Pakistan.* London/ Lahore: Macmillan/Sang-e-Meel.

Rizvi, Hasan-Askari (2003b) "How to Judge Pakistani Democracy?" *Daily Times*, 17 March.

Rizvi, Hasan-Askari (2005) *National Security Council: A Comparative Study of Pakistan and Other Selected Countries*, PILDAT Background Paper. Islamabad: Pakistan Institute of Legislative Development and Transparency, available at: http://fes.org.pk/publications/969-558-015-7.pdf; accessed 2 December 2007.

Rizvi, Hasan-Askari (2008) "Saving Pakistan." *Daily Times*, 20 July.

Rizvi, Hasan-Askari (2009) "Protecting Democracy." *Daily Times*, 20 March.

Robinson, Francis (1992) "Origins." In William E. James and Subroto Roy (eds) *Foundations of Pakistan's Political Economy: Towards an Agenda for the 1990s* (New Delhi: Sage): 33–57.

Robinson, Marguerite (1988) *Local Politics: The Law of the Fishes.* Delhi: Oxford University Press.

Rosen, George (1985) *Western Economists and Eastern Societies: Agents of Change in South Asia, 1950–1970.* Delhi: Oxford University Press.

Rowe, Edward Thomas (1974) "Aid and Coups d'Etat: Aspects of the Impact of American Military Assistance Programs in the Less Developed Countries." *International Studies Quarterly*, 18 (2): 239–55.

Roy, Arundhati (2008) *The Shape of the Beast: Conversations with Arundhati Roy.* New Delhi: Penguin.

Roy, Srirupa (2007) *Beyond Belief: India and the Politics of Postcolonial Nationalism.* Durham, NC/Delhi: Duke University Press/Permanent Black.

Roy, Tirthankar (2007) "Globalisation, Factor Prices, and Poverty in Colonial India." *Australian Economic History Review*, 47 (1): 73–94.

Rubin, Barnett (2008) "Pakistan's Power Puzzle." *Informed Comment, Global Affairs* blog, 1 January, available at: http://icga.blogspot.com/2008/01/pakistans-power-puzzle.html; accessed 3 September 2009.

Rudolph, Lloyd I. and Susanne Hoeber Rudolph (1964) "Generals and Politicians in India." *Pacific Affairs*, 37 (1): 5–19.

Rudolph, Lloyd I. and Susanne Hoeber Rudolph (1978) "To the Brink and Back: Representation and the State in India." *Asian Survey*, 18 (4): 379–400.

Rudolph, Lloyd I. and Susanne Hoeber Rudolph (1980) "The Centrist Future of Indian Politics." *Asian Survey*, 20 (6): 575–94; as reprinted in Rudolph and Rudolph (2008), vol. 2, pp. 160–82.

Rudolph, Lloyd I. and Susanne Hoeber Rudolph (1987) *In Pursuit of Lakshmi: The Political Economy of the Indian State.* Chicago, Ill./Delhi: University of Chicago Press/Orient Longmans.

Rudolph, Lloyd I. and Susanne Hoeber Rudolph (2001a) "Redoing the Constitutional Design: From an Interventionist to a Regulatory State." In Atul Kohli (ed.) *The Success of India's Democracy* (Cambridge: Cambridge University Press): 127–62.

Rudolph, Susanne Hoeber and Lloyd I. Rudolph (2001b) "Living with Difference in India: Legal Pluralism and Legal Universalism in Historical Context." In Gerald James Larson (ed.) *Religion and Personal Law in Secular India* (Delhi: Social Science Press): 36–65.

Rudolph, Lloyd I. and Susanne Hoeber Rudolph (2008) *Explaining Indian Democracy: A Fifty Year Perspective, 1956–2006*, 3 vols. Delhi: Oxford University Press.

Rustow, Dankwart (1970) "Transitions to Democracy: Toward a Dynamic Model." *Comparative Politics*, 2 (3): 337–63.

Rutherford, Bruce K. (2006) "What Do Egypt's Islamists Want? Moderate Islam and the Rise of Islamic Constitutionalism." *Middle East Journal*, 60 (4): 707–31.

Ruud, Arild Engelsen (2000) "Talking Dirty about Politics: A View from a Bengali Village." In C. J. Fuller and Véronique Bénéï (eds) *The Everyday State and Society in Modern India* (New Delhi: Social Sciences Press): 115–36.

Safran, Nadav (1985) *Saudi Arabia: The Ceaseless Quest for Security.* Cambridge, Mass.: Harvard University Press.

Sahni, Ajai (2009) "In a Hurry, Going Nowhere." *South Asia Intelligence Review*, 8 (11), available at: http://www.satp.org/satporgtp/sair; accessed 27 September 2009.

Sarkar, Sumit (2001) "Indian Democracy: The Historical Inheritance." In Atul Kohli (ed.) *The Success of India's Democracy* (Princeton, NJ: Princeton University Press): 23–46.

Sattar, Babar (2007) "The Promise of Law." *News International*, 31 December.

Sayeed, Khalid bin (1959) "Collapse of Parliamentary Democracy in Pakistan." *Middle East Journal*, 13 (4): 389–406.

Sayeed, Khalid bin (1967) *The Political System of Pakistan.* Boston, Mass.: Houghton Mifflin.

Sayeed, Khalid bin (1968) *Pakistan, the Formative Phase, 1857–1948*, 2nd edn. London/New York: Oxford University Press.

Sayeed, Khalid bin (1982) "The Historical Origins of Some of Pakistan's Persistent Political Problems." In A. Jayaratnam Wilson and Dennis Dalton (eds) *The States of South Asia: Problems of National Integration* (London/Delhi: Hurst/Vikas): 27–44.

Schlesinger, Lee (1977) "The Emergency in an Indian Village." *Asian Survey*, 17 (7): 627–47.

Schmidle, Nicholas (2008) "Pakistan Kicked Me Out. Others Were Less Lucky." *Washington Post*, 3 February: B01.

Schmitter, Philippe C. (1992) "The Consolidation of Democracy and Representation of Social Groups." *American Behavioral Scientist*, 35 (4–5): 422–49.

Schmitter, Philippe C. (1996) "The Influence of the International Context upon the Choice of National Institutions and Policies in Neo-Democracies." In Laurence Whitehead (ed.) *The International Dimensions of Democratization: Europe and the Americas* (Oxford/New York: Oxford University Press): 26–58.

Schmitter, Philippe C. (1997) "Clarifying Consolidation." *Journal of Democracy*, 8 (2): 167–74.

Schmitter, Philippe C. and Terry Lynn Karl (1991) "What Democracy Is . . . and Is Not." *Journal of Democracy*, 2 (3): 75–88.

Schmitter, Philippe C. and Javier Santiso (1998) "Three Temporal Dimensions to the Consolidation of Democracy." *International Political Science Review*, 19 (1): 69–92.

Schneider, Carsten Q. and Philippe C. Schmitter (2004) "Liberalization, Transition and Consolidation: Measuring the Components of Democratization." *Democratization*, 11 (5): 59–90.

Schofield, Julian (2000) "Militarized Decision-Making for War in Pakistan: 1947–1971." *Armed Forces and Society*, 27 (1): 131–48.

Schofield, Julian (2009) "Prospects of an Extremist Takeover of Pakistan through a Military Coup, Revolution or Electoral Politics." Manuscript.

Schofield, Julian with Michael Zekulin (2010) "Appraising the Threat of an Islamist Military Coup in Pakistan." *Defense and Security Analysis*, 26 (1).

Scott, James C. (1976) *The Moral Economy of the Peasant.* New Haven, Conn.: Yale University Press.

Scott, James C. (1986) *Weapons of the Weak.* New Haven, Conn.: Yale University Press.

*SDSA* (2008) *see State of Democracy in South Asia: A Report. See also* deSouza et al. (2008).

Sen, Shila (1976) *Muslim Politics in Bengal 1937–1947.* New Delhi: Impex India.

Sethi, Najam (2008) "How to Tame the ISI." *Friday Times*, 1–7 August.

Sethi, Najam (2009) "Discretion and Not Deterrence." *Friday Times*, 7–13 August.

Shafqat, Saeed (1997) *Civil–Military Relations in Pakistan: From Zulfikar Ali Bhutto to Benazir Bhutto.* Boulder, Colo.: Westview.

Shah, Aqil (2006) "Aiding Authoritarianism? Donors, Dollars and Dictators." In Charles H. Kennedy and Cynthia Botteron (eds) *Pakistan 2005* (Karachi: Oxford University Press): 51–81.

Shah, Ghyansham (1994) "Identity, Communal Consciousness, and Politics." *Economic and Political Weekly*, 29 (19): 1133–40.

Shaheed, Farida (2002) *Imagined Citizenship: Women, State and Politics in Pakistan.* Lahore: Shirkat Gah Women's Resource Centre.

Shaikh, Farzana (1986) "Islam and the Quest for Democracy in Pakistan." *Journal of Commonwealth and Comparative Politics*, 24 (1): 74–92.

Shaikh, Farzana (1989) *Community and Consensus in Islam: Muslim Representation in Colonial India, 1860–1947.* Cambridge: Cambridge University Press.

Shaikh, Farzana (2009) *Making Sense of Pakistan.* New York: Columbia University Press.

Sharma, Rita and Thomas T. Poleman (1993) *The New Economics of India's Green Revolution: Income and Employment Diffusion in Uttar Pradesh.* Ithaca, NY: Cornell University Press.

Sheth, D. L. (1999) "Society." In Marshall M. Bouton and Philip Oldenburg (eds) *India Briefing: A Transformative Fifty Years* (Armonk, NY: M. E. Sharpe): 91–120.

Shiva Rao, B., V. K. N. Menon, Subhash C. Kashyap and N. K. N. Iyengar (1968) *The Framing of India's Constitution*, vol. 5, *A Study.* New Delhi: Indian Institute of Public Administration.

Shourie, Arun (1978) *Symptoms of Fascism.* New Delhi: Vikas.

Siddiqa, Ayesha (2007) *Military Inc.: Inside Pakistan's Military Economy.* London: Pluto Press.

Sims, Holly (1988) *Political Regimes, Public Policy, and Economic Development: Agricultural Performance and Rural Change in Two Punjabs.* New Delhi: Sage.

Singh, Himmat (2001) *The Green Revolution Reconsidered; The Rural World of Contemporary Punjab.* Delhi: Oxford University Press.

Singh, Khushwant (1979) *Indira Gandhi Returns.* New Delhi: Orient Paperbacks.

Singh, V. B. (2004) "Rise of the BJP and Decline of the Congress: An Appraisal." In Rajendra Vora and Suhas Palshikar (eds) *Indian Democracy: Meanings and Practices* (New Delhi: Sage): 299–324.

Sinha, Aseema (2005) *The Regional Roods of Developmental Politics in India.* Bloomington, Ind.: Indiana University Press.

Sinha, Sachchidanand (1977) *Emergency in Perspective: Reprieve and Challenge.* New Delhi: Heritage Publishers.

Smith, Brian K. (2003) "Hinduism." In Jacob Neusner (ed.) *God's Rule: The Politics of World Religions* (Washington, DC: Georgetown University Press): 185–211.

Smith, Donald Eugene (1963) *India as a Secular State.* Princeton, NJ: Princeton University Press.

Smith, Donald Eugene (ed.) (1966) *South Asian Politics and Religion.* Princeton, NJ: Princeton University Press.

Sonwalkar, Prasun (2001) "Opposition to the Entry of the Foreign Press in India, 1991–1995: The Hidden Agenda." *Modern Asian Studies*, 35 (3): 743–63.

Spear, Percival (1961) *India: A Modern History.* Ann Arbor: University of Michigan Press.

Sridharan, E. (2002a) "The Origins of the Electoral System: Rules, Representation, and Power-Sharing in Indian Democracy." In Zoya Hasan, E. Sridharan and R. Sudarshan (eds) *India's Living Constitution: Ideas, Practices, Controversies* (Delhi: Permanent Black): 344–69.

Sridharan, E. (2002b) "The Fragmentation of the Indian Party System, 1952–1999: Seven Competing Explanations." In Zoya Hasan (ed.) *Parties and Party Politics in India* (New Delhi: Oxford University Press): 475–503.

Sridharan, E. (2004) "The Growth and Sectoral Composition of India's Middle Class: Its Impact on the Politics of Economic Liberalization." *India Review*, 3 (4): 405–28.

Ståhlberg, Per (2002) *Lucknow Daily: How a Hindi Newspaper Constructs Society.* Stockholm Studies in Social Anthropology, 51. Stockholm: Department of Social Anthropology, Stockholm University.

*State of Democracy in South Asia: A Report* (2008). SDSA team, Lokniti (CSDS). Delhi: Oxford University Press.

Stepan, Alfred (1988) *Rethinking Military Politics: Brazil and the Southern Cone.* Princeton, NJ/London: Princeton University Press.

Stepan, Alfred (2000) "Religion, Democracy, and the 'Twin Tolerations.'" *Journal of Democracy*, 11 (4).

Stepan, Alfred (2007) "Rituals of Respect: Sufis and Secularists in Senegal." Manuscript, available at: http://www.sipa.columbia.edu/cdtr/pdf/AlfredStepan_RitualsofRespect1.pdf; accessed 5 May 2010.

Stepan, Alfred and Graeme B. Robertson (2004) "Arab, Not Muslim, Exceptionalism." *Journal of Democracy*, 15 (4): 140–6.

Stern, Robert W. (2001) *Democracy and Dictatorship in South Asia: Dominant Classes and Political Outcomes in India, Pakistan, and Bangladesh.* Westport, Conn.: Praeger.

Stokes, Eric (1959) *The English Utilitarians and India.* Oxford: Oxford University Press.

Strachey, John (1894) *India*, new and revised edn. London: Kegan Paul, Trench, Trübner.

Suhrawardy, Huseyn Shaheed (1987) *Memoirs of Huseyn Shaheed Suhrawardy, with a Brief Account of His Life and Work.* Edited by Mohammad H. R. Talukdar. Dhaka: University Press.

Sundar, Nandini (2007) *Subalterns and Sovereigns: An Anthropological History of Bastar 1854–2006*, 2nd edn. New Delhi: Oxford University Press.

Svolik, Milan (2008) "Authoritarian Reversals and Democratic Consolidation." *American Political Science Review*, 102 (2): 153–67.

Swami, Praveen (2008) "How to Lose a War against Insurgency." *Hindu Magazine*, 7 August, available at: http://www.thehindu.com/2008/08/07/stories/2008080754761000.htm; accessed 7 August 2008.

Swami, Praveen (2009) "Breaking News: The Media Revolution." In Sumit Ganguly, Larry Diamond and Marc F. Plattner (eds) *The State of India's Democracy* (New Delhi: Oxford University Press): 176–91.

Swamy, Arun (2004) "Ideology, Organization and Electoral Strategy of Hindu Nationalism: What's Religion Got to Do with It?" In Satu P. Limaye, Mohan Malik and Robert G. Wirsing (eds) *Religious Radicalism and Security in South Asia* (Honolulu, Hawaii: Asia-Pacific Center for Security Studies): 73–100.

Syed, Muhammad Aslam (ed.) (1995) *Islam and Democracy in Pakistan.* Islamabad: National Institute of Historical and Cultural Research.

Talbot, Ian (1980) "The 1946 Punjab Elections." *Modern Asian Studies*, 14 (1): 65–91.

Talbot, Ian (1999) *Pakistan: A Modern History.* London/Lahore: Hurst/Vanguard.

Talbot, Ian (2000) *India and Pakistan: Inventing the Nation.* London: Arnold.

Talbot, Phillips (2007) *An American Witness to India's Partition.* New Delhi: Sage.

Tankel, Stephen (2009) "Lashkar-i-Tayyiba: One Year after Mumbai." *CTC Sentinel*, 2 (11): 1–5.

Taseer, Salman (1980) *Bhutto: A Political Biography.* Delhi: Vikas.

Taub, Richard P. (1969) *Bureaucrats under Stress: Administrators and Administration in an Indian State.* Berkeley/Los Angeles: University of California Press.

Tezcür, Günes Murat (2007) "Constitutionalism, Judiciary, and Democracy in Islamic Societies." *Polity*, 39 (4): 479–501.

Tinker, Hugh (1967) "Is There an Indian Nation?" In Philip Mason (ed.) *India and Ceylon: Unity and Diversity* (London: Institute for Race Relations/Oxford University Press): 279–96.

Tinker, Hugh (1968) *The Foundations of Local Self-Government in India, Pakistan, and Burma.* New York: Praeger.

Transparency International (2005) *India Corruption Study (2005) see* Centre for Media Studies (2005).

Transparency International – Pakistan (2009) *National Corruption Perception Survey, TI Pakistan (2009),* available at: http://www.transparency.org.pk/documents/NCPS%202009/NCPS%202009%20%20Report.pdf; accessed 30 November 2009.

Trinkunas, Harold A. (2005) *Crafting Civilian Control of the Military in Venezuela: A Comparative Perspective.* Chapel Hill: The University of North Carolina Press.

Vajpeyi, Ananya (2009) "Resenting the Indian State: For a New Political Practice in the Northeast." In Sanjib Baruah (ed.) *Beyond Counter-Insurgency: Breaking the Impasse in Northeast India* (Delhi: Oxford University Press): 25–48.

Vanaik, Achin (1985) "The Rajiv Congress in Search of Stability." *New Left Review*, I (154): 55–82.

Vanderbok, William and Richard Sisson (1988) "Parties and Electorates from 'Raj' to 'Swaraj': An Historical Analysis of Electoral Behavior in Late Colonial and Early Independent India." *Social Science History*, 12 (2): 121–42.

Varma, Pavan K. (1998) *The Great Indian Middle Class.* New Delhi: Viking.

Varshney, Ashutosh (2000) "Is India Becoming More Democratic?" *Journal of Asian Studies*, 59 (1): 3–25.

Varshney, Ashutosh (2002) *Ethnic Conflict and Civic Life: Hindus and Muslims in India.* New Haven, Conn.: Yale University Press.

Varshney, Ashutosh (2004) "States of Cities? Studying Hindu–Muslim Riots." In Rob Jenkins (ed.) *Regional Reflections: Comparing Politics across India's States* (New Delhi: Oxford University Press): 177–218.

Vicziany, Marika (2007) "Understanding the 1993 Mumbai Bombings: *Madrassas* and the Hierarchy of Terror." *South Asia: Journal of South Asian Studies*, 30 (1): 43–73.

Wade, Robert (1982) "The System of Administrative and Political Corruption: Canal Irrigation in South India." *Journal of Development Studies*, 18 (3): 287–328.

Wade, Robert (1985) "The Market for Public Office: Why the Indian State Is Not Better at Development." *World Development*, 13 (4): 467–97.

Wade, Robert (1988) *Village Republics: Economic Conditions for Collective Action in South India.* New York: Cambridge University Press.

Waseem, Mohammad (1989) *Politics and the State in Pakistan.* Lahore: Progressive.

Waseem, Mohammad (1994) *The 1993 Elections in Pakistan.* Lahore: Vanguard.

Waseem, Mohammad (1998) "The 1997 Elections in Pakistan." *Electoral Studies*, 17 (1): 129–32.

Waseem, Mohammad (2000) "Dynamics of Electoral Politics in Pakistan." In Subho Basu and Suranjan Das (eds) *Electoral Politics in South Asia* (Calcutta: K. P. Bagchi): 123–51.

Waseem, Mohammad (2004) "Origins and Growth Patterns of Islamic Organizations in Pakistan." In Satu P. Limaye, Mohan Malik and Robert G. Wirsing (eds) *Religious Radicalism and Security in South Asia* (Honolulu, Hawaii: Asia-Pacific Center for Security Studies): 17–34.

Waseem, Mohammad (2005) "Causes of Democratic Downslide in Pakistan." In Veena Kukreja and M. P. Singh (eds) *Pakistan: Democracy, Development, and Security Issues* (New Delhi: Sage): 39–58. Also in *Economic and Political Weekly*, 38 (44–5).

Waseem, Mohammad (2007a) "Functioning of Democracy in Pakistan." In Zoya Hasan (ed.) *Democracy in Muslim Societies: The Asian Experience* (New Delhi: Sage): 177–218.

Waseem, Mohammad (2007b) "The 2002 Elections: A Study of Transition from Military to Civilian Rule." In Saeed Shafqat (ed.) *New Perspectives on Pakistan: Visions for the Future* (Karachi: Oxford University Press): 258–75.

Waseem, Mohammad, in association with Sahibzada Shah Saud, Zafar Habib and Najeebullah Khan (2006) *Democratization in Pakistan: A Study of the 2002 Elections.* Karachi: Oxford University Press.

Waterbury, John (1997) "Fortuitous By-Products." *Comparative Politics*, 29 (3): 383–402.

Weinbaum, M. G. (1977) "The March (1977) Elections in Pakistan: Where Everyone Lost." *Asian Survey*, 17 (7): 599–618.

Weinbaum, Marvin G. and Jonathan B. Harder (2008) "Pakistan's Afghan Policies and their Consequences." *Contemporary South Asia*, 16 (1): 25–38.

Weiner, Myron (1957) *Party Politics in India: The Development of a Multi-Party System.* Princeton, NJ: Princeton University Press.

Weiner, Myron (1978) *India at the Polls: The Parliamentary Elections of 1977.* Washington, DC: American Enterprise Institute.

Weiner, Myron (1983) "The Wounded Tiger: Maintaining India's Democratic Institutions." In Peter Lyon and James Manor (eds) *Transfer and Transformation: Political Institutions in the New Commonwealth* (Leicester: Leicester University Press): 49–57.

Weiss, Anita M. and S. Zulfiqar Gilani (eds) (2001) *Power and Civil Society in Pakistan.* Karachi: Oxford University Press.

Wells, Ian Bryant (2005) *Ambassador of Hindu–Muslim Unity: Jinnah's Early Politics.* Delhi: Orient Longmans.

Welzel, Christian and Ronald Inglehart (2008) "The Role of Ordinary People in Democratization." *Journal of Democracy*, 19 (1): 126–40.

White, Joshua T. (2008a) "The Shape of Frontier Rule: Governance and Transition, from the Raj to the Modern Pakistani Frontier." *Asian Security*, 4 (3): 219–43.

White, Joshua T. (2008b) *Pakistan's Islamist Frontier: Islamic Politics and US Policy in Pakistan's North-West Frontier*, Religion and Security Monograph Series No. 1. Arlington, Va : Center on Faith and International Affairs.

Wilcox, Wayne A. (1965) "The Pakistan Coup d'Etat of 1958." *Pacific Affairs*, 38 (2): 142–63.

Wilcox, Wayne A. (1966) "Ideological Dilemmas in Pakistan's Political Culture." In Donald Eugene Smith (ed.) *South Asian Politics and Religion* (Princeton, NJ: Princeton University Press): 339–51.

Wilder, Andrew R. (1999) *The Pakistani Voter: Electoral Politics and Voting Behaviour in the Punjab.* Karachi: Oxford University Press.

Wilder, Andrew R. (2004) "Elections 2002: Legitimizing the Status Quo." In Craig Baxter (ed.) *Pakistan on the Brink: Politics, Economics, and Society* (Karachi: Oxford University Press): 101–30.

Wilder, Andrew R. (2009) "The Politics of Civil Service Reform in Pakistan." *Journal of International Affairs*, 63 (1): 19–37.

Wilke, Boris (2005) "Boundaries of State and Military in Pakistan." In Klaus Schlichte (ed.) *The Dynamics of States: The Formation and Crises of State Domination* (Aldershot: Ashgate): 183–210.

Wilkinson, Steven I. (2004) *Votes and Violence: Electoral Competition and Ethnic* ["Communal" in the Indian edition] *Riots in India.* New York: Cambridge University Press.

Wilkinson, Steven I. (ed.) (2005) *Religious Politics and Communal Violence.* Delhi: Oxford University Press.

Woodruff, Philip [pseudonym for Philip Mason] (1964a [1953]) *The Men Who Ruled India*, vol. 1, *The Founders.* New York: Schocken Books.

Woodruff, Philip [pseudonym for Philip Mason] (1964b [1954]) *The Men Who Ruled India*, vol. 2, *The Guardians.* New York: Schocken Books.

World Bank (2004) *World Development Report 2004.* New York: Oxford University Press.

Yadav, Yogendra (1996) "Electoral Reforms: Beyond Middle Class Fantasies." *Seminar 440: The Election Carnival* (April): 59–72.

Yadav, Yogendra (1999a) "Electoral Politics in a Time of Change: India's Third Electoral System, 1989–99." *Economic and Political Weekly*, 34 (34–5): 2393–9.

Yadav, Yogendra (1999b) "Politics." In Marshall Bouton and Philip Oldenburg (eds) *India Briefing: A Transformative Fifty Years* (Armonk, NY: M. E. Sharpe): 3–38.

Yadav, Yogendra (2000) "Understanding the Second Upsurge." In Francine R. Frankel, Zoya Hasan, Raveev Bhargava and Balveer Arora (eds) *Transforming India: Social and Political Dynamics of Democracy* (Delhi: Oxford University Press): 120–43.

Yadav, Yogendra and Suhas Palshikar (2003) "From Hegemony to Convergence: Party System and Electoral Politics in the Indian States, 1952–2002." *Journal of Indian School of Political Economy*, 15 (1 and 2): 5–44.

Yadav, Yogendra and Suhas Palshikar (2008) "Ten Theses on State Politics in India." *Seminar 591: The Battle for the States* (November): 14–22; available at: http://www.india-seminar.com/; accessed 13 November 2009.

Yadav, Yogendra and Suhas Palshikar (2009) "Between *Fortuna* and *Virtu*: Explaining the Congress' Ambiguous Victory in 2009." *Economic and Political Weekly*, 44 (39): 33–46.

Yasin, Mohammad and Sardar Shah (2004) "System of Justice." In Mohammad Yasin and Tariq Banuri (eds) *The Dispensation of Justice in Pakistan* (Islamabad/Karachi: Sustainable Development Policy Institute/Oxford University Press): 93–114.

Yilmaz, Hakan (2007) "Islam, Sovereignty, and Democracy: A Turkish View." *Middle East Journal*, 61 (3): 477–93.

Yilmaz, Ihsan (2005) *Muslim Laws, Politics and Society in Modern Nation States: Dynamic Legal Pluralisms in England, Turkey, and Pakistan.* Aldershot: Ashgate.

Yong, Tan Tai (1995) "Punjab and the Making of Pakistan: The Roots of a Civil–Military State." *South Asia: Journal of South Asian Studies*, 18, supplement 1: 177–92.

Yong, Tan Tai (2005) *The Garrison State: The Military, Government and Society in Colonial Punjab, 1849–1947.* New Delhi: Sage.

Youngs, Richard (2008) "Is European Democracy Promotion on the Wane?" Centre for European Policy Studies Working Document No. 292 (May); available at: http://shop.ceps.eu/downfree.php?item_id=1653

Zaidi, Mubashir (2003) "Military Raj." *Indian Express*, 24 October [originally published in *Herald* (Karachi)].

Zaidi, S. Akbar (2005a) *Issues in Pakistan's Economy*, 2nd edn. Karachi: Oxford University Press.

Zaidi, S. Akbar (2005b) "State, Military and Social Transition: Improbable Future of Democracy in Pakistan." *Economic and Political Weekly*, 40 (49): 5173–81.

Zaidi, S. Akbar (2005c) *The Political Economy of Decentralisation in Pakistan*, Transversal Theme "Decentralisation and Social Movements" Working Paper No. 1. [Switzerland]: National Centre of Competence in Research; available at: www.nccrnorth-south.unibe.ch (then: Publications).

Zaidi, S. Akbar (2007) "Is Pakistan a Democracy?" *Seminar 576: Experiments with Democracy*: 15–20.

Zaidi, S. Akbar (2008a) "Democracy, Development, Dictatorship and Globalisation: The Complicated Histories of Pakistan." CSDS and IDEA Democracy Round Table 2008, New Delhi, 17–18 June, *Background Papers* (mimeo): 103–19.

Zaidi, S. Akbar (2008b) "A Failed State or a Failure of Pakistan's Elite?" *Economic and Political Weekly*, 43 (28): 10–11.

Zaidi, S. Akbar (2008c) "Pakistan after Musharraf: An Emerging Civil Society?" *Journal of Democracy*, 19 (4): 38–40.

Zaidi, S. Akbar (2008d) *The Political Economy of Military Rule in Pakistan: The Musharraf Years*, Working Paper No. 31, Institute of South Asian Studies, National University of Singapore; available at: http://www.isasnus.org/events/workingpapers/30.pdf; accessed 13 December 2009.

Zehra, Nasim (2008) "Humbled by People's Power." *News International*, 20 August.

Zinkin, Taya (1959) "India and Military Dictatorship." *Pacific Affairs*, 32 (1): 89–91.

# Index